Apologetics

Or Christianity Defensively Stated

By

Alexander Balmain Bruce

Published by Forgotten Books 2012

Originally Published 1892

PIBN 1000339076

INTERNATIONAL THEOLOGICAL LIBRARY.

APOLOGETICS;

OR,

CHRISTIANITY DEFENSIVELY STATED.

BY

ALEXANDER BALMAIN BRUCE, D.D.,

PROFESSOR OF

APOLOGETICS AND NEW TESTAMENT EXEGESIS, FREE CHURCH COLLEGE, GLASGOW;

AUTHOR OF

"THE TRAINING OF THE TWELVE," "THE HUMILIATION OF CHRIST,"
"THE KINGDOM OF GOD," ETC.

EDINBURGH:

T. & T. CLARK, 38 GEORGE STREET.

1892.

STUR

46554

5ᵗ - 11 - 193c

PREFACE.

THE conception of the nature and function of Apologetics which dominates this work is fully explained in the second chapter of the *Introduction*. It will suffice here to say that what is now offered to the public is not an abstract treatise on Apologetics in which all the traditional common places of the subject—*The Theistic Argument, Revelation, Inspiration, Miracles, Prophecy, The Canon,* etc.—are dis cussed, without reference to present needs and trials of faith. It is an apologetic presentation of the Christian faith with reference to whatever in our intellectual environ· ment makes faith difficult at the present time. The con stituency to which it addresses itself consists neither of dogmatic believers for whose satisfaction it seeks to show how triumphantly their faith can at all possible points of assault be defended, nor of dogmatic unbelievers whom it strives to convince or confound, but of men whose sympa thies are with Christianity, but whose faith is "stifled or weakened by anti-Christian prejudices of varied nature and origin." The aim dictates the method. It leads to the selection of topics of pressing concern, burning questions; leaving on one side, or throwing into the background, subjects which formerly occupied the foreground in apolo-

getic treatises.   Such omissions may disappoint those who
are familiar with the older apologetic literature, but it is
hoped that what is here offered as an aid to faith will meet
the wants of those for whose benefit it is designed, and in
so doing be in sympathy with the aim of the projectors of
the INTERNATIONAL THEOLOGICAL LIBRARY.

A. B. BRUCE.

GLASGOW, *November* 1892.

CONTENTS.

———✦———

INTRODUCTION.

CHAPTER I.

HISTORICAL SKETCH.

SEC.

ERRATA.

Page xv. (Contents), under Chapter vi., PAUL, line 8, *for* " Jesus" *read*
" Issues."

Ib., line 9, *for* " His" *read* " his."

Page 68, line 11 from foot, *for* " heat" *read* " heart."

BOOK I. ⸱

THEORIES OF THE UNIVERSE, CHRISTIAN AND ANTI-CHRISTIAN.

CHAPTER I.

THE CHRISTIAN FACTS.

getic treatises.   Such omissions may disappoint those who
are familiar with the older apologetic literature, but it is
hoped that what is here offered as an aid to faith will meet
the wants of those for whose benefit it is designed, and in
so doing be in sympathy with the aim of the projectors of
the INTERNATIONAL THEOLOGICAL LIBRARY.

A. B. BRUCE.

GLASGOW, *November* 1892.

CONTENTS.

INTRODUCTION.

CHAPTER I.

HISTORICAL SKETCH.

CHAPTER II.

THE FUNCTION AND METHOD OF APOLOGETIC.

BOOK I.

THEORIES OF THE UNIVERSE, CHRISTIAN AND ANTI-CHRISTIAN.

CHAPTER I.

THE CHRISTIAN FACTS.

CHAPTER II.

THE CHRISTIAN THEORY OF THE UNIVERSE.

CHAPTER III.

THE PANTHEISTIC THEORY.

CHAPTER IV.

THE MATERIALISTIC THEORY.

CHAPTER V.

THE DEISTIC THEORY.

CHAPTER VI.

MODERN SPECULATIVE THEISM.

CHAPTER VII.

AGNOSTICISM.

BOOK II.

THE HISTORICAL PREPARATION FOR CHRISTIANITY.

CHAPTER I.

THE SOURCES.

CHAPTER II.

THE RELIGION OF THE PROPHETS.

CHAPTER III.

THE PROPHETIC IDEA OF ISRAEL'S VOCATION AND HISTORY.

CHAPTER IV.

MOSAISM.

CHAPTER V.

PROPHETISM.

CHAPTER VI.

PROPHETIC OPTIMISM.

CHAPTER VII.

JUDAISM.

CHAPTER VIII.

THE NIGHT OF LEGALISM.

CHAPTER IX.

THE OLD TESTAMENT LITERATURE.

CONTENTS.

CHAPTER X.

THE DEFECTS OF THE OLD TESTAMENT RELIGION AND ITS LITERATURE.

BOOK III.

THE CHRISTIAN ORIGINS.

CHAPTER I.

JESUS.

CHAPTER II.

JESUS AS THE CHRIST.

CHAPTER III.

JESUS AS FOUNDER OF THE KINGDOM OF GOD.

CHAPTER IV.

JESUS RISEN.

CHAPTER V.

JESUS LORD.

CHAPTER VI.

PAUL.

CHAPTER VII.

PRIMITIVE CHRISTIANITY.

CHAPTER VIII.

THE SYNOPTICAL GOSPELS.

CHAPTER IX.

THE FOURTH GOSPEL.

CHAPTER X.

THE LIGHT OF THE WORLD.

INTRODUCTION.

CHAPTER I.

HISTORICAL SKETCH.

THIS work may fitly begin with a brief statement on some outstanding topics connected with the history of Apologetics, by way of a popular indication of the general nature of the study with which we are to be occupied.

SECTION I.—*The Apologetic Elements in the New Testament.*

These have reference mainly to two topics: the Person of the Messiah, and the Nature of the Messianic Kingdom. As to the former: Jesus came without pomp, political power, or social prestige—"meek and lowly" in state as well as "in heart"; born in poverty, reared amid mean conditions, and appearing in manhood among men utterly denuded of all that tends to secure influence and win the goodwill of those who take their inspiration from the pride of life. This was not the Christ such persons desired; it was not such a Christ, they were persuaded, their sacred Books taught them to expect. The Christ of prophecy, the Christ of their hearts' choice, was a personage who on His advent should be recognisable as a great One. Such being the Christ of expectation, the actual Christ, Jesus of Nazareth, was of course despised and rejected by His countrymen; and on His persisting in giving solid evidence of His Messianic claims in His words and works, was even

A

hated by them, till at length contradiction took the form
of crucifixion. Then it came to pass that the injustice of
one generation became a justification for the unbelief of
the next. Because their fathers crucified Jesus, the Jews
who were contemporaries of the apostles, and witnessed the
founding of the Christian Church, found it difficult or
impossible to accept Him as the Christ. Christ crucified
became to the Jews a σκανδαλον. How could a crucified
man be the fulfilment of Messianic prophecies, the realisa
tion of Old Testament ideals? It was a hard question
even for believing Jews. Many Hebrew Christians found
in the idea of a crucified Christ simply a stumbling-
block.

To this fact *the Epistle to the Hebrews* seems to have
owed, at least in part, its origin. That remarkable writing
is an elaborate apology for the Cross in a twofold aspect;
first and chiefly, for the cross which Jesus bore, and second
and subordinately for the cross that came to Christians in
connection with their profession of faith in the Crucified
One. It may be regarded as the most important contribu
tion to the apologetics of Christianity contained in the
New Testament. It is indeed the one systematic effort of
that sort. Very valuable apologetic ideas occur in Paul's
Epistles, such as that of the "fulness of the time"; but
they are only occasional and undeveloped thoughts. In
the Epistle to the Hebrews, on the other hand, we find a
sustained attempt to meet in a comprehensive spirit the
difficulties of the Christian faith as these presented them
selves to the minds of Hebrews, by setting forth Christ's
death, with all its foregoing and accompanying humiliation,
as an experience which overtook Him in the pursuit of a
high vocation, that of Captain of salvation; an act of self-
sacrifice in virtue of which He realised the ideal of priest
hood whereof only the shadow was given in Leviticalism,
and so inaugurated the eternal religion, the final, because
perfect, form of man's relation to God.

Less obtrusive, but not less significant, are the apologetic elements to be found in the sayings of Jesus. These, however, relate not to the *humiliation-aspect* of His own Person and earthly career, but rather to the nature of His mission. He took no great pains to remove stumbling-blocks to faith arising out of the former. He rather confessed than apologised for the meanness of His state and lot. He did not explain why the Son of man had not where to lay His head, but simply stated the fact for the information of would-be disciples. He seems indeed to have been desirous to increase rather than to diminish the offence of His lowliness, and to have used it as a means of protecting Himself from the patronising attachment of those in whose sincerity and stedfastness as disciples He had no confidence. To this cause in part may be traced His partiality for the self-designation—the Son of man. The same abstention from apologetic speech is observable in His manner of referring to His death. When He began to speak to His disciples of that tragic event, His manner was that of one making an announcement, not that of one offering an explanation or an apology.

Thus reticent in what related to Himself, Jesus was copious in apology in reference to the nature of His mission, and of the kingdom whose advent He proclaimed. The kingdom of heaven He preached was very different from what men looked for. In two respects especially it differed from the Messianic kingdom of popular expectation: in its *spirituality* and in its *universality*.[1] The Jews looked for a political Messiah, and the work they expected Him to do when He came was, not to create a new thing, but to restore an old thing—to give back to Israel her national independence and glory, and to be a second David ruling in wisdom and righteousness over a united, free, strong, and prosperous people. But Jesus, so far as one can judge from the evangelic records, never dreamt of

---

[1] For a discussion of the question, What was Christ's idea of the kingdom of God? *vide* Book III. chap. iii. Here the results of that discussion are taken for granted.

restoring the kingdom. What He had in view was a new creation, not a restoration; a kingdom of heaven, not a kingdom of this world; a kingdom affecting primarily and principally men's souls rather than their bodies. In preaching the kingdom, He addressed Himself to men whom the world accounts miserable, and offered them boons which the world does not value. The most obtuse hearer could not fail to perceive that whatever might be the precise import of such discourse, it related to a king dom very diverse from that of common expectation; and while all might admire the dignity and solemn grandeur of the Beatitudes, not a few probably went away feeling that their hopes were mocked, and their understanding perplexed by sentences which in effect pronounced the wretched blessed.

If the spirituality of the kingdom proclaimed by Jesus was a disappointment to Jewish expectation, its other attribute of universality was in a still greater degree an offence to Jewish prejudice. The spirit of exclusiveness was a prominent feature in the religious character of the Jews. It had its root partly in pride, partly in a mis taken sense of duty. The people of Israel had been chosen of God to be the medium through which the whole world should eventually be blessed. This was God's great pur pose in Israel's election; but the method involved temporary isolation in order to ultimate union in one divine common wealth. That isolation had one unhappy result. It led the chosen race to mistake the means for the end, and to regard the outside world with abhorrence and contempt. Israel fell into the fatal mistake of imagining that election meant a monopoly of divine favour, and imposed the duty of hating all outside the pale. This imaginary duty she performed with great cordiality. The orthodox religious Jews of Christ's time abhorred all dogs without the gates of the holy city; pagans, semi-pagan Samaritans, publicans who, though Jews by birth, were the representatives of foreign dominion, and even the people of their own race who were ignorant and negligent of the commandments of the scribes—the "sinners," or "lost sheep of the house of Israel."

To a people thus minded a universal religion common to Jew and Gentile could not be welcome. Yet such was the religion of Jesus. In proof it is sufficient to point to such sayings as: "Ye are the salt of the earth," "Ye are the light of the world," and to the attitude assumed by Jesus towards the outcasts of Jewish society, the "publicans and sinners," who to orthodox Jews were as pagans, as is implied in the proverbial expression: "Let him be unto thee as an heathen man and a publican."[1] Jesus loved these outcasts, and freely associated with them; and the interest He took in them was the beginning of a social and religious revolution. It was universalism in germ. The man who could be a friend of publicans and sinners, and go to be a guest in their houses, could have no objection on principle to associate with heathens.

With instinctive discernment of what was involved, the strictly religious fellow-countrymen of Jesus earnestly and repeatedly found fault with this part of His public conduct, and so put Him on His defence for the crime of loving the unloved and the morally unlovely. The words He spoke in self-vindication have been preserved, which is not surprising, seeing they are full of poetry and pathos and benignant sympathy with erring humanity, and contain the very quintessence of God's gospel to mankind. These words constitute Christ's apology for His mission as a Saviour, and for the kingdom of God as a kingdom of grace free to all. They are the first apology made for Christianity in its simplest aspect as the good news of God to a sinful world. They are familiar to all readers of the Gospels, but it may not be superfluous to indicate here the principles underlying them, stated in a form adapted to meet objections, which, first raised by the Pharisees, have found numerous sympathisers in all ages, even among men

[1] Matt. xviii. 17.

of a very different stamp from those narrow Jewish religionists.

1. Christianity aims at curing moral evil, and therefore it addresses itself to those who stand in greatest need of its aid. "They that be whole," said Jesus, "need not a physician, but they that are sick."[1] Thereby He intimated that He came to be a physician, and that like every physician, He felt it to be His duty to devote His attention to those who most urgently required the benefit of His skill. Were Christianity a mere philosophy, it might address itself exclusively to the cultivated class, and leave the rude mass of mankind unheeded. Were it a system of religious mysteries, like the sacred rites with which the annual festival of Ceres was celebrated at Eleusis, it might in that case also confine its interests to the privileged few, and neglect the many as unworthy of initiation. But professing to be an effectual remedy for the moral diseases of mankind, it cannot consistently be fastidious and aristocratic, but must address itself to the million, and be ready to lay its healing hand even on such as are afflicted with the most loathsome and deadly maladies.

2. Christianity has faith in the redeemableness of human beings, however sunk in sin and misery. Not deceiving itself as to the grave nature of the ailments with which it finds men afflicted, it yet does not despair of curing them. Philosophy, coldly contemplating mankind from her exalted position, may consider vast numbers of the race incapable of moral improvement, and so regard all philanthropic efforts directed towards that end as wasted labour. But Christianity, cherishing invincible faith in the moral destiny of humanity, refuses to resign itself to a policy of indifference based on hopelessness, and sets itself to the Herculean task of healing men's spiritual diseases, declining to despair even in the most desperate cases. So far from despairing, it even believes in the possibility of

[1] Matt. ix. 12.

the last becoming first, of the greatest sinner becoming the greatest saint. This truth Jesus hinted at when He said : " To whom little is forgiven, the same loveth little," [1] suggesting the correlative doctrine, that to whom much is forgiven, the same loveth much ; in other words, that from among the children of passion, prone to err, may come, when their energies are properly directed, the most devoted and effective citizens and servants of the divine kingdom. It seems a bold and hazardous assertion, but it is one never theless which the history of the Church has fully justified.

3. Christianity thinks the meanest of mankind worth saving. It rejoices over a solitary sinner redeemed, not a picked sample, but any one taken at random. Jesus said : " I say unto you, That joy shall be in heaven over one (such) sinner that repenteth, more than over ninety and nine just persons, which need no repentance." [2] With such joy " in heaven," or among Christlike men, the Pharisees could not sympathise. It seemed to them that people like the publicans were not worth saving, hardly even worth damning ; and in this view many of uncelestial, inhuman temper, in every age, are only too ready to agree with them. But the genius of Christianity is like the good woman in the parable who set value on a single small coin, and could not rest till she found it, and expected all her neighbours to rejoice with her when she had succeeded.[3] Jesus Christ set a high value on every creature endowed with a human soul, seeing in him a lost coin bearing stamped on it, however marred, the image of God, a lost sheep capable of being brought back to the fold, a lost son of God who might any day return to his Father's house.

4. Christianity assumes that God's attitude towards mankind is the same as that of Christ. Jesus believed and said that there was joy in heaven over a sinner repenting, such as He Himself felt. This, in truth, was His radical defence to those who found fault with Him. He pled that

[1] Luke vii. 47.　　　[2] Luke xv. 7.　　　[3] Luke xv. 8, 9.

in taking a keen interest in the erring, He was but doing as they did in heaven. To His accusers it was an effective reply; for while the idea of God it suggested was widely different from that cherished by the Pharisaic mind, yet they could not on reflection quarrel with the doctrine that God is good and ready to forgive, and that it cannot be wrong to be like Him. Yet the alleged "joy in heaven" is, after all, the thing which men have ever found it hardest to believe in : some, because they harbour the incurable suspicion that God's thoughts towards men are thoughts of evil; others, because they cannot conceive of God having thoughts of any kind, loving or the reverse; Christ's whole way of representing God, as a Father who careth for His wayward children, appearing to them, how ever beautiful as poetry, anthropopathic, and from a philo sophic point of view incredible. The Absolute, they tell us, can have no thoughts, no purposes, no joys, no sorrows. A sinner repenting may be an interesting scene to men of philanthropic spirit on earth, but it is not visible from heaven. The difference between a sinner penitent and a sinner impenitent, great as it appears to us, is inappreciable at that distance. If this be true, then apologies for Christi anity are idle, for in that case Christianity is only a lovely dream. Christ is not the revealer of God, His love to man is an amiable weakness, His ministry of mercy a fruitless endeavour; for why strive to bring men to repentance, if repentance have no significance Godwards, and sin be nothing real? We shall have to grapple with this dreary theory hereafter. Meanwhile let us trust the word of Christ, and venture to believe that He uttered truth as well as poetry when He declared "there is joy in heaven over one sinner repenting," and go forward in our apologetic course with such ideas of God and man in our minds as those which underlie the apologies He made in His own behalf as the sinner's Friend.

Section II.—*The Attack of Celsus and the Reply of Origen.*

Literature. — Origen, *Contra Celsum;* Pressense, *The Martyrs and Apologists,* 1871; Theodor Keim, *Celsus' Wahres Wort,* 1873; Patrick, *The Apology of Origen,* 1892.

Apology occupied a very prominent place in the history of the early Church. In the first three centuries of our era Christianity had to defend herself before the civil magistrate, pleading that she was not dangerous to the State and might safely be tolerated; against popular prejudice, pleading that she was not an immoral or inhuman religion ; against the attacks of pagan philosophy, pleading that she was not irrational. Among her most formidable foes of the philosophic class was Celsus, believed to have been a contemporary and friend of Lucian, who has been aptly named the Voltaire of the second century. In the latter half of that century Celsus wrote a work against Christianity, entitled, Ἀληθὴς λογος, to which Origen, by request, wrote a reply about the middle of the century following.[1] In his philosophy, Celsus seems to have been an eclectic. Origen states that in his other works he shows himself an Epicurean, but that in his polemic against Christianity he concealed his connection with the school of Epicurus, lest the avowal of it should weaken the force of his argument against those who believed in a providence, and set God over all. From the extracts out of the *True Word,* preserved in Origen's reply, it appears that Celsus was familiar with, and an admirer of, the writings of Plato, and there is also evidence that in some of his opinions he was in affinity with the Stoics.[2]

---

[1] Keim, in the sub-title of his above-named work, describes the *True Word* as the oldest controversial writing against Christianity from the view point of the ancient theory of the universe (*Antiker Weltanschauung*). He dates it 178 A.D.

[2] Patrick (*The Apology of Origen*) is of opinion that the Celsus of the *True Word* was not Celsus the friend of Lucian ; that he was not an Epicurean, like the latter, but a Platonist, and that the value of his work just lies in its being a work by a Platonist ; *vide* pp. 9–15.

While the attacks of other ancient unbelievers may
without much loss be forgotten, it is important that the
student of Christian apologetics should know something of
the assault made by Celsus, and of the manner in which it
was met by Origen.   The opponents were well matched ;
the attack of the pagan philosopher was deadly, and the
defence of the Church Father wise ; and there is much to
be learned from both.

The objections of Celsus to Christianity may be classed
under two heads : (1) his philosophic prejudices ; (2) his
main argument.

1. To the head of prejudices belongs the decided distaste
manifested by Celsus as a man of letters for the rude
simplicity of style characteristic of the sacred writers
generally, and of the teaching of Christ and His apostles in
particular.   This distaste finds frequent expression in the
" True Discourse."   Thus, *e.g.*, in a passage in which the
author seeks to show the affinity between the good moral
elements of the Christian system and the views of Greek
philosophers, he asserts that what is good and true in
Christianity has been said before, and better, by Plato or
some other Greek writer.   In another place, where he has
occasion to refer to Christ's doctrine of passive submission
to injury, he describes Christ's way of putting the matter :
" Resist not evil ; but whosoever shall smite thee on thy
right cheek, turn to him the other also," as rustic compared
with the elegant manner in which the same moral truth is
put by Plato when he makes Socrates say to Crito : " We
must on no account do injury ; we must not even, as the
multitude think, take revenge for evil done."   Origen's way
of dealing with this petty literary prejudice is characterised
by dignity, magnanimity, and wisdom.   He is not careful to
defend Christianity against the charge of rusticity, nor does
he make any attempt to disparage Greek eloquence.   He
simply puts in a plea of utility.   The simplicity of the
gospel suits its professed character as a message of mercy
from God to the millions of mankind.   The beautiful ornate

style of Plato has profited only a few, while books written in less pretentious style profit many. "This I say," remarks Origen, in a truly philosophic spirit, "not blaming Plato, for the wide world of men has usefully produced him also."[1]

Celsus was further prejudiced against Christianity because of the prominence it gave to *faith*. He represents Christian teachers as unwilling either to give or to ask a reason of their belief, and saying: "Inquire not, but believe, and thy faith will save thee; wisdom is bad, foolishness is good." Origen replies that Celsus caricatures the Christian position; that Christians do not neglect inquiry or despise true wisdom; and that in attaching importance to faith in religion, they but give due prominence to a principle which enters into all human affairs, even into the business of choosing a master in philosophy. It would be well if all could study philosophy; some Christians do, but many have neither the talent nor the leisure. Surely it is good that such without philosophy and by faith are turned from sin unto righteousness. Many have been so turned by faith in the gospel; and this proves it divine, for "nothing useful among men comes into existence without the providence of God."[2]

More violent than either of the foregoing was the prejudice created in the mind of Celsus by the intense interest taken by Christians, following the example of Christ, in the sinful and the miserable. He represents the preacher of the gospel as saying in effect: "Let no one who is educated, wise, or prudent approach; but if any one is illiterate, foolish, or untaught, a babe in knowledge, he may come to us;" and as aiming at making converts only of the silly and senseless, of slaves, women and children. Whence, he asks, this preference for the sinful? contrasting with the strange practice of Christians the more rational way of pagans, in inviting to initiation into their mysteries men of

---

[1] Ὁ γὰρ πολὺς τῶν ἀνθρώπων κόσμος χρησίμως καὶ τοῦτον ἤνεγκεν, lib. vi. c. 2.

[2] Οὐδὲν γὰρ χρηστὸν ἐν ἀνθρώποις ἀθεεὶ γίγνεται, lib. i. c. 9.

pure exemplary lives. This is the old Pharisaic complaint:
" this man receiveth sinners," uttered in perfect good faith
by one who thought he did well to be angry with Christians
for their perverse sympathy with the ignorant and erring.
So new and unfamiliar a thing was the philanthropy of
Jesus and His disciples. What helped to increase the
perplexity of Celsus was his unbelief in conversion. He
held that men who were sinners by nature and habit could
not be changed either by compassion or by severity: for
" to change nature thoroughly is very difficult." [1] Origen's
reply was very simple. In the name of Christianity he
pled guilty to the charge of loving the sinful and the foolish,
but he denied that the Church cared only for them in the
sense meant by the objector.

2. These prejudices are comparatively superficial, but the
main argument of Celsus struck at the heart of the Christian
faith, its conception of God, in the person of Christ, enter
ing into the world as a redeeming power. He assailed the
incarnation on three grounds, maintaining, *first*, that it
degrades God by subjecting Him to change; *second*, that it
unduly exalts man, by making him the object of God's
special care; *third*, that it has in view an unattainable end,
the redemption of man, the cure of moral evil.

"God," said Celsus, enforcing the first of these three
positions, " is good, honourable, happy, the fairest and
the best; but if He descends to men He becomes sub
ject to change—from good to bad, from the honourable to
the base, from happiness to misery, from the best to the
most wicked. Let no such change be ascribed to God." [2]
Origen replied that the descent of God into humanity
implied no such change as Celsus imagined; not from good
to bad, for He did no sin; nor from honour to disgrace,
for He knew no sin; nor from happiness to misery, for
He humbled Himself, remaining none the less blessed.
What is there bad in kindness and philanthropy? Who

---

[1] Φυσιν γαρ αμειψαι τελιως παγχαλιπον, lib. iii. c. 65.

[2] Lib. iv. 14.

would say that a physician seeing horrible things and touching loathsome things, that he may heal the sick, passes from goodness to badness, from honour to disgrace, from happiness to misery ?[1]

More distasteful even than the theological was the anthropological postulate of the incarnation to the mind of Celsus. The central truth of Christianity seemed to him to attach far too much importance to man. What was man that God should be thus mindful of him ? Origen quotes a passage from the *True Word*, in which Jews and Christians, fancying themselves the objects of divine care, are compared to bats, or to ants coming forth from their ant hill, or to frogs holding council in a marsh, or to worms assembling in the corner of a dunghill, disputing with each other which of them were the greater sinners, and claiming a monopoly of God's favour.[2] The insignificance of man is a favourite theme with Celsus, on which he expatiates with cynical delight. He scouts the idea that man was made in God's image ; ridicules the notion that man is an end for God in His works of creation and providence, any more than other creatures ; denies man's lordship over creation ; and enters into elaborate detail to prove that man is not much, if at all superior to the beasts in his intellectual, moral, and religious endowments.[3] His statements on the last mentioned topic may appear only the whimsical exaggerations of one bent on overwhelming with ridicule the pretensions of man to the supreme position in creation, and to a special place in the divine regards. But in the main Celsus was quite in earnest in his anthropological speculations. His views regarding man's position in the world and in relation to God, were in keeping with his attitude as the opponent of Christianity, and formed an essential part of his pantheistic theory of the universe.

Celsus further maintained that the end of the incarnation —the cure of moral evil—is unattainable. His doctrine of evil was to this effect. Evil is not God's work ; it is

---

[1] Lib. iv. 15.   [2] Lib. iv. 23.   [3] Lib. iv. 84-99.

inherent in matter which is eternal and not made by God,
for God makes nothing mortal or material, but only the
spiritual.[1] The origin of evil being traceable to a necessity
of nature, its amount is invariable.[2] Thus the possibility
of redemption is excluded, as it is also by another
doctrine held by Celsus, that all the changes which take
place in the universe are subject to the law of periodicity.
That which has been shall be. The present state of things
will reproduce itself in some future æon, any present state
of things you choose to think of. This law of periodicity,
applied by the Stoics even to the gods, Celsus contended
for chiefly with reference to human history. "Similar,"
he said, "from beginning to end is the period of mortals;
and according to the appointed revolutions the same things
always by necessity have been, are, and shall be."[3] As
Origen remarks, this doctrine, if true, is manifestly sub
versive of Christianity, for it is idle to speak of a redemp
tive economy acting on free agents by moral influence,
where a reign of necessity obtains; and if all beings must
eventually return to the state they once were in, then
man's unredeemed state must have its turn, and Christ
shall have died in vain. A sufficiently gloomy outlook;
but the Celsian theory has its cheering side. For our con
solation we are told that evil, for aught we know, may be
good. "Thou knowest not what is good for thee, or for
another, or for the whole."[4] There is, of course, a sense in
which this is true; but applied, as Celsus meant it to be
applied, to sin or moral evil, it means that sin is not a
reality; that there is no such thing as absolute moral evil;
that, in the words of a modern writer, "evil is only good
in the making." This is the opiate administered by pan
theism in all ages to soothe conscience, deaden human
sensibilities, and enable men to contemplate with philoso
phic indifference the moral condition of the world, as at
once irremediable and not needing remedy.

That Celsus conceived God pantheistically is manifest

[1] Lib. iv. 52.   [2] Lib. iv. 62.   [3] Lib. iv. 67.   [4] Lib. iv. 70.

from the extracts from his work preserved by Origen. God, he taught, cannot be reached by reason, and cannot be named. What the sun is among things visible, being neither eye nor sight, but the cause of seeing to the eye, and to sight of its possibility, and to things visible of their being seen, and yet not the cause for himself of being seen, that is God among the things conceived of by the mind. He is neither mind, nor thought, nor knowledge, but the cause to the mind of knowing, and to thought of its being possible, and to knowledge of its existence, and to all objects of knowledge, and to truth itself, and to being itself, of being; being Himself beyond all things, knowable by a certain ineffable power.[1] This statement is not abso lutely incompatible with theistic conceptions of God, and accordingly Origen does not seem inclined to find much fault with it, here as elsewhere displaying characteristic magnanimity, as one ever ready to receive in a candid spirit things well said by Celsus, or by the Greek philosophers, whose opinions he espouses. But the idea naturally suggested by the comparison of God to the sun is that of a Being unnameable, unknowable, in some sense the cause of all being, yet unlike anything that is, as the sun is unlike the eye, while it is that which enables the eye to see; not even like the human mind, or possessing the properties of mind, thought, and knowledge; a being whose nature cannot be inferred from any of his works, material or mental, of whom nothing can be predicated, not even being itself.

Quite consistently with his pantheistic mode of conceiving God, Celsus was an earnest apologist for polytheism; for all the world over, and in all ages, *pantheism in theory means polytheism in practice.* The supreme deity of this philosopher was quite superior to jealousy, had no desire to enjoy a monopoly of worship, could magnanimously tolerate a host of minor divinities, each receiving his share of homage; for were they not all parts of him, or modes of him? He deemed all religions tolerable (Christianity

[1] Lib. vii. c. 45.

excepted), because all the particular deities were in his view manifestations of the Great Unknown. Polytheism he justified by the simple process of reasoning: whatever is, is part of God, reveals God, serves God, therefore may rationally be worshipped. Christianity he excepted from this wide toleration, because it worshipped a jealous God who was not content to be one of many. This jealousy ascribed to God by monotheistic religions radically signifies that God is a Being to whom moral distinctions are real. The god of Celsus, the god of pantheism, is not jealous, because he is not the Holy One, but simply the Absolute. The category of the ethical is merged in the wider all-embracing category of Being.[1]

SECTION III.—*Free Thought in the Eighteenth Century.*

LITERATURE.—Leland, *A View of the Principal Deistical Writers*, 1754; Lechler, *Geschichte des Englischen Deismus*, 1841; L. Noack, *Die Freidenker in der Religion*, 1853 (this book gives an account of the representatives of religious free thought in England, France, and Germany); A. S. Farrar, Bampton Lectures on *the History of Free Thought in Religion*, 1862; M. Pattison, Essay on "the Tendencies of Religious Thought in England from 1688 to 1750," in *Essays and Reviews*, 1860; Leslie Stephen, *History of English Thought in the Eighteenth Century*, 1876; Cairns, *Unbelief in the Eighteenth Century*, Cunningham Lecture, 1880.

The interest of the attack considered in last section lies in the fact that it was made near the beginning of our era, and shows how Christianity presented itself to hostile minds when it was yet young. The interest of "Deism" lies in its proximity to our own time, and in the fact that it shows how Christianity appeared to a generation whose thoughts, though in many respects antiquated, have been more or less assimilated by the present generation. As was to be expected, the point of view of the eighteenth

---

[1] For the views of Celsus on polytheism, *vide* lib. viii. of Origen's work.

century is greatly changed from that of the second. In the time of Celsus it was the central truth of the Christian faith that was assailed; in the eighteenth century it was its literary documents. The Protestant doctrine of Scripture as the infallible record of a supernatural revelation, setting forth " what man is to believe concerning God, and what duty God requires of man," was presupposed, and the aim of unbelief was to assail the conception of such a revelation as unnecessary and unverifiable, and its record as lacking the characteristics that a book professing to contain such a revelation ought to possess. The movement was European, and found many eager advocates in England, Germany, and France.

In England the history of deism covers a period of about a hundred years, commencing from the middle of the seventeenth and extending to about the middle of the eighteenth century; its rise being represented by Lord Herbert of Cherbury, and its decline by Lord Bolingbroke. The great controversy embraced a large variety of topics, each successive adversary assailing the common object of hostility from his own chosen point of attack, and all combined compelling Christianity, through her champions, to defend herself in every direction in which she appeared weak to the doubting spirit of the age. One assailed the divine Person of the founder of the faith,[1] another its prophetic foundations,[2] a third its miraculous attestations,[3] a fourth its canonical literature.[4] Another group of opponents took up a more general ground, and sought to show that a special revelation was unnecessary, impossible, or unverifiable, the religion of nature being

[1] Charles Blount, in a translation of the two first books of the work of Philostratus on Apollonius of Tyana, furnished with copious and characteristic notes, 1680.

[2] Anthony Collins, in *The Grounds and Reasons of the Christian Religion*, 1713.

[3] Woolston, in *A Discourse on the Miracles of our Saviour*, 1727 ; replied to by Lardner.

[4] Toland, in *Amyntor*, 1698 ; replied to by Jones on the Canon.

sufficient and superior to all religions of positive institution. This was the common position of all deists, but
some made it their business to emphasise it. To this
class belonged Dr. Tyndal, author of *Christianity as Old
as the Creation*,[1] who is entitled to be viewed as the representative and spokesman of English deism, whether regard
be had to the merits of his book, or to the fact that he,
more than any other of the free-thinking fraternity, seems
to have been in the mind of Bishop Butler when he wrote
his famous *Analogy*. The very title of Tyndal's book gives
him a certain claim to the place of representative man,
supplying as it does a fit motto for a scheme of thought
which believed natural uninstructed common reason to
be a sufficient and safe guide in religion, and disclaimed
all indebtedness to Christianity except in so far as it was
a return to the simplicity of nature, a protest against
the corruption of natural religion by superstition, even
as deism was itself a protest against a degenerate Christianity corrupted by professed believers.

Deistical attacks were generally not straightforward, the
real design being masked, and the point formally proved
not the true opinion of the writer, but that which he
deemed it safe to utter. It is, however, not difficult to
ascertain Tyndal's position. It was as follows: God can
be known sufficiently by all men through the use of their
natural faculties. The religion of nature, based on this
naturally acquired knowledge of God's being and character,
is perfect. That it is so is proved by the fact of its being
used as the touchstone of all positive, instituted, traditionary religions; also by the fact that manifold deplorable
mischiefs have arisen wherever the notions dictated by
reason concerning God have been departed from. Being
perfect, the religion of reason excludes all revelation except
such as is merely a republication of the law of nature. A
revelation distinct in its contents from the religion of
reason can differ only in adding to the eternal moral laws

[1] Published in 1730.

of the universe positive precepts, which are simply means towards ends, and derive their obligation from the arbitrary will of the lawgiver. It is, however, not credible that a good God would restrict human liberty by such arbitrary impositions. Nor can it be believed that a professed revelation consisting of such impositions emanates from God, when it is considered what baleful effects—super stition, immorality, falsehood, persecution, strife, division —have sprung from faith in so-called revelations of that kind. Then, apart from these evils, how many instituted religions there are! How shall we choose the true one save by the aid of reason? Nay, this aid is needed even by those whom the chance of education has thrown into the *true* traditionary religion. Mark the epithet " true " : it is printed in italics, as if the author believed *ex animo* that there was a true traditionary religion. But the emphasised adjective simply means the so-called true. It is as if the word had been printed in inverted commas. The " true " traditionary religion needs help from the religion of nature, because its documents are far from clear in meaning, and the agents of revelation were very questionable characters, and the moral tone of the Bible is far from unimpeachable, and even the teaching of Christ is sometimes, as in reference to riches and marriage, very liable to be misunderstood.

But if the religon of nature be so clear and perfect, how comes it that superstition is at all times so very prevalent, and that those who walk in the sunlight of reason are ever a small minority? This is a question for which the deist was bound to find an answer. Tyndal's answer — the answer of all deists—was summed up in one word, *Priest-craft*. Many a hearty curse do those poor priests come in for in the pages of deistical writers. Bentley, in his reply to the *Discourse of Free Thinking*, by Anthony Collins, explaining the significance of the epithet " free " in the title of that book, says that it comprises two ideas—presumption and suspicion. " 'Tis a firm persuasion among them," he remarks, "that there are but two sorts in mankind, deceivers and deceived, cheats and fools. Hence it is that, dreaming and waking, they have one perpetual theme, priestcraft. This is just like the opinion of Nero, who believed for certain that every man was guilty of the same impurities that he was; only some were craftier than others to dissimulate and conceal it. And the surmise in both cases must proceed from the same cause, either a very corrupt, or a crazy and crack-brained head, or, as it often happens, both." [1]

The widespread prevalence of ignorance and darkness might very reasonably be held to show the need of a revelation *at least in the sense of a republication of the religion of nature.* This accordingly was what the apolo gists of last century, such as Dr. Samuel Clarke,[2] chiefly insisted on. No attempt was made by them to disparage reason and natural religion. The fact was so far other wise that one might with more plausibility allege that too much importance was assigned by them to these, and too little to those aspects of Christianity which rise above reason into the region of mystery. Even Butler could write such a sentence as this: "For though natural religion is the foundation and principal part of Christi anity, it is not in any sense the whole of it." [3] Christi anity was regarded by its advocates, in those days, too much as a matter which could be proved by reason, and which existed to be reasoned about, and which could be shown to be true by plain common-sense arguments appreciable by any ordinary man; the aspects of the system which did not admit of such treatment being quietly allowed to fall into the background. "Common-sense" was the watchword of the age; a very good thing

---

[1] *Remarks upon a late Discourse of Free Thinking, by Phileleutheros Lipsiensis,* p. 12.

[2] *Discourses on the Evidences of Natural and Revealed Religion.* A review of this work forms the last chapter of Tyndal's *Christianity as Old as the Creation.*

[3] *Analogy,* Part II. chap. i.

in its way, but a very uncertain test of truth, often a very vulgar thing, and always a very fragmentary thing, viewed as an inventory of man's spiritual endowments. There is a great deal more in man than common sense, and the men of the eighteenth century do not seem to have been aware of the fact. As Mr. Pattison remarks: "The defect of the eighteenth century theology was not in having too much good sense, but in having nothing besides."[1]

Another prominent defect in the apologetic of that time is the low utilitarian view it took of the chief end of revealed religion, as intended to serve the purpose of a moral police to restrain vice and keep men within the bounds of decency. It was strongly insisted on, as a great recommendation of Christianity, that its doctrines had a powerful tendency to reform men's lives and correct their manners. This truth was emphasised very specially in connection with the doctrine of a future life, and its certified solemnities of bliss and woe. The fear of a future hell, it was gravely pointed out, helped to make sinners behave themselves here. What a degradation of religion to convert it into a mere purveyor of motives to morality, and hold it up as a bugbear to frighten evil livers into sobriety and righteousness, their secret inclinations remaining meanwhile unchanged, ready to break forth anew into excess and wrong, if only the external pressure could be got rid of! The aim was mean, and the success, had it been as great as its promoters wished, would have been a gain to the State rather than to the kingdom of God. But the success by all accounts was small. The age of the "Evidences" appears to have been an age of dissolute morals. What else was to be expected? What could a religion whose self-defence appealed to nothing higher than the common sense of the multitude, and which sought to influence men mainly through fear, do for the healing of moral evil? It had nothing to inspire enthusiasm in noble minds, and in the ignoble it was

---

[1] *Essays and Reviews*, p. 297.

more likely to provoke a desire to find it false, than to
drive them, contrary to inclination, into the practice of
virtue.   The cure of infidelity and immorality came from
a different quarter.   When the twilight of deism had
darkened into night, there came from heaven a new
dawn, bringing a restored faith in a more spiritual
Christianity, which was its own witness to regenerated
hearts.

The religious movement in Germany corresponding to
deism in England, goes by the name of *Aufklarung*, which
may be rendered in English *Illuminism*.   The name is
to a certain extent a key to the nature of the thing.   It
traces its origin to the Cartesian philosophy, which made
clearness the test of truth.   Illuminism is the idolatry
of clear ideas.   This idolatry began with Wolff, the
systematiser of the Leibnitzian philosophy, who sought to
place all known truth on a basis of mathematical demon
stration.   It was carried to its height by the so-called
popular philosophers of the *Aufklarung*, who, abandoning
the systematic method of teaching philosophy, discussed
philosophical problems in an easy literary style, adapted to
the taste and capacity of the general public.   In the hands
of these writers the Cartesian principle, "the true is the
clear," degenerated into an overweening value for vulgar
common sense.   This excessive respect for the uninstructed
human understanding meant in religion deism, in philo
sophy aversion to speculation, in morals eudæmonism, and
in all departments of knowledge Indifference to history,
acquaintance with what men of former times thought
being rendered unnecessary by the light each man carries
in his own breast.   From all these characteristics naturally
flowed another, very conspicuous in the writings of the
period, self-conceit.

The authors of the *Aufklarung* were very numerous.
The best known now are Lessing and Reimarus ; Lessing
through the intrinsic merits of his works ; Reimarus by aid
of Lessing, who published extracts from his MS. work

entitled *A Defence of the Rational Worshippers of God*,[1] under the name of *The Wolfenbuttel Fragments*, and by Strauss, who in 1862 published a digest or summary of that work.[2]

Lessing's general attitude is sufficiently indicated in two short writings, entitled *The Testament of John* and *The Religion of Christ;* and in the dramatic composition entitled *Nathan the Wise*. The first-named writing is a dialogue based on a story told by Jerome concerning the Apostle John, that when through great age he was so feeble that he had to be carried into the church, and was unable to speak at length, he was wont to repeat the words, " Children, love one another "; and being asked why he did this, replied, " It is the command of our Lord, and it is enough." The moral pointed by Lessing is, Christianity consists in love, not in holding any particular opinions concerning the founder of Christianity; in Lessing's own words: " At the first the salt of the earth swore by the *Testament* of John (love one another); now the salt of the earth swear by the *Gospel* of John "— as understood by the theologians to teach the dogma of Christ's divinity. The other piece, *The Religion of Christ*, conveys the same thought by suggesting a distinction between the religion which Christ Himself practised, and the Christian religion which worships Christ as God, the two being held to be incompatible. *Nathan the Wise* is a poetic tribute to the religion of reason, and has not inappropriately been called Lessing's poetical confession of faith.[3] The chief characters in the story are persons professing three kindred religions, the Mohammedan, the Jewish, and the Christian; at first they exhibit towards each other the religious pre judices in which they have been educated, but at last they

[1] *Apologie oder Schutzschrift für die vernünftigen Verehrer Gottes.* Hamburg, 1767.

[2] *Hermann Samuel Reimarus und seine Schutzschrift für die vernunftigen* **Verehrer Gottes.**

[3] Zeller, *Geschichte der Deutschen Philosophie.*

are discovered to be members of the same family. The moral is, that those who are divided by different positive religions are brethren as men; that men and religions are to be respected in proportion as they practise or inculcate humane feeling; that that which is common to all religions is of more value than that which is peculiar to any one of them; and that men are to be guided not by what they believe, but by what they do.[1]

While heart and soul devoted to the religion of reason, Lessing was tolerant in his attitude towards positive religion as at least a necessary evil. He did not, like the English deists, regard instituted religions as the inventions of priests and tyrants for selfish ends, but more genially considered them as, if inventions, at least useful inventions suited to the prevailing state of culture; or as the special forms which the religion of nature, the soul of all religion, took among the nations, just as the various forms of civil government are embodiments of natural right. Of this general tolerance for positive religions, the Jewish and the Christian of course got the benefit. Lessing regarded both as useful in their time when the human race was in its spiritual minority, but as destined to be superseded by the pure religion of reason when the race arrived at its majority, and justifiably neglected at all times by such as stand in no need of leading-strings. This view of what believers call revealed religion he developed in the well-known tractate, The Education of the Human Race, the leading idea of which is, that as education in general gives man nothing which he could not have from himself, but gives it sooner and easier, so the religious education conveyed by revelation gives to the human race nothing to which human reason left to itself would not eventually come, but only gave and gives the most important of these things, the essential truths of religion, earlier and more easily. In this process of education the Old Testament

---

[1] Those who desire full information concerning Lessing and his writings may consult Lessing: His Life and Writings, by James Sime, 1877.

is the primer, and the New Testament the second lesson-book, the latter superseding the former, and being destined itself to be superseded by the gospel of reason ; for the end of all education is to make the pupil independent of the means by which his training is carried on.

In propounding the foregoing theory as to a divine plan for the religious training of mankind, Lessing may be said to have acted rather as the apologist than as the assailant of revelation. His large genial nature gave houseroom to ideas and tendencies not easily reconciled. He was no mere creature of the *Aufklarung*. He possessed virtues which he did not acquire in that school, and he was free from some of its most characteristic vices. Herder called him the "right thinker among the free thinkers." The eulogy was not undeserved, and it pos-sesses value as coming from one who was worthy to be associated with Lessing, as occupying a far more appreciative attitude towards revelation and the Bible than that of the illuminists. Herder taught the Germans of his time to set a high value on the prophetical and poetical portions of the Old Testament, and so in his own way did good service as an apologist.[1]

While thus tolerant and genial in his attitude towards all positive religions, Lessing felt lively sympathy with men of more truculent temper. Hence the publication of *The Wolf-enbuttel Fragments*, which, like the whole work from which they were extracted, exhibit the worst features of eighteenth century unbelief, and especially that scurrilous treatment of the Bible and of Bible characters which makes the literature of deism now so unsavoury reading. Of this no

[1] An apologetic literature like that of England can hardly be said to have existed in Germany in last century. One book, however, of a professedly apologetic character may here be mentioned, that of F. V. Reinhard, *Versuch über den Plan welchen der Stifter der Christlichen Religion zum Besten der Menschen entwarf*. This book was published in 1781, and ran through several editions. It argues from the mere plan which Jesus formed for the wellbeing of mankind to the truth, and divine, incomparable value of His religion. It is a book still worth reading.

samples need here be given. For one thing only Reimarus deserves mention in a rapid sketch of the free thought of his time, viz. the distinct manner in which he formulates his fundamental objections to the Bible as the record of a supposed revelation. His criticism is based on two assumptions : that if a revelation was to be made it would be given in the form of a system of doctrine expressed in precise terms, and that men of blameless lives would be chosen to be the agents of revelation. Of course he had no difficulty in showing that neither of these requirements is satisfied by the Scriptures, and proceeding triumphantly to the conclusion that they are not the word of God. But his inference is to be disallowed because his assumptions are false. In making these assumptions he showed himself to be a disciple at once of the philosopher Wolf and of the Protestant dogmatists of the seventeenth century ; of the former in his love of system, of the latter in taking over from them the doctrinaire conception of revelation, as consisting in the supernatural communication of a body of theological truth through the writers of the sacred books. The use he made of that old orthodox conception as a weapon of attack on the faith shows the need for revising the idea of revelation, and for asking whether revelation and the Bible are synonymous terms, and whether the chief end of re velation be indeed to communicate theological instruction.[1]

In the closing chapter of his book on Reimarus, Strauss remarks on the inconsistency of which eighteenth century unbelievers, like Reimarus, were guilty in freely imputing to the agents of revelation, not excepting Jesus and the apostles, trickery and fraud, while recognising the purity of Christ's teaching, and the enthusiasm with which the apostles propagated the lying invention of the resurrection. The explanation of the riddle he offers is to this effect: The men of the eighteenth century assumed the historical truth of the Bible narratives, and yet were unbelievers in the miraculous. But the *caput mortuum* which remains

---

[1] On this *vide* my book on *The Chief End of Revelation.*

after the spirit of the divine has departed out of a revela
tion and miracle — history is deceit. The nineteenth
century gets over the difficulty by not assuming the truth
of the narratives, but rather regarding the miraculous as an
after-growth, a moss overspreading in the course of ages
the historical foundation, without conscious intention on
the part of any one to gain currency for falsehood. It
also recognises the importance of the imagination as a
factor in human history, in contrast to the men of the
earlier century, who set value only on common sense, and
saw in man only a reasoning being. Hence the difference
between the two ages in their respective treatment of
positive religions. The former traced the origin of all
positive religions to conscious fraud; the latter refuses to
believe that any religion had its origin in fraud. The
former levelled down all positive religions to one low moral
level of imposture; the latter levels up all positive religions
to the same high level of sincere, though it may be
mistaken, hallucinated conviction. Broadly speaking, the
distinction thus taken between the two ages is well
founded. Whether the modern method of disposing of the
miraculous be more successful than that which it has
superseded is another question. Deceivers, or self-
deceived, such are the alternatives. The alternative now
in favour is certainly the less injurious to human nature,
and the less offensive to religious feeling.

Of French free thought in last century, which was to
some extent an echo or product of English deism,
Voltaire and Rousseau are the leading representatives.
A full history of the movement would have to speak of
both, but in this hasty outline Rousseau alone need be
referred to. He is much the more worthy spokesman of
the religion of nature. Voltaire's works are now unread-
able, but the *Confession of Faith of a Savoyard Vicar*,[1] in

---

[1] It forms a part of *Emile*, a treatise on education in the shape of an ideal
history, and sets forth what the author thinks should be taught the pupil,
at the proper age, on the subject of religion.

which Rousseau expounds his religious position, can still
be read with a thrill of delight.   It is worthy to be
associated with *Nathan the Wise* as a poetical eulogium on
natural religion, and it is charged with a passion and a
pathos all its own.   It is in keeping throughout with the
spirit of the eighteenth century, both in method and in
substance, so that it is unnecessary to offer an elaborate
analysis of its contents.   The source of truth for the
confessor is plain common sense, the inner light, *la lumière
intérieure*, and the revelation such as we might expect from
such a quarter.   He proves the being and attributes of God
to his own satisfaction by familiar processes of reasoning,
including the argument from design.   He assigns to man,
in virtue of his intelligence and freedom, a sovereign place
in the world.   While claiming for man this exalted position,
he at the same time owns that he is a slave, through the power
of the passions inherent in the body.   He acknowledges the
existence of moral evil, but strives to clear God of all
blame for it, and to reduce its amount to a minimum, in
this as in other respects true to the optimism characteristic
of the deistic type of thought.[1]   He asserts the competency
of conscience to be the guide of life, and follows its guid
ance as far as the body with its imperious desires will
allow.   He cherishes devout sentiments towards the Deity,
refusing, however, to pray for any blessing, spiritual or
temporal, and contenting himself with the one all-sufficient
utterance of the pious mind, " Thy will be done."

Having finished his exposition of the creed of natural
theism, the author of *Emile* makes the vicar of Savoy
indicate his attitude towards revealed religion.   He starts
with the assertion that natural religion is sufficient for all
practical purposes.   What need for more ?   What purity of
morals, what dogma useful to man can be drawn from a
positive religion that cannot be reached by the use of
reason ?   But suppose a positive religion to be required.

---

[1] This will be more fully explained in Book I. chap. v., on "The
Deistic Theory of the Universe."

There are many such; how find out the right one? Either they are all alike good, as various embodiments of the one Catholic religion of nature, or there must be signs by which the solitary acceptable one can be known—proofs accessible to all men everywhere; for if there were a religion on earth outside of which salvation was impossible, and in one place in the world a single honest mortal had not been impressed with its evidence, the God of that religion would be an unjust, cruel tyrant. But the examination of these evidences is a very serious affair, so serious as to amount to a *reductio ad absurdum* of the theory which makes a revealed religion necessary to salvation. In view of what the task involves, it is not credible that God can have required such an amount of toil and trouble in order to salva tion. " I, for one," protests the vicar, " have never been able to believe that God ordained me under pain of damnation to be learned. I have therefore shut all the books. There is one only, open to the eyes of all, the Book of Nature."

While thus declining to believe in the necessity of a revelation recorded in a book written in learned tongues, Rousseau speaks with marked respect of Christianity and its Author. The holiness of the gospel, he confesses, is an argument which speaks to his heart, and to which he should be sorry to find a good reply. Can a book at once so sublime and so simple be the work of men? Can it be that He whose history it relates is no more than a man? Shall we say that the history of the Gospels is an invention? No Jewish authors could invent that tone, that morality. The gospel has characters of truth so striking, so perfectly inimitable, that the inventor would be more astonishing than the hero. Yet, on the other hand, that same gospel is full of incredible things opposed to reason which no man of sense can receive. What is to be done in presence of such contradictions? " To be modest and circumspect, to respect in silence what one can neither reject nor compre hend, and to humble oneself before the Great Being, who alone knows the truth."

SECTION IV.—*Free Thought in the Present Time.*

The contrast drawn by Strauss between eighteenth and nineteenth century unbelief might be indefinitely extended. We live in a different world, and, whether believers or unbelievers, find ourselves related to a greatly altered environment. Science has made a mighty advance, new philosophies have arisen, biblical criticism has been at work, the religions of mankind have been studied on the comparative method. The result is that new questions have come to the front, unbelief has assumed new forms, and faith has been compelled to defend itself with new weapons. To indicate the full extent of the change would take longer space than can be spared; it must suffice here to point out the altered attitude in reference to the subject of revelation and the Scriptures.[1]

In two respects the free thought of our time differs from that of the eighteenth century. The first is that referred to by Strauss. The offensive depreciatory criticism of the Bible, its authors, and principal characters, too common in the earlier period, especially in England, has given place to a sincere recognition of the sacred volume as of exceptional value, and worthy of "an high and reverend esteem." Modern unbelief, however, does not, any more than that of the eighteenth century, concede the claim advanced for the Bible to authority as a rule of faith. Not only so; it does not admit that the Bible itself supplies any basis or justification for such a claim, and this is the second point of difference between it and the unbelief of the earlier time. The free thinkers of the eighteenth century accepted from Protestant scholastic theologians their doctrinaire conception of revelation as consisting in the communication of dogmas concerning God, man, the world, and their relations, and of the Bible as the repository of such dogmas, and reasoned destructively from

---

[1] For a more extended contrast between the free thought of the two centuries, *vide* Book I. chap. vi., on "Modern Speculative Theism."

this idea. The tendency of our time, on the contrary, is to regard the Bible as profitable, not for doctrine but for life, as edifying " literature " rather than as divinely - given instruction in " dogma "; as fitted and intended solely for religious edification, and laying no claim to any such function as scholastic theology has ascribed to it.

In this altered view of the Bible, the nineteenth century is in close sympathy with a great free thinker of the seventeenth. Spinoza is nearer us than are the deists and illuminists. He is indeed, as the late Mr. Matthew Arnold remarked, coming to the front,[1] insomuch that there is no man whose writings it is more worth while studying in order to understand modern thought in philo sophy and religion. The work in which his views on the Bible are stated is the *Tractatus Theologico-Politicus*, the professed design of which is to offer an apology for free thought—a defence of the liberty of philosophising on all subjects human and divine, as not forbidden by a right use of the Scriptures, and not contrary to the true interest of the State.[2] The position contended for by the author is that the Bible was not intended to teach, and does not in fact teach, any definite doctrines concerning God, man, or the world, but has for its sole object to promote the practice of piety, justice, and charity. A man may make a very wise, good use of these holy writings, and be a true believer in the Scripture sense, and hold all manner of opinions concerning God, faith and piety requiring not true but pious opinions. To support this position Spinoza enters on a discussion of the nature of prophecy, and the value of miracles, real or supposed, as a source of know ledge concerning God. With regard to the former, he arrives at the conclusion that we must not seek in the

[1] *Vide* Essay on " Spinoza and the Bible " in *Essays in Criticism*.

[2] The *Tractatus* was published anonymously in 1670, two years after the publication of Hobbes' *Leviathan*, to which in its political part it bears a close resemblance. The occasion of its being written, as the author in forms us in the preface, was the disputes between Calvinists and Arminians, which led to the assembling of the Synod of Dort.

prophetic writings for accurate views concerning God, but merely for such teaching as tends to promote piety and morality, the prophets not being raised by their prophetic gift above liability to ignorance and error, in reference to matters which have no bearing on charity or practice. On the subject of miracles he maintains that from miraculous events, however viewed, we can learn neither the essence, the existence, nor the providence of God, all these being best perceived from the fixed and immutable order of nature. With regard to the apostolic writings in the New Testament, he admits that they do contain dogmatic or philosophic elements, but he seeks to rob these of all claim to be authoritative statements, by the suggestion that the apostles wrote not as prophets but as theological doctors, not prefacing their utterances with a " Thus saith the Lord," but addressing their views to reason, and supporting them by argument, so that they are to be taken for what they are intrinsically worth.

As a protest against a purely scholastic conception o revelation, these views of Spinoza, however extreme, are of real and permanent value. How far they are from being out of date may be seen from such a work as *Literature and Dogma*, which is simply the *Tractatus* done into modern English. This revival in recent years of the bold opinions of the philosophic Jew of Amsterdam by a distinguished British man of letters, whose works have been widely and sympathetically read, seems to give urgency to the questions, What is the *raison d'être* of the Bible ? what is the true conception of revelation ? Two widely contrasted theories, which may be distinguished as the theological and the ethical, have been propounded. Which of the two is the true theory, or are they both erroneous in different directions ?

Spinoza's view of the Bible was based on a preliminary inquiry into its literary characteristics, along the lines of investigation made familiar to us by the modern science of biblical introduction. Whatever we may think of his final conclusion, there can be no doubt that his method was sound. Criticism must precede theological construc tion. We must learn all we can about the history of these holy writings before we can be in a position to determine with confidence to what extent or intent they are profit able for doctrine. Modern critics are busily engaged in the study in which Spinoza played the part of a pioneer, and their labours cannot be ignored by any one who would wisely speak as to the didactic value of the Scriptures.

CHAPTER II.

THE FUNCTION AND METHOD OF APOLOGETIC.

LITERATURE.—Sack, *Christliche Apologetik*, 1829; Drey, *Die Apologetik*, etc., 1838; Lechler, *Ueber den Begriff der Apologetik, Studien und Kritiken*, 1839; Schleiermacher, *Kurze Darstellung des Theologischen Studiums*, 1810; Delitzsch, *System der Christlichen Apologetik*, 1869; Baumstark, *Christliche Apologetik auf Anthropologischer Grundl. r.* 1872–89; Ebrard, *Apologetik*, 1874-5 (translated by T. & T. Clark); Chalmers, *Evidences of the Christian Revelation*.

The foregoing historical sketch may suffice to convey a rudimentary and popular idea of the need for and the nature and aim of Christian Apologetic. In this chapter an attempt will be made to define more exactly the function and method of this branch of theological study, and to indicate the plan on which the present work is constructed.

Some topics of a scholastic nature discussed in recent apologetic treatises may here receive a passing notice.

German writers, always systematic, are careful to dis tinguish between *Apology* and *Apologetic*. There is, of course, an obvious difference. An apology is a particular defence of the Christian faith with reference to a definite attack; apologetic, on the other hand, is the science of apology, or the defence of Christianity reduced to system. A recent writer thus puts the distinction :—

"Apologetic differs from simple apology by method based on a distinct principle. There are apologies which consist of replies to definite attacks on Christianity, and allow their method to be determined by these. Such, *e.g.*, were the two apologies of Justin Martyr, which deal with a series of single attacks, and are excellent as apologies, though very insufficient as apologetic. Christian apologetic differs from apology in this that, instead of allowing its course to be fixed by the accidental assaults made at a particular time, it deduces the method of defence and the defence itself out of the essence of Christianity. Every apologetic is apology, but not every apology is apologetic. Apologetic is that science which, from the essence of Christianity itself, de termines what kinds of attacks are possible, what sides of Christian truth are open to attack, and what false principles lie at the foundation of all attacks actual or possible. ˮ

According to this definition, the business of the sys tematic apologist is not, either to make a full historical collection of all past apologies for Christianity, or to add to the list a new apology directed against the most recent efforts of anti-Christian thinkers, but to make students in this department acquainted with the sources of attack and the science of defence, so that as occasion arises they may be able to play the part of expert apologists themselves. Accepting this as so far a true enough account of the matter, it still remains open to consideration whether the method of historical induction would not be a good way of ascertaining both the sources of attack and the laws of defence; also whether it be either desirable or possible so to isolate apologetic from contemporary influences, that it shall give no more prominence to prevailing forms of unbelief than to others which were prevalent in former times. These two things it is certainly important to know: what answer believers of other ages gave to those who

¹ Ebrard, *Apologetik*, i. 3.

examined them concerning their faith, and what answer we ourselves should give to those who examine us now; in other words, the history of past apologies, and the apology which befits the present hour.

At one in regard to the verbal distinction between apology and apologetic, the German apologists are by no means agreed as to the precise nature of this theological discipline. The idea of apologetic has been very variously defined. Sack defines it as the theological discipline of the ground of the Christian religion as a *divine fact*.[1] He distinguishes between an ideal and a real side of Christianity, and while assigning to systematic theology the task of developing the former aspect as doctrine, he gives to apologetic the function of dealing with the reality of Christianity, and so laying the foundation of dogmatic. Sack was doubtless led into this obviously one-sided view by the circumstance that in his day the attack against Christianity, as conducted, *e.g.*, by Strauss in his first *Leben Jesu*, was directed mainly against its historical foundation —a fact illustrating the manner in which contemporary unbelief almost involuntarily directs the course of apologetic thought. Another writer, Drey, belonging to the same period, and subject to the same influences, defines apologetic as the philosophy of the Christian revelation and of its history. With Lechler, the well-known author of an excellent history of English deism, the point of view changes, and apologetic becomes the scientific demonstration of the Christian religion as the absolute religion, the exclusively and ideally true, alone satisfying the need of man as a religious being, and setting forth the pure unmixed truth concerning God.[2] This view is not less one-sided than the former, and accordingly a third class of writers, including Ebrard and Delitzsch, combine the two aspects, and assign to apologetic a double function; on the one

---

[1] *Christliche Apologetik*, p. 4.

[2] *Vide* the article in *Studien und Kritiken* referred to at the beginning of this chapter.

hand, that of defending the eternal truth contained in Christianity as tested by the facts of nature and of human consciousness, and on the other, that of defending Christianity as a historical fact viewed in its organic connection with the general history of religion.

Of less moment is the question as to the proper place of apologetic in a curriculum of theological study. Some have disputed its claim to any place on such grounds as these: that apologetic has no distinct material to work upon, but borrows its material from other sciences; that its function of defence is one which has to be performed by every positive science for itself, and by theology in particular; that what unbelievers attack is always some dogmatic truth, and if the truth assailed be properly stated and handled by the systematic theologian, nothing remains to be said by the apologist; finally, that the truths of Christianity are self-evidencing, and that the evidences in which apologists usually deal are of little intrinsic value as means of exorcising doubt and propagating faith. The larger number take a more favourable view of the claims of apologetic, and are also on the whole agreed as to the position to be assigned to it in the systematic study of theology. The view expressed by Schleiermacher is pretty generally accepted, viz. that apologetic is a branch of philosophical theology, and as such ought to be studied at the commencement of a theological course.[1] It may indeed be regarded as the mediator between philosophy and theology. The need for such mediation has been indicated by representing philosophy as ending with blank strokes and signs of interrogation, pointing to theology as the science which starts where philosophy terminates, and answers the questions it has left unanswered.[2] But the attitude of philosophy is not always so modest. Not unfrequently it leaves the mind of the student prepossessed with opinions concerning God, man, and the world opposed to those which underlie

[1] Vide Kurze Darstellung des Theologischen Studiums.
[2] So Delitzsch, System der Christlichen Apologetik, p. 30.

the Christian faith, so that at least one, if not the principal, function of apologetic must be to deal with anti-Christian prejudices, that Christianity may get a fair hearing.

These last words indicate the point of view from which the subject on hand is to be contemplated in the present work, and which, dismissing scholastic questions, I now proceed more fully to explain.

Apologetic, then, as I conceive it, is a preparer of the way of faith, an aid to faith against doubts whencesoever arising, especially such as are engendered by philosophy and science. Its specific aim is to help men of ingenuous spirit who, while assailed by such doubts, are morally in sympathy with believers. It addresses itself to such as are drawn in two directions, towards and away from Christ, as distinct from such as are confirmed either in unbelief or in faith. Defence presupposes a foe, but the foe is not the dogmatic infidel who has finally made up his mind that Christianity is a delusion, but anti-Christian thought in the believing man's own heart. "A man's foes shall be they of his own household." The wise apologist instinctively shuns conflict with dogmatic unbelief as futile. He desiderates and assumes in those for whom he writes a certain fairness and openness of mind, a generous spirit under hostile bias which he seeks to remove, a bias due to no ignoble cause, animated even in its hostility by worthy motives. But, on the other hand, with equal decision he avoids partisanship with dogmatic belief. He regards himself as a defender of the catholic faith, not as a hired advocate or special pleader for a particular theological system. He distinguishes between religion and theology, between faith and opinion, between essential doctrines and the debateable dogmas of the schools. There are many special views held by believers, of which, whether true or false, he takes no cognisance; many controversies internal to faith, such as that between Calvinists and Arminians, with which he does not intermeddle.

The attitude and temper characteristic of the apologist

disappoint extremists on both sides. The thoroughgoing
unbeliever is dissatisfied with him because, while conceding
much, he does not give up everything. The dogmatising
believer, on the other hand, is displeased because he con
cedes anything, or even seems indifferent to the minutest
items of an elaborate creed, and is ready to call him
deserter and traitor. Between the two the apologist is apt
to fare ill, and he may well be tempted to shun a task which
is more likely to expose him to misunderstanding than to
earn thanks and honour. But he must take his risk, and
be satisfied if his efforts prove useful to those for whose
benefit they are undertaken, and help some honest doubters
to sincere stable faith.

The end proposed may seem to restrict within very
narrow limits the sphere of the apologist's influence.
" Honest doubters," sincere inquirers, earnest seekers after
God and truth, groping their way amid the darkness of
involuntary misapprehensions, how few they are at any
time! How much more numerous the contented slaves
of opinion, Christian or non-Christian, according to the
accidents of birth and education! It may be so, yet, even
if few, men of the class contemplated are supremely worth
caring for. One such straying sheep is more worth the
shepherd's care than ninety-and-nine who have never
known what it is to doubt. But they are not so few as on
first impressions we may think, especially if we do not
form too ideal a conception of the state, but include in the
class all in whom there is a sincere sympathy with the
good, an implicit rudimentary faith in God, a spiritual
receptivity that would readily respond to such teaching as
that of Christ, a vague, restless longing for light on the
dark problems of life, that under proper guidance might
ripen into Christian discipleship. This widened definition
takes us outside the Church, and even outside Christendom,
and includes among our possible readers many belonging to
the Churchless mass of men and women living in nominally
Christian countries, and who shall say how many even

among the vast millions whom we, with a pity tinged with a little self-righteousness, call "the heathen"? The common people of Judæa heard Jesus gladly. How many of the same class who are never seen in our churches would gladly hear Him now, if His own true voice could only reach their ear! And are there not many in heathen lands who are nearer God, and the kingdom of God, and the Lord Jesus Christ, than are not a few of the "Christians" who find their way into India, China, and other parts of the non-Christian world on commercial, political, scientific, or other errands? As he ponders such questions, the apologist begins to feel that he may be addressing himself to a very large constituency, including, besides professional students of theology fresh from the study of philosophy, and no longer resting peacefully in the faith of their childhood, young men of all ranks and professions keenly sensitive to the higher influences of their time, honest, thoughtful artisans, who amid their daily toil remember that life is more than meat, good pagans who show themselves to be implicit Christians by deeds of kindness to Christ's brethren the poor and needy.[1]

On the subject of *method* great diversity of opinion and practice has prevailed among apologetic writers. In England it has been customary, following the traditions of the deistic controversy, to distribute the topics belonging to apologetics under the two heads of the Evidences of Natural Religion and the Evidences of Revealed Religion, the former including all that can be known from the works of nature and the spiritual constitution of man, the latter all that tends to confirm the supernatural teaching concerning God contained in the Scriptures. The evidences of revealed religion have been subdivided into the "external" and the "internal," the one term, in its simplest acceptation, signifying the evidence for Christianity derivable from sources

---

[1] I do not remember to have read anything more to my taste on the proper aim and temper of the apologist than Harrison's *Problems of Christianity and Scepticism.* Longmans & Co., 1891.

outside Scripture, *e.g.* from heathen writers; the other denoting the evidence derivable from the Bible itself, such as the consistency of its teaching, the loftiness of its morality, the character of Christ. Neither the general division nor the special subdivision supplies a satisfactory scheme of distribution. Not the former, because by isolating the topics falling under the head of natural theology for independent discussion, it deprives them of the interest arising out of a conscious connection with the burning questions of Christianity. Whatever we discuss, whether it be the being of God, or the reality of a righteous benignant Providence, or the certainty of a life to come, it ought to be felt that the discussion is carried on in the interest of the Christian faith. The traditional subdivision of the Christian evidences is still less satisfactory. The distinction between " external " and " internal " is neither clear in itself nor susceptible of consistent application, as is frankly acknowledged by Dr. Chalmers in his treatise on the *Evidences of the Christian Revelation*,[1] and as any one can ascertain for himself by subjecting his own mind and memory to a process of interrogation on the subject. He will find that he is liable to forget which are the evidences usually reckoned external and which the internal, and that he is not quite sure to which of the two categories any particular piece of evidence, say that from miracles, belongs; or, in case he remembers how it is classed in the books, able at once to give a reason for the classification. The wise course to be pursued by any one who has occasion to deal with the subject is to discard the confused and misleading distinction altogether, and to look out for some other principle of classification.

In Germany writers on apologetics base their method on a scientific principle, instead of on a purely outward, arbitrary, and formal arrangement, as has been customary in England. As yet, however, no proposed method has secured general concurrence, each writer adopting a plan of

[1] Vol. ii. pp. 8–10.

his own for which he claims peculiar advantages. Baumstark builds on an anthropological foundation. Taking man, his nature and his needs, for his starting-point, he seeks to show that Christianity corresponds perfectly to the religious wants of humanity, confirming the positive argument by a negative one directed to prove that no other religion satisfies these wants. He claims for his plan that it admits of the whole apologetic material being easily grouped around the psychological demonstration, and, further, that it transfers the argument to a field on which we engage on advantageous terms in direct conflict with the chief modern foes of Christianity—pantheism and materialism. This method is, to say the least, very legitimate. It conducts us into the heart of the subject, and gives greatest prominence to those aspects of it which at the present time are of pressing importance.

With Delitzsch the centre is not man, but the idea or essence of Christianity itself. His method is, first of all, to determine what Christianity is, then to analyse the idea into its elements, and thereafter to show in detail that these are, one and all, in harmony with the moral and religious consciousness of man, and contain at once the refutation and the truth of all opposing philosophies and religions. The result of the argument is to exhibit the idea of Christianity as being the truth of theism as opposed to polytheism and pantheism, the truth of pantheism as opposed to deism, and the truth of polytheism as opposed to simple theism. It is a fine conception, though, in the working out of it, the author gives the impression of a man so fully persuaded in his own mind, and so utterly at rest in his conviction of the truth of Christianity, as to be disinclined to enter into much detail in dealing with the position of opponents.

The method of Ebrard is somewhat similar to that of Delitzsch. Having briefly stated the presuppositions of Christianity as the religion of redemption,—viz. the existence of a living God, an everlasting moral law, the freedom and responsibility of the human will, the existence in man of a state of opposition to the law, and the impossibility of self-redemption,—he asks and answers at length the question, Whether these are or are not in harmony with the facts of nature and of human consciousness? He then proceeds to the negative part of his task, which undertakes the refutation of anti-Christian systems, and more especially those of materialism and pantheism. Finally, he considers Christianity comparatively as one of the religions of the world, with a view to establish its claim to be the one true divinely-given religion, the perfect realisation of the religious ideal.

These samples may suffice to illustrate the variety in plan with which it is possible to construct an apologetic system aspiring to scientific form and completeness.[1] It is now time to explain the course to be pursued in the present less ambitious attempt.

The aim naturally determines the method. The aim is to secure for Christianity a fair hearing with conscious or implicit believers whose faith is stifled or weakened by anti-Christian prejudices of varied nature and origin. The purpose of apologetic, as thus conceived, is not so much scientific as practical. It is not designed to give theoretical instruction in a branch of theological knowledge, but rather to serve the purpose of a moral discipline, by dispossessing ingenuous truth-loving minds of opinions which tend to make faith difficult, presenting Christianity under aspects which they had not previously contemplated, suggesting explanations of difficulties which they had not before thought of, and so making it possible for them to be Christians with their whole mind and heart.

For the accomplishment of this end, the first step

---

[1] Among writers who have treated the subject from still different points of view may be mentioned: Fr. H. R. Frank, *System der Christlichen Gewissheit*, 1870. His starting-point is the Christian consciousness. Kaftan, *Die Wahrheit der Christlichen Religion*, 1888. His guiding thought is the Christian idea of the kingdom of God as the highest good.

obviously is to make sure that men know what Christianity really is. Much of the weak, half-hearted attachment to the Christian faith which prevails arises from lack of such knowledge. And if we wish to dispel this baleful ignorance, we must not begin with any ready-made idea of the Christian religion extracted from the creeds or current in the Churches, but, remembering that much prejudice against both creeds and Churches exists in many minds which we should desire to influence, we must remount to the fountainhead, and learn the nature of our faith from the records of Christ's life and teaching contained in the Gospels. Nay, to avoid outrunning the sympathies of honest doubt by seeming to forestall the solution of any grave apologetic problems, we must impose on ourselves a still further restriction, and gather our information regarding nascent Christianity, in the first place, from the first three Gospels, leaving the fourth on one side to be dealt with at a subsequent stage. An honest endeavour to extract from these Gospels a simple account of what Jesus was and taught might, without further trouble, win to hearty faith many whose alienation has its root in social grievances rather than in science or philosophy or biblical criticism.

But all doubt cannot be so easily healed. There are prejudices against Christianity to be dealt with arising out of philosophy, science, history, criticism. In view of these, we must consider not merely what are the Christian facts, but what are the presuppositions of Christianity. There are two classes of presuppositions to be considered—the speculative or philosophical and the historical. As to the former, Christianity is not a philosophy, but it implies nevertheless, as indeed does every religion, certain characteristic ways of regarding God, man, and the world, and their relations; in other words, a certain *theory of the universe*. It will be of service to ascertain what the Christian theory of the universe is, and, having done that, to state and compare with it other more or less antagonistic theories, so that it may appear which of them, in view of all interests, is most worthy to be entertained. The consideration of this speculative class of questions will occupy our attention in the first book of this work. On a narrow view of the function of Christian apologetic, it may seem as if such abstruse discussions might be omitted. Why cannot we take for granted the being of God, for example, and go on at once to consider the positive evi dences of the Christian faith? But taking for granted the being of God will not do much for us. The great matter is not *that* God is, but *what* He is. All men, in one fashion or another, admit the existence of somewhat that may be called God. Where they differ widely is in their conceptions of God's nature and character. And what the Christian apologist is concerned to show is not that a God of some sort exists, but that the Christian idea of God is worthier to be received than that of the pantheist or the deist, or of any rival theory of the uni verse. This task he cannot shirk if he would thoroughly perform the duty he has undertaken, that of establishing doubters in the Christian faith. For it cannot be ques tioned that what keeps many in a semi-sceptical state of mind is that they consciously or unconsciously cherish a thought of God belonging to an entirely different theory of the universe from that which is in harmony with Christian belief.

Christianity has also its historical presuppositions. Jesus belonged to a peculiar people, which had a singular history, possessed a remarkable literature, and cherished extraordinary ideas of its destiny. In its literature that people is called an *elect* race, implying an exceptional relation to God, and a position of distinction as compared with other peoples. It will be of importance to form just conceptions of the nature of Israel's privilege, what it involved with regard to herself, and also what it signified in regard to the outside nations, and to inquire how far the religious history of the ancient world justifies Israel's claim to be a people near to God in knowledge and in life.

In the course of this study we may learn to recognise as a fact the superiority of Israel, as in possession of a divine revelation, while doing full justice to all that is good in heathenism. We may also learn, independently of all doubtful questions of criticism, to set a high value on the Hebrew Scriptures, in which Israel's history is related, her religion unfolded, her sin exposed, and her undying hope proclaimed. These topics will occupy us in a second book, having for its general heading, "The Historical Preparation for Christianity."

A third book will treat of Christianity itself, or the Christian origins, including such topics as these: Jesus in Himself, and as the Christ; His work; His resurrection; the faith of the early Church concerning Him; Paul as a factor in the nascent religion; primitive Christianity; the historic value of the evangelic documents. The considera tion of these weighty themes will help us to appreciate the claim of Christianity to be the consummation of all that was best in Old Testament piety, and the absolute religion, and of Christ to be the *Light of the world.*

BOOK I.

THEORIES OF THE UNIVERSE, CHRISTIAN AND ANTI-CHRISTIAN.

———◆———

CHAPTER I.

THE CHRISTIAN FACTS.

LITERATURE.—The Gospels of Matthew, Mark, and Luke.

In making an attempt in the present chapter to state the Christian facts, it may be well, in order to prevent mis understanding, to begin by explaining that by the expression is not meant all that a Christian man believes to be true concerning the person, life, and teaching of Jesus, but only the things related in the Synoptical Gospels on these topics which possess such a high degree of probability that they may be provisionally accepted as facts, even by those who scan the evangelic records with a critical eye. The task now on hand is beset with difficulty, arising from the cir cumstance that these records cannot, without proof, be assumed to contain only pure objective history, but may at least plausibly be regarded as history coloured more or less by the faith of the narrators. How much or how little solid fact any one finds in them depends partly on the philosophical bias which he brings to the examination, partly on the extent to which, on grounds of historical criticism, he thinks he can trace the colouring influence of faith. The estimates formed of the amount of historical matter in the Gospels are, accordingly, very diverse. Some reduce the kernel of hard fact to a meagre minimum : the beautiful moral teaching in the Sermon on the Mount, or a new method and secret for attaining the reward of righteousness—the method of inwardness, the secret of self-denial.[1] Some even go the length of doubting whether anything whatever can be definitely ascertained concerning Jesus; whether "the Sermon on the Mount" was ever preached, and whether "the Lord's Prayer" was ever prayed by Him.[2] Such style themselves, with reference to the history of Christ, *agnostics*, men who do not know, and who maintain that it is impossible to know. The imposing authority of great names that could be cited in support of such sceptical views might well scare one from attempting to determine the outlines of the Christianity of Christ. Nevertheless, in spite of discouragement we must try.

We may find a good clue, to begin with, as to what was central in the thought and religion of Jesus, in the apologetic elements contained among His recorded sayings. What was He above all things obliged to apologise for ? It was, as we have already learned, His love to the outcast sinful, the "publicans and sinners" of Jewish society. That love, then, we may take to be the first and fundamental Christian fact. It is a very instructive fact. It shows us for one thing that Christ is not to be thought of primarily and principally as a teacher coming with some wonderful new doctrines, moral or religious, revealing to the initiated some unheard of method and secret for the attainment of felicity. This needs to be said and to be reiterated; for there is an inveterate tendency among believers and unbelievers alike to assume that revelation must consist in the communication of instruction, and that the founder of a religion must before all things be a great original teacher.[3] And, beyond doubt, Jesus was such a teacher;

---

[1] So the late Mr. Matthew Arnold in *Literature and Dogma.*

[2] So Mr. Huxley in the *Nineteenth Century,* April 1889, p. 487.

[3] On this *vide* my *Chief End of Revelation,* chap. i.

but the thing to be insisted on is that, great though He
was as a teacher, He was still greater in His love.   His
love was the great novelty, the primary revelation He
had to make—a revelation made, as all God's greatest
revelations have been made, by deeds rather than by
words.   But by words likewise.   For no recorded word
of Jesus is more characteristic, more credibly authentic,
and more significant as an index of His own con
ception of His mission, than this : " The Son of man is
come to save that which was lost," with which may be
associated that other parabolic saying : "They that be
whole need not a physician, but they that are sick."
Thereby He intimated that His proper vocation was that
of a Saviour or Healer of spiritual disease, and suggested
the thought that Christianity is the religion of redemption,
a religion which announces and applies a new divine power
of love to cure moral evil.   That power He splendidly
exemplified in His own ministry, effecting marvellous
spiritual recoveries among the depraved by a sympathy
which no moral vileness could repel, drawing the sinful to
Him in perfect confidence of welcome, and making credible
the existence of similar love in the heart of God.

Jesus healed men's bodies as well as their souls.   The
same sympathy which made Him pity them in their sin,
caused Him also to bear on His heart the burden of their
sicknesses.   Some of the best authenticated narratives in
the Gospels are accounts of cures wrought instantaneously
on the bodies of sick persons.   The stories are found in
all the three first Gospels, and may be regarded as belonging to the original stock of apostolic tradition.[1]   They
are all very marvellous ; some, if not all, seem positively
miraculous, not explicable otherwise than by the assump
tion that Jesus had at His command a supernatural divine
power.   That one so exceptionally humane should desire,
if possible, to remove all evil, physical as well as moral,

---

[1] *Vide* my *Miraculous Element in the Gospels*, chap. iv. ; also Book III.
chap. iv. of this work.

was perfectly natural ; that He was able by a word to heal a *leper* seems to show that in some preternatural manner " God was with Him." [1]

Apart from their miraculous aspect, these works of healing possess permanent significance as showing the comprehensiveness of Christ's conception of salvation. Nothing lay out of His way which in any respect concerned the wellbeing of man. In His healing ministry He was the pioneer of Christian philanthropy, and lent the sanction of His example to all movements which aim at social amelioration.

Though Jesus was not a philosopher or mere ethical teacher, yet He did teach, and in a most characteristic style. What a religious teacher has to say concerning God and man is always important and worth noting. Now Christ's doctrine of God was not elaborate. It was remarked of Him by shrewd observers among the common people of Judæa that He taught " not as the scribes," which was as if we should say now of any new religious teacher arising among us, " He teaches not as a professional theologian." Jesus taught His doctrine of God by a single word. He always called God " Father " and that in connections which gave His thought about God a very new and startling aspect, offensive to those who were reputedly holy and righteous called " Pharisees," very welcome to all others, that is to the great mass of the Jewish people. The name as He used it implied that God had paternal goodwill to the unthankful and evil, to the immoral and irreligious, to the outcasts ; that He was the God and Father of the mob, of the publicans and sinners, of the lost sheep of the house of Israel, not merely of Pharisees, scribes, and priests. It was only an extension of Christ's thought about God when Paul said that God was not the God of the Jews only, but also of the Gentiles ; and we simply apply His grand inspiring doctrine to our modern circumstances when we say God is the God and

[1] *Vide Miraculous Element in the Gospels*, chap. v.

Father of the churchless, of the proletariat, of the denizens of the lanes and slums of our great cities, of society's out casts and non-elect. It was a new idea of God, whose import is not yet fully realised, a revelation full of hope for humanity.

Christ's idea of man was kindred to His idea of God. It was as remote as possible from that of Celsus, whose feeling towards mankind was one of cynical contempt. Jesus thought a man a being of infinite value, in view of his spiritual endowments and possibilities. He said with an emphasis previously unknown, a man *is* a man, yea a son of God. He said this not with reference to picked samples—holy, wise, learned men; on the contrary, of the holiness, wisdom, and learning in vogue He seemed to have a very poor opinion; still less with reference to men that were rich, for of mere material wealth He always spoke with a compassionate disdain. He affirmed the indefeasible worth of human nature with reference to the poor, the ignorant, the foolish, the immoral, the irreligious; to the amazement and disgust of those belonging to the upper select classes of society. He taught this revolutionary doctrine not as a Rabbi delivering theoretical lectures in the school to his disciples, but chiefly by the far harder and more testing method of action; freely associ ating with people low down in the social scale, whose worth to God and men, in spite of degradation, He per sistently proclaimed. The reality and extent of the degrada tion He was well aware of, and often described by the pathetic term "lost." He knew that His outcast friends much needed saving, but He believed, in defiance of all appearances and assertions to the contrary, that they were capable of being saved and worth saving; that, though lost, they were still lost *sons*. This genial, hopeful, optimistic humanitarianism of Jesus was an astonishment and scandal to His contemporaries. It is not more than half sym‧ pathised with yet, even by Christendom. Were all that bear the Christian name earnestly of Christ's mind, how many degraded ones would be raised, and, what is more important, how many would be kept from ever sinking down ! What countless possible victims of lust and greed would be rescued from wrong by the spirit of humanity expelling these evil demons from the heart ! So, not otherwise, will God's kingdom come.

But it is not merely through care for the good of others that Christ's doctrine of man works for the establishment of the divine moral order. It tends thereto with equal power through the stimulus it brings to bear on the individual conscience to realise the ideal of sonship. For the doctrine that man is the son of God has two sides—the one the side of privilege, the other that of duty. It is a great privilege to be able to call God our Father. But the grace in which we stand imposes high obligations. God's sons must be God-like. They must realise in their character the Christian ethical ideal. It is a very high, exacting ideal as set forth, *e.g.*, in the Beatitudes, implying a passion for the right, and a willingness even to suffer for righteousness' sake. That ideal, not less than God's gracious love to all, is a part of Christ's gospel for the million. And though it seems too high for all but the few elect ones, the aristocracy of the kingdom of heaven, it ought to be proclaimed in all its Alpine elevation in the hearing of all. For its elevation is its charm. Christ's moral ideal commands universal respect, and to lower its claims to adapt it to average capacity, a policy too often pursued, is only to expose Christianity to contempt.

The foregoing facts suggest the thought that Jesus was a very remarkable person, exceptional, unique in goodness and wisdom, a moral phenomenon difficult to account for in any age and country, and especially in such an arid spiritual wilderness as Judæa was at the beginning of our era. Men of all shades of opinion acquainted with His history are agreed in this. All subscribe to this creed at least, that Jesus was an extraordinary man, a religious genius. The Church believes Him to be God. If this

solemn affirmation be true, then the story recorded in the
Gospels presents to our view this great spectacle: God
entering into the world in human form and under the
limited conditions of humanity, as a redemptive force, to
battle with the moral evil that afflicts mankind. If we
form the highest idea possible of divine love and grace,
the amazing thing will not appear utterly incredible. On
the physical and metaphysical side the doctrine may seem
to present a difficulty bordering on impossibility, but on the
moral side it is worthy of all acceptation. The world has
a religious interest in the faith that Jesus is divine; for
what can be more welcome than the idea that God is like
Him, loves men as He loved them—nay, is Himself per
sonally present and active in that Good Friend of publicans
and sinners ?

There is good reason to believe that Jesus was conscious
of being in some sense an exceptional person. He had a
peculiar way of designating Himself. He called Himself
sometimes the Son of God, but oftenest the Son of man.
What the precise import of these names may be is a sub
ject for careful inquiry. But they at once suggest thoughts
of a notable personage, and provoke the question, Who can
this be ? The titles are in harmony with what He who
wore them taught concerning God and man. " Son of man,"
to mention the more familiar and less mysterious title first,
probably expresses sympathy and solidarity with mankind.
It is the embodiment in a name of the faith, hope, and love
of Jesus for the human race. The other title, Son of God,
expresses the consciousness of intimate relations to God;
not necessarily exclusive, possibly common to Jesus with
other men, but certainly implying affinity of nature between
God and man, and great possibilities of loving fellowship.
It is in that view the correlate of the name " Father "
employed by Jesus to express His conception of the
Divine Being. If God be our Father, we are, of course, His
sons. In one recorded saying Jesus seems to claim for
Himself some special and exceptional privilege in the

matter of Sonship: "No man knoweth the Son, but the Father; neither knoweth any man the Father save the Son." The use of the definite article before Son and Father instead of the pronoun "my," seems to express an absolute antithesis and suggest a unique relation.[1] But this need not be insisted on here. It is enough to signalise in general Christ's manner of self-designation as expressing His consciousness of being in some sense an exceptional person, and, as, in that view, one of the notable Christian facts.

Two other features in Christ's teaching claim attention here: His proclamation of the advent of the kingdom of God, and His allusions to the Messianic hope. These both imply something going before, and are suggestive of the historical presuppositions of Christianity, an elect race, a sacred literature, and the expectation ever cherished in Israel, amid present trouble, of brighter days to come. The utterances of Jesus on these topics were rooted in the past history of His people. It was perfectly natural that He as a Jew should speak about a kingdom of God and a Christ as coming, or possibly, if there were apparently good reasons for thinking so, as come. But did He think and call Himself the Christ? It is a momentous question, on which there is not, as yet, entire agreement of opinion. That Jesus might have His Messianic idea, and, in common with His countrymen, cherish the Messianic hope, and even believe in Messiah's speedy advent, no one denies; but that He actually identified Himself with the Messiah, or complacently allowed His disciples to make the identification, some are extremely unwilling to admit. The able and eloquent author of *The Seat of Authority in Religion* regards the ascription of Messiahship to Jesus as the earliest of several theories concerning His person formed by the

[1] In *The Seat of Authority in Religion*, p. 585, Dr. Martineau represents the use of the article as a feature due to the influence of a later time, "when the Logos theory had need to distinguish two constituents or participants in the Godhead." He traces the same influence of a later theology in the saying, "Of that day or that hour knoweth no one, not even the angels in heaven, neither the Son but the Father," *v*. 590.

Primitive Church, and finds in all gospel texts that impute
to Jesus Himself Messianic pretensions the reflection of
this later faith. Among His reasons for adopting this
view is a regard to the modesty of Jesus, and to the unity
and harmony of His spiritual nature. Now unquestionably
these are to be respected and even jealously guarded; and
if the Messianic consciousness ascribed to Jesus really
involved an "inner breach of character," it would have to
be discarded at all hazards. But let us see how the case
actually stands. What does "Messiah" translated into our
modern European dialect mean? It signifies the bringer-
in of the *summum bonum*, the realiser of all religious ideals,
the establisher of the loving fellowship between God and
man, and between man and man, for which the Hebrew
equivalent is the kingdom of heaven. Now is this not
what Jesus actually did? He introduced the religion of
the spirit, the final, ideal, absolute religion. He brought
into the world supremely valuable and imperishable boons:
a God who is a Father, a regenerated human brotherhood,
a love that had in it purpose and power to redeem from
sin, a love that could die, and that expected to die a
"ransom" for the million. To say that Jesus thought of
Himself as Messiah is to say that He was aware what He
was doing, that He understood His endowments and the
tasks they imposed on Him. The name is foreign to us,
and if we do not like it we can translate it into our own
tongue. The thing it denotes is good, and we owe it to
Jesus. Why should we hesitate to say that He knew He
was bringing to the world that good? It is not necessary
to think of that knowledge as involving pretension and
claim. We should think of it rather as involving simply
recognition of a vocation arising out of endowment, above
all out of the unparalleled wealth of human sympathy
with which the heart of Jesus was filled. Recognition, or
better still, *submission;* for the hardships and sorrows of
the Messianic vocation were such as effectually excluded
all vain ambitious thoughts, and insured that the Elect

One in entering on His high career should be simply suffering Himself to be led into a path from which all egoistic feelings would instinctively shrink.[1] But be this as it may, Jesus *was* the Christ, if He did not call Himself Christ. He did Messiah's work, and that is another of the essential Christian facts.

Jesus represented the kingdom of God, whose advent He announced, as the chief good and the chief end of man, for the acquisition of which one should be ready cheerfully to part with all other possessions, and to whose sovereign claims all other interests should be subordinated. He further taught that that kingdom is a chief end for God as well as for men. He strongly and repeatedly asserted the reality of a paternal providence continually working for the good of those who make the kingdom of God their chief end. "Seek ye," He said, "the kingdom of God, and all these things shall be added unto you;"[2] "The very hairs of your head are all numbered;"[3] "Fear not, little flock; for it is your Father's good pleasure to give you the king dom."[4] His absolute faith in the fortunes of the kingdom, and in God's power and will to promote its interest in spite of all untoward influences, found emphatic expression in reference to His own personal concern therein in the words: "All things are delivered unto me of my Father."[5] These simple, pathetic utterances are profoundly significant. They implicitly enunciate Christ's doctrine of God's rela tion to the world, and teach in effect that the universe has a moral end, and that the creation is an instrument in God's hands for the advancement of that end—the establish ment of His kindgom of love.

It would be a very incomplete account of the Christian facts which omitted mention of Christ's conflict with Pharisaism, and of the important service which He ren-

---

[1] On this *vide The Kingdom of God*, chap. vi. *Vide* also on the whole question of Christ's Messianic claims, Book III. chap. ii. of this work.

[2] Matt. vi. 33.   [3] Matt. x. 30.

[4] Luke xii. 32.   [5] Matt. xi. 27 ; Luke x. 22.

dered to the kingdom as a critic of counterfeit goodness. The function of moral criticism forms a regular part of the prophetic vocation, but Jesus performed the unwelcome though necessary task under peculiarly urgent conditions. It has been stated that Christianity had three historical presuppositions—an elect race, a sacred literature, and a Messianic hope.[1] But in reality there are three more which it is equally necessary to take into account, if we would fully understand the work of Jesus—an election mistaken for a monopoly of divine favour, a literature turned by the scribes into an idol, a high holy hope degraded and vulgarised. When both these opposite sets of conditions met, the hour for Messiah's appearing had arrived. He came when He was most needed, when His task was supremely difficult, and when His work well done would have its maximum of influence. In such circumstances realisation of the ideal inevitably involved conflict with its caricature. Righteousness of the heart had to be put in contrast to a righteousness of conformity to external rules; the Scriptures had to be rescued from the scribes by a free spiritual interpretation ; an election for self had to be set aside to make way for the nobler election for the benefit of others originally intended, and the true idea of Messiah had to be differentiated from all current false conceptions. All this Jesus accomplished in an effectual manner, but at a great cost. The inevitable collision with Rabbinism brought Him to the cross. It was not an unforeseen catastrophe. How could it be ? One who had such perfect insight into the radical viciousness of the prevailing religion, must have had equal insight into the wicked hearts of those who practised it, and known what evil spirits of envy, malice, and hatred harboured there. The predictions of his violent death ascribed to Jesus in the Gospels are perfectly credible. So also are the interpretations He is reported to have put upon it: that His suffering was for righteousness' sake, for the benefit of men,

---

[1] *Vide* p. 53.

endured in a spirit of self-sacrificing love, and not in vain, being destined, though meant for evil, to do good to many.

Christ's exposure of Rabbinism, important in many ways as a feature of His public ministry, is specially significant as throwing light on His view of *sin*. The severity of His tone in speaking of the Pharisees and their ways, is startling when contrasted with His compassionate gentle ness towards "the publicans and sinners." The difference is not to be explained by class prejudices or sentimental partialities; it must be held to indicate a deliberate judg ment as to the relative intensity of moral evil, as manifested in the two sections of society. That is to say, in the judgment of Jesus the vices of the Pharisaic character must have been in a higher degree opposed to the spirit of the kingdom of God than those which appeared in the conduct of the lower class. That this was actually His view is evident from the words He is reported to have spoken to the priests and elders in the temple shortly before His passion : "The publicans and the harlots go into the king dom of God before you."[1] The grounds of this comparative estimate are obvious. The sins of "the people of the land" were acts of wayward impulse, and had their seat and source in the flesh : the sins of the Pharisees were vices of the spirit, and had their seat and source in the soul. In the one class the power of evil left the inner man to a certain extent untouched, the moral nature not so much depraved as undeveloped. The sinner was still human, still had in him possibilities of good that might be appealed to. In the other class, on the contrary, sin had taken possession of the inner man, of the will, the heart, the conscience, the whole spiritual nature. Hence it came that Jesus was so much more hopeful of making acquisitions for the kingdom of God from the irreligious class, than from those who were religious after the prevail ing fashion. In the one case all that was necessary was to rouse the man against the brute, to appeal to latent moral

[1] Matt. xxi. 31.

energies, and utilise them for worthy ends. In the other case there was no man to appeal to; the man had been perverted into a kind of devil; all that of right belonged to God, and the kingdom of God, and the spirit of the kingdom, love, had been taken possession of by an antigod, a Satanic usurper, a spirit of selfishness disguising its hatefulness under the cloak of zeal for religion.

In the light of this judgment of Christ, and its grounds, we see how far He was from entertaining the view as to the nature and origin of sin held by the Greeks and by deists, that it has its seat in the flesh, and makes its appearance in human conduct because man is a being possessed of a material organisation which exercises a misleading, disturbing influence upon his rational nature. He rather believed that sin appears only in mitigated form when it springs out of bodily appetites and passions, and that it is seen in its true malignity when it has its origin in the soul, and reveals an evil will, a selfish heart, and a perverted conscience. This idea of sin is one of the most characteristic among the Christian facts.

CHAPTER II.

THE CHRISTIAN THEORY OF THE UNIVERSE.

LITERATURE. — Schleiermacher, *Der Christliche Glaube;* Bushnell, *Nature and the Supernatural;* Ebrard, *Apologetik;* Delitzsch, *System der Christlichen Apologetik;* Bruce, *The Chief End of Revelation;* Matheson, *Can the Old Faith Live with the New?* Kaftan, *Das Wesen der Christlichen Religion,* 1888; Bornemann, *Unterricht im Christenthum,* 1891; Aubrey L. Moore, *Science and the Faith,* 1889.

It is in no spirit of mere philosophical curiosity that the apologist sets himself to ascertain the speculative presuppositions of Christianity, its characteristic ways of thinking concerning God, man, and the world, and their relations;

that is to say, its distinctive theory of the universe. He becomes keenly sensible of the practical importance of the inquiry when he considers how desirable it is that all professed Christians should be able to maintain perfect solidarity in thought and feeling with Christ, to sympathise unreservedly with His manner of thinking and speaking on all subjects pertaining to morals and religion. Ability to do this depends largely on the question, How far our theoretical conceptions are distinctively Christian?[1] To decide that question, we must first know what the Christian theory is. This knowledge we now attempt to extract from the Christian facts as stated in the previous chapter.

1. From Christ's view of God as a Father. and of men as His sons, we can infer as a first speculative presupposition of Christianity the *personality* of God, using the term in essentially the same sense in which we apply it to men. The relations asserted by Jesus to exist between God and men imply an essential likeness between the divine nature and human nature. But man is essentially a being who reasons and wills and distinguishes between right and wrong. Therefore God also has reason, will, and a moral nature. He thinks and purposes, and right and wrong have a meaning for Him not less than for us. He is a rational, ethical personality, self-conscious and self-determining.

2. Christ's view of man as indefeasibly a son of God involves that in the Christian theory of the universe man occupies a very important place. Nothing is more characteristic of any theory of the universe than the place it assigns to man. Pantheism and materialism degrade him. Christianism, on the other hand, exalts him. It commands all men to respect themselves as the sons of God; it enjoins on all men respect for each other as brethren, sons of the same Father; on the highest respect for the lowest, on the

---

[1] Aubrey L. Moore truly remarks that "it is on the ground of presuppositions that the battle must be fought out."—*Science and the Faith*, p. 148.

wisest respect for the most foolish, on the best respect for the worst. It insists on the meanest reality of human society being regarded in the light of the lofty ideal of man as made in God's image. For the Christian theory man cannot be a mere child of time. The relation in which he stands to God compels faith in immortality. God is not the *Father* of the dead, but of the living. This is the true Christian foundation for belief in "a future life"; not processes of reasoning concerning the changes of state living creatures are known to survive, or the abstract possibility of living agents surviving the greatest known change—death such as those contained in the opening chapter of Butler's *Analogy*. The only true convincing ground of faith in eternal life is the dignity of human nature, and the fact that a man at his worst is a son of God.

The Christian, then, who desires to be in harmony with the mind of Christ, will firmly believe in the immortality of man. And, be it noted, of the *whole* man, not merely of the human soul. Herein lies the difference between the Christian view of eternal life and that of deism. For deists, as for pagan philosophers like Socrates and Plato, the hope for the future was the immortality of the soul; in both cases for the same reason, because the vile material body was the seat and source of sin, and the sooner it was got rid of finally and for ever, the better. For the Christian, thinking as Christ thought, the body is not inherently vile, or the sole or chief source of moral evil; not more in need of redemption than the soul, and not less capable of it.

3. The relation of sin to the body is one aspect of a large subject, the specifically Christian doctrine of sin. It is a momentous question, What is the view of moral evil required by the Christian facts, and appropriate to a Christian theory of the universe? The following statements may serve as a contribution to the answer:—

(1) Sin is a *reality*. Every one must firmly hold this who regards Christ as He regarded Himself, as a moral

physician, and believes that God in the person of Christ entered into the world as a redemptive force with fixed intent to fight with and destroy moral evil.   God does not fight with a shadow, or undertake labour in vain. Every one must firmly hold this who believes with Christ in the dignity of human nature; for all minimising views of sin, which treat it as a triviality, an infirmity, a necessity, or as the negative side of good, though humane and charitable in appearance, are in truth insulting to human nature.   They virtually represent man as a being so weak that it is idle to expect virtue from him; as a victim of necessity, who only deludes himself when he imagines that he is free; as a thing not a person, as a human animal not a rational and responsible creature. Christianity commits no such offence against man's dignity. It shows its respect for man as a moral personality, by imputing to him the guilt of his evil actions; and its charity towards him, not by denying his responsibility, but by making his sin a burden even to the heart of God.

(2) Sin does not originate with God.   What Jesus Christ, the Son of God, was grieved by and waged war with, cannot have come into the world by His Father's will or with His consent.   In the teaching of Christ we find no account of the origin of sin : it is there dealt with simply as a fact.   But that beautiful saying, "Joy shall be in heaven over one sinner that *repenteth,*" which formed a part of His apology for loving the sinful, excludes the idea of sin having God for its ultimate cause.   Joy over repentance implies sorrow over sin.   But why should God sorrow over that which He Himself has brought into being?   Sin, however originating, is eternally contrary to the divine will.

(3) Sin is not to be conceived of as a necessity, a fatal incurable vice of nature, inevitable for all men living in the body, for the first man and the last, and all between, Jesus Christ not excepted.   The fact that Jesus represented Himself as a moral physician teaches us rather to regard sin as a disease foreign to the normal condition of human

nature, and, being curable, capable also of being prevented.
From the Christian point of view, sin might not have been,
was not always and necessarily in existence.   How it ever
came to be may be a great mystery, a difficult even an
insoluble problem.   But the worst solution possible is
virtually to annihilate the phenomenon to be explained by
regarding it as a physical necessity.   The best and wisest
solution, with whatever difficulties it may be beset, is to
conceive of sin as the result of a wrong choice on the part
of primitive man.   This is the view quaintly embodied in
the story of the temptation and fall of Adam in the book
of Genesis.   In its essential features that product of ancient
wisdom still approves itself to our minds as the best that
can be said on the subject.   Nor are we called on to
surrender the view therein presented by the discoveries
or speculations of recent science.   It is not irreconcilable
with the doctrine of evolution.   That doctrine teaches that
in the gradual course of the ascent of life there arrived in
the world at a certain period a being who was not merely
an animal, but in rudimentary form *human*.   The advent
of this being was a great event, for with it began the
possibility of moral life.   It was a great step in advance, in
which the Creator might well take pleasure.   Its signifi
cance lay not in this that a man had appeared already as
perfect as it is possible for man to be, for perfection can
be reached only by a process of moral development, but in
this that a man had appeared at all—a being made in
God's image, with reason and will and affection.   But this
step in advance, involving indefinite possibilities of further
advance in a new region of life, involved also risks of
degeneracy, or development downwards.   For in the new
type of being there were two natures: a lower animal, and
a higher human, and their possessor would be constantly
called on to choose which of them he was to follow.   To
choose the guidance of the higher nature was to go on in
a career of moral advancement ; to choose the guidance of
the lower nature was to fall from the dignity he had

attained in becoming human.   This is the story of the fall
from the point of view of modern science.   Is it very
widely different from the account given in the book of
Genesis ?

(4) Besides sin, or moral evil, there is in the world
much physical evil, disease, pain, sorrow, calamity, death.
What connection is there between the two kinds of evils ?
They were, as we have seen, closely connected in Christ's
ministry.   He was a healer of bodily as well as of spiritual
maladies.   In one case, that of the palsied man, He seems
to have looked on the physical ailment as the effect and
penalty of sin.   And there can be no question that very
much of the misery that is in the world is directly caused
by men's evil deeds.   Can we say that physical evil
universally is the God-appointed penalty of moral evil ?
Does this view enter as a necessary element into the
Christian theory of the universe ?   It is a question of great
difficulty and delicacy, demanding careful handling, seeing
that at this point Christianity comes into contact with
science, which has its own way of dealing with the subject.
The tendencies of science and religion lie in opposite directions
here, that of science being to explain physical evil as far as
possible without taking moral evil into account, while that
of religion is to find the ultimate explanation of all physical
evil in the existence of moral evil.   It is very easy to carry
to false extremes either view, and the wisest position seems
to be that which aims at maintaining a balance between
them.   Schleiermacher, who as much as any modern theo
logian strove to do justice to the claims of both science and
religion, laid down the thesis that the collective evil in the
world is to be regarded as penalty of sin, social evil directly,
natural evil indirectly.   The meaning of the thesis, in
reference to natural evil, is that, viewed objectively, or from
the scientific point of view, such evil is not caused by sin,
but that, viewed subjectively, or as it affects us, it is the
penalty of sin, because without sin it would not be felt to
be an evil.   Applied to death, it means that man was

mortal irrespective of his fall, and that nevertheless mortality was properly regarded by man fallen as the fruit and punishment of his transgression. This position appears to be as satisfactory as any one that could be stated. It certainly well accords with the spirit of Christianity as an ethical religion, that we should conceive of the present state of the physical universe as in a divinely established correspondence with the moral condition of its human inhabitants. This view does not imply that the order of nature was altered after sin entered into the world. It need imply only that in the framing of nature God had regard to the eventual incoming of moral evil. Death, decay, violence, according to the testimony of science, were in the world not only before man sinned, but long before man existed. But it is conceivable that they were, because he was to be, prior in time, yet posterior in creative intention. We may imagine God, in making the world, providing that it should be a suitable abode for a race of morally fallible beings, furnished with all that was needful for their moral discipline—with evil of diverse sorts to be regarded as penalty of sin, and also with manifold forms of good, revealing the divine benignity, summoning to repentance, and inspiring in the penitent hope of pardon. This view of the universe harmonises with the tendency of Christianity in all things to make the moral category supreme. It has the further recommendation that it steers a middle course between optimism, which tries hard to see no dark side in nature, and pessimism, which with equal determination shuts its eyes to its good side. Christianity sees in the world both evil and good; evil because man hath sinned, and God desired that man sinning should find sin to be a bitter thing; good because God is gracious and dealeth not with men according to their deserts; the evil and the good serving the opposite purposes of judgment and mercy, and forming together one redemptive economy, working in different ways towards the fulfilment of God's gracious purpose in Christ, to which the whole constitution of nature and the whole course of history are subservient.

4. In the foregoing statement it has been assumed that God stands to the world in the relation of a *Creator.* It is, however, important that this should be formally enunciated as a distinct and most characteristic feature in the Christian theory of the universe. This position is involved in the conception, suggested in certain sayings of Christ already quoted, of the world as an instrument in God's hands for the advancement of the divine kingdom. The world cannot be a perfectly pliant instrument in the hand of God unless it be dependent on Him for its being. If it existed independently of Him there might be something in its constitution that would prove intractable, the source of evil that could not be cured, and tending seriously to frustrate His beneficent purposes. Whether the idea of creation necessarily implies that the matter of the world had a historical beginning, is a question upon which theists are divided, some holding it possible for the universe to be the creature and the abode of God, even though it never came into being, but was like God, eternal.[1] Possibly it might guard all Christian interests to say that the world *might have had* a beginning, and that if eternal it was so by God's will. It may not be contrary to Christian theism to say that the world did always exist, but only to say that it must have existed from eternity, and that God could no more exist without a world than the world could exist without God. But it must be admitted that a creation implying a historical beginning most effectually guards the supremacy of God, and the dependence of the world upon Him. A world eternally existing is apt to land us in one of two anti-Christian conceptions. Either the eternally existent world assumes in its primitive state the aspect of a *chaos* which at a given date God takes in hand to shape

---

[1] So Dr. Matheson in *Can the Old Faith Live with the New?* p. 105 ; also Dr. Martineau, *The Seat of Authority in Religion,* p. 11. Schleiermacher and Rothe held the same view.

into a cosmos, or it becomes a stream eternally flowing out of the divine fountain of being. The former was the view of Greek philosophers who conceived of the raw material of the world, the ὕλη, as independent of God for its being, and thought of God merely as the shaper of chaos into a world of order, as far as that was possible with material pre-existing as a ready-made *datum*. This theory obviously involves an endless incurable dualism. The other concep tion is not less fatal to Christian interests. Under it creation becomes a process of necessary emanation, exclud ing freedom if not consciousness, and God becomes con founded with the universe, differing from it only in name, as the *natura naturans* of Spinoza's system differs from *natura naturata*.[1] The alternatives before us, if we con ceive of the world as eternal, are thus likely to be either Manichæan dualism or pantheism. God becomes either one of two, or He is not even one.

5. The Christian faith demands not only that God be the ultimate source of the world, but also, and for the same reason, viz. that the natural may subserve the moral order, its sustainer, as active now and always as in creation. He is not necessarily sole actor as in the Bible view, in which nature and second causes are virtually blotted out, and God becomes all in all. This biblical pantheism, by which nature is absorbed into God, is not to be regarded as a dogmatic or theoretical negation of nature, but simply as an intensely religious mode of contemplating the world. Compatibly therewith we can recognise a nature, a fixed physical order, presenting the appearance of a self-acting machine. Yet the *appearance* only. To Christian faith the world is not a machine to which God stands related as an artisan, with which, the more it approaches perfection, the less He has to do. It is rather an organism of which God is, as it were, the living soul. This view does not bind us to any theory as to the method by which the present order of things was produced. It is perfectly compatible, for example, with

---

[1] On the speculative system of Spinoza, *vide* chap. iii. of this book.

the evolutionary theory as to the origin of the existing universe.   There is no need to contend for special creations of plants and animals, as if to provide some work for God to do; or to regard life as something which God alone could produce by His immediate and absolute causality. We can admit everywhere natural law, yet believe also that everywhere is divine agency.

6. It is characteristic of the Christian view of the world to cherish a large hope for the future of humanity.   It looks for a *palingenesis,* "new heavens and a new earth wherein dwelleth righteousness." [1]   This hope is justified by the doctrine that the creation has the kingdom of God for its moral end.   This being so, it stands to reason that the kingdom of God should eventually attain dimensions corresponding to the vast preparations made for its coming. Turning to Christ's teaching and life, we find much to encourage high expectations.   His own spirit was pre eminently hopeful.   He hoped where others despaired. The outcasts of society appeared to His loving eye all capable of being transformed into good citizens of the kingdom.   Some of His sayings are suggestive of a great future for redemptive regenerative effort — those, for ex ample, which compare the kingdom of heaven to leaven and to a grain of mustard seed.   Very significant also in this connection is the apologetic word: "They that be whole need not a physician, but they that are sick."   The imme diate purpose of the word is to claim for the speaker the privilege of having His conduct judged in the light of His claim to be a physician.   But its permanent didactic significance goes far beyond that.   It teaches by implication Christian universalism, for if the patient's need is to be the physician's justification and guide, then he must go where-

[1] This striking phrase expressive of Christian optimism first occurs in Isa. lxv. 17.   Canon Cheyne, in his Bampton Lectures on *The Origin and Religious Contents of the Psalter* (1891), expresses the opinion that the author of Isa. lxv. and lxvi. was stimulated to cherish the hope embodied in the phrase by Zoroastrianism, "which from the Gathas to the Bundahis so con stantly proclaims this doctrine," p. 405.

ever he is needed. The sphere of redemption must be coextensive with the sphere of sin—wide as humanity. It casts a gleam of hope on the most desperate forms of spiritual disease; for the very occasion for self-defensive speech arose out of the attempt to bring spiritual healing to classes generally regarded as hopelessly lost to God and goodness. This simple pathetic utterance thus proclaims that the redeeming love of God can go down to the lowest depths of human depravity, and raise its victims up to heavenly heights, and that its breadth and length are those of the wide world.

The Christian hope embraces in its scope *both* worlds, both the present life and that which is to come. It looks for new heavens and also for a new earth wherein dwelleth righteousness. It expects great beneficent social changes here, as well as a great salvation hereafter. It is not necessarily *other-worldly*, whatever one-sidedness in that direction it may have exhibited at certain periods in the history of the Church. The object of its loving solicitude is *man*, not merely man's *soul*; and to no legitimate human interest can it possibly be indifferent. Still, while not dwarfing into insignificance the present earthly life, the life eternal occupies a large place in the Christian system of thought, as it cannot fail to do in the case of all who really believe that man survives death. And the question, Who shall share in that eternal life? weighs heavily on the Christian heat. Some cherish the belief that all with out exception shall participate in its bliss, and that such as pass out of this life unprepared for the glorious inheritance shall be fitted for it by a disciplinary process in an inter mediate state of being. General apologetic can recognise the legitimacy of this generous forecast, while not pronounc ing dogmatically on the question. For the Christian theory of the universe, universal salvation is not an article of faith any more than it is a heresy. One thing introduces an element of uncertainty and doubt—the human will. The Christian philosopher does not believe that there is anything in the ὑλη, in the elements of matter out of which the universe is built, capable of frustrating the divine purpose. But he does recognise in the will of man a possible barrier to the realisation of the Creator's beneficent intentions. He remembers the ominous words of Jesus, " I would, ye would not," [1] and is content to cherish large hope, without dogmatically asserting the larger and largest possible. It involves no injury to the sovereignty of God to ascribe to man this power of resisting His will. God freely imposed on Himself the limitation arising out of the existence of human wills, that He might have a realm in which He could reign by love, and not by mere omnipotent force, as in the lower animate and inanimate spheres of being.

While recognising human freedom as a factor in determining the fortunes of the kingdom of God, the Christian theorist has profound trust in the goodwill of God. He believes that God "will have all men to be saved," and that He desires His will to be done on earth as it is done in heaven, and that He is constantly working towards the accomplishment of these beneficent ends. Fully convinced that the divine will supports and guides the lower physical evolution of the universe, he is, if possible, still more assured that it is the firm ground and animating spirit of the higher spiritual evolution. He believes in the Holy Ghost, and in His incessant struggle for the birth of the better world. He sees in the great crises of history His action as a mighty *wind ;* in quiet times he traces His blessed presence and influence as a still, noiseless, yet vital *air,* the breath of human souls.

In reference to all things future the thoughts of men, even of inspired men, are very vague. It was so with the Hebrew prophets when they gave eloquent utterance to their sublime Messianic hopes, and with Christian apostles when they foreshadowed the advent of the divine kingdom. With regard to the precise nature of the good time coming, and the hour of its arrival, they were left to their own

[1] Matt. xxiii. 37.

imaginations very much as we are. The apostolic age
expected the coming of the kingdom to be apocalyptic in
character, sudden, and soon. The lapse of time has
corrected these early impressions, and taught us to expect
the grand consummation as the gradual result of a slow
secular process of development, rather than as the astound
ing effect of a sudden, speedy, miraculous catastrophe.
But we must beware lest, with the natural mistakes of the
primitive Church, its hope also pass away. It becomes
the disciple of Christ to cherish a spirit of high hope
for himself, for the Church, for mankind; to believe in
progress along the whole line, and not to settle down into
the sluggish creed of an inert religious conservatism which
believes that the divine redemptive force has spent itself,
and that all God's great achievements lie in the past. We
ought, on the contrary, to expect God to do greater things
in the future than He has done in any past age, greater
things than are recorded in the pages of history, or than it
enters into the mind of the average Christian to ask or
even imagine. We must look for results more worthy of
the love of God, more commensurate with the moral
grandeur of Christ's self-sacrifice, more clearly demonstrat
ing that Christ is the centre of the universe. The Chris
tian theory of the universe is inherently and invincibly
optimistic. Its optimism is not shallow or impatient. Its
eyes are open to the evil that is everywhere in the world,
and it does not expect these evils to be cured in a day, or
a generation, or a century, or even a millennium. Never
theless its fixed faith is that cured they shall be in the
long-run.

CHAPTER III.

THE PANTHEISTIC THEORY.

LITERATURE.—Spinoza, *Ethica ord. geom. demonstrata ;* Pollock, *Life of Spinoza,* 1880 ; Martineau, *Study of Spinoza,* 1882 ; Principal Caird, *Spinoza,* 1888 ; Hegel, *Philosophie der Religion ;* Seth, *Hegelianism and Personality,* 1887 ; Strauss, *Glaubenslehre ;* Lotze, *Mikrokosmus,* 2te Aun. 1869-72 (translated by T. & T. Clark); Flint, *Antitheistic Theories,* 1877; Hartmann, *Die Krisis des Christenthums,* 1880.

The pantheistic theory of the universe is in deadly antagonism to Christianity at all points. It negatives all the cardinal Christian ideas—the personality of God, the creation of the world, the freedom of man, the reality of sin, providence, redemption, immortality. The radical principle of the theory is that God and the world are one. It denies to God any being distinct from the world, and to the world any being distinct from God. It may assume different forms according to the manner in which the divine nature is conceived. God may be conceived as spirit, or as substance ; in the one case there results an idealistic form of pantheism, in the other a materialistic. The former species of pantheism regards the world as the garment through which the Great Spirit reveals Himself ; the latter views all particular beings, animate or inanimate, as accidents or modes of one universal substance, waves on the surface of an infinite ocean, which is God. To all practical intents the two are one.

Pantheistic modes of contemplating the universe have prevailed more or less from the earliest ages, and in different countries, *e.g.* India and Greece ; but the father of modern European pantheism, by general acknowledgment, is Benedict Spinoza, of whose views on the subject of Revelation and the Scriptures a brief account has already been given. On many grounds Spinoza is entitled to be regarded as the typical exponent of the pantheistic system as a component element of modern European thought: very specially because of the great extent to which he has influenced the minds of leading philosophers and theologians during the last hundred years. Instead of discussing pantheism in the abstract, or attempting to sketch the history of this type of speculative thought, it will best serve our purpose to study the extremely significant sample presented to our view in Spinoza's great work, *Ethica ordine geometrico demonstrata*. No better or more direct way to acquaintance with the genius of pantheism can be taken than to make ourselves familiar with the contents of this treatise, which in five books discourses successively of God, the nature and origin of the mind, the origin and nature of the affections, human servitude or the power of the affections, and human liberty or the power of the intellect.

Spinoza was a disciple of Descartes, and his philosophy may be viewed as an attempt to improve on that of the illustrious Frenchman, by reducing its dualism to unity. Descartes recognised besides God two mutually independent substances, matter and mind, the characteristic property of the former being extension, and of the latter thought. Spinoza, on the other hand, acknowledged only one infinite indivisible substance, whereof thought and extension are attributes, and all particular beings, extended or thinking, modes. This one substance he called God. In his famous treatise on *Ethics* it is Spinoza's humour to prove all things in mathematical fashion, his theses being marshalled in array like the propositions of Euclid, each proposition in succession being provided with its formal demonstration, and the demonstration being occasionally followed up by corollaries and scholia. The fourteenth proposition of the first book of the *Ethics* is: "Besides God no substance can exist or be conceived." The proof of this proposition is rendered very easy by the definition of substance given at the beginning of the treatise, which is in these terms: "By substance I understand that which is in itself, and is conceived by itself; that is, that whose concept does not need for its formation the concept of any other thing." Of course if it belong to the nature of substance to be self-existent and self-caused, then there can be only one sub stance, that is God. God being the sole substance, it follows that He is both an extended and a thinking being : at once "*res extensa*" and "*res cogitans*," the cause of all particular beings which are extended and which think, in virtue of the attribute corresponding to the nature of each being, the cause of things extended in so far as He is *res extensa*, the cause of things which think in so far as He is *res cogitans.* He is therefore the cause of the human intellect, and as such is Himself an intellectual being. The human mind is indeed a part of the infinite intellect of God. But we are warned not to infer from this that God's intellect is like man's. The intellect and will which con- stitute the essence of God agree with the intellect and will of man only in name, not otherwise than the celestial sign of the dog and the animal called dog which barks. All actual intellect is to be referred not to God Himself, but to God in man; in Spinoza's terminology : *ad naturam naturatam,* not *ad naturam naturantem.* The two uncouth phrases, *natura naturans* and *natura naturata,* are employed by Spinoza to indicate precisely the relations of God and nature. They imply that God and nature are the same thing under different aspects. God is nature viewed actively, or as cause; nature is the universal substance with its attributes and modes viewed passively, or as effect.

Such being the relation between God and nature, we know what doctrine of creation to expect from the Spinozan system. It is as follows : All things exist eternally by necessity. All things exist which can exist; everything possible is actual and necessary. God eternally produces all He has power to produce, His power being identical with His essence, and that in turn being identical with His existence. Things could not have been produced in any other mode nor in any other order than they have been produced. There is no such thing as contingency in the world, except in respect of our ignorance. Of all things whatever God is the immanent not the transient cause. Finally, God, or nature viewed actively, produces all things without reference to an aim : there is no design or purpose in the universe. The eternal infinite *Ens* which we call God acts with the same necessity with which He exists. Therefore the words perfect and imperfect have no sense in reference to the intrinsic nature of things, but are simply relative to our human way of conceiving things as belonging to species, and expressive of our opinion as to the comparative degree of completeness with which the characteristics of the species are reproduced in the individuals. Whatever is real is perfect; reality and perfection are the same thing. The common notion that nature, like man, acts for an end, or that God directs all things towards an end, Spinoza treats as a delusion and vain deceit, due partly to ignorance and partly to self-importance, and fraught with mischievous consequences, as when men see in the inconvenient phenomena of nature an expression of divine anger against them for their sins. The truth is, there is no purpose in events; all things, whether good or evil so-called, proceed by an eternal necessity of nature, and with the greatest possible perfection, but without design or final causes. This doctrine implies that even moral evil, as we call it, belongs to the eternal order, and is in reality good. From this inference Spinoza does not shrink. To the question, Why did God not create all men so that they should be guided by the sole governance of reason ? he acknowledges that he has no other reply to give than this : " Because there was not wanting to God matter wherewith to create all things from the highest to the lowest grade of perfection ; or, to speak more properly, because the laws of nature were so ample that they sufficed for the production of all things which can be conceived by an infinite intellect."

These words, which form the conclusion of Spinoza's

discussion of the doctrine of final causes at the end of the first book of the *Ethics*, signify that the idea of the universe demands the existence of all sorts of beings, that therefore sinners and fools are needed to make a world not less than saints and wise men. Such a sentiment could be entertained only by one who had no belief in the reality of moral distinctions from the divine point of view, or in the freedom of man. Accordingly Spinoza makes no pretence of believing in either. He admits, of course, that there is a difference between a wise man and a fool, but he sees in the difference, admitted as a matter of fact, no ground for feelings of approbation and disapprobation. God, he teaches, has no resentment against the evil and foolish, seeing He has brought them into existence, and we ought to imitate God in this. Against this doctrine that evil and good are alike to God it might seem to be a valid objection that the evil and the good, the wise and the foolish, do not fare alike. Spinoza touches on the point in one of his letters in reply to a correspondent who had started the difficulty. " God," he remarks, "is not angry with any, for all things happen according to His mind, but I deny that therefore all ought to be happy, for men can be excusable and nevertheless want happiness and be tormented in many ways. A horse is excusable for being a horse and not a man, nevertheless he ought to be a horse in lot and not a man. He who is mad from the bite of a dog is excusable, nevertheless he is justly suffocated; and in like manner he who is unable to govern his desires is indeed to be excused for his infirmity, nevertheless he cannot enjoy peace of mind, and the knowledge and love of God, but necessarily perishes." [1] Moral responsibility could not be more expressly denied than by such comparisons. *The denial is an essential characteristic of true pantheism.*

Spinoza's doctrine as to the nature and origin of the mind may now be briefly explained. His definition of a

[1] Epistola xxv.

mind is peculiar. "The first thing," he tells us, "which constitutes the actual being of the human mind is nothing else than the idea of some particular thing actually exist ing."[1] This vague thesis is explained in a subsequent proposition by the more definite statement that the object of the idea constituting the human mind is a body, or a certain mode of extension actually existing. Our mind, in short, is neither more nor less than the idea of our body. Mind and body are the same thing conceived under different aspects, under the attribute of thought as mind, under the attribute of extension as body. Hence it follows that the order of the actions and passions of the body corresponds to the order of the actions and passions of the mind. This correspondence, however, is no proof, as is com monly supposed, of interaction. The mind exerts no causal influence on the body; its states are produced by the laws of corporeal nature alone. On this theory the body is as independent of the mind as a cause of motion as if it were a mere machine. On the other hand, the mind is dependent on the body, not indeed as a cause of thought, but as a condition of the continuance of its being. The mind, according to Spinoza, can imagine and remember nothing save while the body lasts. When the body perishes the mind ceases to exist except as an eternal idea in God. Such is the only immortality possible on the Spinozan system. When the body dies no individual mind survives, but merely an idea of a thing that has been in the divine mind, all whose thoughts are eternal. Nothing else was to be expected from the definition of mind with which we set out. My mind is the idea of my body as actually existing. Of course when the body is dissolved, the mind perishes along with it. Take away the substance and the shadow vanishes.

Such is the pantheistic creed as frankly expounded by Spinoza. The universe is bound in an iron chain of necessity, which leaves no room for freedom either in God

----

[1] Book II. prop. xi.

or in man. The course of nature is unalterably fixed, and needs no alteration. Whatever is must be, and whatever is is right. All individual life is transient, only the one infinite substance is eternal. Nature is the ever-abiding, yet superficially ever-changing ocean of being, and we men and all things we see are the waves or the foam on its surface; here to-day, gone to-morrow, as the winds determine. To this system all religions must be pretty much alike—all tolerable as modes under which the great One and All is worshipped. One may rise higher than another in the scale of rationality, and approach more nearly to that pure intellectual love of God in which, according to Spinoza, wisdom and true felicity lie. In that respect Christianity may be entitled to occupy the first place, and Christ its author worthy to be regarded as the wisest of the sons of men. In justice to Spinoza, it ought to be stated that he ungrudgingly conceded this position to Christ.

Regard to space forbids the exposition at similar length of any of the more recent presentations of the pantheistic theory. One is, indeed, glad to escape the task, not only on account of its difficulty, but because, in view of the moral aspects of the system, it is invidious to apply the epithet pantheistic to any philosophy which has not become a matter of history. The philosophy most worthy of attention in the present connection is that of Hegel. But the disciples of this great master have not been agreed as to the tendency of his doctrines, some putting on them a Christian construction, while others, such as Strauss, have used them for the subversion of Christianity. The former section of the school may be considered the more faithful to the spirit and aim of the master, who claimed to be a defender of the faith, and regarded his philosophy as a translation into the forms of speculative thought of the articles embodied in the Christian creed. But into the delicate question of the religious tendency of the Hegelian philosophy it is unnecessary here to enter. It will suffice

to point out the difference between it and the Spinozan
system in their respective ways of conceiving God, and His
relation to the universe.[1]

The points of contrast between the two philosophies
are chiefly these: In the Hegelian system, the absolute
Being, God, is conceived as Spirit; whereas in the Spinozan
He is represented more materialistically as substance.
Again, in the former, God, the world, and man are connected together by a process involving succession, if not in
time, at least in logical thought. The absolute spirit
becomes objective to himself, becomes another, in the
world of nature; makes for himself, as it were, a body in
the material universe, and loses himself therein. Then in
man he returns to himself, recognises himself, becomes
conscious of himself, and the great world-process is complete. In the Spinozan system, on the other hand,
material things, modes of extension, and mental things,
modes of thought, are, so to speak, contemporaneous and
mutually independent manifestations of the one eternal
indivisible substance. There is not one process binding
God, nature, and man together, but two parallel processes,
which are mutually exclusive though not without correspondence, the manifestation of the eternal substance as a
res extensa in things material, and the manifestation of
the same substance as a *res cogitans* in human minds. In
this respect there is a clearer affinity between Spinoza and

[1] The late Professor Green, of Oxford, gives this statement of the vital
truth which Hegel had to teach: "That there is one spiritual self-consciousness, of which all that is real is the activity and expression; that we
are related to this spiritual being, not merely as parts of the world which is
its expression, but as partakers in some inchoate measure of the self-consciousness through which it at once constitutes and distinguishes itself from
the world; that this participation is the source of morality and religion."
He adds: "It still remains to be presented in a form which will command
some general acceptance among serious and scientific men."— *Works*, iii.
146. With reference to the epithet "Hegelian," he remarks that "No one
who by trial has become aware of the difficulty of mastering, still more of
appreciating, Hegel's system would be in a hurry to accept the title for himself or to bestow it on another."— *Works*, iii. 129.

Schelling than between Spinoza and Hegel. In philosophy Schelling was a chameleon, and assumed in succession very diverse aspects. It has been remarked of him, that in all phases of his ever-varying speculative career he always leaned on some great name. Among his philosophic heroes and models Spinoza had his turn, and when his star was in the ascendant Schelling adopted at once his views and his demonstrative method of exhibiting them, and taught an Absolute which was neither subject nor object, neither mind nor matter, but the indifference or the identity of both, yet revealing itself at once as matter and as mind, as object and as subject, as nature and as thought.

In proceeding now to criticise the pantheistic theory in the interest of the Christian mode of conceiving God and the world and their relations, I begin with the obser vation that this theory could not have taken the place it holds in the history of speculative thought, nor have fascinated so many noble truth-loving minds in all ages, unless it had contained elements of real value. And it is not difficult to divine where its strength lies. Pantheism has attractions for all parts of our spiritual nature, for the intellect, for the religious feeling, for the heart. Its fascination for the intellect lies in its imposing conception of the universe as a unity. The one and the all—the mere combination of the two ideas has a charm for the imagination. God the one, and at the same time the all : the universe of being and its ground not two but one, the sublime thought gratifies the craving of the mind for unity in knowledge, tracing all existence to one fountain-head, and reducing all mysteries to a single all-compre hending one, that of God's eternal being. Its fascination for the religious feeling lies in its doctrine of divine immanence. The God of pantheism is not, like that of deism, outside the world, but within it, its life and soul, present in everything that is or that lives ; in the clouds and the winds, in the leaves of the trees and in every blade of grass, in the bee and the bird, endowing them with skill to build their cell or nest; in man, inspiring him with lofty thoughts and noble purposes. Finally, its fascination for the heart lies in its doctrines of necessity and of the perishableness of all individual life. These supply an opiate to deaden the feeling of pity awakened by the contemplation of the world's sin and misery. In moments of depression the heart that bleeds over the crime and wretchedness everywhere visible is tempted to clutch at a theory which relieves the weak of a burden of moral responsibility too heavy for them, and to accept as the future destiny of man annihilation, rather than face the dread alternative of the bare possibility of eternal loss involved in every theory that is in earnest in asserting the reality of moral distinctions.

Besides these practical attractions, pantheism may appear on a superficial view to possess some speculative advantages as compared with Christian theism. Among the subjects on which it may seem to offer the best solution of speculative problems are *the personality of God* and *the creation of the world*.

Pantheism meets the theistic assertion of divine person ality with the counter-assertion that personality is not compatible with the idea of the absolute, that an absolute personality is simply a contradiction in terms. This posi tion is essential to the pantheistic theory. That it was held by Spinoza may be inferred from several characteristic elements in his teaching, such as that will and intellect are one, that the intellect of God resembles intellect in man in name only, that all actual intellect is to be referred to *natura naturata*, that all human minds together consti tute the eternal and infinite intellect of God, which, as Strauss has pointed out, implies that the divine mind is nothing distinct from particular human intellects, but simply their immanent unity.[1] In this connection it is not irrelevant to mention the curious fact that a brief,

---

[1] *Vide* his *Glaubenslehre*, i. 507-8. Spinoza's words are : "Omnes (mentes) simul Dei æternum et infinitum intellectum constituunt."— *Ethic.* v. 40 schol.

pithy sentence of Spinoza's, occurring casually in one of his letters, has been made the basis of all modern argumentation against the personality of God. The sentence is *determinatio negatio est*—definition is negation. Spinoza made the statement in connection with an attempt to prove that the figure of a body is a purely negative thing. The modern application to the subject now under consideration is as follows: All determination is negation, personality is a determination, therefore personality is a negation; but negation can have no place in connection with the most real Being, therefore personality cannot properly be ascribed to God. Fichte puts the argument thus:

"You insist that God has personality and consciousness. What do you call personality and consciousness? No doubt that which you find in yourselves. But the least attention will satisfy you that you cannot think this without limitation and finitude. Therefore you make the divine Being a limited being like yourselves by ascribing to Him that attribute, and you have not thought God, as you wished, but only multiplied yourself in thought."[1]

Strauss expresses the same view, with his usual clearness, in these terms:

"To speak of a personal God appears a combination of ideas of which the one excludes the other. Personality is self-collected selfhood as against another from which it separates itself. Absoluteness, on the other hand, is the comprehensive, unlimited, which excludes from itself nothing save that very exclusiveness which lies in the idea of personality. An absolute personality, therefore, is a *non-ens*, which is really unthinkable."[2]

This attribute of personality implicitly excluded from the Spinozan system, and explicitly denied and reasoned out of existence by modern philosophy, Christian theism cannot afford to part with. The maintenance of the divine personality may be beset with speculative difficulty,

[1] *Werke*, v. 157.   [2] *Glaubenslehre*, i. 504-5.

but the price which pantheism pays for riddance from the
difficulty is too dear.[1] For no divine personality means no
real fellowship with the Supreme. The intellectual love
of God, wherein Spinoza placed man's chief good, is, by his
own admission, simply God's love of Himself, and as God
loves Himself only in man, it is on man's part simply the
enjoyment of his own existence as a rational being.

But how is the difficulty of reconciling personality with
absoluteness to be got over? How can we think of God
as a self-conscious, self-determining Ego without making
Him dependent on something outside of Him which helps
Him to attain self - consciousness, as we ourselves are
dependent on the world around us, as an aid to the consciousness of being a distinct whole over against the
universe? Now, let it be remarked, in the first place, that
if personality, as involving limitation, must be denied to
the Absolute, then every attribute whatever must be denied
to God for the same reason, even because *determinatio
negatio est.* God must be conceived as a Being of whom,
or which rather, no affirmation can be made, as pure
abstract being, equal to nothing because it is nothing in
particular. Yet not thus did Spinoza conceive God. He
ascribed to the infinite substance at least two attributes,
those, viz. of extension and thought, whereof all things
known to us are modes. Nay, he ascribed to it an infinite
number of attributes, apparently seeking to guard the abso
luteness of God from violation, not by denying to Him
possession of any attributes, but by multiplying the number
of attributes *ad infinitum,* making God, in the expressive
phrase of Gregory Nazianzen, "a sea of being." On this
view, what objection can there be to include personality
among the infinite number of attributes?

Some pantheists do conceive of God as the absolutely

---

[1] Lipsius, who represents the neo-Kantian Philosophy in Dogmatic, while
admitting divine personality to be speculatively a contradiction, yet holds
it to be a religious necessity. *Vide* his *Lehrbuch der Evangelisch-Pro-
testantisch Dogmatik*, § 228.

undetermined, and their view is perhaps the more con
sistent with the genius of the system. Accepting this view,
what have we for a God? Not a real being, but a logical
abstraction. Is there no absolute but this? Is there not
an absolute which really and necessarily exists, as even
Spinoza believed? And if there be such an absolute, will
he not be the very opposite of the logical one? The
logical absolute being the utterly indeterminate, the real
absolute will be the infinitely self-determined; the logical
absolute being absolute emptiness, the real absolute will
be absolute fulness; the logical absolute being incapable of
relations, the real absolute, while not needing, will be
capable of all sorts of relations. Pantheistic philosophers
do not settle the question as to the existence of such an
absolute simply by not choosing to believe in Him, and
preferring in the pursuit of an *a priori* method to com
mence with the most abstract notion the mind can frame,
thence to proceed from the abstract to the concrete by the
addition of attributes, and then to conclude that the pro
cess of the universe is identical with the process of their
thought, that is, that all particular determinate being
emerges out of absolutely undetermined being.

Returning now to the question, How can we conceive
of God as a self-conscious personality without making Him
dependent on an outside world through which He attains
self-consciousness? it is obvious that this question raises
another. Is limitation by a *not-self* an indispensable
condition of self-consciousness? Theists, with one voice,
reply in the negative. The question has been well handled
by Lotze, who sums up a most suggestive discussion on
the subject in these three propositions: 1. Selfhood, the
essence of all personality, rests not on a positing of the *ego*
against a *non-ego*, but on an immediate being-for-self which
forms the ground of the possibility of such a contraposition.
2. In the nature of the finite spirit lies the reason why the
development of its personal consciousness can take place
only through the exciting influence of a *non-ego* in the

form of an outside world. It is not because it needs the opposition of a foreign object in order to be a self, but because in this respect, as in all others, it has not the conditions of existence within itself. This limit has no place in the being of the Infinite Spirit. To Him alone, therefore, is a being-for-self possible, which needs neither for its initiation nor for its progressive development the help of anything outside itself, but maintains itself in eternal unoriginated inner movement. 3. Complete personality is only in God; in all finite spirits is only a weak imitation thereof. The finitude of the finite spirit is not the producing cause of personality, but rather a hindering limit in the way of its development.[1] In short, the drift of the reply given to the deniers of the divine personality by the theistic philosopher is this — Pantheists make personality consist in that which is really the defect of human personality, viz. that it needs an external object to help it to self-consciousness, and outside stimuli to promote its development. Our idea of self-consciousness should be formed, not from its beginning and progress, but from that to which it tends, viz. ever-increasing independence of outward stimuli, ever-enlarging fulness of contents, ever growing conquest over the limits of space and time. That to which we tend, but never reach, God has in perfection and from eternity, a self-consciousness absolutely independent of outside stimulus, infinite in contents, and utterly unaffected by limits of space and time. Hence it is our own personality, rather than God's, that we should doubt, human personality being only a very imperfect embodiment of an ideal which is perfectly realised in the Infinite and Absolute One.

The creation of the world, viewed as involving a beginning in time, is a very difficult conception. As already indicated, it has been doubted whether it be necessary to the interests of Christian theism to maintain that the world had a historical commencement,[2] but it

---

[1] *Mikrokosmus*, iii. 575 (Eng. trans. ii. 679).　　　　[2] *Vide* p. 65.

cannot be questioned that this mode of conceiving creation is more in affinity with a theistic theory of the universe than that which conceives of the elements of the world as co-eternal with, while ever dependent on, God. In arguing with pantheists, therefore, it is only fair to accept as part of the theistic position, the idea of a creation in time, with all its drawbacks. These drawbacks are manifest. It is easy to ask puzzling questions with reference to creation so conceived : How was God occupied before He created the world ?   Why did God make a world if He could do without one throughout eternal ages ?   Supposing that question to have been satisfactorily answered by Plato when he said, God as the Good is not envious, and therefore was pleased to communicate Him self to beings like Himself, is not the very idea of an aim injurious to the perfection of God, and incompatible with the notion of the absolute, as implying that while the aim is unrealised God wants something ?   Finally, does not creation so conceived violate the absoluteness of God in these further respects, that it makes Him subject to the category of Time in His own being, inasmuch as it involves His entrance into a new relationship, that of Lord, and that it represents Him as performing a particular act, whereby it seems to degrade Him to the level of a human artist who sets himself the task of painting a particular picture at a given point of time ?

Pantheism gets rid of these troublesome questions by adopting as its doctrine that God by necessity produces eternally all things possible.   But it escapes difficulties in one direction only to encounter others not less serious in another direction ; or rather, we may say that it covers over the inherent difficulties of the question by skilfully chosen phrases.   For, in the first place, it gives really no account of the existence of the universe.   It is easy to say that God, by necessity of His nature, produces all things. The world is here, and some account of its existence must be given, and you may say if you will that it is an eternal

necessary efflux out of the absolute substance or spirit.
But what is there in the idea of the Absolute that would
lead you to expect the existence of this world, or of
any world? Pantheism has no answer to this question.
Spinoza did not attempt to answer it. His infinite
substance is abstract, lifeless; it is the monotonous,
characterless One into which the realities of the world
have been resolved, but how out of this One come the Many
he did not even inquire, far less explain. Hegel felt the
pressure of the problem, and tried to solve it by introduc
ing into the Absolute a principle of finitude, self-limitation,
or negation, which is supposed to give rise to an eternal
process resulting in the manifold being which constitutes
the universe. But capable critics concur in the opinion
that Hegel's explanation of the universe is neither more
nor less than the hypostatising of a logical process, and
that he has left the problem of existence where he found
it.[1]

Pantheism seems to leave no place for the existence of
a world in which there is progress, development, evolution,
steady onward advance from lower to higher stages of
being, each step in advance bringing into existence new
things. Such a world is full of incessant change. New
phenomena are constantly appearing—new effects of new
causes, or of new combinations of existing causes; if not
absolutely new in the sense that such phenomena always
may have been in existence in some part of the universe,
yet new in this or that part, say in our own planet. Thus
by general consent of men of science there must have been
a time in the history of the earth when there was no life
in it, though there may never have been a time when life
was not to be found anywhere in the universe. Such a
world created piecemeal, even though the process never
had a beginning, subjects the Creator in some sense to the
categories of time and space, making Him enter into new

[1] Among those who have criticised Hegel to this effect may be mentioned
Strauss, Dorner, Zeller, Hartmann.

creative and proprietary relations in this or that part of the creation. To escape this it would be necessary to invest the world with God's unchangeableness, and say that all things possible were always and everywhere actual. But this would be in effect to deny the existence of a world. Change is involved in the idea of a world; a world without change is either a nonentity or it is God under another name. The actual world is undeniably a world full of change, and with reference to God's relation to it we must choose between two alternatives: either to save His absoluteness we must assert that He stands in no relation whatever to the world, whether as creator or as preserver; or we must admit that His eternal being is somehow reconcilable with change,[1] that without prejudice to His absoluteness He can, as Hebrew prophets teach, create new things—living beings, thinking men—at a given time, in a given part of the world. The admission covers the theistic idea of creation in time, at least in detail; and there seems to be no cogent reason why it should not cover the idea of a historical commencement of the world as a whole. If life or man may begin to be, why not a universe?

It thus appears that even on its speculative side the pantheistic theory is not so invulnerable as at first view it may seem. But it is on the moral side that its weakness is most easily discerned. Questions concerning the Divine Being and His relations to the universe are abstruse, but on such as refer to man, his nature and destiny, we are able to form more definite views, and to pronounce more confident judgments. And no one who in any measure

---

[1] Hartmann denies that simplicity and unchangeableness are attributes of God, doing so in the name of what he calls *concrete monism*, which he dis tinguishes from abstract monism in this wise. Abstract monism makes the Many, as simple appearance, lose itself in the abstract Unity. Concrete monism, on the other hand, recognises the reality and independence of the existing Concrete over against the Unity of being. According to his view the dogma of divine unchangeableness belongs to abstract monism. *Vide Die Krisis des Christenthums*, pp. 88, 92.

sympathises with the teaching and spirit of Christ can
hesitate what to think of pantheistic views on these topics.
Pantheistic anthropology is at all points antagonistic to
Christian thought. First, in its general conception of man's
place in the world. Pantheism in all its forms degrades
man. It may seem as if we ought to except from this
statement that fascinating type which makes man the
medium through which the absolute spirit attains to self-
consciousness. But even on this view the individual man
is only a shadowy, fleeting phenomenon, a mere temporary
apparition, manifestation, and individualisation of the great
impersonal spirit of nature. Neither God nor man pos
sesses stable personality. The soul of the world attains to
reality and self-consciousness only in the single souls of
men; man, on the other hand, has no being-for-self, but is
merely a medium of divine self-manifestation and self-
consciousness, used for a season, then dispensed with.
Whence it appears that the personality of God and that of
man stand and fall together. Each is the guarantee of the
other, and the denial of either is the destruction of both.
Admit the independent personality of God, then man can
be recognised as a distinct, though finite and subordinate
personality. Deny the personality of God, except in so
far as it is realised in man, then individual men are
degraded into the position of mere temporary instruments,
and only the human race, if even it, possesses abiding
significance.

The fatal bearing of the pantheistic theory on the moral
nature of man is made very apparent by the frank utterances of Spinoza. For him human freedom is a dream,
moral distinctions purely relative, and good and bad men
alike entitled to recognition as constituent parts of a
universe in which all that is real is perfect. Human
actions of whatever nature are subject to the inexorable
law of causality, and all alike tend to one goal. Evil and
good from the divine point of view, regarded *sub specie
æternitatis*, are one; error, sin, wickedness are words that

have no absolute significance, but merely denote things that are evil relatively to our present feeling, comfort, and convenience. In the great system of the universe they are but the discords in the divine music of the spheres, which resolve into concords, and make these by contrast more exquisite to the ear.

From the pantheistic point of view, the hope of individual immortality is a delusion. Strauss acted as the spokesman of the system when he wrote these remarkable words: "The Beyond is the one in all, but in the form of a *future* it is the last enemy which speculative criticism has to fight with, and if possible to overcome."[1] It is the utterance of an ex-pantheist gone over to the ranks of materialism, but it none the less expresses the genuine thought of pantheism on the subject of immortality. While recognising an eternal within the temporal, it mocks at the idea of a life that survives death, and declares that with the last breath individual existence ends. The finite spirit then loses itself in the infinite, like a burst bubble in the stream.

Against these views it is unnecessary to argue, the only question to be considered is whether they be truly charac teristic of the theory under discussion. If they be, then pantheism is self-condemned for all who belong to the school of Jesus, or even to the school of Kant, who built his faith in God and in immortality on human freedom, and on the absolute validity of moral distinctions.

It has already been acknowledged that pantheism pos sesses powerful attractions for our religious nature in its doctrine of divine immanence (of which, however, it has no monopoly, for that God is immanent in the world is the belief of every intelligent theist). Nevertheless, the deity of pantheism is too vague, shadowy, and intangible to be a satisfactory object of worship. The human heart craves

---

[1] *Glaubenslehre*, ii. 739. For an instructive discussion on the bearings of Hegelianism on the question of individual immortality, *vide* Strauss's *Christian Marklin, ein Lebens- und Charakterbild aus der Gegenwart*, 1851.

a more comprehensible, definite, and congenial object of religious devotion than the universal substance of Spinoza, or the Urgeist of Hegel, or the moral order of the world with which Fichte identified the divine being. Hence, wherever the pantheistic theory is accepted, polytheism, in a more or less refined form, prevails. The One in All for practical religious purposes breaks up into the Many; the modes of the Absolute take the place of the Absolute itself as objects of worship ; sun, moon, and stars, birds, beasts, and creeping things, in ruder times ; the beautiful in nature, as reproduced by art, and genius in man, as expressed in literature, in highly cultured epochs.

CHAPTER IV.

THE MATERIALISTIC THEORY.

LITERATURE.—Cudworth, *True Intellectual System of the Universe;* Lange, *Geschichte des Materialismus,* 2te Aufl. 1873 ; Lotze *Mikrokosmus* (translated by T. & T. Clark, Edinburgh); Strauss *Der alte und der neue Glaube,* 1874 ; Ulrici, *Gott und die Natur,* 1866 ; Du Bois-Reymond, *Ueber die Grenzen des Naturerkennens; Die Sieben Welträthsel,* 1872, 1880 (published together 1891); Bain, *Mind and Body;* Clifford, *Lectures and Essays,* 1879 ; Havelock Ellis, *The Criminal,* 1890 ; Flint *Antitheistic Theories;* Martineau, *Essays, Reviews, and Addresses,* 1891 (two on Modern Materialism in Relation to Religion and Theology); Le Conte, *Evolution and its Rela tion to Religious Thought,* 2nd ed. 1891.

Superficially viewed, the materialistic mode of contemplating the universe differs widely from the pantheistic. In Spinoza's system thought and extension are two independent attributes of the eternal and infinite Substance, standing in no causal relation to each other. According to the materialistic theory, on the contrary, thought is a function of the brain and a mere mode of motion. In modern forms of pantheism the contrast to materialism is even more striking. The Absolute therein appears not as sub stance, but as spirit, the material world being its negation, and the end of the whole world-process is declared to be the manifestation of spirit. Notwithstanding this super ficial difference, however, the two systems are closely allied. For both the world, nature, is the great reality, and God and the human soul the shadowy and insubstan- tial. To the pantheist the physical universe is the reality *of* God; to the materialist it is the reality *without* God. God for the one is an idea, an abstraction apart from nature, and man a development out of nature; for the other God is a nonentity, a word without meaning, and man a curiously-organised piece of matter characterised by some very remarkable and not easily explicable properties.

Materialism is the most thoroughgoing and the most formidable opponent of the Christian theory of the universe. It is the foe which is at present in the ascendant. It owes its prevalence to various causes. In Germany, in recent years, a spirit of reaction against an extravagant idealism has been at work, which has issued in the rapid spread of materialistic tendencies. But doubtless the main cause has been the signal progress of physical science within the present generation. The physical sciences are not, indeed, to be confounded with materialism. The aim of these sciences is not to propound a speculative theory of the uni verse, but simply to make us as fully acquainted as possible with the universe as it actually exists; with the properties and relations of the elements of which it is composed. It has indeed been said that it is the interest of science that there should be no God,[1] but that is true only in the sense

---

[1] So Jacobi, *Werke*, Band III. pp. 384-5. " It is therefore the interest of science that there be no God, no supernatural, extramundane, supramun- dane Being. Only under this condition, viz. that nature alone exists, as independent and all in all, can science reach the goal of perfection and flatter itself that it can become like its object all in all." Commenting on this statement in another place, Jacobi remarks that the science which has this interest is different from the true science which has an entirely opposite interest. *Vide Werke*, iv., Erste Abth., Vorbericht, pp. xxvii. xxviii.

that science cannot allow the being of God to put an arrest on its endeavours to ascertain the causes of existing phenomena, or to interdict the carrying of its inquiries as far back as possible. If, for example, it thinks it can account for the appearance of design in nature without postulating a designer, it declines to regard it as a good reason for foregoing the attempt that theologians will thereby be deprived of a favourite argument for the being of God. If, again, science thinks it can establish a doctrine of evolution, according to which all existing forms of life have arisen by a slow secular process out of a few prim ordial living germs, it refuses to be stopped in its course by the consideration that the establishment of such a doctrine would leave the Creator so little to do as to suggest the thought that He might be dispensed with altogether. The scientific man might meet such objections by the reply : "If God be put into a corner I cannot help it. Nay, if He should be shut out of the universe altogether, I still cannot help it. I have no wish to do so : the motive of my scientific labour is not a desire to carry on a crusade against the existence of God. But as little is it my busi ness to protect that existence from peril. I must go on my own course of inquiry, and leave the divine existence to look after itself." [1]

Modern science prosecuted in this spirit of stony indifference to theological interests, or to any interest whatever but the ascertainment of truth, has established many doctrines, and thrown out not a few hypotheses, which have given much comfort to the heart of the materialist, and inspired him with great confidence in asserting that his theory of the universe may now be regarded as conclusively proved. Hence materialism has

---

[1] On the bearing of evolution on theism, Le Conte remarks : "To the deep thinker now and always there is and has been the alternative—materi alism or theism. God operates Nature or Nature operates itself ; but evolu tion puts no new phase on this old question."—*Evolution and its Relation to Religious Thought*, p. 289, 2nd ed.

been much in vogue of late, and has won over to its ranks many ardent supporters who have devoted themselves to its exposition and defence, using for this purpose all the materials lying ready to their hands in scientific treatises. Germany has been specially prolific in materialistic litera ture. In that land of thinkers every theory has its turn, and every subject which engages attention is gone into with characteristic thoroughness and unreserve. In English- speaking countries men are not supremely interested in speculative theories, but give themselves, by preference, to patient prosecution of special lines of inquiry, and if the results arrived at are, from the theological point of view, questionable or suspicious, such aspects of the matter under consideration are either quietly ignored, or only noticed by a passing word. But in Germany the bearing of any particular scientific discovery on the theory of the universe is for many the thing of predominant interest, and what the Englishman passes over in discreet silence the German proclaims from the house-top. Hence the land of idealism has taken the lead also in a materialistic propa- gandism, which has given birth to many publications of various merit, including an elaborate history of materialism from the earliest times till now.[1]

In view of that history, and of the many phases of opinion it reveals, in view also of the extent to which the story of modern materialism is interwoven with that of recent scientific discovery, it seems vain to attempt a state ment and criticism of the materialistic theory of the universe within the compass of a single chapter. Yet let us hope that the task may not prove so hard as at first it looks.

What then is the materialistic theory? Briefly and roughly it is this: that to account for all the phenomena of nature, including those of life, animal and vegetable, and of thought, nothing more is needed than matter and its properties. Matter and force have built up the universe, the former being the stuff out of which the structure has

---

[1] Lange, *Geschichte des Materialismus.*

been raised, the latter the architect by whose unconscious skill it has been shaped into a *cosmos.* The world-process is throughout an affair of mechanism. The substitute for God in this theory is the *hyle*, matter in its original element- ary state conceived of as existing from eternity, and con- sisting of an infinite number of atoms moving about in empty space. By this conception of matter as eternal the need for a Creator is excluded. Equally unnecessary, according to the materialist, is a Divine Being at all stages of the process by which the world arose out of the eternal atoms Not even at those critical points in the world- process, when life, feeling, and thought first appeared, is it necessary to postulate more than matter and the properties it possessed before these remarkable phenomena appeared, in order to account for them sufficiently.

The consistent maintenance of this theory would seem to require no small measure of audacity, a quality in which, it must be acknowledged, the materialist has never been lacking The origin of *life*, even in its most elementary form, might well appear a *crux* to any modest theorist desirous to ascertain how far lifeless matter and its properties will carry us in the explanation of the world. For the testi mony of experimental science is decidedly against spon taneous generation —that is, the appearance of life where there is no reason to suspect the presence of living germs antecedently existing. Yet, in spite of that testimony, modern materialists, with one consent, refuse to regard the origin of life in a world in which the phenomenon of life had not previously appeared as a crisis demanding the supernatural interposition of a Creator. They assume the conceivability of the world, its explicability by natural causes, throughout, as an axiom, and therefore they look on the origin of organisms out of dead matter as possible and certain, whether such an event fall within our present experience or not. Life must have so arisen in our planet, for it is here now, and yet it is certain that there once was a time when no life could have existed on the earth. We may not yet be able to explain the process, or to specify the conditions under which atoms of carbon, hydrogen, oxygen, and nitrogen combine so as to yield the wondrous phenomenon we call life. But we ought not to despair of one day discovering the secret, but simply to regard it as " a very difficult mechanical problem." [1] The common faith of materialists in reference to the origin of life is expressed by a well-known scientific expert in these explicit terms :—

" If it were given me to look beyond the abyss of geologi cally-recorded time to the still more remote period when the earth was passing through physical and chemical conditions, which it can no more see again than a man can recall his infancy, I should expect to be a witness of the evolution of living protoplasm from not living matter. I should expect to see it appear under forms of great simplicity, endowed, like existing fungi, with the power of determining the forma tion of new protoplasm from such matters as ammonium carbonates, oxalates and tartrates, alkaline and earthy phos phates, and water, without the aid of light." [2]

Life once introduced, no crucial difficulty emerges for the theorist who undertakes to account for all things by matter and its properties, by atoms and their motions, till in the onward course of evolution the marvellous phenomena of feeling, consciousness, thought make their appearance. Apart from these perplexing mysteries, the materialist, by aid of Darwin's theory, can explain the boundless world of living beings, with its infinite variety of species, from the

[1] The expression is quoted from Du Bois-Reymond. In his Vortrag, Ueber die Grenzen des Naturerkennens, p. 31, this eminent man of science says : " It is a mistake to see in the first appearance of living beings upon earth or on another planet anything supernatural, anything else than a very difficult mechanical problem" (ein uberaus schwieriges mechanisches Problem). This Vortrag is published along with another, Die Sieben Welträthsel. Among the seven riddles of the world Du Bois-Reymond includes the origin of life, but he does not regard it as, like the nature of matter, or the origin of feeling, "transcendent," i.e. absolutely insoluble.

[2] Huxley, Critiques and Addresses, p. 239. Similar views are expressed by Fiske, Outlines of Cosmic Philosophy, i. 430-4.

lowest forms of vegetable and animal life to the highest and latest achievement of the evolutionary process, the animal that can speak and think called *man*. *Corporeal* life in all its phases may be resolved into mechanics ; but *conscious* life, is that not a puzzle ? Feeling, even in its most rudimentary manifestations, still more as a phenomenon in the vast world of mind opened up to view in the human species, can it be explained by the movements of atoms ? Surely materialists will hesitate to answer this question in the affirmative ? Some do, but not all. With character istic boldness, some of the most prominent advocates of the theory under consideration maintain that feeling and thought are modes of motion. "Thought," says one, "is a motion, a translocation of the cerebral substance ; think ing is a necessary and inseparable property of the brain ;" and "consciousness itself is but an attribute of matter."[1] Another asks, "What stronger proof for the necessary connection of soul and brain can one desire than that which the knife of the anatomist yields when it cuts the soul to pieces ?"[2] A third expresses himself in this cynical fashion : "Every student of nature must, if he think at all consistently, arrive at the conclusion that all those capacities which we comprehend under the name of the soul's activities are only functions of the brain sub stance ; or, to express myself here somewhat coarsely, that thought stands in the same relation to the brain as the gall to the liver or the urine to the kidneys."[3]

Other writers, materialistic in tendency, shrink from such positions, and frankly acknowledge that mental states are not explicable in terms of motion ; that the phenomena of thought and feeling are separated by an impassable gulf

---

[1] Moleschott, *Der Kreislauf des Lebens*, pp. 439, 445.

[2] Büchner, *Kraft und Stoff*, 6te Aufl. p. 113.

[3] Vogt, *Physiologische Briefe für Gebildete aller Stände*, p. 206 ; *Köhler-glaube und Wissenschaft*, p. 32. The blunt declaration above quoted created a great sensation. Du Bois-Reymond, in his paper on the "Limits to our Knowledge of Nature," states that it gave rise in the fifties to a sort of tournament about the soul (p. 49).

from, while intimately connected with, movements in the
brain and nervous system. They even affect to treat such
utterances as those above quoted as mere extravagances not
demanded by the system. But it is by no means certain
that the views of the moderate and cautious materialist are
the more consistent with the theory. The urine-simile may
be offensive in expression, but it is in essence true to the
materialistic mode of viewing the world. Is it not the
very *rationale* of materialism to resolve the phenomena of
mind into phenomena of matter? On this point the most
competent judges are agreed. Thus Lotze says that
materialism consists in explaining psychical by physical
states, thought by motion.[1] And Lange, the historian of
materialism, represents Strauss as a correct exponent of
materialism.[2] Yet Strauss, recognised by many of his
countrymen as the father of modern materialism, treats the
relation of thought to motion as a question of the conserva
tion of force, as the following passage will show :—

" It is not long since the law of the conservation of force
was discovered, and it will take long to clear up and define
its application to the conversion of heat into motion and of
motion into heat. But the time cannot be far off when they
will begin to make application of the law to the problem of
feeling and thinking. If under certain conditions motion
changes itself into heat, why should there not also be con
ditions under which it changes itself into sensation? The
conditions, the apparatus for the purpose, we have in the
brain and nervous system of the higher animals, and in those
organs of the lower animals which take their place. On the
one side the nerve is touched and set into internal movement,
on the other a feeling, a perception, takes place, a thought
arises ; and inversely the feeling and the thought on the way
outward translate themselves into motion of the members.
When Helmholtz says: in the generation of heat through
rubbing and pushing the motion of the whole mass passes
over into a motion of its smallest parts; inversely in the
production of driving power through heat the motion of the

---

[1] *Mikrokosmus*, i. 168.
[2] *Geschichte des Materialismus*, ii. 533.

G

smallest parts passes over into a motion of the whole mass—
I ask : is this anything essentially different; is the above
account of the connection between the movement of the body
and the thought of the mind not the necessary continuation
of that law ? One may say I speak of things I do not under
stand. Good, but others will come who do understand, and
who have also understood me." [1]

Strauss was not in the technical sense a man of science,
but few are better able to judge what belongs to a con
nected system of theoretic thought. Those who hesitate to
apply to feeling and thought the law of the conservation of
force may be wiser men than he, but they are less con
sistent materialists. It is as incumbent on materialism to
maintain that thought or consciousness is a mode of motion
as it is to maintain that life in its primordial forms originated in lifeless matter.[2] All attempts to formulate a
materialistic doctrine without accepting the former of these
two positions amount to a virtual abandonment of the
theory. Among these falls to be classed the conception
of psychical and physical phenomena as the attributes of
" one substance, with two sets of properties, two sides, the
physical and the mental, a *double-faced unity* "[3]—a modern
reproduction of Spinoza's thought. Another favourite way
of meeting the difficulty is to introduce into the component
elements of matter the attributes of mind—not merely life,
after the manner of the ancient hylozoists,[4] but consciousness, feeling, "mind-stuff." [5] Of course it is easy to bring
out of matter what you have once put into it, and to find
in it so endowed the " promise and potency " of the highest

---

[1] *Der alte und der neue Glaube,* p. 211.

[2] Lange remarks that the special case of the motions named rational must
be explained from the general laws of all motion, else nothing is explained.
Geschichte, i. 20.

[3] Bain, *Mind and Body,* p. 196.

[4] On the views of the hylozoic atheists or corporealists, as represented by
Strabo Lampsacenus, *vide* Cudworth's *True Intellectual System of the
Universe,* i. 237-41.

[5] Clifford, *Lectures and Essays,* ii. 85. " Mind-stuff is the reality which
we perceive as matter."

spiritual life.	But to ascribe to matter feeling and thought
is to abandon rather than to defend materialism.	A third
conceivable method of making the problem easy would be
to deny, if that were possible, the existence of psychical
states, at least as phenomena demanding scientific explana
tion.	This device seems to be hinted at in these sentences
of Lange: " Feeling is not another member of the chain of
organic changes, but, as it were, the consideration of any
one of these from another side.	We come here upon a
limit of materialism, but only because we carry it through
with the strictest consequence.	We are of the opinion that
in feeling outside and beside the nerve-processes there is
hardly anything to seek; only these processes themselves
have a wholly different mode of manifestation, viz. that
which the individual calls feeling." [1]	It seems scarcely worth
while to formulate such a statement unless one can dispense
with such qualifying phrases as " hardly " and " as it were."

Such, in brief, is the *physical* aspect of materialism.
Turning now to the *ethical* side of the theory, it is unneces
sary to say that of course the materialist repudiates all
belief in human freedom.	Men, in his view, are what Des
cartes held the lower animals to be, *automata*, only not
unconscious ones, and not without an idea that they are
voluntary agents.	" We are," writes Mr. Huxley, " con
scious *automata*, endowed with free will in the only
intelligible sense of this much-abused term, inasmuch as
in many respects we are able to do as we like ; but, none
the less, parts of the great series of causes and effects
which, in unbroken continuity, composes that which is, and
has been, and shall be, the sum of existence." [2]	The con
cession here made to free will does not amount to much ;
for the likings of men are the result of causes over which
they have no control.	We do what we like, and we like
what we must.	In proof of the illusory character of
human freedom, materialists appeal to the results of the

---

[1] *Geschichte des Materialismus*, p. 374.
[2] *Science and Culture, and other Essays*, pp. 239, 240.

modern science of statistics, according to which it is approximately determinable how many out of a given number of men will commit crimes in a year, and even what will be the percentage for each species of crime, and for the mode in which it will be committed. It is held that it would be impossible to frame such formulæ unless there were physical causes at work determining the actions of men with as much certainty as the occurrence of eclipses.

There is no charge to which materialism seems more justly liable than that it renders anything like a fixed code of morals impossible. The logic of a system which denies freedom and regards human action as the product of causes over which the actor has no control, appears to justify the conclusion that all actions are equally right or legitimate, those of the man who is the slave of animal passion not less than those of the man who obeys reason and lives a sober, benevolent life. Conduct is the necessary result of nature, and as is the nature so will be the quality of the conduct. In one case the quality may be higher than in another, but that constitutes no ground for condemning the man whose conduct is judged to be inferior, for it is as reasonable as it is inevitable that nature varying conduct should vary accordingly.

The materialists of last century were not at all concerned to deny this consequence of their system, but frankly acknowledged that morality was a purely personal affair, and that the only rule of conduct that could be laid down was: Every man to his taste. Every man, it was argued, desires to be happy, but no man can be happy at the bidding of another; therefore let every man pursue the common aim in his own way. If one think he can best reach the goal by what is called virtue, let him do so by all means. If another think he can attain happiness by a life of libertinage, he has an equal right to follow his bent. If a third has come to feel that happiness is no longer possible to him on any terms, he may, if he pleases, hang himself. In the spirit of such free and easy morality

Hume defended suicide. "A hair, a fly, an insect, is able to destroy this mighty being whose life is of such import ance. Is it an absurdity to suppose that human prudence may lawfully dispose of what depends on such insignificant causes? It would be no crime in me to divert the Nile or Danube from its course, were I able to effect such pur poses. Where, then, is the crime of turning a few ounces of blood from their natural channel?"[1] Even eighteenth century materialism might have something to say by way of reply to this cynical argument for the right of the individual to do with his life as he pleased. It might mildly suggest that every man owed something to others, to his family, to his friends, to the state. It might go so far as to lay down the rule: the interest of the state the supreme law for the individual. But how uncertain the code of morals based on this principle might be, we may learn from Helvetius, who argued in favour of libertinage as useful to France, and reminded purists that it was to the mud of the Nile that Egypt owed its fertility.[2]

Some modern materialists are not less frank than Hume or Helvetius, but others show a noticeable anxiety to obviate the prejudice against their system arising from a consideration of its relation to morality, by discovering an objective basis for moral distinctions that lifts conduct out of the region of individual caprice. And, of course, the materialist is quite entitled to use for this purpose all that is consistent with his conception of man as a being whose conduct is necessarily determined by his corporeal organisa- tion. With this conception it is impossible for him to rise above *egoism*, but it is competent for him to press the question, What is the *Ego*? What am I? What is the actual nature of my physical organisation as determined by the process

---

[1] From *Unpublished Essays*. *Vide* Hume's *Works*, by Green & Grose, ii. 410.

[2] *Oeuvres, Tome Premier*, p. 304. Helvetius regarded the vices of the libertine as an inevitable accompaniment of luxury, and the evil incidental to them as quite insignificant compared to the wealth which fosters them.

of evolution? It is also competent to insist on the distinction between a healthy and a morbid condition of the organisation.

Taking his stand upon the latter, the materialist may say: It does not follow from my theory that what we call a criminal is as much in his right as what we call a virtuous man. The criminal is a man whose brain and nervous system are more or less diseased; the virtuous man is one whose whole body is in a normal state of health. On this distinction between disease and health moral distinctions rest; into this distinction they ultimately resolve themselves, and by this distinction they are justified. Will is the necessary result of a condition of the brain produced by external influences which may be either normal or abnormal, and according as it is the one or the other is conduct virtuous or vicious, wise or foolish. It may be wrong to condemn or punish a criminal, the proper mode of treating him may not be to put him in prison or to inflict on him stripes, but to put him under medical care in "a moral hospital"; but it is not contrary to my theory to recognise moral distinctions as having a foundation in physics. A materialist may speak of lying, deceit, murder, theft, inordinate sexual appetite as evils, just as a Christian does, only not for the same reasons.[1]

Of much more interest and importance is the other line of inquiry along which materialists may seek, in accordance with their principles, to discover a stable basis for ethical distinctions, as generally recognised among civilised men. The question here is, What is the nature of the

---

[1] The study of criminal anthropology has made great progress in recent years, and already it has begun to exercise an influence on criminal jurisprudence in the direction of practically setting aside the idea of culpability, while of course recognising the reasonableness and necessity of social reaction in self-defence against the criminal, in proportion to his *dangerousness* as distinct from his guilt. A good popular guide to the literature of this subject and its various aspects is supplied in the work of Havelock Ellis, *The Criminal*, 1890. The lead has been taken by Italians, and especially by Lombroso of Turin. The subject and the modern method of treating it have no necessary connection with materialism.

nervous organisation which I have received by inheritance
from a long line of ancestors? More definitely, Can I
discover in it any principle which raises us above mere
vulgar egoism into the region of that benevolent regard to
others with which human morality may be said to begin?
Now it is open to the materialist to point to the feeling
of sympathy as such a principle, claiming for it to be as
natural, as much the outcome of our organisation, as
hunger, or any other animal instinct; much weaker in the
ordinary man than the imperious appetites common to him
with the brutes, but not less than they a real feature of
human nature as now constituted. If the question be
asked, Why should man have a fellow-feeling with others?
he may reply, Why should man not be a social animal like
the bee or the beaver? Of course, given the social nature
a regard to the interests of society is as natural as a regard
to individual interest. But the materialist may not con
tent himself with a reference to the existence of a social
instinct in other parts of the animal kingdom. He may
undertake to point out circumstances connected with the
evolution of the human race which tend to develop into
exceptional strength the social affections which form the
foundation of the noblest morality. In this connection
stress might be laid on the influence of the senses making
men acquainted with the experiences of beings whom they
recognised as like themselves. Thus, it might be con
tended, "the virtues gradually came into men through the
eyes and the ears." "Through the connection of the senses
gradually, in course of millenniums, a community of the
human race in all interests is established, resting on this
that each individual lives through the destiny of the whole
in the harmony or disharmony of his own feelings and
thoughts."[1] Or, again, the humanising effect of prolonged
infancy, and dependence on parents, in the human species,

---

[1] *Vide* Lange, *Geschichte des Materialismus*, i. 379, 380. Lange thinks
that in this way might be founded a materialistic moral philosophy which
is still a desideratum

giving occasion for the formation of family affections, might be insisted on as powerfully contributing to the moralisation of the race.[1] In short, the whole ethics of naturalism, as developed by the modern school of evolutionary philo sophy, might be utilised for the purpose of showing how, compatibly with a purely materialistic conception of the universe, an ethical system may be held scientific in its basis and satisfactory in its results.

A few words, finally, as to the *religious* aspect of materialism. It may appear mockery or banter to speak of a religious aspect in connection with a system which recognises no God but atoms, and out of these constructs the universe of being animate and inanimate. Was it not the very aim of ancient materialism, as represented by Epicurus and Lucretius, to get rid of religion as the source of infinite mischief to mankind ? But contemporary materialists recognise the fact that man is a religious being, and are not willing to be thought indifferent to that side of human nature, or incapable of making some provision for it. What provision then do they make ? God having been eliminated, there remains as a possible object of worship the universe. Universe-worship in detail, after the manner of polytheists, is not possible in a scientific era, but the most advanced scientist and philosopher may, it is thought, still bow in reverence before the universe as a whole, conceived of as revealing to the instructed eye an æsthetic, a rational, and a moral order ; the first appealing to and satisfying the sense of beauty and harmony, the second supplying the intellect with ample materials for de vout contemplation, the third embodying and approximately realising the idea of the good, and offering to the conscience a sufficiently satisfactory substitute for a righteous God.[2] This new cult, adapted to the tastes of artists, scientists,

[1] Mr. Fiske has worked out this line of thought in *Outlines of Cosmic Philosophy*, vol. ii. chap. xxii.

[2] *Vide* Strauss, *Der alte und der neue Glaube*, p. 142 ; also Seeley's *Natural Religion*.

and moralists, who can no longer believe in the old-fashioned anthropomorphic Deity, may not commend itself to all materialists. To some it may appear too optimistic, ascribing to the universe a character it does not deserve, and investing it with qualities that have no place in the realm of reality, but only in the poetic imagination of the worshipper. The world, it may be said, is not a unity except in our thought, nor is it really full of order, æsthetic, rational, and righteous, except for the man of optimistic temper who creates a perfect world as a congenial home for his spirit. The unity and the order are mere *ideals*. For those who thus think the ideals themselves may become gods. Religion may be relegated to the realm of poetry, and men may gratify their devout feelings by dreaming of a world of truth, beauty, and goodness which never has had and never will have any real existence.[1]

In proceeding to criticise this bold and pretentious theory, I commence by remarking that it constructs the universe out of it knows not what. Materialism begins with an unknown quantity, and ends with an insoluble problem. What is this matter of which all things consist, and by whose motions all phenomena are explained? Is it atoms, or is it force, or is it both, and how are the two related? Whence comes the motion that builds up the universe? Is it inherent in matter, or does it come to it from without? These are unanswerable questions. Science, even when biassed in favour of materialism, is obliged to confess two limits: ignorance of the ultimate elements of the universe, and the impossibility of accounting for consciousness.[2] The further question may even be asked, Is it quite certain there is such a thing as matter? Of the two substances which have been supposed to exist, mind and matter, which is intrinsically the more probable?

---

[1] *Vide* Lange, *Geschichte des Materialismus*, ii. 644.

[2] *Vide* Du Bois-Reymond's *Ueber die Grenzen des Naturerkennens.* Du Bois-Reymond recognises two insurmountable limits: the nature of matter and the origin of feeling.

If we must have a monistic system of the universe, why should a materialistic monism be preferred to a spiritual or idealistic ? Is there not force in the observation of Lotze : " Among all the errors of the human mind it has always seemed to me the strangest that it could come to doubt its own existence, of which alone it has direct ex perience, or to take it at second hand as the product of an external nature which we know only indirectly, only by means of the knowledge of the very mind to which we would fain deny existence " ?[1] Even Lange, the historian of materialism, in sympathy with the system, though conscious of its weakness in certain directions, is con strained to acknowledge that while it remains for material ism an insurmountable difficulty to explain how out of the motions of matter a conscious feeling can arise, it is, on the other hand, not difficult to think that our whole idea of matter and its motions is the result of an organisation purely spiritual in its nature.[2]

As to the manner in which materialists deal with the problem of the origin of life, it is not necessary that the Christian theist should meet dogmatism with dogmatism. That topic offers certainly a suitable occasion for remark ing on the tendency to dogmatise on disputed points characteristic of the advocates of the materialistic theory. Science leaves spontaneous generation an open question, but the materialist does not. He cannot afford to do so. He must assume that life under favourable conditions can emerge out of lifeless matter by a purely natural process, for if that were not true his theory would break down, and he would be forced to recognise the creative hand of God. On the other hand, the believer in God is under no neces sity to maintain as matter of religious faith the opposite thesis. His faith is that God is the cause of the world and all things therein ; but he is not tied to any particular view as to the method of creation. He can admit that the

[1] *Mikrokosmus*, i. 296 (Eng. trans. i. 263).
[2] *Geschichte des Materialismus*, ii. 430.

creation in its incipient stage would to an onlooker have had the appearance of things coming out of an invisible into a visible state, and that no unmistakable trace of the divine agent would be observable. In like manner he can admit that when life first appeared it would seem to be a case of spontaneous generation, that it would be impossible to prove the contrary to one who denied it, or to force him to recognise in the new phenomenon the presence and power of the Creator. He does not need, in order to magnify the wonder and make it appear *dignus vindice nodus*, to insist on the mysterious character of life, on the supposed difference between organic and inorganic chemistry, or to contend for the existence of a peculiar life-force. It is enough for him, with the Psalmist, to believe that with God is the fountain of life. It is not necessary in maintaining this faith to regard the first emergence of life as due to the immediate and absolute causality of God apart from all natural conditions. We may accept the view which steadily gains ground that the antecedent state of things contained the needful preparation for the appearance of the new phenomenon, and that its origination was simply the next step onwards in the steady march of the great evolutionary process. This view may eliminate miracle, or the purely supernatural, but not the divine activity which underlies the whole.

The relation of materialism to the problem of consciousness possesses exceptional interest and significance. There can be no doubt what philosophical consistency requires of the theory. It is bound to regard consciousness as a phenomenon ultimately resolvable, if one only knew how, into a mode of motion. There can be as little doubt that the feat is not only difficult but impossible. Thought is accompanied by agitation of the brain; there is a close correspondence between mental states and antecedent or accompanying movements in the nervous system; but the mental and the physical series of states are distinct and irreducible into each other. Here it is emphatically true

that the consistency of materialism is its overthrow.   The
fact is confessed by those who in recent times have
suggested modified forms of materialism; the confession
is indeed the chief value of their suggestions.   Mr. Bain's
hypothesis of "one substance with two sets of properties,"
is a frank admission that motion cannot be transmuted
into mind.   As for the hypothesis itself, it has little to
recommend it.   It may very reasonably be asked whether
it be scientific to conceive of two sets of utterly heterogen
eous qualities as inhering in the same substance.   It is
doubtless the interest of science to bring all phenomena, if
possible, under a single principle, but it is still more its
interest to recognise a plurality of grounds when the
phenomena cannot be traced to one source, or ultimately
reduced to one kind.[1]   A soul, though inaccessible to the
senses, is therefore a reasonable postulate.   But theists do
not need to dogmatise on the soul question, any more than
on the question as to the origin of life.   They may take
up this attitude: What matter is and what soul is I cannot
tell.   Whether either or both exist I know not.   Whether
one substance can possess properties so diverse as those of
mind and matter, I do not undertake to say.   That the
hypothesis of a soul or spirit as the substratum of mental
phenomenon does not explain all difficulties, and even
introduces new ones, I am aware.   All I know is that the
phenomena of mind are here, constituting a whole spiritual
world in which materialism has no part.   I magnify this
world, and refuse to think less of it because it may have
been reached by insensible gradations, proceeding from
inanimate matter to life in its most rudimentary vegetable
form, from vegetable life to the simplest form of animal
life, and thence onwards to man.[2]   My spiritual life has as

---

[1] Lotze, *Mikrokosmus*, i. 165, 166.

[2] Some theists unhesitatingly accept the doctrine of the evolution of mind
out of matter.   Thus Le Conte says: "I believe that the spirit of man was
developed out of the *anima*, or conscious principle of animals, and that this
again was developed out of the lower forms of life-force, and this in its turn
out of the chemical and physical forces of nature, and that at a certain

much value for me as if it had come to me immediately
from God. And I believe it has equal value for God, and
that He will not suffer it to perish. Whether mind-life
be possible apart from a bodily organism I cannot tell. It
may be that the brain is so needful to the soul that the
latter is reduced to the condition of mere latent potency
in the disembodied state.[1] But there is no reason to think
that death is the destruction of the thinking principle, and
whatever is necessary to the full exercise of its powers in
a future state God will provide.

The other form of prudent or moderate materialism, that
which endows the elements of matter with spiritual
qualities, is an equally decisive, though not equally frank,
confession that the consistent thoroughgoing application
of materialistic principles is impracticable. Epicurus
ascribed to atoms no qualities save size, figure, and weight,
and, according to Lange, this view forms one of the stand
ing features of genuine materialism. " With the assumption
of inner conditions you turn atoms into monads, and pass
over into idealism or pantheistic naturalism."[2] It is,
however, easier for a German philosopher to see this than
for an English scientist, who may discern in matter the
promise and potency of all that exists, and define matter as
the mysterious thing by which all has been accomplished,
without being aware that he may thus be combining two
incompatible theoretical view points; first making matter
everything, then to fit it for its gigantic task turning
matter into spirit, or at least making spiritual qualities
a part of its miscellaneous outfit. Such a "see-saw
doctrine, which now touches solid ground and now escapes

stage in this gradual development, viz. with man, it acquired the property
of immortality, precisely as it now, in the individual history of each man
at a certain stage, acquires the capacity of abstract thought."—*Evolution
and its Relation to Religious Thought*, p. 313, 2nd ed.

[1] This is the view of Ulrici. *Vide* his *Gott und die Natur*, pp. 329, 330.
A similar view was held by the late Archbishop Whately. *Vide* his *View
of the Scripture Revelations of a Future State*, Lecture 4.

[2] *Geschichte des Materialismus*, i. 80.

it," [1] is a not uncommon feature of English scientific materialism, having its origin in part in a national indifference to philosophic consistency and proneness to eclectic habits of thought. One wonders, indeed, how persons accustomed to scientific methods of inquiry, however defective in philosophy, could identify themselves with such crude speculations as to the ultimate nature of the *hyle*. What is gained by ascribing to elementary matter, "mind-stuff," will, thought, feeling? There is no ground in observation for the assertion, and no evidence as to how the consciousness of the human organism as a whole arises out of the obscure feelings of the component parts. That matter feels is simply an inference from the general axiom that whatever is in the effect must have been in the cause, or that whatever comes out at the end of the evolutionary process must have been there from the beginning. And granting both the inference and the axiom, what do they amount to? Simply to the abandonment of materialism and a transition to its opposite, spiritualism. Materialism means explaining the highest by the lowest, the end by the beginning, mind by motion. Spiritualism means explaining the lowest by the highest, the beginning by the end, matter and motion by mind. [2]

On the ethical and religious aspects of materialism it is not needful to remark at great length. With every wish to be fair and even generous, it may truly be asserted that materialistic ethics must differ seriously from those of Christianity. We have seen of what complexion they were in the eighteenth century. It may be thought that the modern doctrine of evolution has greatly altered the situation for the better. But does it after all make such a difference? It may be affirmed that the evolutionary process tends to develop in a steadily increasing degree

---

[1] So Martineau expresses himself in reference to the materialism of Professor Tyndal. *Vide* his able Essay on "Modern Materialism in its Attitude towards Theology," in *Essays, Reviews, and Addresses*, iv. p. 206.

[2] *Vide* on this Professor Caird's *Critical Philosophy of Kant*, ii. 33–35; also Professor Jones, *Browning as a Philosophical and Religious Teacher*, pp. 202-212.

right moral sentiments, and corresponding right conduct, and that we may look for a golden age when men generally will think and act wisely and well. Be it so; but the evolutionary process has not reached that stage yet, and meantime the human race consists of individuals of very diverse feelings and characters. Some are wise, some foolish, some generous, some selfish, some temperate, some self-indulgent. What ground is there on materialistic principles for condemning the foolish, selfish, and self-indulgent, or for their condemning themselves? They are what they have been made; they act by necessity of nature; they cannot be other than they are. They are physically different from the wise, generous, and temperate, but not ethically, in the sense of being the proper subjects of moral reprobation; for sin cannot be imputed where there is no freedom. They cannot even be justly treated as diseased. What ground is there for thinking that the brain of every selfish or violent man is in a morbid con dition? The quantity of brain and the proportions of the various parts of the cerebral organ may vary, as between the virtuous and the vicious, but the organ may neverthe less be equally healthy in both classes. The brain of a wolf or tiger is not to be considered unhealthy because he is ferocious. But on the Darwinian theory it is to be expected that there should be men with a wolf-like or tiger-like constitution of the nervous system, and when this leads them to commit acts of violence it is no more an evidence of diseased brain than similar acts in the case of the wild beasts whose dispositions they inherit. Then, as Ulrici has remarked, the number of men who are thoroughly righteous and good is comparatively small. But the test of soundness is naturally that which is usual, and the unusual and exceptional the evidence of an abnormal diseased condition. From these premises the conclusion would be that the healthy state of the brain is to be found in the sinner, and the diseased state in the saint.[1]

[1] *Gott und der Mensch*, ii. 12.

There appears to be good reason to doubt whether biological or evolutionary ethics bring us into the region of ethics at all. But waiving this, it may be observed that the moral standard supplied by modern science is a shifting one. There is no such thing as "eternal and immutable morality." Morality has no absolute worth irrespective of interests and opinions. Some modern materialists, indeed, frankly own and glory in the variableness of right and wrong from age to age, according to the condition of a tribe or nation. That entirely diverse ideas of right and wrong, even in fundamental matters, are among the possibilities of evolution is admitted by the most careful expositors of the doctrine. Thus Darwin, who makes conscience an outgrowth of the social instinct, remarks:

"I do not wish to maintain that any strictly social animal, if its intellectual faculties were to become as active and as highly developed as in man, would acquire exactly the same moral sense as ours. In the same manner as various animals have some sense of beauty, though they admire widely different objects, so they might have a sense of right and wrong, though led by it to follow widely different lines of conduct. If, for instance, to take an extreme case, men were reared under precisely the same conditions as hive-bees, there can hardly be a doubt that our unmarried females would, like the worker bees, think it a sacred duty to kill their brothers, and mothers would strive to kill their fertile daughters, and no one would think of interfering."[1]

This is one illustration of what "Darwinism in morals" might conceivably mean. According to the same high authority another might be the adoption of the policy of improving the human race by killing off the weak:

"With savages the weak in body or mind are soon eliminated, and those that survive commonly exhibit a vigorous state of health. We civilised men, on the other hand, do our utmost to check the process of elimination. . . . No one who has attended to the breeding of domestic animals will doubt that this must be highly injurious to the race.

[1] *The Descent of Man*, p. 99, 2nd ed.

It is surprising how soon a want of care, or care wrongly directed, leads to the degeneration of a domestic race ; but, excepting in the case of man himself, hardly any one is so ignorant as to allow his worst animals to breed."[1]

All risk of a return to the savage mode of dealing with the weak may be considered to be excluded by the tendency of civilisation to develop humane affection and an increasing sense of the value of those qualities which constitute the difference between a civilised man and a savage. Granting this, are we equally safe against an anti-Christian ethical drift in the shape of a tendency to underestimate personal virtues in comparison with those which make for the material interests of society ? It has been supposed that the great merit of Christ was that He gave currency to the "method of inwardness," taught men, that is to say, to seek their happiness within through the practice of self-denial. But the advocates of a form of socialism which describes itself as "atheistic humanism" tell us that Christ's teach ing in this aspect was the reverse of meritorious, and ostentatiously declare that they have no sympathy with the "morbid eternally-revolving-in-upon-itself, transcendent morality of the gospel discourses."[2] They encourage in the industrial class total disregard of the ethical ideal embodied, say, in the Sermon on the Mount. "The work man of the great industry has never, as a rule, paid much attention to his soul, to the *vrai*, the *beau*, the *bien*, as embodied in his character. Personal holiness has never been his ethical aim. . . . The idea of a 'holy' working man is even grotesque. The virtues which the working classes at their best have recognised have been rather those of integrity, generosity, sincerity, good comradeship, than those of 'meekness,' 'purity,' 'piety,' 'self - abnegation,' and the like ; in short, social and objective virtues—those immediately referable to the social environment—rather than those individual and subjective ones referable to the

---

[1] *Descent of Man*, pp. 133, 134.
[2] Bax, *The Religion of Socialism*, p. 97.

H

personality as such."[1]   This is ethical materialism for the million. Its error does not lie in its care for the interests of society. Christ cared for society. He laid upon His disciples the duty of being the salt of the earth. The question is, What qualifies for that high vocation?   Wherewith shall society be salted, if not by the personal inward moralities inculcated by Jesus?

Materialism popularised would probably be not less irreligious than morally lax. Against the worship of the universe, as expounded by Strauss, nothing need be said. Better worship the *universum* than nothing at all. Indeed, as has been remarked, Strauss invests his *universum* with such worshipful attributes that his religious attitude does not greatly differ from that of deism, and it seems little more than a matter of taste whether the object of worship be called God, or Nature, or the All?[2]   The trouble is, that for one who has discarded a living God it is difficult to think so well of the world as is necessary for the sincere practice of this new cult.   Does not scientific materialism insist on the defectiveness of the world in every sphere of existence as a proof that it cannot have proceeded from an almighty, intelligent, and beneficent Maker?   The world, on its showing, is not full of reason, beauty, and goodness, but largely irrational, hideous, immoral, suggesting a pessimistic rather than an optimistic view of its constitution and destiny. What then, must religion be given up for want of anything worth worshipping?   No; there is one refuge left—Ideals ! You may dream of a world rational, fair, making for righteousness, though the world of reality be far otherwise. You may be optimist in feeling, though pessimist in creed under compulsion of facts. You not only may; you must. There is, we are assured, an innate

---

[1] Bax, *The Ethics of Socialism*, p. 16. Similar views are taught by the leaders of the social democratic movement in Germany. They practically deny Christ's doctrine that life is more than meat, and assert that food and raiment, not the kingdom of God and its righteousness, are man's chief end.

[2] Lange, *Geschichte des Materialismus*, ii. 543.

tendency in the human spirit to create for itself a harmonious ideal world, and in this perfect world of fancy to
find solace amid the struggles and miseries of life. This
is religion; legitimate and praiseworthy, so long as the
pleasant fond dream does not crystallise into an earnest
faith in a living Providence, making all things work
together for good![1]

CHAPTER V.

THE DEISTIC THEORY.

LITERATURE. — Leland's *View of the Principal Deistical Writers;* Lechler's *Geschichte des Englischen Deismus;* Noack's *Freidenker in der Religion;* Zeller, *Geschichte der Deutschen Philosophie,* 1873 ; Rousseau's *Emile ;* Kant, *Religion innerhalb der Grenzen der blosen Vernunft ;* Butler's *Analogy of Religion ;* John Stuart Mill, *Three Essays in Religion ;* Schopenhauer, *Die Welt als Wille und Vorstellung.* *Vide* also list at head of Section 3, Chapter I., Introduction.

The deistic mode of regarding the great objects of philosophic contemplation—God, man, and the world—differs widely from that of either of the systems previously considered. Deism recognises a God distinct from the world, who stands to it in the relation of creator to creation. It not only recognises such a distinction between God and the world, but lays exaggerated emphasis upon it, making God stand outside the world He has made, a mere spectator of the universe He has ushered into being, rigidly excluded from all subsequent interference with the course of nature He Himself established at the first. The Creator of the world it conceives of as a being possessing self-conscious intelligence and will, capable of forming designs and of executing them with consummate skill. The world it regards as a theatre in which the divine

[1] Lange, *Geschichte des Materialismus,* ii. 544.

wisdom is conspicuously displayed. To the eye of the deist, as to the eye of the Psalmist, the heavens declare the glory of God, and not less the earth and all the creatures therein. Universal nature shows forth the glory of its Author, the glory of His *wisdom* and of His *goodness*. For these are the two attributes chiefly insisted on in the scheme of thought now to be considered. God is first of all good, a benevolent Being having only one end in view, to make the sentient creatures He has brought into being happy. "The earth is full of the goodness of the Lord;" "Oh that men would praise the Lord for His goodness!" —to such scriptural utterances the deist said Amen with all his heart. The divine wisdom he saw in the manner in which the Author of nature has arranged all things so as to promote the happiness of His creatures, and especially of man. Hence the evidences of beneficent design skilfully worked out were for many deists a favourite theme of study and discourse.

The deistic view of man differs not less widely from that of pantheism or materialism. Man, as the deist conceives him, is a very important being. He is the chief of God's works, the lord and the end of creation. He is endowed with sublime gifts, reason, conscience, freedom. And he has before him a splendid prospect, a blessed immortality. He does not always make the best use of his powers, and behave himself as becomes one destined to live for ever. But this is only his infirmity; his faults are but pardonable errors which an indulgent Maker will readily overlook; errors into which he is led by "this muddy vesture of decay" that for the present grossly closeth in the celestial element of reason, from which, therefore, he will be emancipated by death, when his soul will remount to its native sphere to mingle with pure spirits that delight in virtue.

This sketch of deism, in contrast to pantheism and materialism, suggests at the same time the characteristics by which, while apparently allied to, it is really dis tinguished from, Christianity. Four features have to be

noted in this connection—the conception of God's relation ⟨ ⟨⟩
to the world characteristic of deism ; its extreme optimism ;)
its lenient view of human shortcoming ; and its pagan view)
of the future life. The first of these topics will be most
conveniently considered in next chapter in connection with
the modern descendant and representative of deism which
goes by the name of "speculative theism." The other
three may be dealt with here.

1. The optimistic tendencies of deists were revealed by
the use they made of the teleological argument, and the
views they expressed on such subjects as those of provi
dence, prayer, and miracle.

As already hinted, it was characteristic of deistical
writers, especially in Germany, to dwell with much com
placency on the evidences of beneficent design everywhere
discernible in the world. To point out the manifold proofs
of the goodness of God in providing for human happiness
was one of the pet tasks to which the Aufklärung philo
sophers addressed themselves. Arguments were drawn from
all parts of nature, and books appeared on bronto-theology,
seismo-theolog﹐, litho-theology, phyto-theology, melitt﹐-
theology, etc. Some of the arguments were such as to
provoke a smile. One writer found proofs of the divine
goodness in the important facts that cherries do not ripen
in the cold of winter, when they do not taste at all so
well, and that grapes do not ripen in the heat of summer,
which would convert the new wine into vinegar.[1] One
can understand how Kant lost conceit of a method of
demonstrating the divine existence which had degenerated
into such utter bathos, and looked about for arguments of
a more dignified description.

There is nothing in the deistic conception of God in His
relation to the world that involves of necessity a denial
of divine interference in human affairs. Pantheism and
materialism both necessarily exclude the supernatural, for
a God distinct from the course of nature has no existence

[1] Zeller, *Geschichte der Deutschen Philosophie*, p. 311.

on these theories. But deism does believe in a Supreme Being
distinct from the world; and, in the creation of the world
by His power at the first, it recognises a stupendous miracle.
But if a miracle could be wrought once, why not a second
time, or any number of times, as might seem desirable?
The answer of deists to this question was, in substance,
this: Miracle is excluded, now that nature is in existence,
not by any want of power in God, but by the absence of
any occasion. Nature, God's handiwork, is a perfect con-
trivance; and all that is needed is that God sustain it in
being, and for the rest leave it to its course. To introduce the disturbing element of miraculous interference
would be to pay a compliment to the power of Deity at
the expense of His wisdom. God made all things so good
at the first that the best thing He can do is to let the
world alone.[1] On similar grounds, a special providence
was denied by some deists, *e.g.* Bolingbroke, who thought
that the "ordinary course of things, preserved and con
ducted by a general providence, is sufficient to confirm
what the law of nature and reason teaches us,"—that is,
that to do right is for our advantage, and to do wrong for
our ultimate loss. It must here be remarked, however,
that deists were not all of one mind on this subject; and
the same remark applies to other topics. Our account of
deistic tendencies, therefore, is to be regarded as a descrip
tion of average deism, leaving room for individual varia
tions. This statement applies especially to deistic views
on the subject of *prayer*. On this important subject
English deists gave an uncertain sound, possibly due to
prudential considerations. Rousseau's utterance, referred
to in a former chapter,[2] is the most explicit and the most

---

[1] *Vide* Lechler's *Geschichte des Englischen Deismus*, p. 321, where he gives
an account of the views of Annet, who gave the apologists considerable
trouble. Annet argued, "A proper government must be all of a piece. If
we think of God as displeased with this or the other event, and therefore
altering things, we get a system which it might perhaps be too strong to
call atheism, but, to say the least, there is little of God in it."

[2] *Vide* p. 28.

in accordance with the optimistic spirit of the system. It pronounced prayer inadmissible both in the physical and in the spiritual sphere; in the former, because it amounted to asking God to work needless miracles in our behalf; in the latter, because it was virtually asking God to do our work. Our duty is to acquiesce in the established order as the best possible, and to say, Thy will be done.

2. The deistic view of human nature might be characterised as _Pelagian_. Of man's moral shortcoming deists generally took a genial and tolerant view. They did not, indeed, like pantheists and materialists, get rid of sin, altogether by denying human freedom. On the contrary, they asserted with emphasis the freedom of the will as one of man's highest attributes, and claimed for him power to give practical proof of his freedom by a life of virtue and wisdom. Freedom was one of three great watchwords in the deistic creed—"God, Freedom, Immortality." "Thou canst because thou oughtest," said Kant, herein acting as the spokesman of his time. But average deists did not take the moral imperative by any means so earnestly as did the great critical philosopher. They weakened the "shall" to make the "can" easier. In other words, they represented man as placed in circumstances which rendered it unreasonable to expect from him high moral attainment, and made it possible to regard him as essentially good, while admitting his faults. In this way they made sin a light thing, while not treating it absolutely as a nonentity. Misconduct arose from the "passions wild and strong," on which Robert Burns threw the blame of his delinquencies; from the senses, which, as Rousseau pled, make men, especially in youth, the victims of delusions; from the limitation of the spirit, which, according to Bahrdt,[1] makes error in the earthly stage of man's career a thing of course. It all comes of this body of death, this gross fleshly prison of the soul. But we are exhorted not to

---

[1] For an account of the opinions of this member of the Aufklärung fraternity, _vide_ Noack's _Freidenker_, 3ter Theil, pp. 103-136.

lament too bitterly that our spirit in the present life is
subject to sense, and chained to a body which enslaves it.
" If the spirit had been unconnected with a body, it would
have had no merit in loving and pursuing a moral order
which it had no temptation to violate. Human virtue in
that case would have fallen short of the sublime, and sunk
to the level of angelic goodness." [1]   Where to be virtuous
is heroic, failure must be venial. Therefore those who are
conscious of moral frailty need not greatly vex themselves.
Nor need they fear the frown of an indulgent Deity.
Pardon is a matter of course; no atonement is necessary;
no scheme of redemption called for. The true redeemer is
death; not Christ's death, but our own. When death
comes, to quote once more the eloquent author of *Emile*,
" I am delivered from the trammels of the body, and am
myself without contradiction."

3. These words help us to pass easily to the third
characteristic of the deistic system—its pagan view of the
future life. By the epithet "pagan" I mean to convey
the idea that the hope of deism regarding the life beyond,
like that of Greek philosophy, contemplates only a disembodied form of existence. The watchword of deism is
the immortality of the soul; whereas that of Christianity
is the resurrection of the body. On this point there is
general agreement among the freethinkers of the eighteenth
century. The re-embodiment of the soul in the life beyond
is not merely not affirmed, but expressly denied and argued
against. " Immortality," writes the German illuminist
Bahrdt, "what does that mean? The word *man* cannot
here be taken in the full sense, since the greatest part of
that which we name man enters into the circular course of
nature, becomes earth and then plants, and distributes itself
through a thousand forms of being. It can therefore be
the ' I ' only that is meant when it is maintained that man
is immortal. I, the possessor of so many thousands of
ideas, with the consciousness of my former and present

[1] Rousseau, *Emile*, Liv. iv.

condition, will continue, when my visible part, my body, has been for ever annihilated." [1]   The deistic habit of thought was to regard the body as a hindrance to the life of the soul, from which one should be thankful to be for ever rid.   The Kantian sentiment, "What would this clod of a body do in the eternal world?" all deists cordially endorsed.

On one point connected with the doctrine of a future life the representatives of deistic tendencies betray perplexity and exhibit contrarieties of opinion. With one consent they predict a blessed life after death for the good. But what of those who are not good, who have loved vice rather than virtue, folly rather than wisdom? Are their souls, too, immortal, and how does it fare with these? Some were tempted to get rid of the perplexing problem by denying the future life altogether, choosing to forego the hope of an eternal reward to escape the unwelcome alternative of eternal punishment. This course, however, could hardly find general approval in a school of thinkers with whom the necessity of a future state to redress the inequalities of the present was a favourite theme. It was rather to be expected that they would follow the example of Reimarus, and boldly proclaim their belief in a future involving both alternatives—an infinite Fear, as well as an infinite Hope.[2]   Yet they could not but be in a strait betwixt two, for so robust a creed was distasteful and repellant to deistical soft-heartedness; and many, accordingly, were at a loss what to believe. Chubb thought it questionable whether the retributions of the future state, if there were such, would apply to any but a small number of conspicuous offenders and benefactors, consigning the rest of mankind to annihilation, as not worthy either of eternal weal or eternal woe.[3]   Rousseau's statement is the most typical and pathetic, giving vivid

---

[1] Noack, *Die Friedenker*, 3ter Theil, p. 123.

[2] For the views of Reimarus, *vide* Noack, 3ter Theil, pp. 90-92.

[3] Leland's *Deists*, i. 198, 199.

eloquent expression to the conflict between two classes of feelings — respect for divine justice and abhorrence of wickedness on the one side; faith in divine benevolence and pity for the suffering, however bad, on the other.[1] The antinomy is one with which all thoughtful humane men are familiar; and its effect is the same now as then, to abate dogmatism and produce suspense of judgment.

Reviewing now this brief sketch of the deistic mode of contemplating the universe, it must be admitted that the picture presented is a very genial one. There is so much light and so little darkness in the deist's world; so much joy and so little misery—at least so little misery that has not a bright side to relieve the gloom; so much goodness and so little absolute wickedness. The deist moves about on this earth well pleased with God, with the creation, with his fellow-men, and above all with himself; his heart filled with tender sentiments, intoxicated with a sense of the beautiful in nature, passionately in love with virtue, cherishing high hopes of human progress in wisdom and goodness, until all the curses under which the race groans shall have disappeared, and the dark shadows of superstition been chased away, and the age of reason and common-sense been ushered in with millennial glory. You would not be surprised to hear him singing: "O Lord, how manifold are Thy works! in wisdom hast Thou made them all: the earth is full of Thy riches."[2] And again: "The glory of the Lord shall endure for ever: the Lord shall rejoice in His works. I will sing unto the Lord as long as I live. . . . My meditation of Him shall be sweet: I will be glad in the Lord."[3] The next stanza: "Let the sinners be consumed out of the earth, and let the wicked be no more,"[4] he would of course omit as unworthy of an enlightened age. He might say to himself, What a pity the pages of that otherwise excellent Hebrew book should be disfigured by so inhuman a sentiment, and that there should be so much

[1] Vide *Emile*, Liv. iv.
[3] Ps. civ. 31, 33, 34.
[2] Ps. civ. 24.
[4] Ps. civ. 35.

in it about sin and judgment, and wrath and sacrifice ! And
we in turn may say, What a pity there is so much in the
world to justify these darker elements in the biblical mode
of viewing God, man, and the course of providence, and to
make the deist's theory appear the romantic dream of one
who refuses to see whatever is disagreeable to his feelings.

Deistic optimism is superficial and extravagant. It may
be distinguished from Christian optimism by saying that,
whereas the Christian hopes that evil will eventually be
overcome by good, the deist virtually denies the existence
of evil, and proclaims the present prevalence of good. The
deistical use of the argument from design in the service
of this shallow and one-sided optimism is very open to
criticism. Two questions might be raised in regard to it :
whether the argument be at all competent, and, granting its
competency, whether it supplies as unequivocal evidence of
the goodness of God as deists imagined.

The former of these two questions does not properly
belong to the criticism of deism ; seeing that the employ
ment of the teleological argument in proof of the being and
attributes of God was not confined to deists, but was
common to them and their Christian opponents. It may
be said indeed with truth that this argument belongs not to
a party but to mankind. Since the days of Socrates, and
long before, the aspect of design everywhere exhibited in
the works of nature has attracted the attention of thought
ful men, and been regarded as evidence that this world is
the product of a Great Wise Mind. Even now, when the
recent advance of science has rendered the argument in its
old form antiquated, men thoroughly imbued with the
modern scientific spirit are constrained to acknowledge its
irresistible force, and Christian apologists claim for it, as
readjusted to new intellectual surroundings, undiminished
cogency. Another opportunity will occur for referring to
this venerable line of proof ; meantime it may suffice to say
with reference to the deists, that as men who maintained
the sufficiency of the light of nature they naturally made

the most of all sources of knowledge concerning God accessible to reason, and especially of those traces of adaptive skill with which, by common consent, the world was filled. The only question that may fairly be asked is whether they read aright the lesson which the frame of nature teaches.

Now it certainly is not the part of a Christian theist to meet the deistic inference of an omnipresent, all-pervading divine benevolence with a chilling, unsympathetic negative. It becomes a believer in the Bible, and in Christ, to affirm with emphasis that "the earth is full of the goodness of the Lord," and the average Christian is probably not by any means so optimistic as the genius of his faith requires him to be. But the interest of that faith demands that the doctrine of divine benevolence should be balanced by another doctrine, which is not indeed contrary, but complimentary to it, that, viz., which asserts the reality of a moral order in the world. Facts as well as the faith demand recognition of this truth. There is much in the world that may indeed be capable of reconciliation with divine benevolence, viewed as a disposition to make sentient creatures, and especially human beings, happy, but is far from being direct evidence of it. There is all that which has supplied food for superstitious fears and given rise to the worship of nature's destructive powers, and which, to a Christian way of contemplating nature, affords evidence that the world is a theatre of judgment as well as of mercy, and a school of virtue in which the supreme aim is not to make man happy as an animal, but to make him partaker of holiness, and train him for heroic behaviour in suffering and in doing. This sterner side of nature the deists were unwilling to see. Human superstition they traced to the scheming of priests, not to the elements of nature working on man's fears; on evil, the existence of which could not be denied, they put the best face: it was evil that looked at closely was really good, or it was evil resulting directly from man's own fault, or it was temporary evil that would

be put right, and abundantly compensated for in a future
state. Rousseau gave classic expression to the deistic
point of view in the following words :— -

"Moral evil is incontestably our work. The physical evil
would be nothing without our vices which render us sensible
to them. Is it not for the purpose of self-preservation that
nature makes us feel our wants? The pain of the body, is
it not a sign that the machine is out of order, and a hint
to take care of it? Death—do not the wicked poison their
own life and ours? Who would wish to live always among
them? Death is the remedy for the evils you inflict on
yourselves. Nature has wished that you should not suffer
always. To how few evils man is subject living in primitive
simplicity; he lives almost without disease, as without
passions, and neither foresees nor feels death; when he
feels it his miseries render it desirable, and it ceases to be
an evil for him."[1]

The representation is not wholly false, but its one-sided
tendency is manifest. The bias is that for which Butler
supplied the needful corrective in his chapters on the
Moral Government of God, and which he gently reproved
in these terms : "Perhaps divine goodness, with which, if
I mistake not, we make very free in our speculations, may
not be a bare single disposition to produce happiness, but
a disposition to make the good, the faithful, the honest
man happy."[2] The tone of the *Analogy of Religion* is not
itself, any more than that of deism, altogether true to
the spirit of Christianity. It errs on the side of gloom, as
deism erred on the side of gaiety. The general impression
the book leaves on the mind of a reader is sombre and
depressing. But the position taken up is unassailable, and
might with truth be more strongly expressed than in the
modest terms just quoted. God's end in constructing the
world was not, so far as we can see, to make men happy,
irrespective of character, but to make character and lot
correspond, or to use lot as a discipline for the develop-

[1] *Emile*, Liv. iv. [2] *Analogy*, chap. ii.

ment of character. This view, it will be observed, is in entire accordance with the Christian theory of the universe, in so far as it teaches that the world has a moral end, and that the creation is an instrument for the advancement of that end—the end being the establishment of the kingdom of God.

One reason why the modern reader is apt to find Butler's *Analogy* dreary is that he reads it apart from its historical environment. If we came to its perusal fresh from a course of reading in deistic literature, we should thankfully imbibe its teaching as a wholesome tonic after dipping into the honey-pots of optimism. We could even stand a stronger dose in the shape of a draught of the bitter medicine of pessimism. For such as desire it this medicine is supplied in full strength by certain modern physicians.

John Stuart Mill, in his essay on *Nature*, takes a very dark and gloomy view of the world. Discussing the question what is meant by following nature, he remarks that if by that be meant doing what we see physical nature doing, then we ought not to follow nature, because she does so many evil things. "In sober truth," he solemnly avers, "nearly all the things which men are hanged or imprisoned for doing to one another are nature's everyday performances."[1] After endeavouring to make good this grave charge by an enumeration of dismal particulars, he draws this conclusion with reference to the Author of nature: that He can be supposed to be good only on the assumption that His power is limited, so that He cannot help many of the evils which occur, and that nature affords no evidence whatever in favour of His being just. The net results of natural theology he thus sums up: "A Being of great but limited power, how or by what limited we cannot even conjecture; of great and perhaps unlimited intelligence, but perhaps also more narrowly limited than His power; who desires and pays some regard to the happiness of His creatures, but who seems to have other

[1] *Three Essays on Religion*, pp. 28-30.

motives of action which He cares more for, and who can hardly be supposed to have created the universe for that purpose alone." [1] What would the men of the Auf- klarung have thought of such doctrine ? How they would have held up their hands in virtuous horror at the profane Philistine who presumed to speak in this fashion of the omnipotent, omniscient, and utterly beneficent Creator ! But Schopenhauer goes still further, so that even Strauss is shocked, and in his tender feeling for the *universum* deems his brother philosopher guilty of something like blasphemy. Schopenhauer's doctrine in brief is that the world is as bad as a world can be and yet be able to exist. Optimism he regards as an utter platitude and triviality, and a heartless mockery of human misery. A pessimistic view of the world is in accordance with fact, and has been recognised as such by thoughtful earnest men of all times and countries. The present state of the world is hopelessly bad, and there is no prospect of improvement in the future. Physical and moral evil will go on unabated for ever, and the only redemption or escape possible is the resignation of despair.[2] Against this doctrine, which sees neither reason nor morality in the universe or its imaginary Author, Strauss contends that both a rational and a moral order are dis cernible in the world.[3] And without doubt he is right The pessimism of such writers as Schopenhauer or Hart- mann is wilful and passionate, and ignores the patent facts that there is a Power in the world, conscious or uncon scious, making for righteousness, and an all-pervading order, law, and reason, and manifold traces of a spirit of goodness. Nineteenth century pessimism is as far astray as was eighteenth century optimism. Both alike follow fancy and indulge their humour, and believe what is to their liking, rather than what, whether pleasant or otherwise, can on good grounds be shown to be true. Schopenhauer is a

[1] *Three Essays on Religion*, p. 194.
[2] *Vide Die Welt als Wille und Vorstellung*, Buch IV. p. 59.
[3] *Der alte und der neue Glaube*, p. 147.

cynic who views all things with jaundiced eye. The deist
was a self-complacent wiseacre who constituted himself a
special pleader for God against priests and bigots. The
one reminds us of Job sitting on a dunghill cursing his
day, and making desperate speeches against Providence;
the other resembles one of Job's friends dealing in weari-
some platitudes, refusing to see any mystery in God's ways,
and comforting his afflicted friend by telling him he must
be very wicked, seeing he is so miserable, for "who ever
perished, being innocent."

If the deist's view of the world and of providence was
very superficial, not less so was his view of *man*. Naturally
good, but often weak, liable to be enslaved by his passions,
which have their seat in the body, from which, therefore,
he will be released by death, error only what was to be
looked for in the circumstances, therefore pardonable, and
certain to be pardoned by an indulgent Deity—such was
man in nature and destiny, as conceived by the apostles of
common-sense philosophy. It was a theory not in accord
ance with fact, contradicted by the conscience of humanity,
and anything but complimentary to the dignity of human
nature. No man who knows the world, or whose moral
sentiments have any vigour, can accept deistical anthropology. Kant, in many respects at one with deists in
religious opinion, was not in accord with them at this point.
With the characteristic dislike of a strong man for senti
mental twaddle, he virtually pronounced the Aufklärung
philosophers, in their view of human nature and character,
a crew of quack-doctors, who told their patient pleasant
lies and administered to him drugs unsuited to the gravity
of his disease. Such is the import of the opening sentences
of his treatise on *Religion within the Bounds of Pure
Reason* :

"That the world lies in the wicked one is a complaint
which is as old as history—as old as the yet older art of
poetry—nay, as old as the oldest of all inventions, priestly
religion. All make the world begin from the good, from the

golden age, from life in Paradise, or happier still, from fellow ship with heavenly beings. But this felicity they represent as passing away quickly as a dream, through a fall into moral evil, which ever since the fall has gone on increasing with constantly accelerating pace."

Of the contrary view prevalent among the philosophers of his own time that the world was steadily advancing onwards, he remarks:

" It is certainly not drawn from experience, if it be of the morally good and bad, not of civilisation they speak, for the history of all times is decidedly against them. It is probably simply a good-hearted assumption of the moralists from Seneca to Rousseau, who wished to carry on unweariedly the culture of the seed of goodness possibly lying in us, and for that end thought good to start with the postulate that a natural foundation for such progressive culture was to be found in men."

Kant himself believed in a radical evil, appealing in proof to the wanton barbarities of savages, and to the characteristic vices of civilisation, insincerity, ingratitude, secret joy in the misfortunes of even the most intimate friends, not to speak of sins of the flesh, which are of no account in an otherwise cultivated man. Referring to the remark of Walpole that " every man has his price," he observes :

" If this be true, and every one can satisfy himself on the point, if there be no virtue for which a measure of tempta tion cannot be found able to overcome it ; if the question which side we shall take, the good or the bad, turns on this: who offers most and pays most promptly—then, indeed, were true of men what the apostle says : ' There is no dif ference, for all have sinned ; there is none that doeth good, no, not one.' "

While not affirming that Walpole's cynical judgment was correct, Kant in these words plainly indicates what he thinks of men of whom it holds good. This suggests the reflection that in forming an estimate of man's moral condition much depends on our moral ideal. Lenient judgments of character and sanguine views of man's ability to fulfil the requirements of duty, may simply be the result of low-pitched views of what righteousness is and man ought to be. What, for example, do I think of the corruptibility charged by Walpole against mankind? Do I regard it with abhorrence, or simply as a thing to be laughed at, done by nearly everybody, and no great harm in it? In the latter case it may be easy for me to entertain a favourable opinion of men, even of politicians; the only question will be, What is my opinion worth? But in the former case I may find it hard to cherish a favourable view of average human character; for when it is remembered how easily men can be induced to tamper with truth, justice, and mercy for a very little gain, not only in the sphere of politics, but in commerce, and indeed in all departments of life, it has to be acknowledged that if all men have not their price, at least very many have. Meditating on this fact I, in case I do from the heart abhor the subordination of righteousness to interest, will be apt to regard human goodness as a deceitful appearance, and to be reminded of Christ's picture of the Pharisees: whited sepulchres, fair without, within full of rottenness and dead men's bones. And when I extend my views to other sins besides that of venality, my sense of human depravity will only be deepened till I am constrained to acquiesce in Christ's verdict on human sinfulness as strictly true: "Out of the heart proceed evil thoughts, murders, adulteries, fornications, thefts, false witness, blasphemies." This verdict I will not merely admit to be true of others, but take home to myself. To flattering optimists I will reply: "In me, that is in my flesh, dwelleth no good thing. Nay, I cannot throw all blame on my flesh. There is evil in my mind, envy, vanity, pride, *schadenfreude*, meanness, selfishness, hateful indifference to, and lack of sympathy with, the wellbeing of my fellow-men. Wretched man! who shall deliver me, not merely from this body of death, but from these evil satanic spirits?"

On the deistic view of the future life it is not necessary to dilate. Here, as elsewhere, the characteristic shallowness of the system appears. In its conception of the life to come pagan rather than Christian, it was slipshod in its method of proof. The body dies but not the soul, because it is immaterial; the good get not what they deserve here, therefore God in justice is bound to give them a second life hereafter by way of compensation. If there be a God who wills the happiness of men, He must will their virtue, and He must further supply them with sufficient motives to virtue. But sufficient motives to virtue exist not, if my ego do not continue, and virtue have no enduring consequences. Therefore I must expect continued existence from God. How characteristic this over-confident fore cast! These genial optimists are sure that God will give them everything they wish or fancy that they need. The world to come is necessary to their happiness, therefore they will certainly have it. No wonder such men were surprised to find next to no traces of the doctrine of immortality in the Old Testament. A professed revelation without a doctrine of immortality—impossible! exclaimed Reimarus, all true sons of the Aufklarung vehemently assenting. Yet, after listening for some time to the oracular utterances of the apostles of reason on "the great enigma," one begins to be conscious of a profound respect for the reticence of Hebrew prophets and poets, who, whatever their thoughts on hereafter might be, were content to be silent on a theme concerning which they had no sure message to communicate. The silence of the Old Testament about immortality, so surprising to deists, is much more divine than their own copious effusive speech.

CHAPTER VI.

MODERN SPECULATIVE THEISM.

LITERATURE.—F. W. Newman, *The Soul* and *Phases of Faith;* Theodore Parker's works, especially *A Discourse on Religion*, vol. i., and *Of Speculative Theism*, vol. xi.; Miss F. P. Cobbe, *Broken Lights* and *Darwinism in Morals and other Essays;* W. R. Greg, *Creed of Christendom* and *Enigmas of Life;* Pécaut, *Le Christ et La Conscience* and *sur L'Avenir du Theisme Chretienne;* Schwartz, *Zur Geschichte der neuesten Theologie;* Pfleiderer, *Die Religion;* Martineau, *A Study of Religion;* Aubrey L. Moore, *Science and the Faith.*

In most, if not in all, essential particulars, the system of thought which goes by the name of modern speculative theism represents the same religious tendency as that which in the eighteenth century was known as deism, free thought, Aufklarung. In the more recent system there is the same rejection of revelation, the same reduction of religion to a few elementary beliefs made accessible to all by the light of nature, the same optimistic view of the world, the same naturalistic conception of God's relation to the world, the same sceptical attitude towards the miraculous in every shape and sphere. Yet the leading expositors of the system are very anxious not to be confounded with deists. Hence the choice of the title theists, which, so far as etymology is concerned, ought to mean the same thing as deists, the only difference between the words being that the former is derived from the Greek name for God, θεος, while the latter is derived from the Latin name, *Deus.* An English representative of the new school thus distinguishes between it and the old :

The deism of the last century, with its cold and dry negations of Christianity, has passed away for ever, and given place to a theism which, in the writings of Newman and Theodore Parker, may vie for spirituality and warmth of religious feeling with any other faith in the world. God is no longer to us the Great First Cause discoverable through chains of inductive argument, and dwelling far away in unapproachable majesty, where only our awe and homage and not our prayers and love might follow Him. He is our Father in heaven once more, the God who reveals Himself hourly to our consciences and our hearts; who is nearer and dearer than earthly friend may ever be; in whom we desire consciously to live and move and have our being here, in the joy of whose love we trust to spend our immortality hereafter." [1]

The American apostle of theism referred to in this extract defines his position, as distinct from that of deists, in these terms:

"I use the word theism as distinguished from deism, which affirms a God without the ferocious character of the popular theology, but still starts from the sensational philosophy, abuts on materialism, derives its idea of God solely by induction from the phenomena of material nature or of human history, leaving out of sight the intuition of human nature; and so gets its idea of God solely from external observation, and not at all from consciousness, and thus accordingly represents God as finite and imperfect." [2]

The difference between modern theism and deism is to a considerable extent one of tone rather than of principle. The more recent system is warmer in temperament; speaking generally that is to say, for the deists were not all frigid, some of them being almost as emotional in their religious character as Miss Cobbe herself. There is observable also in the literature of the later movement an appreciative manner of speaking concerning the Holy Scriptures and Christ which we miss in most deistical writings. While denying to the Bible all claim to be or to contain a divine revelation in any exclusive sense, and to be regarded as the literary product of an inspiration

---

[1] Miss Cobbe, *Broken Lights*, p. 175.

[2] "Of Speculative Theism regarded as a Theory of the Universe," *Works*, vi. 105.

limited to its writers, modern theists are effusive in their eulogies on the sacred writings as the most excellent of all known productions of human genius within the sphere of religion. Of Christ also, while denying His divinity and even His absolute moral perfection, they are reverential admirers, as a man of unsurpassed, if not unsurpassable, wisdom and goodness. Therefore they claim to be Chris tians, and call themselves Christian theists, and even hold that they have a better right to the name than those who confess the Catholic creed of Christendom, which they regard as a monstrous and melancholy perversion of Chris tianity as taught and exemplified by Jesus Christ Himself.

Of this modern movement of religious thought, as claiming to be something new and distinctive, and as entitled to respect for the earnestness and ability displayed by its leading advocates, it is meet that some account should here be given. A brief statement and criticism of its characteristic views may help the believer to a clearer understanding of his own position in relation to con temporary opinion. The task is not altogether easy; for the representatives of the system, while all professing to derive their inspiration from one source, the moral con sciousness, are by no means at one in their sentiments. It is even doubtful who are to be taken as representatives, whether, for example, the author of *The Creed of Christendom* and Dr. Martineau may be classed with Francis Newman, Frances Power Cobbe, and Theodore Parker, who may without hesitation be regarded as typical exponents.

The subject of chief interest is the conception of God in relation to the world. Theism of the type now under review may be broadly distinguished from deism by saying that the former conceives of God's relation to the world as one of *immanence*, and the latter as one of *transcendence*. These philosophic terms, which have recently obtained currency in the sphere of speculative thought, do not con- vey a very definite meaning to minds unaccustomed to their use. For popular purposes the distinction may be

identified with that between within and without. An
immanent God is a God who abides within the world, a
transcendent God is a God who dwells above and beyond
the world. The distinction may be made vivid to the
imagination by representing the immanent Deity as
imprisoned, in respect of His being and energy, within the
world, and the transcendent Deity as in the same respects
banished to the outside of the world ; the imprisoned God
being the God of modern theism, the banished God the
God of deism. Delitzsch, having in view chiefly German
representatives of the theistic creed, states the difference
thus :

" While speculative theism in a one-sided manner em
phasises the immanence of God, the old deism emphasised
with equal one-sidedness His transcendence. The former
makes God the active ground of the world-development
according to natural law, which is dependent on Him, He
in turn being dependent on it ; the latter placed Him above
the *perpetuum mobile* of the universe, and made Him a mere
spectator of human history; both agreeing in the opinion
that there is no need or room for a supernatural incursion
of God into the natural course of development, and refusing
to recognise in Christ a new creative beginning and all
that goes along with that." [1]

No intelligent Christian in our time can hesitate as to
which of the two contrasted views of God's relation to
the world is to be preferred. The deistic conception of
God as an artificer who long ago made a perfect machine,
and then left it to work in obedience to its own self-
acting forces, is entirely out of date. The mechanical
conception of the universe has given place in modern
thought to the organic, and that has brought along with
it an altered view of God's relation to the universe as
somewhat analogous to the relation of soul to body. Thus
far all are agreed, influenced by the spirit of an age
dominated in all departments of human thought by the

[1] *System der Christlichen Apologetik*, p. 157.

great idea of evolution. But on looking more narrowly into the matter, one soon discovers that the Christian theory of the universe and that of speculative theism part company.

The distinctive view of speculative theism, when it aims at philosophic precision, is that God, while not to be confounded with the world, as in pantheism, is still so far one with the world that His activity is rigidly confined within the course of nature. All the energy displayed in the world is His, and therein consists His immanence; there is in Him no activity which does not reveal itself in the world of matter and of mind according to the laws of each, and this amounts to a denial of transcendence. Theodore Parker, however, who, perhaps, of all English-speaking representatives of the school, has the greatest pretensions to a speculative habit of thought, does not admit that his doctrine is one of mere immanence. He thus defines his position as against pantheism :

" If God be infinite, then He must be immanent, perfectly and totally present in nature and in spirit. Thus there is no point of space, no atom of matter, but God is there ; no point of spirit, and no atom of soul, but God is there. And yet finite matter and finite spirit do not exhaust God. He transcends the world of matter and of spirit, and in virtue of that transcendence continually makes the world of matter fairer, and the world of spirit wiser. So there is really a progress in the manifestation of God, not a progress in God the manifesting. In thought you may annihilate the world of matter and of man ; but you do not thereby in thought annihilate the Infinite God, or subtract anything from the existence of God. In thought you may double the world of matter and of man ; but in so doing you do not in thought double the Being of the Infinite God ; that remains the same as before. That is what I mean when I say that God is infinite, and transcends matter and spirit, and is different in kind from the finite universe." [1]

The doctrine that God is both immanent and transcend-

[1] " Of Speculative Theism regarded as a Theory of the Universe," *Works,* xi. 108.

ent is the distinctively Christian one, and we might
therefore expect to find Mr. Parker, after laying down such
a position, prepared to assign a place in his system to a
supernatural divine activity.   Yet this was far from his
thoughts.   His doctrine on the miraculous is: " No whim
in God, therefore no miracle in nature.   The law of nature
represents the modes of God Himself, who is the only true
cause and the only true power, and as He is infinite, un
changeably perfect, and perfectly unchangeable, His mode
of action is therefore constant and universal, so that there
can be no such thing as a violation of God's constant mode
of action." [1]   Thus, so far as the fixity of nature's course
is concerned, it is as if there were no God distinct from
nature, no God other than the *natura naturans* of Spinoza.
Supernatural incursion is inconceivable, impossible.

The immanence of God in the human spirit is asserted
by Mr. Parker not less unqualifiedly than in reference
to the world of matter.   All human thought and will, in
his view, is in reality God's thought and will.   He identifies
divine inspiration with the exercise of the human intellect
on all subjects.   " It is the light of all our being ; the
background of all human faculties ; the sole means by
which we gain a knowledge of what is not seen and felt,
the logical condition of all sensual knowledge ; our high
way to the world of spirit." [2]   It belongs to all men in
varying measure, proportioned to the amount of their
mental powers and the extent to which they have exercised
these.   It reveals itself in varying forms according to the
diversity of gifts, making one man a philosopher, another a
poet, a third a musician, and a fourth a prophet.   It be
longs to no man in a supernatural form, or in absolute
degree, not even to a Christ ; for absolute inspiration would
be a miracle.   In effect this is to resolve the intellect of
man into the intellect of God.

The absorption of the human will into the divine is

[1] *Works*, xi. 114.
[2] " A Discourse on Religion," *Works*, i. 141.

asserted by this author with equal emphasis, not indeed on purely speculative grounds so much as in the interests of a sweeping optimism. Holding that God not only wills, but is bound, to save all men, and even to provide a heaven for the sparrow, he sacrifices human freedom to escape all risk of miscarriage. "In that part of the world not endowed with animal life there is no margin of oscillation, and you may know just where the moon will be to-night, and where it will be a thousand years hence." "In the world of animals there is a small margin of oscillation, but you are pretty sure to know what the animals will do." "But man has a certain amount of freedom, a larger margin of oscillation wherein he vibrates from side to side." But what then? "The perfect cause must know the consequences of His own creation, and knowing the cause and the effects thereof, as perfect providence, and working from a perfect motive, for a perfect purpose, with perfect material and by perfect means, He must so arrange all things that the material shall be capable of ultimate welfare."[1] In short, men must be saved without exception, and God's goodness vindicated, come what will of human freedom.

Theism of this type seems to approach indefinitely near to pantheism. We are therefore not surprised to find Parker hesitating to ascribe to God personality. "As the Absolute Cause God must contain in Himself, potentially, the ground of consciousness, of personality—yes, of unconsciousness and impersonality. But to apply these terms to Him seems a vain attempt to fathom the abyss of the Godhead, and report the soundings."[2] On this subject, however, other members of the school lean more to theistic than to pantheistic views. The warm temperament of modern theists, despite their philosophic tendencies, inclines them to affirm with more or less emphasis the personality of Deity. From the same cause they love to think of God as a Father. Parker in his exuberant, extravagant way

---

[1] *Works*, xi. 116-119. [2] *Works*, i. 104.

was wont in his prayers to address God not only as Father but as Mother. Miss Cobbe makes the very essence of the new theism, that which distinguishes it from every other creed in the world, consist in the assertion of God's absolutely paternal goodness. "Negatively it will reject all doctrines of atheism or pantheism on the one hand, and of a plurality of divine persons on the other. Affirmatively it will assert not only the unity, and eternity, and wisdom, and justice of God, but above all that one great attribute which is our principal concern, His goodness."[1]

If God be a Father, then we His children may make known to Him our needs; but what room can there be for prayer in a system which restricts divine activity to the fixed course of nature? Are modern theists not conscious of a difficulty here? They are, and the manner in which some have attempted to meet the difficulty is instructive. On this topic the new theistic school, as represented by Miss Cobbe, differs from the old deistic school, as represented by Rousseau, when he said, "I bless God, but I pray not." Miss Cobbe insists, with much emphasis, on the value of prayer as a safeguard for theists against ultimate lapse into pantheism. "Theism to be a religion at all, and not a philosophy leading off into pantheism, must be a religion of prayer." "If we abandon prayer, the personality of God recedes away into the dimness of distance. We begin to think of a Creative Power, a World-Spirit, a Demiurge,—the All of things."[2] This is a very frank, though incidental acknowledgment of the pantheistic tendency of the system, and it is quite natural and proper that one conscious of the danger and dreading it should have recourse to prayer as an antidote. But the habit of prayer is not likely to be persisted in merely as an aid to a theistic way of thinking concerning God. Perseverance in the pious exercise can spring only out of earnest belief in the possibility of obtaining thereby

[1] *Broken Lights*, p. 157.   [2] *Ibid.* pp. 179, 180.

some practical benefit greatly desired. But is such belief reconcilable with the doctrine that the divine activity is rigidly restricted to, and indeed synonymous with, the fixed course of nature? The answer given by those who plead for the reasonableness and utility of petitionary prayer consists in a distinction taken between the physical and the spiritual worlds, to the effect of confining such prayer to the latter as its sole legitimate sphere. Prayer, it is maintained, is irrational when the benefit desired is physical,—health, wealth, good weather,— but competent and prevailing when our requests are directed to spiritual blessings, for such requests amount to asking God to fulfil His own laws of the spirit. "It is not irreligious to ask that God should perform His will on us, that will which we know is our sanctification, our purification from all taint of sin, our elevation to all heights of spiritual good and glory."[1] It may not be irreligious, but the question is, Is it not superfluous on a thoroughgoing doctrine of immanence, just as much so as it is on a thoroughgoing doctrine of transcendence? On the latter doctrine divine activity is entirely excluded from the sphere of the human spirit, and God, as Rousseau taught, can only look on, while man, in the exercise of his freedom, does or neglects his duty. On the former doctrine, on the other hand, the divine activity is identical with that of the human spirit. It is God that thinks and wills and struggles against evil in us, and He does all, not by free concurrence in answer to our prayers, but by the same necessity by which He acts through the law of gravitation. Thus the two extremes meet in a common exclusion of prayer, for the justification of which, even in the spiritual sphere, it is necessary to combine in our conception of God's relation to our spirit the two con trasted ideas of immanence and transcendence, believing that He is in us "both to will and to do," but not so that He "under the mask of our personality does our

[1] *Broken Lights*, p. 177.

thinking, and prays against our temptations, and weeps our tears," but rather through "a sympathy free to answer, spirit to spirit, neither merging in the other, but both at one in the same inmost preferences and affections."[1] Nor does any reason appear why prayer thus justifiable should be confined to the spiritual sphere. It may, indeed, be contended that God is wholly immanent in the physical sphere, wherein therefore His action can only take the form of invariable natural law, and that He is transcendent only with reference to the spiritual sphere, wherein He may act supernaturally as "free cause in an unpledged sphere," communicating His grace in answer to prayer.[2] The truth seems to be that He is both immanent and transcendent in all spheres.

Modern theism, in spite of superficial differences, betrays its affinity with the older deism, very specially in its optimistic views of divine providence and human destiny. Parker is here the most characteristic representative of the school. According to his sunny creed, all things work together surely for the good of men, nay, of all living creatures. "The sparrow that falls to-day does not fall to ruin, but to ultimate welfare. Though we know not the mode of operation, there must be another world for the sparrow, as for man."[3] This is not only a matter of fact, but a matter of right. Every creature has a right to be made for a perfect purpose. The right is inherent in creaturehood; it depends not on the position any particular creature occupies in the scale of being, and therefore it is equal for all. It cannot be voided by any accident of their history. It is easy to see what view this involves of pain and error, physical and moral evil. These are to be regarded as divinely ordered economies,—temporary

---

[1] Martineau, *A Study of Religion*, ii. 190.

[2] This seems to be the view maintained by Martineau. *Vide A Study of Religion*, ii. 190-194, where, however, the subject of discussion is not the limit of legitimate prayer, but the personality of God, its grounds and implications, in vindication of theism as against pantheism.

[3] *Works*, xi. 115.

ills working toward a higher good for man and beast, now
or hereafter. At this point modern theism is at its greatest
distance from pantheism; for while the latter denies
abiding significance in the universe even to man, the
former claims an eternal value for the meanest creature
that lives or exists.

By way of criticism on this recent system of religious
thought, two points only need be insisted on. In the
first place, it is obviously a theism in a state of very
unstable equilibrium, tending to topple over into pantheism,
and conscious of its need for the culture of a devotional
spirit to avert the catastrophe. It is not a consistent,
carefully - thought - out theory of the universe, but an
eclectic system, with elements borrowed from pantheism
and Christianity; on the emotional side Christian, on
the philosophic side pantheistic, and destined eventually
to go wholly over either to the one side or to the other.

Secondly, on the religious side this system is scarcely
more satisfactory than on the speculative. The far-off,
transcendent God of deism is admittedly an unsatisfactory
object of faith and worship. But is the immanent Deity of
modern theism a great improvement? Can a God eternally
immured within the prison walls of the universe meet the
wants of our religious nature? What great difference
is there between this immanent God and the *natura
naturans* of Spinoza? Is it replied that this God is
personal, the self-conscious benignant author of the world?
Good, but whence comes this knowledge? From the
moral consciousness. The heart demands such a God;
there is really no other evidence for His existence. But
is the heart satisfied to stop there? If the heart is to be
listened to, let us hear all it has to say. Does it not
demand a God not only personal but free, a God who can
hear prayer in all spheres, exercise a constant providence
over men through the ordinary course of nature or other
wise, work miracles, become man, demonstrate His love
by that extreme act of condescension?

This question reminds us that in another aspect of funda
mental moment the system now under review is weak on
its religious side. It totally fails to satisfy the craving
of our minds for religious certainty. The exclusive organ
of revelation for the modern theist is the moral consciousness. Discarding a historical revelation as out of date,
useless, incredible, impossible, he looks to the light within
—conscience, the spiritual nature of man. And surely if
there were no other light available than that of our own soul
it would be natural and right that we should make the
most of it. Nor can one have any wish to disparage that
light, far less to deny its existence, for God has not left
Himself without a witness in the human spirit, and there
is truth in the saying of Tertullian, *conscientia naturaliter
Christiana*. But it may without hesitation be affirmed
that the light within is dim, to be used thankfully and
hopefully in the absence of a better, yet not such as to
justify a contemptuous attitude towards that which is
offered us as a more sure word of prophecy. In proof
it is enough to point to the utterances of those who in
recent years have professed to derive all their religious
inspiration from the human soul. Illustrative instances
may legitimately be taken from all who make this pro
fession. It will be found on inquiry to be almost the
only thing on which they are agreed. On hardly one of
the great questions of religion does the oracle give a
certain sound. Take the personality of God. Miss Cobbe
affirms confidently, Mr. W. R. Greg affirms timidly,
Theodore Parker almost denies, that God is a Personal
Being; all on the authority of the moral consciousness.
Or take the goodness of God. The moral consciousness of
Mr. Parker enables him to trace throughout human history
the constant action of an infinitely benignant Providence.
Mr. Greg's consciousness tells him a less flattering tale,
bearing witness indeed to divine goodness, but finding it
impossible to save that goodness from suspicion, except
by a limitation of divine power, which makes it impossible

to prevent many evils overtaking man. Or, take the great question of a future life, and what it will bring. Mr. Parker believes in a life to come; in a heaven for man, beast, and bird; in an absolutely universal salvation from sin and misery. This comfortable creed Mr. Greg is not able to accept. The future for him is "the great enigma." The intellect may imagine it, but could never have discovered it, and can never prove it. The "soul" alone can reveal it. The revelation is a purely personal affair. If my soul does not speak to me, it is in vain that another man's soul has spoken to him; that will not help me. The soul does not speak to Mr. Greg in very audible or distinct tones. It tells him that there are abundant possibilities for a dreadful hell in the spirit of man con ceived as continuing after death, but that probably the morally crude specimens of humanity will escape this doom by ceasing to exist. "Probably what God bestows at birth is a germ, not a finished entity, not an immortal soul, but a nature capable of being worked up into a soul worthy of immortality, an organisation rich in the strangest and grandest potentialities; not a possession, but an opportunity; not an inheritance, but the chance of winning one. Perhaps it may be only such natures as develop adequately, and in the right direction in this life, that will be heirs of heaven, and that all others may, as it were, never pass beyond the embryonic or earthly stage of existence."[1] Take one other instance, the utility of prayer, a vital question in practical religion. Here, too, the prophets of the soul are at variance. Miss Cobbe declares prayer to be both legitimate and useful within the spiritual sphere, and neither legitimate nor useful within the physical. Mr. Greg pronounces prayer theo retically indefensible in all spheres, therefore impossible for those who possess insight into the truth of things, but permissible and harmless for the weak and ignorant.[2]

These examples of variation do not encourage us to

[1] *Enigmas of Life*, p. 221.   [2] *Creed of Christendom*, ii. 196-209.

cherish a high opinion of the moral consciousness as an independent and reliable guide in religion. They seem to prove that the inner light is not a sun but a moon, not a lamp but a mirror, reflecting rays which fall upon it from other sources. Plato, who gave all diligence to make the best possible use of this light, was conscious of its dimness, and sighed for a surer word concerning human destiny than his own conjectures. The surer word came, and for a while the world was thankful. Now a different temper prevails; men place overweening trust in the light within, and despise the light without, though, to a large extent, it is the real though unacknowledged source of the light within. The altered mood finds eloquent expression in the sentences which follow—the enthusiastic utterance of a prophetess of the new revelation :

" In the long pilgrimage of our race we have reached a point where the way to the celestial city is no longer clear, and where no angel or interpreter stands by to direct us. To the right lies the old road which our fathers trod, and where we can yet recognise their venerable footsteps. But that path is a quicksand now, hardly able to bear the weight of a traveller who would plant his feet firmly as he goes. To the left there is another path, but it turns visibly before our eyes away from that city of God which has been hitherto our goal, and passes down fathomless abysses of lonely darkness where our hearts quail to follow. Straight before us lies a field hardly tracked as yet by the pilgrim feet which have passed over it, a vast field full of flowers and open to the sun. May the king of that country guide us, so that walking thereon we may find a new, straighter road to the celestial city on high, beyond the dark river, and to the Beulah land of peaceful faith here upon earth." [1]

The same tone of buoyant confidence in the sole and sufficient guidance of reason or spiritual intuition is audible in the more recent utterances of a greater prophet. Dr. Martineau recognises the claim neither of Church nor Bible to be an authoritative guide in religion. Not

[1] Miss Cobbe, *Darwinism in Morals and other Essays,* p. 146.

even to Jesus will he concede the right to be regarded as the Light of the world. For negative criticism has enveloped His history in a thick mist of uncertainty, and a series of faith-woven veils have hid His face beyond recognition. We cannot now truly know or clearly see the Son of man. Nor does it greatly matter. We have within ourselves, each man apart, the light that can be implicitly trusted. In spiritual intuition, God immediately reveals Himself to every faithful soul. That is the true, first-hand, authoritative revelation.[1]

CHAPTER VII.

AGNOSTICISM.

LITERATURE.—Herbert Spencer, *First Principles;* Fiske, *Outlines of Cosmic Philosophy;* Flint, *Theism;* Martineau, *Study of Religion* (vol. i., " Restatement of Teleological Argu ment "); Lotze, *Mikrokosmus;* Janet, *Final Causes;* Principal Caird, *Introduction to the Philosophy of Religion;* Professor Edward Caird, *The Social Philosophy and Religion of Comte;* Green, *Prolegomena of Ethics;* Aubrey L. Moore, *Science and the Faith;* Kennedy, *Natural Theology and Modern Thought;* Kaftan, *Die Wahrheit der Christlichen Religion;* W. Hermann, *Der Verkehr des Christen mit Gott;* Chapman, *Preorganic Evolution and the Christian Idea of God;* Royce, *The Religious Aspect of Philosophy.*

In the foregoing chapters the aim has been, by the method of comparison, to make the Christian mode of conceiving God, man, and the world, and their relations, appear theoretically satisfactory, and on practical ethical grounds, preferable. This done, we might consider our speculative task achieved. But it seems meet, ere passing from this division of the subject, to take notice of a prevailing attitude of mind which does not express itself by pro pounding a distinctive theory, but rather by declining

[1] *Vide The Seat of Authority in Religion,* Books III. and V.

to have one, and by pronouncing all actual or possible theories incompetent. This attitude in our time is called *agnosticism*. It is the negation of real or possible knowledge concerning God and His relations to man and the world. God is, for this modern mood, an unknown quantity, of which we are not in a position to affirm anything. That He is may be admitted, but what He is no man it is held can know.

This doctrine of nescience is prominently associated with the name of Mr. Herbert Spencer, the author of *A System of Synthetic Philosophy*. In his statement of *First Principles*, Mr. Spencer devotes a chapter to the discussion of *ultimate religious ideas*, which ends with these ominous words: "The Power which the universe manifests to us is utterly inscrutable."[1] The bearing of this position on the important problem of the origin of the world is clearly indicated in the following sentences:— "Respecting the origin of the universe, three verbally intelligible suppositions may be made. We may assert that it is self-existent, or that it is self-created, or that it is created by an external agency. Which of these suppositions is most credible it is not needful here to inquire. The deeper question, into which this finally merges, is, whether any one of them is even conceivable in the true sense of the word."[2] That is to say, in the opinion of the writer, atheism, pantheism, and theism are all alike incompetent attempts to solve a problem which is really insoluble. The obvious practical lesson is that we should abstain from all such vain efforts, and rest in the conviction "that it is alike our highest wisdom and our highest duty to regard that through which all things exist as The Unknowable."[3]

From the terms in which the founder of modern agnosticism formulates his doctrine, it appears that this much is known about The Unknowable: that it is a "Power which the universe manifests," and "through

[1] *First Principles*, p. 46.   [2] *Ibid.* p. 30.   [3] *Ibid.* p. 113.

which all things exist." One might hope that if so much can be known, a little more knowledge might be attainable ; that, *e.g.*, something might be learned concerning the ultimate Source of being from the world which it has brought into existence. This, however, is peremptorily denied. While holding that the phenomenal universe is the manifestation of a Power that cannot be identified with the totality of the phenomena, the agnostic philosopher maintains that we can learn nothing as to the nature of this Power from the qualities of the phenomena. The ultimate Cause of the world cannot be known through its effects. An American disciple of Mr. Spencer seeks to prove the incompetency of this method of knowing God by a *reductio ad absurdum*. " Since the universe contains material as well as psychical phenomena, its first Cause must partake of all the differential qualities of those phenomena. If it reasons and wills, like the higher animals, it must also, like minerals, plants, and the lowest animals, be unintelligent and unendowed with the power of volition, which requires in the first Cause a more than Hegelian capacity for uniting contradictory attributes." [1]

That the agnostic position is fatal, or at least most hostile, to all earnest Christian faith, does not need to be pointed out. If from nature, history, or the human soul no hints of truth concerning God, except, perhaps, that He is, can be derived, a higher revelation, if not impossible, is at least apt to appear incredible. Such faith in a self-revealing God, as one imbued with the agnostic temper still cherishes, can be but an evening twilight, after sunset, destined soon to fade into darkness. If the teaching of Christ concerning God be true, it ought to be in harmony with what nature in all its spheres suggests, not to say proves. The Christian doctrine of God, to be valid, must be a hypothesis which all we know tends to verify. If this be found to be the fact, if the Christian

[1] Fiske, *Outlines of Cosmic Philosophy*, ii. 388, 389.

God be not without a witness in all parts of the world accessible to observation, then the believer will feel himself confirmed in his faith by the consciousness of being in harmony with the universe, of which he forms a part. On the opposite alternative, faith is in the air, unsupported, isolated, struggling to maintain itself in spite of the chilling negations of reason and science.

The sceptical attitude of agnostics may seem to be justified by the mutual contradictions of the advocates of theism. For it is the fact that, while those who profess nescience assert the valuelessness of all attempts to know what God is, there are few believers in the possibility of knowing God who do not deny the validity of some theistic arguments, and that there is little agreement among those who hold in common a theistic creed as to what proofs are valid, and what sources of knowledge available. Hardly any argument has been advanced which has not been assailed not merely by unbelievers but by believers. Apologists, accepting unanimously theistic conclusions, have differed widely as to the premises from which these ought to be drawn. Speaking generally, it may be said that there is a close connection between the line of proof adopted by the theistic advocate and the school of philo sophy to which he belongs. Disciples of Locke, Kant, and Hegel all disallow arguments alien to their respective philosophies, and advance others more akin to these, which to minds outside the school have not infrequently appeared less conclusive than the arguments supplanted.

Among the theistic proofs which have commanded wide acceptance, the foremost place is due to the three entitled respectively the *cosmological*, the *teleological*, and the *ontological*, which may be called the standard arguments for the existence of a great First Cause, almighty, wise, good, and perfect. The first argues from the mere existence of a world to an absolutely necessary Being from whom it took its origin. The world as a whole it regards as an effect whose cause is God. The argument implies that the world as we know it is contingent, that is, does not necessarily exist, and that it is an event, or had a commencement. The principle on which it proceeds is that for all contingent being the ultimate source must be a cause necessarily and eternally existing. Its force may be evaded either by denying that the world had a beginning;[1] or by denying that any contingent system of things needs any cause other than an antecedent system also contingent, explicable in turn by a third, and so on *ad infinitum* in an eternal succession of causes and effects; or yet again, more boldly, by maintaining that the category of causality is inapplicable to God as the Supersensible and the Infinite.[2]

The *teleological* argument is based on the manifold instances of adaptation discernible in the world, as of the parts of an organism to its function, or of an organ to its environment. These adaptations wear the aspect of design, and suggest the thought that a world full of them must be the work of an infinitely wise Mind. " He that planted the ear, shall He not hear? He that formed the eye, shall He not see?" To the religious spirit the reasoning quaintly conveyed in these questions of the Psalmist will never cease to appeal. Science and philosophy may criticise, but science itself only supplies new materials for an argument, which, suggested by a single instance of adaptation, acquires through the indefinite multiplication of examples a cumulative force which many feel to be irresistible. Living in a *cosmos* everywhere pervaded by

---

[1] Flint says that the question whether the universe had a commencement is *the* question in the theistic argument from causality. — *Theism*, p. 101.

[2] Kant maintained that the principle of causality cannot take us beyond the limits of the sensible world. Principal Caird contends that the category can be applied only to the finite. His argument is to this effect. The relation of cause and effect implies the succession or the coexistence of its members. In the latter case things exist externally to each other, mutually acting on each other. In the former the cause passes into the effect and ceases to be ; heat produces and passes into motion. Both aspects of the relation imply a limitation in space and time that cannot have place with reference to God as infinite and eternal. *Vide* his *Spinoza*, pp. 167, 168.

order, the man of unsophisticated mind finds it impossible to acquiesce in the *dictum* of Strauss: "This world was not planned by a highest reason, though it has the highest reason for its goal."[1] He rather endorses with emphasis the verdict of Mr. J. S. Mill, no prejudiced witness, that "It must be allowed that in the present state of our know ledge the adaptations in nature afford a large balance of probability in favour of creation by intelligence."[2]

Yet since the days of Kant this ancient, popular, and still impressive argument has been regarded with more or less disfavour by many philosophers and theologians. Kant himself, while treating it with respect, strove to minimise its value, partly in order to read a lesson of moderation to the men of the Aufklarung, who did their best to make it ridiculous. He held that it yields at most a World-Architect, not a creator, Author of the form not of the matter of the universe, and only a very wise Architect, not an absolutely wise, and doubted if in strict logic it can give us so much. He robbed it of all support in the internal adaptations of an organism such as the eye, by his conception of an organism as a structure in which all the parts mutually condition and produce each other, are mutually to each other at once cause and effect, and all alike are possible only through their relation to the whole and owe their existence to their relation. In this bearing of all the parts on the whole he recognised a teleology of nature, yet not such as implies a cause outside of them who has an idea of their design. He admitted that it comes very natural to us to think of such an outside designing cause, but held nevertheless that the conception comes from our own spirit, and has no objective value.[3] In this view he was followed by Hegel, who, in his lectures on the proofs of the existence of God, remarks: "The inner construction of the bodily organism, the functions of the nerve and

---

[1] *Der alte und der neue Glaube*, p. 143.

[2] *Three Essays on Religion*, p. 174.

[3] *Kritik der Urtheilskraft*

blood system, of the lungs, liver, stomach, and their mutual harmony, are certainly very surprising. Does not this harmony demand Another besides the organic subject as its cause? This question we may leave on one side, as if one grasps the notion of an organism, this develop ment of teleological adaptation is a necessary consequence of the vitality of the subject."

The Darwinian theory has largely restricted the material available for the teleological argument, by inverting the mode of conceiving the relation between an organ and its environment. Whereas of old the fitness between the two was regarded as the result of intentional adaptation of organ to environment, according to the new scientific point of view the fitness is the result of the slow, unconscious action of environment on organ, producing in the course of ages development from a crude condition to a very high state of perfection. While thus accounting for all cases of useful adaptation, the theory claims to have this advantage over the old teleological view of the world, that it can explain such phenomena as are presented in rudimentary and useless organs, which it is difficult to imagine being made by design.

Some scientific writers have sought to bring discredit on the teleological view of the world by pointing out defects in organs which, on that view, would have to be regarded as instances of blundering on the part of the Creator. The eye, formerly a favourite theme for the teleologist, has been carefully studied in this controversial interest. Generally the tendency of physical inquiry has been to enlarge the sphere of the unintentional in nature. Thus a well-known writer, himself a theist, and very com petent to speak on the topic, remarks: "It is not in accordance with the facts of experience that all parts of nature point to ideal significance and definite aims. Along with a thousand appearances which give this im pression go a thousand others which look like aimless by products of an accidental self-formed combination of atoms, which by no means ought to arise under a preconceived plan, and which have arisen and maintained themselves in being because they did not contradict the mechanical conditions of continued existence."[1]

The *ontological* argument infers the existence of God from the idea of Him necessarily entertained by the human mind. The idea we cannot help forming of God is that of a Being than which a higher cannot be conceived, absolutely perfect in all respects. Into this conception existence necessarily enters as an element, for a supposed highest, most perfect Being not conceived as existing would not be the highest conceivable. Therefore a most perfect Being exists. Such is the gist of the argument as first formulated by Anselm. It wears a subtle scholastic air, which puzzles the mind and makes it difficult to decide whether to regard it as a very profound and conclusive piece of reasoning, or as a sample of ratiocinative trifling. On the whole, one inclines to the view of Kant, who, in his criticism of this argument, while conceding that the *idea* of existence entered into the idea of the most perfect Being, argued that the idea no more involves the reality of existence than the notion of a hundred dollars in my mind proves that I have them in my purse.[2]

Through lengthened and continuous criticism of these famous arguments, it has come to pass that in their old forms they are no longer available, and that they must therefore either be abandoned or transformed. Some pursue the one course, some the other. It was not to be expected that so valuable a line of proof as that supplied in the second of the three would be lightly given up by theists, and accordingly efforts have been made recently to restate the "design argument" so as to fit it to the present condition of scientific knowledge and thought. Those who have laboured in this sphere have striven to show that accepting the modern doctrine of evolution and

[1] Lotze's *Mikrokosmus*, Bd. II. p. 29.
[2] *Kritik der reinen Vernunft*, p. 409.

the account which it gives of the order and method of
creation, there is still ample scope for an argument which
aims at proving that the world has been made, and its
upward development guided, by an almighty, wise, and
beneficent Creator.[1]   Others have sought a foundation for
their theistic convictions in entirely different directions.
Abandoning the region of teleology to the tender mercies
of sceptical scientists, they have justified belief in God
either by an appeal to the facts of the moral world, or by
an analysis of self-consciousness ; in the one case following
Kant, in the other Hegel.   Kant, failing to find any sure
trace of God in the region within which the theoretic
reason bears sway, turned to the domain of practical
reason, and found there as an actual existence the Being
who had hitherto been only a regulative idea.   Virtue and
happiness ought to correspond, but happiness depends
largely on external conditions over which we have no
control ; therefore we must postulate a moral Governor
who is able to bring the order of nature into harmony
with the moral world—such was the gist of the argument
which certified for him the reality of Deity.   To some it
has appeared not less weak than the arguments it super
seded, as, *e.g.*, to Strauss, who criticises it in these terms :
" The agreement of virtue and happiness from which the
argument starts is in one respect, in the inner man,
already present ; that the two should be harmonised in
outward conditions is our natural wish and rightful
endeavour ; but the ever incomplete realisation of the
wish is to be found not in the postulate of a *Deus ex
machinâ*, but in a correct view of the world and of

---

[1] Among those who deserve honourable mention here are Flint (*Theism*)
and Martineau (*A Study of Religion*, vol. i.). They have at least tried well,
whatever may be thought of their success.   With their contributions may
be associated that of Kennedy, who, in the Donellan Lectures for 1888–89,
strives to show that whatever may be thought of the validity of the design
argument in other spheres, it still holds in the region of the beautiful, which
it is contended cannot be accounted for on Darwinian principles.   *Vide*
Lecture iv.

fortune."[1]   Nevertheless for many the "moral argument" of the great critical philosopher in one form or another remains the sheet-anchor of faith.   A recent apologetic writer of the Neo-Kantian school thus indicates his preference for it as compared with the "design argument":

"The rationalising mode of viewing the world starts from the teleological order. Finding in the world interrelated ends and means, while in the things themselves is neither consciousness nor will, it infers an intelligent wise Originator and Guide of all things. It is the very soul of this point of view that it understands and knows how to interpret the means in single instances, whilst it becomes uncertain as soon as it attempts to complete itself through the recognition of a supreme all-dominating idea of an aim. The Christian's faith in Providence inverts the point of view. Its starting-point is not the world as exhibiting the aspect of design, but the certainty of divine love, which has chosen him from eternity, and therefore orders all so that it must promote his best interest. Not the teleological connection of things and events is the object of his contemplation, but the divine purpose to confer on him blessedness."[2]

For writers imbued with the spirit of the Hegelian philosophy, the chief source of the knowledge of God is the self-consciousness of man, or the nature of human thought. The line of proof may be said to be a modification of the

---

[1] *Der alte und der neue Glaube*, p. 119.

[2] Kaftan, *Die Wahrheit der Christlichen Religion*, p. 60. It is characteristic of Kaftan and the school of theology to which he belongs, that of Ritschl, to restrict the function of theology to showing how for the members of the Christian community the religious view of the world, as existing for the sake of the kingdom of God and the realisation of the good, is possible. Attempts either at proving from the general non-ethical features of the world the existence of God, or at deducing from the idea of God these features, such writers as Kaftan and Hermann (*Die Metaphysik in der Theologie*, 1876 ; *Der Verkehr der Christen mit seinem Gott*, 1890) regard as extraneous, injurious, and even incompetent. They would be agnostics but for Christ, whose presence as a fact in this world, through His sinlessness and His faith in a Power bent on realising the good, brings light where otherwise deepest darkness would brood. With the stress laid on Christ one can cordially sympathise, but surely if Christ's idea of God be true there should be something in the world to verify it !

ontological argument. It is an inference from thought to being; not merely from the thought of God as the most perfect being to His existence, but from the very nature of thought in general to the Great Eternal Thinker. God is very near us, on this view. We do not need to roam the world over in quest of proofs that the world was made by a Being of infinite skill; we have only to consider what is involved in being conscious of ourselves, or in a single act of thinking. For the consciousness of self involves the consciousness of a not-self. Self and not-self are thus, in every act of consciousness, at once opposed and embraced in a higher unity. Consciousness posits a self, a not-self, and a higher Being in whom the two opposites meet and are reconciled. " Thus all our conscious life rests on and implies a consciousness that is universal. We cannot think save on the presupposition of a thought or conscious ness which is the unity of thought and being, or on which all individual thought and existence rest."[1] Nor is it alone in our highest thoughts that the Universal Thinker is revealed. He is present in the humblest act of percep tion. What we have to recognise in all our perceptions of the external world is an animal organism, which has its history in time, gradually becoming "the vehicle of an eternally complete consciousness."[2] To this eternally com plete consciousness the system of relations which constitute the universe is ever present in its totality as an object of contemplation; through our human consciousness it attains to knowledge of the system piecemeal by a gradual process. It would serve no purpose to comment on these positions, in the way either of explanation or of criticism. To those within the school they seem clear and certain ; to those without they are apt to appear abstruse, unintelligible, and baseless.[3]

---

[1] Principal Caird, *An Introduction to the Philosophy of Religion*, pp. 131, 132.

[2] Green, *Prolegomena to Ethics*, p. 72.

[3] For a criticism of the views of the British Neo-Kantian school of philo sophy, *vide* Veitch's *Knowing and Being*, and Seth's *Hegelianism and Personality*.

When one considers the facts connected with the history
of theistic evidence: how few arguments command the
general assent even of theists, how much the line of
proof adopted depends on the advocate's philosophic view-
point, and how little respect the rival schools of philosophy
pay to all methods of establishing the common faith but
their own, he is tempted to think that that faith is without
sure foundation, and that the agnostic is right when he
asserts that knowledge of God is unattainable. But there
is another way of looking at the matter which deserves
serious attention. While differing as to what proofs are
valid and valuable, all theists are agreed as to the thing to
be proved: that God is, and to a certain extent what God
is. This harmony in belief ought to weigh more in our
judgment than the variation in evidence. It suggests the
thought that the belief in God is antecedent to evidence,
and that in our theistic reasonings we formulate proof of a
foregone conclusion innate and inevitable. How otherwise
can it be explained that men who have demolished what
have passed for the strongest arguments for the theistic
creed are not content to be done with it, but hold on to
the conviction that God is, on grounds which to all others
but themselves appear weak and whimsical? Thus a
recent writer, after searching in vain the whole universe of
matter and of mind for traces of Deity, finds rest at last
for his weary spirit in this train of thought: There is such
a thing as error, but error is inconceivable unless there be
such a thing as truth, and truth is inconceivable unless
there be a seat of truth, an infinite all-including Thought
or Mind, therefore such a Mind exists. That Mind is
God, the "infinite Seer," whose nature it is to think,
not to act. "No power it is to be resisted, no plan-
maker to be foiled by fallen angels, nothing finite,
nothing striving, seeking, losing, altering, growing weary;
the All-Enfolder it is, and we know its name. Not
Heart, nor Love, though these also are in it and of it;
Thought it is, and all things are for Thought, and in

it we live and move."[1]　How weak the proof here, but how strong the conviction! So it is, more or less, with us all. In our formal argumentation we feebly and blunderingly try to assign reasons for a belief that is rooted in our being. In perusing works by others devoted to the advocacy of theism, we are conscious of disappointment, and possibly even of doubt suggested rather than of faith established, only to recover serene and strong conviction when the book is forgotten.[2] It would seem as if the way of wisdom were to abstain from all attempts at proving the divine existence, and, assuming as a *datum that* God is, to restrict our inquiries to *what* He is. Without pronouncing dogmatically as to the incompetency of any other method of procedure, I shall here adopt this policy, and confine myself in the remainder of this chapter to a few hints in answer to the question, How far is the Christian idea of God "a hypothesis which all we know tends to verify"?

Christ taught that God is a Father and that man is His son, and that it is a leading purpose of God to establish between Himself and men a kingdom of filial relations and loving fellowship. This doctrine implies that there is a close affinity of nature between God and man, that, indeed, the most direct and certain way to the knowledge of God is through human nature. Now the view thus suggested of the man-like nature of God is in accordance with the teaching of the most recent science. Man, according to science not less than Scripture, stands at the head of creation as we know it. He is the crown and consummation of the evolutionary process, by the frank admission of one of the most brilliant expounders of the modern theory. "So far from degrading humanity," writes Mr. Fiske, "or putting it on a level with the animal world in general, the doctrine of evolution shows us distinctly for the first time

---

[1] Royce, *The Religious Aspect of Philosophy*, p. 435.

[2] Lipsius says that the various "proofs" for the being of God are no proofs, but only the various momenta of the elevation of the human spirit to God, and that their root is not *à priori* thought, but religious experience. —*Lehrbuch der Dogmatik*, p. 231.

how the creation and the perfecting of man is the goal towards which Nature's work has been tending from the first. We can now see clearly that our new knowledge enlarges tenfold the significance of human life, and makes it seem more than ever the chief object of divine care, the consummate fruition of that creative energy which is mani fested throughout the knowable universe."[1] It is a reason able inference that from the creature who occupies this distinguished place something may be learned concerning the nature of the Creator. The author just quoted, indeed, protests against this inference, and maintains, as we have seen, that God's nature cannot be known from one part of the creation more than from another. But this view is compatible only with such a conception of the universe as that of Spinoza—a mere monotonous wilderness of being in which all things are equally significant or insignificant, not to be distinguished as lower and higher. This is not the conception of the evolution theory, which teaches us to regard the universe as the result of a process which, beginning with a fiery cloud, passed through many suc cessive stages in an ever-ascending scale, from star-vapour to stars, from dead planets to life, from plants to animals, from apes to men. It is in keeping with this grand con- ception to see in the final stage of the process a key to the meaning of the whole, and in man a revelation of God as a Being possessing mind and guided by purpose.[2]

If the Creator be not only like man in nature, but had man in view from the first as the end of creation, we may expect to find traces of a purposeful guidance of the evolu-

[1] *Man's Destiny*, p. 116. The same doctrine is very strongly asserted by another American writer. Le Conte says : "Without spirit-immortality this beautiful cosmos, which has been developing into increasing beauty for so many millions of years, when its evolution has run its course and all is over, would be precisely as if it had never been—an idle dream, an idiot tale signifying nothing."—*Evolution and its Relation to Religious Thought*, p. 329. Le Conte is an enthusiastic advocate of the evolution theory of crea tion, but also a not less enthusiastic defender of Christian theism.

[2] *Vide The Miraculous Element in the Gospels*, chap. i., where the line of thought here indicated is more fully developed.

tionary process so as to insure that it should reach its end.
There is reason to believe that such traces are not wanting,
and recent theistic writers have done good service in
pointing them out, and in so doing have furnished the
restatement of the teleological argument rendered necessary
by the dislodgment of it from its old ground through the
influence of the Darwinian theory as to the origin of species.
The details cannot be gone into here. Suffice it to say
that the end has been reached: man is here, and it has
been reached through a steadily upward process, not as a
matter of course, but through manifold risks of miscarriage,
which have not been escaped by happy accident, but by crea
tive control. There is no known law of necessary advance
ment, no reason in the nature of the case why variation
should proceed in an upward direction. "Apart from the
internal constitution of an organism having been so planned,
and its external circumstances so arranged as to favour
the one rather than the other, its variations could not have
been more towards self-perfection than self-destruction." [1]

The Christian doctrine of God, as in nature like man, is
in accordance with the latest teaching of science regarding
the nature of _force_. According to that teaching, all physical
forces are convertible into each other, and are all but
diverse manifestations of one ultimate force. Thus the
question arises, What is the nature of that ultimate force?
The agnostic replies, It is inscrutable. But reason suggests,
What if the Power that is at work in the universe be like
that form of power with which we are most familiar, the
power exercised by the being who stands at the head of
creation, and reveals the mind of the Creator—Will-power?

Once more, if God, as Christ teaches, be like man, He
possesses not only Intellect, Purpose, and Will, but moral
character. Many have seen in the moral nature of man,
the conscience, a powerful witness to the _existence_ of God.

[1] Flint, _Theism_, p. 202. For a spirited attempt to base a theistic argu
ment on the evolutionary process antecedent to the introduction of life,
vide Chapman's _Preorganic Evolution and the Biblical Idea of God_, 1891.

Without calling in question the validity of the argument, my present purpose is to point to the human sense of right and wrong as showing not that God is, but what He is. Man's place in the universe, as assigned to him by science, makes it legitimate and reasonable to do so. And history confirms the inference to morality in God suggested by an inspection of man's moral nature. Men of all schools, pessimists excepted, are agreed that a moral order is revealed in the story of the human race. Carlyle and Arnold interpret its lesson in much the same way as the Hebrew prophets. Whether the Power that makes for righteousness be conscious and personal or otherwise may be a subject of dispute or doubt. The main point is that the Power exists—imperfectly manifested, it may be, a tendency rather than a completely realised fact, yet indubitably there. As revealed in human affairs, it possesses some noticeable characteristics. It is slow in action, especially on the punitive side, and it seems, not now and then, as if by accident, but with all the regularity of a law, to treat the best of men as if they were the worst, making the good suffer as the bad ought. Prophetically interpreted, and expressed in religious language, these facts mean : that God is patient, slow to anger, prone to pardon, giving evil men ample space to repent ; and that in the moral world the good are called to the heroic function of redeemers, propagators of righteousness, and as such have to suffer, the just by and for the unjust. In other words, the moral order of the world is not only a reign of retributive justice, but a reign of grace, under which love is the supreme law, with full scope for the display of its nature as a spirit of self-sacrifice, and the stream of tendency is steadily towards the grand consummation, the bringing in of the kingdom of God.

In the foregoing observations, man, his nature and position in the universe, is made the basis of the theistic argument. And this is as it ought to be. Science aims at explaining man from the world, but religion explains the world, in its first Cause and last End, from man.

The two attitudes are not incompatible, but their tend
encies are as diverse as their points of view. The one
tends to minimise, the other to magnify, the peculiarity of
man. The patrons of the two methods are apt to be
unjust to each other, either undervaluing the aim of the
other, and remaining comparatively unimpressed by his
lines of proof. In the case of the scientific man this
defect may appear specially excusable. For the demon
strations offered by the representatives of the religious
view of the world are not of that strict order to which the
scientist is accustomed. The results arrived at are not
logically inevitable conclusions from absolutely certain
premises. They are value-judgments resting on moral
grounds, and involving an exercise of freedom, or, to speak
more correctly, a bias due to the esteem in which we hold
man as a moral personality, and to the habit of regarding
his moral nature and destiny as the key to the riddle of
the universe. A man can be an agnostic if he pleases.
Faith in God is an affair of personal conviction. No
offence is meant by this statement. It is not intended to
insinuate that unbelief is the effect of an unsatisfactory
moral condition. It may be frankly acknowledged that
many worthy men are agnostics, as many worthless men
are theists. Nevertheless it remains true that it is with
the heart man believeth. God is the postulate of a soul
that finds the world without God utterly dark and unintelligible. And those who believe in God most firmly
best know what it is to doubt. Faith is the result of a
successful struggle against all that tends to produce reli
gious atrophy, including too exclusive devotion to scientific
habits of thought, which may turn the mind into "a
machine for grinding out general laws out of large collec
tions of facts," and prove fatal not only to religious faith,
but even to all taste for poetry, music, and pictures.[1]

[1] For an instructive example of this, *vide The Life and Letters of Charles
Darwin*, i. 313. For remarks on the candid confession of Mr. Darwin,
vide Aubrey L. Moore's *Sc* and *the Faith*, pp. 216-218.

The agnostic, however, need not be altogether without God. There remains for him the absolute unknown Reality, deanthropomorphised and devoid of all qualities, capable of awakening an awe like that produced by a sandy desert. For more thoroughgoing agnostics who profess nescience as regards even the existence of the ultimate Reality, and for whom the universe is reduced to mere phenomenalism, there is available as an object of worship or service Comte's Supreme Being—Humanity, the "subjective synthesis" which meets the demands of the heart, in absence of the objective synthesis, wherein the universe finds its centre of unity, denied by the intellect.[1]

[1] For an acute criticism of the religion of humanity, *vide* Martineau's *Types of Ethical Theory*, i. 472. *Vide* also Professor Edward Caird's *Social Philosophy and Religion of Comte*, where the religion of humanity is criticised from the view-point of the Hegelian philosophy, and it is argued "that the true synthesis of philosophy must be objective as well as subjective, and that there can be no religion of humanity which is not also a religion of God" (Preface, p. xvii).

BOOK II.

THE HISTORICAL PREPARATION FOR CHRISTIANITY.

CHAPTER I.

THE SOURCES.

LITERATURE.—Ewald, *Die Geschichte des Volkes Israel*, Band I.; Graf, *Die Geschichtlichen Bucher des Alten Testa ments;* Reuss, *La Bible* (new translation, with Introductions and Commentaries); Kuenen, *Origin and Composition of the Hexateuch* (translated from the Dutch); Wellhausen, *The History of Israel* (including *Prolegomena to the History of Israel* and article "Israel" from the *Encyc. Brit.*); Bissell (of Hartford Theol. Sem.), *The Pentateuch: its Origin and Structure* (Conservative); Driver, *Introduction to the Litera ture of the Old Testament.*

On a comprehensive view, the whole previous history of the world and of its religion might be said to be a divinely ordered preparation for the coming of Christ. But in the present work our attention must be concentrated mainly on the people from whom as concerning the flesh Christ came. This limitation, while bringing the subject within man ageable dimensions, involves no serious sacrifice of truth. For Christ was emphatically a Jew in mind as well as in body. So far as His religious character is capable of being explained by historic antecedents, it is sufficiently accounted for by the religion of Israel, without reference to any supposed influence emanating from other quarters, as,

104

e.g., the philosophy of Greece.[1] What we have therefore to do is to make ourselves acquainted with the religious history of that remarkable race to which belonged "the adoption, and the glory, and the covenants, and the giving of the law, and the service of God, and the promises."

The sources of this knowledge are the *Hebrew Scriptures.* The characteristics of these writings as the literature of Revelation will come up for consideration at a later stage; meantime we regard them simply as a channel of informa tion concerning the people who physically and spiritually were the ancestors of Jesus. In using them for this pur pose, the apologists of the present day are in a very dif ferent position from that of those who lived before modern Biblical Criticism took its rise. Then to exhibit the his torical preparation for Christianity was a comparatively simple task. Accepting the Jewish tradition respecting dates and authorship of books, the apologist opened the Old Testament and read it as the plain uncultured man reads it still. Thence he drew out with unsuspecting confidence the history of Redemption in its various stages; beginning with the quaint picturesque simplicity of the patriarchal age, the era of the *Promise;* passing on to the *Lawgiving* under Moses, who was conceived to be the human author of all the laws recorded in the Pentateuch; advancing through the chequered narrative of judges and kings—mostly transgressors of the God-given law, and by their conduct helping to justify Paul's view of the law as given only for the knowledge of sin—to the splendid period of the *Prophets*, who grasped the full significance of the promise and purpose of God concerning Israel, and taught the people to fear Jehovah, to do His will, and to trust in His mercy, and warned them of coming judgment upon persistent disobedience. Thereon followed in due course

---

[1] It is well known that Dr. Ferdinand Baur represented Christ as indebted indirectly for His conception of man as a moral subject to the Socratic philosophy. *Vide* his *Geschichte der Christlichen Kirche*, i. 10-16.

the story of the exile, of the restoration, of the religious revival under Ezra, and of the long night of legalism which ensued when the sun of prophecy set, till at length the dawn came with the advent of Jesus, in whom promise, law, and prophecy all found their fulfilment.

It is an altogether imposing picture of Divine Provi dence marching on with a redemptive purpose from the call of Abraham in the grey dawn of time to the coming of Him through whom the whole earth was to be blessed throughout an unending era of grace. But criticism has rudely assailed the foundations of this historical construc tion. It tells us that the narratives concerning the patriarchs cannot be implicitly accepted as history, that Genesis, the book of origins, was not written by Moses, but is of much later date, and of composite nature, a story woven out of separate documents, with diverse literary characteristics, as, *e.g.*, distinct names for God, one preferring the title *Jehovah*, another *Elohim*.[1] The order in which these two documents were produced is as yet an unsolved problem, some critics regarding the Elohistic document as prior and the original base of the present composite narrative, others holding it to be long pos terior, and even as late as the period of the Babylonian exile. The Jehovist document most critics regard as belonging to the great prophetic period, and as imbued with the prophetic spirit. To it we owe the charming

---

[1] This of course is a very inadequate account of critical views as to the composition of Genesis. When the matter belonging to the Elohistic docu ment has been removed, it is found on close examination that the remainder is not homogeneous in structure. It resolves into two parts, in one of which the name Elohim is used (without the other literary characteristics of the Elohistic document), and in the other Jehovah. These are regarded as remnants of two independent narratives by authors belonging respectively to the northern and southern kingdoms. The two together, as used in Genesis and elsewhere, are distinguished as JE from the Elohist document, whose symbol is P (*Priests' Code*, with special reference to the ceremonial sections in Exodus, Leviticus, and Numbers). The fact of there being two Elohists is puzzling to novices. *Vide* Driver's *Introduction to the Literature of the Old Testament*, pp. 9–12.

stories of the patriarchs, which we are to take not as exact history, but as the embodiment of prophetic ideas.

Modern criticism further tells us that the collections of laws contained in the books of the Pentateuch which follow Genesis are for the most part post-Mosaic. The only exception to this statement with regard to which there is anything like unanimity is the Decalogue, and even to it a Mosaic origin is denied by some leading critical authorities. At least three distinct strata of legis-lation, of different dates, but all subsequent to the time of Moses, as written compilations, are discovered in these four books: the short code in Ex. xx. 22–xxiii. 19, designated in Ex. xxiv. 7 *the Book of the Covenant;* the more extended body of laws contained in Deuteronomy, espe cially in chapters xii.-xxvi., distinguished as *the Deutero-nomic Code;* and the large collection of laws relating to religious ritual, uncleanness, and kindred topics, scattered throughout the middle books of the Pentateuch — Exodus, Leviticus, Numbers — appropriately called *the Priestly Code.* Even within this code distinct strata are recog nised, the group of laws in Lev. xviii.-xxvi. being specially recognised as outstanding, and called with refer ence to its subject-matter *the Law of Holiness.* It is supposed to have been originally a separate work, and to have been incorporated in the priestly code by the compiler.

As to the order in which these three codes came into existence critics are by no means agreed. There is, indeed, a general agreement as to *the Book of the Covenant* being the earliest, but there is serious difference of opinion as to the relative position of the other two. During the earlier period of the critical movement, the opinion prevailed that the priestly code was prior to the Deuteronomic, finding its place in the Elohistic document, which was supposed to be the *Grundschrift,* or basis of the present composite work called the Pentateuch, or including Joshua the

Hexateuch.[1] But more recently the strong drift of criti
cism has been towards the view that the priestly code was
the latest product of legal literary industry, and that it
did not take shape till after the Babylonish exile.   The
Deuteronomic code is believed to be definitely fixed down
to a certain date by the statement in 2 Kings xxii. 10
concerning a book which Hilkiah the high priest found in
the house of the Lord, and gave to Shaphan the scribe, and
which Shaphan read to King Josiah.   This book, it is held,
was none other than the Deuteronomic code, not merely
found but composed then, somewhere about the middle of
the seventh century before Christ.

It is not necessary for our present purpose to under
take the elaborate task of setting forth in detail the grounds
on which these critical views rest.   Suffice it to say that
two questions figure prominently in the argument: those,
viz., relating to the restriction of worship to one central
sanctuary, and to the distinction between the priests and
the Levites.   By reference to the former point, the order
of the three codes is determined to be, first, the Book of
the Covenant; second, the Deuteronomic code; third, the
priestly.   The argument is: in the Book of the Covenant
a plurality of sanctuaries is recognised as legitimate;[2] in
the Deuteronomic code one central sanctuary, the sole
legitimate place of worship, is insisted on with an emphasis
and iteration which imply recent innovation on old custom;
in the priestly code one sanctuary is treated as a matter of
course, gainsaid by no one, and held to be as ancient as the
time of Moses.   By reference to the distinction between
priests and Levites, it is held by Wellhausen and others
to be easy to determine the relative age of the Deuteronomic and priestly codes.   In the former no such distinction exists, the phrase constantly used being "the priests the

---

[1] The literary diversities noticeable in the book of Genesis, referred to on
p. 166, run through the Pentateuch and Joshua, so that P and JE are
sources not only for Genesis, but for the whole Hexateuch.
[1] *Vide* Ex. xx. 24.

Levites"; in the latter the distinction is carefully made, a
fact naturally pointing to later legislative changes. That the
change was post-exilic is argued from a significant passage
in Ezekiel, in which priests and Levites are still spoken of
as one, but an intimation is given of future differentiation
based on the misconduct of a certain class of Levitical
priests, those, viz., who had served at heathen sanctuaries.
For their sin they are to be degraded into mere minis
terial drudges at the sanctuary, having charge at the gates
and slaying the sacrifices, but not permitted to approach
Jehovah in the discharge of proper priestly functions. On
the other hand, " the priests the Levites, the sons of Zadok,
that kept the charge of my sanctuary when the children of
Israel went astray from me," are to be confirmed in their
priestly office in reward of their fidelity. Thus henceforth
there shall no longer be priests who are at the same time
Levites, or Levites who are at the same time priests, but
two orders of religious officials, a higher order of priests
and a lower order of Levites.[1]

From the foregoing brief outline it will be seen that
the effect of modern criticism on the mode of viewing the
religious history of Israel is serious. It amounts to an
inversion of the order subsisting between law and prophecy.
Instead of saying, the law and the prophets, we must say,
the prophets and the law. The law, in the comprehensive
sense, was not given by Moses; it came not till the great
prophets Micah, Hosea, Amos, Isaiah had delivered their
message. Their scathing criticisms of the religious services
of a people ungodly in life are therefore not to be regarded
as a protest against the exaltation of ritual, legitimate,
ancient, and even divinely given, above the supreme claims
of morality—a declaration that to obey is better than sacri
fice, however important sacrifice in its own place may be—
but as indirect yet sure evidence that a priestly code, pur
porting to be of Mosaic origin, was not then in existence.
That code, we are given to understand, could not have pro-

[1] *Vide* Ezek. xliv. 9-16.

ceeded from Moses, who, as is indicated in Deuteronomy and in Hosea,[1] was a prophet in vocation and spirit, and must therefore, like all the prophets, have attached more value to the ethical than to the ritual. It belongs rather to the post-prophetic period, to the time when the spirit which animated the great prophets began to lose its influence, and the legal spirit sought to usurp its place, and men under its guidance strove to please God by anxious compli ance with innumerable technical rules; in a word, to the time of the return from exile and of the scribe Ezra. And if we are to take a critically well-founded view of the religious development of Israel, we must recognise three great periods or stages in the onward march : *Mosaism*, having for its salient feature the *Decalogue ; Prophetism*, true to Mosaism, and carrying it on to higher issues ; *Judaism*, not without valuable characteristics, but inaugurating an era in which the prophetic motto, "to obey is better than sacrifice," might be said to have been finally transformed into "sacrifice the sum of obedience."

In comparison with the *Law* and the *Prophets*, the *Hagiographa* are of subordinate importance as sources for a study of the religion of Israel. Yet from some of the books contained in this division of the Hebrew Scriptures, and very specially from the *Psalter*, much can be learned concerning the spiritual life of the Jewish people. According to the traditional view, very many of the Psalms are of Davidic authorship, and ex hibit a type of religious thought and feeling prevailing among devout Israelites as far back as the eleventh century B.C. The tendency of recent criticism, however, has been greatly to reduce the number of Psalms belonging to so early a time, and to assign to the collection as a whole a post-exilic origin. According to this view, the Psalter is to be regarded as the song-book of the second temple, and its value for the history of Israel's religion consists in the bright light which it throws on the inner life of the spirit during the legal period. It is a pendant to the history of Judaism.

[1] Deut. xviii. 15 ; Hosea xii. 13.

A very important question now arises for the apologist. What is to be his attitude towards these critical views as to the authorship and dates of the component parts of Old Testament literature ? To this question it may be answered, first, that the apologist is not called upon to accept the results of modern criticism, or to constitute himself an advocate of its claims to scientific certainty. He is en titled to hold himself aloof from critical dogmatism, and to keep his personal opinions in a state of suspense. He may reasonably excuse himself from coming to a final decision on the questions raised on various grounds. He may without shame plead the lack of an expert's knowledge. He may further plead that the discussion and solution of critical problems do not fall within the scope of general apologetic, but belong to a distinct theological discipline, that of Biblical Introduction. Once more, he may plead the unsettled state of critical opinion. It will be time enough for the apologist to dogmatise when criticism has arrived at the stage of finality. It is far enough from having reached that stage as yet. Not to mention endless diversity of view on special points, there are broad contrasts between different schools even with reference to the leading critical problems. One set of critics call in question the Mosaic origin even of the Decalogue,[1] another bring under the cate gory of Mosaism, not only the Ten Words, but the principles common to the various legal codes.[2] Not only is there conflict between critics of different schools regarding the relative priority of the Deuteronomic and priestly codes, but instances are not unknown of the same critic changing his mind on the question. Thus Vatke, who in 1835 in his great work on the *Religion of the Old Testament* maintained the post-exilic origin of the priestly code, in his posthumous work on *Introduction*, published in 1886, repre-

---

[1] So Wellhausen, who thinks that it perhaps belongs to the time of Manasseh's reign. *Vide* his *Prolegomena*, p. 486. Kuenen, on the other hand, regards Moses as the author of the *Ten Words*. *Vide The Religion of Israel*, p. 274.

[2] So Riehm, in his *Altestamentliche Theologie*, p. 57.

sents it as prior to the Deuteronomic code, viewing it as
a programme of reform, an ideal legislation not actually
realised till after the exile.[1] Nor are the contradictions of
criticism confined to the legal portions of the Old Testa
ment. Even with reference to the prophets wide con
trariety of view obtains. The majority of critics indeed
regard it as beyond doubt that not a few of the prophetic
writings can be definitely fixed down to dates antecedent to
the exile. But there have not been wanting men with suffi
cient hardihood to maintain that this is a mistake, and that
the whole Hebrew Scriptures, including the prophets, are
post-exilic, and show us merely what the Jews of that late
period believed concerning their past history.[2]

For these reasons and in these circumstances the attitude
of the apologist must necessarily be that of one who refuses
to be deeply committed on critical questions. But on the
other hand, he cannot go on his way as if nothing had
happened, or as if he had never heard of modern higher
criticism. He must adjust himself to the new situation.
He must take into account opinions confidently advanced
by others for which he declines to be personally respon
sible, to the extent at least of considering how far they
are compatible or the reverse with the faith he is concerned
to defend. In this connection it is incumbent on him to
be on his guard against a jealous temper. Avoiding care -
fully dogmatism in favour of criticism, he must with at
least equal care avoid dogmatism against it, in the form of
hasty conclusions that if the critics are right it is all over
with revelation, or with the claim of the Scriptures to be in

---

[1] *Einleitung*, p. 402.

[2] So Maurice Vernes in *Les resultats de L'Exegese Biblique*, 1890. With
him agree Ernest Havet and d'Eichtal. *Vide* Havet's *La Modernité des
Prophetes*. In a review of this work, reprinted in *Les Prophetes d'Israel*,
pp. 121-151, Darmesteter has given a convincing refutation of Havet's
theory that the prophetic literature originated at the end of the second
century B.C., in connection with the struggle of the Jews against the Greek
kings of Syria. On this theory Assyria really means the Syria of the Seleu-
cidæ, and Tiglath Pileser, Sargon, and Sennacherib represent Antiochus
Epiphanes, Demetrius Nicator, etc.

any sense a divine book, or of Israel to be an elect people, and that therefore the believer must renounce the critics and all their works. In the interest of faith it is absolutely necessary to make it as independent as possible of all dogmatism in reference to matters coming within the sphere of scientific inquiry. To this sphere the questions dealt with by criticism certainly belong. If the date of a book, say of the second half of Isaiah, or of Daniel, can be ascertained by careful observation of its own characteristics, why should it not be? How inept to interdict such an inquiry in the supposed interest of faith, how foolish to proclaim on the housetop that if the inquiry lead to a certain result the faith must be destroyed!

The proper apologetic attitude towards criticism is essentially the same as that towards the evolutionary theory of the origin of the universe. Modern criticism yields what may be called an evolutionary theory of the origin of Old Testament literature and religion; and the two evolutions should be faced with the same spirit of fearless trust. The business of the apologist is, in both cases alike, to recognise the legitimacy of the inquiry, while not dogmatising as to the truth of its results, to acquire such an acquaintance with the main lines of thought as shall enable him to grasp their drift, and to show if he can that the old faith can live with the new science. or hypo thesis. With reference to the evolution in the sphere of nature, the task has been achieved to the satisfaction of a large section of the believing world. With reference to the evolution in the sphere of religion, apologetic endeavours have hitherto been less abundant and less successful in commanding general assent.

Proceeding in the spirit just explained, we must allow our method to be controlled by criticism, so far as to make our starting-point what critics of greatest weight and authority regard as certain. On this principle we must begin our study of the religion of Israel with the prophets. In their writings we escape from the mists of critical doubt

into the daylight of acknowledged history. The oracles of
Hosea, Amos, Isaiah, Jeremiah, etc., are for the Old Testament what the four Epistles of Paul to the Galatian,
Corinthian, and Roman Churches are. for the New Testament,—a firm foundation on which the student of Israel's
religious history may safely plant his foot. In both cases
the authenticity of the relative writings has been called in
question by a few extremists, but in the judgment of the
vast majority of critics we may confidently gather from the
prophetic writings the religious view of the universe cherished
by the best minds in Israel from the eighth to the sixth
century B.C., as we may gather from the four above-named
Epistles of Paul the conception of Christianity entertained
by the man who was second only to the great Master.

Our plan, then, is as follows :—

First, we shall endeavour to form a preliminary general
idea of the religion of the prophets, noting how they
thought concerning God, man, the world, and kindred
topics. Next, we shall try to learn from their writings
what idea the prophets cherished concerning the nation to
which they belonged. Happily there are scattered hints
available for this purpose, not so copious as one might
wish, yet sufficient ; only occasional, yet on that account
all the more reliable. From these we gather that the
people of Israel had a remarkable history reaching far back
into the ancient time ; that their fathers had sojourned in
Egypt, and had been brought out of that land by a remark
able man and a remarkable Providence, which seemed to
point them out as an elect people with a peculiar destiny.
The prophetic view of Israel's vocation and history will
form the subject of a chapter, which will naturally be
followed by one on the hero of the Exodus, through whom
a horde of slaves was organised into a nation—that is to
say, on *Moses* and *Mosaism*. From that topic we shall
revert to *Prophetism*, now to be regarded as a stage in the
onward progress of revelation ; in which connection we shall
have to consider some of the more special characteristics

of Hebrew prophecy, and, above all, these two—its stern
assertion of the moral order of the world, and its bright
inspiring proclamation of the Messianic hope. Thence we
shall proceed to the study of *Judaism,* or the religion of
Israel in the period subsequent to the exile, when we shall
have to consider the connection of this phase of Israel's
religion with the earlier stages, what elements of good
were in it, and how far it contained the seeds of that
degenerate type of piety with which the Gospels make us
familiar under the title of "the righteousness of the scribes
and Pharisees." With that counterfeit righteousness
Judaism, as it appeared within the period covered by
the Hebrew canonical literature, cannot certainly be
identified. With whatever defects, it was, on the whole,
a boon to Israel, and the chief agents connected with it
were men of pure intention, acting under divine guidance
and inspiration. To understand Pharisaism, that dark
religious background which throws into such bright relief
the fair image of Jesus, we must pass from the twilight of
Judaism into the *night of legalism,* which will form the
subject of a separate chapter. Having thus considered in
succession the various stages of Israel's history from Moses
to the Christian era, we shall, in two concluding chapters,
have to consider the *Hebrew Scriptures* as a literature of
revelation, treating of their origin and value, and also of
their defects arising out of their being the literature of the
preparatory stage of revelation.

One other remark is needful to complete the explanation
of the method of procedure. The conception of Israel as
an *elect* people, having a special religious vocation and
enjoying peculiar privileges, naturally leads to comparison
of her religious ideas and practices with those of other
peoples. Such comparisons accordingly will be made, as
opportunity offers, with the aim of establishing the reality
of Israel's election and the superior value of her religion.
Happily, as will appear, this aim can be attained without
unjust or ungenerous disparagement of ethnic religion.

CHAPTER II.

THE RELIGION OF THE PROPHETS.

LITERATURE.—Vatke, *Die Religion des Alten Testaments,* 1835; Duhm, *Die Theologie der Propheten;* Kuenen, *The Prophets and Prophecy in Israel* (translated from the Dutch); Professor Robertson Smith, *The Prophets of Israel;* Green (W. H., of Princeton Theol. Sem.), *Moses and the Prophets* (a review of Robertson Smith's *Old Testament in the Jewish Church* and *The Prophets of Israel,* and of Kuenen's *Prophets and Prophecy in Israel*); Schultz, *Altestamentliche Theologie;* Riehm, *Altestamentliche Theologie;* Duff, *Old Testament Theology,* or *The History of Hebrew Religion from the Year 800 B.C.,* 1891; Professor Robertson, *The Early Religion of Israel* (Baird Lectures for 1889).

The following sketch is based upon the utterances of the series of prophets ranging from Amos to Jeremiah, and covering a period of about two centuries.

In the writings of these prophets Jehovah is, with ever growing clearness and emphasis, represented as the one supreme true God. The great religious teachers of Israel in the eighth and seventh centuries were, speaking broadly, *monotheists.* By this statement is not meant that these prophets taught in modern fashion an abstract or meta physical doctrine of monotheism. This was not the way of the Hebrew prophets, or of the race to which they belonged, at any time. Their monotheism was practical and religious, not theoretical and philosophical. They affirmed, not that their God Jehovah was the only possible deity, but that He was the Highest, the Mightiest, and the Best, and that whatever other gods existed were unworthy of regard. Their attitude towards the gods of the surround ing peoples was not one of philosophic scepticism, but rather of religious contempt. This contempt, however, is expressed in terms so incisive that it amounts to dogmatic denial. The heathen deities are called "lies,"[1] "vanities,"[2] "the work of men's hands."[3] This dialect of scorn is common to all the prophets, and grows in intensity in each succeeding prophet. It reaches its culmination in Jeremiah, in whose prophecies religious monotheism may be said to develop into theoretical monotheism, and con tempt to issue in downright denial. He calls heathen gods "no gods,"[4] charges them with utter impotence to do either good or evil,[5] and ridicules the idea of trusting in them.[6] On the other hand, he calls Jehovah the King of nations, and declares Him to be the true God, the living God, and the everlasting King.[7]

This prophetic doctrine of God may be regarded as the implicit or instinctive faith of the best in Israel from the days of Moses downwards. But there can be no doubt that, from the eighth century onwards, it was proclaimed by the prophets with an emphasis which made it virtually a new faith. A prophet is never a repeater of common places; when we find him affirming any truth with intensity and iteration, we may be sure it is a new truth, at least in respect of the amount of conviction with which it is uttered, and the connections of thought in which it is introduced. The historical situation in which the prophets of the eighth and seventh centuries found themselves explains the strength with which they asserted the supremacy of Jehovah. At that period the fate of Israel began to be involved in the movements of the great Eastern monarchies. First the Assyrian empire, then the Chaldean, menaced the inde pendence and even the existence of the petty kingdom lying between the Jordan and the Mediterranean. When these great powers of the East rose above the horizon, monotheism became a necessity for the chosen people. It

---

[1] Amos ii. 4.

[2] Isa. ii. 18, 20 ; x. 10 ; xix. 3. In Hebrew, אֱלִילִם, translated in Authorised Version "idols."

[3] Hos. xiv. 3 ; Micah v. 13.   [4] Jer. v. 7.

[5] Jer. x. 5.   [6] Jer. x 2–5.   [7] Jer. x. 7, 10.

was the only way of escape from submission to the vic
torious gods of the conqueror. Thus the political calamities
of Israel became an important factor in her religious educa
tion. She learned therefrom to rise above the idea of a
merely national God, whose relative might, as compared
with that of other national deities, was decided by the
issue of battle, to the idea of a God over all, exercising a
providence over all the nations, and using them alternately
as the instruments of His righteous government.

The prophets learnt first, and promptly, the momentous
lesson. Amos, the earliest of the prophets whose writings
have been preserved, very distinctly declares Jehovah to
be the God of all the nations, when he represents Him as
claiming to have brought the Philistines from Caphtor, and
the Syrians from Kir, even as He had brought up Israel
out of the land of Egypt.[1] Micah, in the same spirit, calls
Jehovah "the Lord of the whole earth."[2] Jeremiah, as
we have seen, addresses Jehovah as the " King of nations,"
and claims for Him, as such, universal reverence. " Who
would not fear Thee, O King of the nations? for to Thee
doth it appertain. . . . Jehovah is the true God, He is
the living God, and an everlasting king : at His wrath the
earth shall tremble, and the nations shall not be able to
abide His indignation."[3]

Along with this doctrine of Jehovah's supremacy over
the nations naturally goes the conception of Him as
creating and sustaining the world. Accordingly we find
these functions very expressly ascribed to the God of Israel
in the prophetic writings. Thus Amos describes Jehovah
as Him " that formeth the mountains, and createth the wind,
and declareth unto man what is his thought, that maketh
the morning darkness, and treadeth upon the high places
of the earth ; "[4] and, again, as one " that maketh the seven
stars and Orion, and turneth the shadow of death into the
morning, and maketh the day dark with night : that calleth
for the waters of the sea, and poureth them out upon the

[1] Amos ix. 7.   [2] Micah iv. 13.   [3] Jer. x. 10.   [4] Amos iv. 13.

face of the earth."[1] In these animated passages God appears as the Maker of all things in heaven and on earth, and as the sustainer of the course of nature ; the ultimate cause of all that happens, of the succession of day and night, of the ebbing and flowing of the tides, of the tempest and the following calm. As was to be expected, the doctrine of God's creative power and universal providence appears full-blown in the pages of Jeremiah. " He hath made the earth by His power, He hath established the world by His wisdom, and hath stretched out the heavens by His discretion. When He uttereth His voice, there is a multitude of waters in the heavens, and He causeth the vapours to ascend from the ends of the earth ; He maketh lightnings with rain, and bringeth forth the wind out of His treasures."[2] These prophetic representations, it will be observed, are in full accord with the Jehovistic records of the beginnings of things, wherein the heavens and the earth are spoken of as owing their origin to Jehovah Elohim.[3]

The Hebrew prophets, however, it must not be forgotten, were not alone in ascribing to their God the attribute of creator. Other peoples, such as the Babylonians and Phœnicians, bestowed on their national divinities the same title. From this it might plausibly be inferred that the prophetic doctrine of creation is quite compatible with a purely national conception of the creator. If every nation thought of its god as a creator, why should we attach any importance to the fact that the prophets claimed this distinction for the God of Israel ? The answer to this is, that the prophets did not use the title creator as a mere

---

[1] Amos v. 8. These two texts are regarded by Wellhausen and Stade as later interpolations, on the ground that they disturb the connection. Professor Robertson remarks : " Any one with the least sympathy with the writers will recognise in them (the passages suspected) the outpouring of hearts that were full of the noblest conceptions of the God whom they celebrate, and will perceive that they come in most fitly to emphasise the context."—*The Early Religion of Israel*, p. 320.

[2] Jer. x. 12, 13.　　　　　　　　　　[3] Gen. ii. 4.

expletive, by way of lip-homage, in accordance with Semitic fashion. They believed that only one God could create, as there was only one world to create; and they argued, not from divinity to creative power, but from creative power to true divinity. They made power to create the test of divinity. Thus Jeremiah asks: "Are there any among the vanities of the heathen that can cause rain? or can the heavens give showers? Art not Thou He, O Jehovah our God? therefore we will wait upon Thee; for Thou hast made all these things." [1]

That the Jehovah of Hebrew prophecy is not merely the national God of Israel, but the one true God over all, appears very conspicuously from the fact that He is con stantly represented as exercising a *universal* and *impartial justice*. Very instructive in this connection are the two opening chapters of Amos, in which Jehovah is exhibited as threatening with condign punishment for their sins, through the instrumentality of the Assyrian invader not named but ominously referred to as "it," the various nations in and around Palestine lying on the line of the conqueror's march. Three things in this judgment pro gramme are noteworthy, all suggesting the same inference: Jehovah, not the national God of Israel, partial to His people, but the just Ruler over all. The offences to be punished are moral; they are not in all cases offences against Israel; and Israel herself is not to be exempted from the invading scourge. Damascus, Gaza, Tyre, Edom, Ammon, and Moab are to be subjected to the judicial fire, not because they are heathen and do not worship Israel's God, but because they have been guilty of barbarities which outrage the laws of universal morality. Damascus has threshed Gilead with threshing instruments of iron, and Ammon has done to the devoted city something worse; Gaza and Tyre have been the seats of an inhuman traffic in slaves; Edom has pursued his brother in a too relentless blood-feud, and "kept his wrath for ever." In these cases

[1] Jer. xiv. 22.

Israel was the sufferer, and it is mentioned as an aggrava
tion of the offence in the case of Tyre, that in making
slaves of Israelites she had been unmindful of the old
alliance between herself and Israel. But as if to show
that it is not because they affect Israel, but because they
are grave moral offences, that these crimes of nations are
singled out for punishment, one other offence, that of Moab,
is mentioned, in which Jehovah's people is not concerned.
The offence of Moab is that she has burned the bones of
the king of Edom into lime—a wanton outrage on the
common feeling of respect for the dead.

Still, five out of six of the sins specified are offences
against Israel, and the fact may seem to justify a suspicion
of partiality. But the suspicion vanishes when it is
observed that Israel herself comes in for a share of the
impending chastisement. Far from being exempted, she is
to be in a special degree the subject of Jehovah's judicial
severity, just because she is His peculiar people. To the
race which He has brought up out of the land of Egypt
Jehovah by the mouth of His prophet says : "You only
have I known of all the families of the earth : therefore I
will visit upon you all your iniquities." [1] This is not the
kind of utterance we expect from a merely national God,
whom it would rather suit to say : You only have I known,
therefore I will defend you, right or wrong, against all
comers, and with special zeal against this boastful Assyrian
who approaches my land. This is the language of One
who has to do with all the nations of the earth, while
standing in special relations to a particular people, and who
has a fixed moral character which no special relations can
be allowed to compromise in the way either of injustice to
the outside nations or of favouritism to the chosen people.
Accordingly the transgressions of that people are not slurred
over, but enumerated with a fulness of detail that in more
than any other instance justifies the formula, "for three
transgressions and for four." "Because they sold the

[1] Amos iii. 2.

righteous for silver, and the needy for a pair of shoes ; that
pant after the dust of the earth on the head of the poor,
and turn aside the way of the meek : and a man and his
father will go in unto the same maid, to profane my holy
name : and they lay themselves down beside every altar
upon clothes taken in pledge, and in the house of their
god they drink the wine of such as have been fined."
Such is the black damning list of Israel's sins, wherein two
stand out above all others—shameless covetousness and
shameless sensuality.   Such iniquities the God in whom
the herdman of Tekoa believes cannot endure.   He did
not choose Israel in order to become the patron of inhumanity and vileness ; perish the chosen race rather than
that such enormities should go unpunished.   This is the
creed not only of monotheism, but of *ethical* monotheism.
It is a high, pure faith in a moral order of the world that
without respect of persons deals with men and nations
according to their works.

In view of such an august moral order it may seem
difficult to vindicate the idea of *election,* or special relations,
in any sense or to any extent.   This is a question we shall
have to consider hereafter.   Meantime we remark that the
very idea of election, or of a special relation sustained by
God to a particular people, constituted by an act of choice,
is incompatible with the notion of Jehovah being merely
the national God of Israel.   A national god is not the god
of his people by choice, but by natural affinity and necessity.
Bel could no more help being the god of Babylon, than a
Babylonian could help being born in a country where Bel
was worshipped as the national deity.   On the other hand,
a God who becomes related to a particular people by choice
or covenant is a God who, before the choice, stood in the
same relations to all, and might have made no choice or a
different one.   He is further a God who, after making a
choice, does not feel bound by it to partiality in favour of
the elected people, or to permanence in His relations

---

[1] Amos ii. 6–8.

thereto. He chooses from a purpose in harmony with His absolute character, and He will be guided by that purpose in all His relations to the chosen. Thus the electing God of Hebrew prophecy is in all respects the very antithesis of the national gods of heathen Semitic peoples.

The title, *the Holy One of Israel*, frequently applied to Jehovah by the prophets, especially by Isaiah, seems to savour of religious nationalism. When, however, the import of the title is carefully considered, it is seen to be in entire accord with the monotheistic conception of deity ascribed to the prophets on the grounds already mentioned. No stress, indeed, is to be laid on the mere epithet " holy." All the gods of all peoples are holy ; even the infamous gods of the pagan Semites, the patrons of prostitution. [1] Even the worshippers of these foul divinities who gave themselves up to the vile practices prescribed in the name of religion, were called holy women and holy men. The term thus applied simply means separated from common to religious use, and is perfectly compatible with any degree of immorality. The holiness of Jehovah as conceived by the prophets is something very different, as we may learn from examining the connection in which the title, " The Holy One of Israel," first occurs in Isaiah's prophecies. It is introduced in connection with a severe condemnation of the sin of Israel : " Ah sinful nation, a people laden with iniquity, a seed of evildoers, children that deal corruptly : they have forsaken Jehovah, they have despised the Holy One of Israel, they are estranged and gone backward." And note what the sins are that have insulted the divine holiness. They are not ritual offences, ignorant or wilful breaches of ceremonial rules, neglect of religious services. On the contrary, the sinners complained of are scrupulously careful in these respects ; they are religious *ad nauseam*. What the Holy One finds fault with in Israel is her moral offences : sins of injustice and inhumanity. " Thy princes are rebellious, and companions of thieves ; every one loveth

[1] Isa. i. 4.

gifts, and followeth after rewards; they judge not the
fatherless, neither doth the cause of the widow come unto
them." [1]   This charge throws light on the nature of
Jehovah's holiness.   It means above all aloofness from
such misconduct as Israel is guilty of—disapprobation of
moral evil.   The Holy One of Israel is exalted in all
senses.   He is, as Hosea and Micah call Him, God on high,
raised far above the world of created and finite being; He
is so exalted in virtue of His being God, so that holiness
and deity are in a sense synonymous.   But the moral
element in the divine holiness is what the prophets chiefly
emphasise.   And just on that account the Holy One of
Israel does not in their view belong to Israel.   His holiness
imposes on Israel obligations to be holy, not ritually only
but really, and exposes her to the risk of forfeiting His
favour in case she fail to satisfy His just demands.   In
other words, the Holy One of Israel is the Holy One of
the universe.   He is high and lifted up, and "the whole
earth is full of His glory." [2]

It does not follow from this that the chosen people, or
the temple which Isaiah in vision saw filled with the train
of the Holy One, was nothing to Jehovah, or that the pro
phets who had risen above religious nationalism in their
conception of deity must therefore lightly reconcile themselves to the abandonment of either.   For them as for
Providence, it is true, the religious interest was supreme,
and they understood more or less clearly that that interest
might be promoted even by the misfortunes of Israel.
Nevertheless, it might well appear to them that the ex
istence of Israel in whole or in part, and of the holy place,
was necessary to the preservation of the true religion.   So
long as they believed this they would maintain the inde
structibility of the divine state and the inviolability of
Jehovah's sanctuary; for with all the prophets it was
an axiom that God's end in choosing Israel could not fail,
His gracious purpose must be fulfilled.   This accordingly

[1] Isa. i. 23.   [2] Isa. vi. 3.

is the position taken up by the prophet Isaiah. That
Jerusalem or Zion, Jehovah's seat, is inviolable, is for him
a fixed principle, which he resolutely maintains in the
most desperate circumstances. Even when the Eastern
conqueror is at the gate with a mighty army, and destruc
tion seems inevitable, he hurls defiance at the invader in
such terms as these : "The virgin, the daughter of Zion,
hath despised thee, and laughed thee to scorn ; the daughter
of Jerusalem hath shaken her head at thee. Whom hast
thou reproached and blasphemed ? and against whom hast
thou exalted thy voice, and lifted up thine eyes on high ?
even against the Holy One of Israel ;" concluding with
the firm declaration that Sennacherib's army should not
enter Jerusalem : "For I will defend this city to save it,
for mine own sake, and my servant David's sake." [1] Isaiah
was prepared for much in the way of judgment on Jehovah's
people for her sins. He predicted that in threescore and
five years Ephraim should be broken in pieces, and cease
to be a people. [2] He expected that even Judah would
suffer severely, so as to resemble a tree cut down to the
stump. But he believed that in her case a stock would
survive all calamities, a holy seed, a faithful remnant. [3] It
was this faith that supported him through the crisis of
the Assyrian invasion, and which was so marvellously
justified by the sudden destruction of Sennacherib's host.
It was not faith in a merely national god, bound in
honour and as a matter of course to defend his people. It
was at bottom faith in the indestructibility of the true
religion, with which at the moment the continuance of the
state of Judah seemed inseparably bound up.

In Isaiah's time the interest of the true religion and
the maintenance of the Jewish state were indeed practically
one. And, owing to the limitations of prophetic vision, it
might well be that he deemed the two things permanently
inseparable. The fact, however, was not so, and within a
century this had become clear to recipients of prophetic

[1] Isa. xxxvii. 22, 23, 35.   [2] Isa. vii. 8.   [3] Isa. vi. 13.

inspiration. Jeremiah, holding firmly Isaiah's principle, the common faith of all Hebrew prophets, that the true religion must prosper and Jehovah's purpose be fulfilled, draws from it an opposite inference; not that Judah must be saved, and Zion remain inviolable, but that Judah must go into captivity, and Jerusalem and the temple be de stroyed. Jeremiah believed negatively that these calamities might happen without detriment to the religious interest, and positively that by their occurrence that interest would be advanced. What had happened in the interval between the two prophets to bring about this marked change of view? Well, for one thing, Isaiah's long ministry had borne its natural fruit. He had raised up a band of dis ciples, "a community of true faith able to hold together even in times of persecution, and conscious that its re ligion rested on a different basis from that of the idolatrous masses." [1] This was the birth of a *Church* as distinct from a nation: a community of men united not by mere nationality, though belonging to the same people, but by fellowship in religious faith.[2] If we accept the view that the concentration of worship at the one sanctuary insisted on in Deuteronomy had taken place shortly before Jeremiah began to prophesy, this event also would not be without influence in making religion independent of political con ditions. It involved that devout souls had to learn to be religious without daily access to sanctuaries such as they enjoyed when every town and district had its high place. Dispensing with sacrifices and sacred festivals, except at stated intervals at the central sanctuary, was an education for dispensing with them altogether during the exile, with out degenerating into heathenism. In some such way it came to pass that Jeremiah could contemplate the destruc tion of state and temple without fear. He felt sure that the divine interest would survive these disasters. Nay, as

---

[1] W. Robertson Smith, *The Prophets of Israel*, p. 262.

[2] *The Prophets of Israel*, p. 275. Professor Smith's whole discussion of the contrast between Isaiah and Jeremiah is very instructive.

has been said, he ventured to hope that it would be promoted thereby, that through exile God's people would be brought nearer to the happy times of the *New Covenant*, when all, from the least to the greatest, should know Jehovah. Hence the sublime calmness with which he intimates to those whose constant cry was, " The temple of Jehovah, the temple of Jehovah, the temple of Jehovah," that the temple in which they trusted might share the fate of the holy place at Shiloh. " Go ye now unto my place which was in Shiloh, where I set my name at the first, and see what I did to it for the wickedness of my people Israel." [1]

We have thus satisfied ourselves from every point of view that the religion of the prophets did not consist in the worship of a merely national God called Jehovah. It may be strictly described as an ethical monotheism. Of such a faith, individualism and universalism are obvious consequences, and we naturally inquire whether any traces of these developments can be discovered in the prophetic writings. Now, as to the former, which points to a personal relation of God to the individual spirit, it has to be remembered that in the ancient Hebrew way of thinking, the nation not the individual is the unit. Jehovah is the God of Israel as a whole. He is the Maker of Israel, who has given her her place in history. His covenant is with Israel. His promises and threatenings, His mercies and judgments, concern immediately the people at large, and only indirectly the individuals who belong to it. We need not therefore be surprised if we find this point of view predominant in Hebrew prophecy. And yet we should feel disappointed if we failed to discover at least the rudiments of a new way of thinking in harmony with a monotheistic creed, traces of the idea that the individual man is of some account to God. Prophecy itself, by its very existence, is a witness to this truth. For what does it mean but this, that God reveals Himself, " His secret,' [2]

---

[1] Jer. vii. 4, 12. [2] Amos iii. 7.

the present truth, not to or through the nation, but to and through the individual spirit.   It would be strange, indeed, if the men whom God so highly favoured, "His servants the prophets,"[1] had not a word to say in behalf of ordinary men, but allowed them to lose themselves in the national organism.   But the fact is not so.   Even in Isaiah the dawn of individualism may be descried.   The Maker of Israel is also called the Maker of *man*.   "At that day shall a man look to his Maker, and his eyes shall have respect to the Holy One of Israel."[2]   A century later the new thought has assumed larger dimensions.   In two ways Jeremiah constitutes himself an advocate of the claims of the individual : by contradicting the old adage about the fathers eating sour grapes and the children's teeth being set on edge, and by claiming for the individual, however insignificant, an immediate knowledge of God.[3]   In the one case he asserts personal responsibility against the law of heredity, and in the other he vindicates the independ ence of the individual in his religious relations to God of all mediation by priestly representatives.   It is a great word, that spoken by the prophet in his oracle of the New Covenant, concerning the immediate knowledge of God : greater than he knows.   It portends religious revolution ; it anticipates a time when the true worshipper in every land shall worship the Father in spirit and in truth.

In every land, for the fellowship of the individual spirit with God involves universalism.   That a universal world wide religion was a necessary consequence of their own principles, was not as clear to the prophets as it is to us. God never reveals to men truth, with daylight brightness, so long before the time of fulfilment.   In the prophetic age, the light of universalism was but the light of a star in the night.   But to that extent it did shine even in the eighth century B.C. witness the oracle of *the mountain of Jehovah's house*, preserved both by Isaiah and by Micah.[4]

---

[1] Amos iii. 7.   [2] Isa. xvii. 7.
[3] Jer. xxxi. 30, 34.   [4] Isa. ii. 1-5 ; Micah iv. 1-5.

This remarkable prophecy, apparently proceeding from some older prophet, points to something higher than a political influence exerted on surrounding tribes by a reformed Israel, in which the ideal of a holy nation with a just, wise king at its head has been realised. The very fact that both Isaiah and Micah deemed the anonymous utter ance worthy of embodiment in their own prophecies, may be taken as evidence that its meaning is not exhausted by so comparatively commonplace an idea. It predicts, surely, the extension of Israel's religion among the nations, the spread of the knowledge and fear of Jehovah, and the establishment of peace through community in faith and worship. The fair picture is similar to that presented in Isaiah's own prediction of a happy time when Israel shall be a third with Egypt and with Assyria, all three blessed of Jehovah and owned by Him as His united people: " Blessed be Egypt my people, and Assyria the work of my hands, and Israel mine inheritance."[1] Egypt and Assyria, the great rival powers between which the petty state of Israel was ever in danger of being crushed, repre sent the outside nations—the world beyond the pale of the chosen people. And the meaning is that in the good time coming the distinction between that people and heathendom shall cease. Jehovah shall own as His chosen all the representative heathen nations, applying to each of them epithets expressive of peculiar and intimate relations: " My people," " the works of my hands," equivalent in import to the epithet, "mine inheritance," applied to Israel. A beautiful poetic dream, we may think, but very unlikely, this union in the true religion. But is it more unlikely than concord and peace between three such peoples in the lower sphere of politics ? The prophetic mind lived in the region of improbable and apparently impossible ideals. And this dream of Isaiah's, whether realisable or not, is one which would naturally suggest itself to one who believed that Jehovah was the sole true God. What

[1] Isa. xix. 24, 25.

more desirable than that the true God should be universally recognised; how could earnest believers in Him help cherishing such a desire?

Such was the religion of the prophets, such their conception of God and of His relations to the world, to the nations, to Israel, and to man. It is admittedly a unique phenomenon in the religious history of the human race, rising above all other ancient thoughts of deity in solitary grandeur. Whence came it, how is it to be accounted for? This is a question not easy to answer on naturalistic principles. Various suggestions have been made, the most plausible being that of Renan, that the religion of Israel as seen at its best in the prophets was the outcome of a monotheistic tendency inherent in the Semitic races. Granting the tendency, which however has been gravely disputed, how did it come about that it attained its proper development only in the Hebrew member of a large family? Reference has already been made to the educative effect of the appearance on Israel's horizon of the great Eastern power · and there can be no question that the new political situation would tend to widen the thoughts of observing and reflecting men. But the rise of the Assyrian power could not create the prophets, or the prophetic type of religious thought; at most it could only stimulate into a quicker and ampler growth seeds of thought pre-existing in prophetic minds. It is unnecessary to say that the religious ideas of the prophets are not a mere reflection of the current opinion of their countrymen. Their constant complaints against prevailing religious fashions are conclusive evidence of this. The prophets were not echoes. They were not the mouthpiece of the majority. They were in a hopeless minority—a remark, by the way, which applies to all the men of revelation. The men whose golden imperishable utterances are recorded in the Bible whether in the Old or in the New Testament, were all men whose back was at the wall fighting against heavy odds and who seemed to their contemporaries heretics and blasphemers. For their message was ever some *new* word of God, which blind followers of religious tradition refused to hear. How strange that those who pay the most ostentatious homage to a book thus originating should be in spirit the children of the men who did their best to prevent it from coming into existence!

The prophets themselves had no doubt as to whence their knowledge of God came. It was, they felt, a revelation direct from heaven. It was in this belief they spoke unfamiliar, unwelcome truth; by this belief they were emboldened to speak in the face of all possible contradiction. They could not help themselves: they must utter the thought that by divine inspiration had arisen in their minds. The word of Jehovah was as a fire in their heart. In the expressive language of Amos: "The lion hath roared, who will not fear? the Lord God hath spoken, who can but prophesy?"[1] What had God spoken? That Israel, just because she was Jehovah's chosen, must be specially punished for her iniquities. In this practical ethical manner does the truth come home to the prophet's heart that Jehovah is no merely national partial deity. And in this instance we can see how true is the saying that the secret of the Lord is with them that fear Him in other words, that moral simplicity is a condition of receiving divine revelations. "Surely," says Amos, "the Lord God will do nothing, but He revealeth His secret unto His servants the prophets."[2] Unless the prophets had been exceptionally pure-hearted men they would have remained as ignorant of God's secret as their fellow-countrymen. They enjoyed the privilege of initiation because they were proof against common prejudices and passions, and loved righteousness more than country. They so heartily hated wrong—greed, oppression, cruelty, vileness—that it was impossible for them to believe that any prerogative, supposed or real, could screen a wicked nation from the punitive action of the moral order of the world. Israel

[1] Amos iii. 8. [2] Amos iii 7.

might be God's beloved, but Israel must suffer and even perish if she played the harlot. In a word, the ethical monotheism of Hebrew prophecy has for one of its neces sary presuppositions the intense ethicalism of the prophets themselves.

CHAPTER III.

THE PROPHETIC IDEA OF ISRAEL'S VOCATION AND HISTORY.

LITERATURE.—Trench, *The Desire of all Nations* (the Hul-sean Lecture for 1846); Maurice, *The Religions of the World and their Relations to Christianity* (Boyle Lecture for 1846); Ewald, *Die Lehre der Bibel vom Gott*, Band I. (translated by T. & T. Clark, contains Theory of Revelation and State ment on Revelation in Heathendom and the Worth of Pagan Religion); Duhm, *Die Theologie der Propheten;* Bunsen, *God in History;* Hegel, *Religions-Philosophie;* Temple, " The Edu cation of the World " in *Essays and Reviews;* Bruce, *The Chief End of Revelation; Lux Mundi* (Essay 4th, " The Preparation in History for Christ ").

In last chapter we saw that the prophets regarded Israel as an elect people. There this view came before us inci dentally, simply in its bearing on the prophetic idea of God, as contributing to the proof that Jehovah was not merely the national God of Israel, but the God of the whole earth who had freely chosen Israel to be a peculiar people. In the present chapter the subject of Israel's election will be considered under a wider aspect and in more varied relations, in connection with prophetic ideas of Israel's vocation and past history, and with the religious condition of the world at large.

It will hardly be necessary to offer further proof that the idea of election was present to the mind of the prophets from the eighth century onwards. It has been asserted, indeed, that it is only in the writings of the unknown prophet of the exile, to whom we owe the second part of

Isaiah, that that idea begins to play its part,[1] and it is certainly true that it occupies a place of exceptional prominence in that remarkable group of prophecies. But the idea, if not the very word election, is traceable in all the prophets of the eighth century.

It finds very distinct expression in the words of Amos, already quoted: "You only have I known of all the families of the earth."[2] It underlies the words put into the mouth of Jehovah by Hosea, "When Israel was a child, then I loved him, and called my son out of Egypt,"[3] which carry the election back to the time of the Exodus. Isaiah echoes Hosea's thought when he represents God as complaining, "Hear, O heavens, and give ear, O earth : for Jehovah hath spoken : I have nourished and brought up children, and they have rebelled against me. The ox knoweth his owner, and the ass his master's crib : but Israel doth not know, my people doth not consider."[4] The thought recurs in the song of the vineyard, in which Israel is compared to a choice vine planted in Jehovah's vineyard and tended with the utmost care.[5] In varied language Micah repeats the divine complaint, as reported by his brother prophet : "Hear ye, O mountains, Jehovah's controversy, and ye strong foundations of the earth : for Jehovah hath a controversy with His people, and he will plead with Israel. O my people, what have I done unto thee ? and wherein have I wearied thee ? testify against me. For I brought thee up out of the land of Egypt, and redeemed thee out of the house of servants; and I sent before thee Moses, Aaron, and Miriam."[6]

The one thought running through all these passages is : special favours conferred by God on Israel, imposing on her special obligations. The God of the whole earth has distinguished Israel from other nations by making her His peculiar people, His son, His vine, and He expects from the chosen race corresponding fidelity, obedience, and fruitfulness. And He complains that His just expectations have

---

[1] Duhm, *Die Theologie der Propheten*, p. 282. [2] Amos iii. 2.
[3] Hos. xi. 1. The same idea is still more pathetically expressed by the comparison of Israel to a wife, which pervades Hosea's prophecies.
[4] Isa. i. 2, 3. [5] Isa v 1-7. [6] Micah vi. 2-4.

not been realised, making His complaint to the heavens and the earth, to the universe of being, of which not less than of Israel He is Maker and Lord.

From these prophetic utterances it is obvious that Israel is not only an elect people, but that she has been elected for a purpose. God has chosen her not merely to privilege, that she may be more fortunate than other peoples, but that she may fulfil a high vocation. The nature of that vocation is variously indicated. The prophet of the exile puts it thus · "This people have I formed for myself; they shall show forth my praise."[1] The most distinct statement of God's purpose in choosing Israel is given in Ex. xix. 5, a sentence which, at whatever date written, has a genuine prophetic ring: "Now therefore, if ye will obey my voice indeed, and keep my covenant, ye shall be a peculiar treasure unto me above all people: for all the earth is mine: and ye shall be unto me a kingdom of priests, and an holy nation." Israel called to be a kingdom of God, a community of men devoted to God and to righteousness— such is the divine ideal as proclaimed from Mount Sinai, with which all prophetic utterances consent. In this view of Israel's vocation it may be difficult to satisfy impartial students of her history that her election was a reality. It is by what a people does that the world judges whether she be an elect people or not. But did Israel realise in her history the divine ideal of a holy nation? Was it not the constant complaint of the prophets that she had failed to do so? God looked for grapes, and behold wild grapes; "for judgment, but behold oppression; for righteousness but behold a cry."[2] It is easier to see the reality of Israel's election when we think of her as chosen to receive the knowledge of the true God and to be the home of the true religion. In that view her election is a fact, not merely a theological idea. As a matter of fact the religion of Israel, by comparison with the religions of the Gentiles, is the true religion—the best thing the world has seen,

[1] Isa. xliii. 21.   [2] Isa. v. 7.

the best thing possible. Her idea of God, as formulated by her noblest sons, is her glory.[1] As the vehicle through which God communicated to the world the worthiest thoughts concerning Himself, Israel realised her vocation by producing the *prophets*. No matter how far short the mass of the people fell in thought and in conduct, God's purpose was saved from being stultified by the appearance in due time of men like Amos, Hosea, Isaiah, Jeremiah, and the great prophet of the exile. It was worth while planting a vine that was to bear such generous fruit. If the chosen people perish, no matter; Hebrew prophecy remains, an imperishable treasure, proof to all time that God took in hand no vain task when He became the religious instructor of the child whom He brought out of Egypt, beginning at the beginning, and playing the part of nurse to the infant Ephraim, teaching him to go, taking him by the arms to encourage him in his first attempts.[2] The permanent results of that divine training are the sum of moral duty in the Decalogue, the grand conception of a kingdom of God acting as a ferment in society, the true idea of God as the Maker and Ruler of the world, as One who Himself delights in the exercise of lovingkindness, judgment, and righteousness,[3] and who requires of His worshippers, above all things, "to do justly, and to love mercy, and to walk humbly with God."[4]

The prophetic references to Israel's past history are all dominated by the idea of election. The interest of the prophets in that history lies in the proofs it affords of God's gracious favour and of the obligations thence arising. They use the past to enforce the lessons of the present. Their references, therefore, to ancient times are incidental and comparatively few, their business being not to chronicle but to preach. Though few, however, these occasional allusions are important, and cover the outstanding events of the memorable story of Israel's beginnings. There are slight

---

[1] Isa. lx. 19 : "Thy God thy glory."   [2] Hos. xi. 3
[3] Jer. ix. 24.   [4] Micah vi 8.

hints concerning the patriarchs Abraham, Isaac, and Jacob,[1] more numerous and explicit statements concerning the Egyptian bondage, the Exodus, and the sojourn in the wilderness[2] These historical allusions, taken together, give us an outline of Israel's early fortunes, such as might have been gathered from one of the documents out of which the Pentateuch was ultimately constructed, say the Jehovistic, and which may actually have been the source whence the prophets drew their information. The question has been asked What is the value of these notices? and the answer of some critics is that they yield us only the idea which was entertained of Israel's early history in the eighth century B C Some have gone so far as to doubt the reality of the sojourn in Egypt and the Exodus, and to regard even Moses as a legendary personage, not to speak of ---- patriarchs, whose names are supposed to denote tribes rather than individuals, and whose family story is con ceived to be a legendary representation of the relations subsisting between the group of peoples to which the Beni-Israel belonged. The more sober-minded critics, however regard the Egyptian episode and the redemptive work of Moses as unquestionable facts, and are not indisposed to find some historic material even in the patriarchal story. These critical questions do not vitally concern us here: they may seriously affect the view to be taken of the Hebrew Scriptures, but they are of subordinate importance in relation to the purpose we have now in view. The important question for us is, Is the prophetic concep tion of Israel's past true, at least in principle

As has been stated, the prophets look at Israel's past in the light of the idea of election. Thus Micah writes: "Thou wilt perform the truth to Jacob, and the mercy to Abraham, which Thou hast sworn unto our father

---

[1] Hos. xii. 4 13 ; Micah vii. 20 ; Isa. xxix. 22.
[2] Amos ii. 9, 10 ; v. 25 ; ix. 7 ; Hos. ii. 15 ; viii. 13 ; ix. 3, 6 ; xi. 1 ; xii. 9, 13 ; xiii. 4, 5 ; Micah vi. 3, 4 ; vii. 15.

the days of old," [1] implying that God made a covenant with the patriarchs, and promised them special blessings. And Hosea introduces Jehovah, saying, " I am the Lord thy God from the land of Egypt, and thou shalt know no god but me : for there is no saviour beside me." [2] In general form the prophetic doctrine is that in the beginning of Israel's history God in His providence acted towards her as an electing God. If they were mistaken in that, their prophetic inspiration is compromised ; but if they were not mistaken, their prophetic inspiration stands intact, even if they were not perfectly informed in special matters of fact ; for their function, as already said, was not to narrate facts, but to teach the right point of view for reading truly the religious significance of Israel's whole history. The creation of Israel, like the creation of the world, may have been a much more complicated process than it appears in the sacred page ; and the secular history of the process, if it could be written, might assume a very different appearance in many respects to the biblical, just as the scientific history of the physical creation differs widely from that given in the first chapter of Genesis. But the main point is that throughout the period of obscure beginnings God was forming a people whose destiny it was to give to the world the true religion. As the story of the beginnings is told in the Pentateuch, and more briefly in the Prophets, that is very apparent ; and the merit of the story so told is that it does make the religious lesson so apparent. And if we are inclined to receive the lesson we shall not feel tempted to undue scepticism, but be ready to receive the story of the patriarchs, and of the Exodus, and of Moses, as substantially true ; as just such a history as Israel was likely to have, if she was to be the divine instrument for introducing the true religion.

It is not necessary to suppose that the early generations of Israelites were conscious of their high destiny, or conceived of the events that were happening as signs of a

[1] Micah vii. 20. [2] Hos. xiii. 4.

divine elective purpose towards them. They might be an elect people, yet for a while remain unconscious of the fact. It is conceivable that Israel first attained to clear consciousness of her vocation through the prophets, and that in the initial stage of her history she thought of Jehovah, not as the God of the whole earth choosing her for a peculiar people, but simply as a national god doing his best for the people to which he was nationally related. Even if the fact were so, she might still be the subject of such a choice from the first. I am far from thinking that the fact was indeed so, or that the generation of the Exodus was as completely in the dark as some modern critics imagine. An event of such magnitude as the deliverance out of Egypt could hardly take place without exercising an illuminating influence on susceptible spirits, and one can well believe that the prophetic mind of Moses anticipated the great discovery of the eighth century B.C., and read the Exodus in the light of an elective purpose of grace towards the emancipated people. The gospel of the Exodus, contained in Ex. xix. 5, already quoted, may have been formulated as it there stands long after the time of Moses, but there is no good reason to doubt that it truly reflects his thought. Looking back on what Jehovah had done unto the Egyptians, and considering how He had borne the enslaved race, as on eagle's wings, out of the land of bondage, he took out of the wondrous story this meaning: the one true God is going to make out of my despised and down-trodden people a great nation—great, not in numbers or in warlike power, but in character, a kingdom of God in the earth.

It may not be so easy to feel quite sure that the gospel of election in Abraham's call is historical, and not a projection backwards into the dawn of Israel's history of the prophetic conception of her destiny. The latter alternative might be admitted compatibly with the recognition of the ideal truth of the construction put by the prophets on the story of Abraham's life, and even of the

substantial accuracy of the main outlines of the story.
The call of the patriarch implies some such fact basis as
this, that he left the land of his birth partly, at least, from
motives of religious discontent, that he wandered westward
in search of another place of abode, and that on his arrival
in Canaan the thought took possession of his heart that
that land would become the home of a people sprung from
his loins, destined to play a remarkable part in history.
These facts, read with a prophetic eye, were sufficient to re
veal a divine intention such as is expressed in the call, to
separate Abraham from his own people, and make him the
father of a new race that should occupy a land specially
prepared for them, and be there a peculiar people, worship
ping the true God, and communicating eventually the true
religion to the world.   To Abraham himself the facts
might mean much less.   His departure from his native
country might be to his consciousness the result of an
irresistible impulse, rather than of a deliberate purpose ; the
religious motive might be a vague dissatisfaction with
prevalent religious beliefs and practices, rather than a new
clearly conceived idea of God ; the hope of founding a
nation, peculiar in character and vocation, might be to his
feeling only a persistent presentiment of which no account
could be given, a sort of fixed idea, for cherishing which a
man might be reckoned a madman or a sage, according to
the event.   If this were Abraham's state of mind at the
period of the migration, then he would not be conscious of
receiving such a call as the narrative in Genesis reports.
Nevertheless that call gives the true ideal significance of
the events as I have supposed them to happen.

The closing words of the call of Abraham, " In thee
shall all the families of the earth be blessed (or bless
themselves)," imply that Israel's election had a reference
to the general good of the world, that she was chosen, not
for her own sake merely, but for the sake of mankind at
large.   It must be so.   Election involves universalism.
It is a method by which the few are qualified to bless the

many. The election of Israel, we saw, involved universalism in reference to the idea of God: the electing God is *ipso facto* the God over all. What is now insisted on is that election equally involves universalism in reference to the vocation of the elect. Nations are never chosen for their own sakes, and therefore nations which have never done any good worth speaking of, except to themselves, cannot with any propriety be called elect nations. The Chinese nation has lasted so long, and is still so vigorous, that one might be tempted to think her a chosen people peculiarly favoured of Heaven. But, populous and long-lasting beyond comparison though she be, China is not worthy of the name, because she has lived only for herself. More deserving the honourable designation is a small people which gives birth to a great boon for mankind, and dies in childbirth. Such a people was Israel. A very insignificant people numerically, compared with China; but that is no drawback. It is the way of Providence to select small nations to be its chosen instruments; and it is a way of wisdom, because it serves to make clear that the importance of a people lies not in its numbers, but in the contribution which it makes to the higher good of the world.

Though a petty people, Israel seemed destined by her whole history, and even by her very geographical position, to be the source of a universal influence in the sphere of religion. From first to last she came into contact with all the great nations of antiquity. She came originally from the valley of the Euphrates, the seat of great Eastern monarchies. She went down to Egypt and sojourned long enough there to learn the ways of the children of Ham. Then she settled in the land of promise, through which ran the great highway between Egypt and the East, along which in later centuries the armies of mighty nations were to march to conquest or defeat. To the ambition of Oriental despotism she at length fell a victim, and in consequence returned a captive to the land whence she

had migrated. Her later fortunes brought her under the
dominion of the great powers of the West. Egypt, Assyria,
Babylon, Persia, Greece, Rome were in succession her
masters and her teachers. It might have been expected
that such an experience would have developed in her a
cosmopolitan spirit. It did not, except in the few. But
the "great dialectic of the world's history"[1] did tend
to develop in this people the true idea of God, and when
that had gained adequate expression through the voice of
prophecy it was a permanent gain to the world, whatever
became of the people among whom it originated, and
however they might fail to realise the value of their own
discovery.

The principle of election applied to religion creates an
apologetic problem with reference to the heathen world.
Election to distinction in philosophy or art causes no
difficulty, because, however important in their own place,
these things can hardly be said to belong to the chief end
or chief good of man. But religion, and conduct as
affected by it, are of vital concern to every man, both for
this life and for the next, and if the election of one people
meant the exclusion from divine mercy and grace of all
other peoples it would necessarily appear to the enlightened
Christian conscience open to grave objection, and even
altogether incredible. The question thus raised must
always have presented a difficulty to men imbued with the
spirit of Christ, but it has become more acute within the
last half century, since the religions of the world have been
made the subject of comparative study. Within that
period the apologetic attitude towards Gentile religion has
undergone a great change. Since the science of compara
tive religion came into vogue the modern mind has resiled
from the pessimistic views of ethnic religions entertained

---

[1] The expression is Vatke's. *Vide Die Religion des Alten Testaments*,
p. 440. Vatke deals with the religion of Israel on the principles of the
Hegelian philosophy in a masterly way, and with a breadth of treatment
worthy of Hegel himself.

by the early apologists, and still widely prevalent in the
Church. The point of view occupied by the apologists of
the patristic period was a very simple one. They held,
and sought to prove, that the pagan religions, and especi
ally those of Greece and Rome, were false, corrupt, and
corrupting, and that the little truth that was in them was
borrowed from Hebrew sources. Some, indeed, of the
more large-minded and philosophic fathers, such as Justin
Martyr, recognised elements of truth in pagan writers which
had not come to them from without by a borrowing
process, but rather from the inward illumination of the
Logos, the light "which lighteth every man that cometh
into the world." Now Christian apologists are more
inclined to sympathise with the opinion expressed by an
eminent student of the science of religion that "every
religion had some truth, nay, was a true religion, was the
only religion possible at the time."[1]   No professed
apologist, probably, would care to adopt this precise
language, or to endorse so optimistic an estimate; but
most recent writers on apologetic have shown a disposition
to go as far in that direction as is consistent with main
taining the supreme worth of the Christian faith. The
keynote of this more genial modern apologetic was struck
by Archbishop Trench in his Hulsean Lectures for 1846,
entitled, *Christ the Desire of all Nations; or, The Uncon
scious Prophecies of Heathendom*.   In the same year Mr.
Maurice delivered a course of lectures on the Boyle founda
tion on *The Religions of the World, and their Relations
to Christianity*, in which the same general view was set
forth, which was only what was to be expected from one
who, more than most men, believed in the possibility of
finding sermons in stones, and good in everything.

Besides the phrase, "the desire of all nations," so happily
chosen by Trench to suggest and justify a hopeful, kindly
view of pagan religion, use has been made, for the same
purpose, of another biblical expression, that of Paul in his

[1] Max Müller, *Lectures on the Science of Religion*, p. 261.

Epistle to the Galatians, "the fulness of the time." The apostle himself employed the expression in an apologetic interest, his purpose being so to exhibit the relation between Judaism and Christianity as at once to recognise the importance of the former as a preparatory discipline, and to justify its supersession by the latter when it had served its end. In modern times attempts have been made to give to Paul's idea a wider application, and to use his happy phrase as a compendious formula for the whole religious history of mankind, its attraction for philosophic minds being that it makes it possible to recognise the relative value of all the great historical religions, while reserving for Christianity the distinction of being the absolute reli gion.[1] The general truth underlying such attempts is that the whole religious history of mankind, up till the birth of Christ, may be brought under the category of *preparation*, which does not commit us to an optimistic view of ethnic religions, as these might be to a large extent fruitless experiments to find out God, and yet help to prepare the nations for welcoming Christ as the Light of the world.

These modern views may be justified by the facts brought to light by the scientific study of religion, and they are certainly such as it well becomes Christians to cherish. But the question is, Can they be entertained compatibly with acceptance of the prophetic view of Israel as an elect race chosen by Providence to receive and transmit the true knowledge of God ? If not, then our Christian geniality is in conflict with our reverence for prophetic revelation, and we are painfully divided against ourselves.

The question here is not whether the tone of the modern Christian mind in reference to Gentile religion is reflected in all parts of the Hebrew Scriptures. It is conceivable that the prophetic idea of Israel as an elect people, properly understood, justifies and even demands a more hopeful view of Gentile religion, and a more kindly feeling towards

---

[1] *Vide* Hegel, *Religions-Philosophie ;* Bunsen, *God in History ;* Bishop Temple on "The Education of the World" in *Essays and Reviews.*

pagans than is to be found in some parts of these writings.
It has been said that the people of Israel did not at first
think of themselves as a chosen race, and that when at
length they did begin to entertain this opinion, their attitude
towards Gentiles was one of bitter exclusiveness. It may
be so, but what then? We should simply have to include
the indications of such a state of feeling to be found in
Old Testament literature among the element of legalism
traceable therein — the elements which show that that
literature, however excellent, is still the literature of the
early rudimentary stage of revelation. It is incidental to
the method of election that the favour of God to the
elect is apt to be more laid to heart by them than their
vocation, the privilege rather than the duty, the present
separateness rather than the ultimate comprehension. This
is the tendency of all privileged races, societies, and indi
viduals. It needs a high order of mind to resist the
temptation, and to remember that the elect are chosen, not
for their own sakes, but to serve others. There always
were those in Israel who fully comprehended this truth,
and constantly kept it in view, and it finds frequent and
noble expression in the Hebrew Scriptures, especially in
the later chapters of Isaiah, and in certain of the psalms,
which breathe the genuine spirit of universalism. If a less
heroic type of feeling here and there crops out, there is no
cause for surprise.

The question, therefore, is not how all members of the
chosen race felt towards the heathen world, but what atti
tude is in harmony with the hypothesis of an election.
Now, to arrive at a right answer, we must keep clearly
before our minds what the hypothesis is. It is that the
God of the whole earth, having in view the religions wellbeing of all mankind, adopted as His method the selection
of a particular people to be the subject of special training,
so as to become eventually a light to lighten the Gentiles.
It is the universal Lord pursuing a universally beneficent
end by a temporary religious particularism. No sooner

have we grasped this idea than we perceive that three inferences suggest themselves.

The first is, that the universal aim involves a beneficent regard towards the outside nations on God's part all along. For we cannot reasonably conceive of God as hostile to the heathen world up to a certain date, the beginning of the Christian era, and then suddenly changing His attitude from hostility to friendliness, as earthly monarchs change their tone towards each other for reasons of state policy. We must believe that He desired unchangeably the good of all everywhere, in all ages, and while reserving some great boon for a future age, took care that at no time should any people be entirely without some token of His goodwill, even in the sphere of religion. That means that even in the pre-Christian era God gave to the Gentiles at least the *starlight* of religious knowledge. We should therefore not be surprised to find that the pagan peoples had their pro phets and seers, or think it necessary, in jealousy for the honour of Hebrew prophets and Christian apostles, to disparage the teaching of the wise men of the heathen world. On the contrary, our very belief in an election of one for the good of the many should lead us to look for traces of inspiration among pre-Christian races, seeing the total absence of these would cast doubt upon the reality of God's gracious purpose to bless the many through the one. That a beneficent Being should cherish such a purpose, and for a time, even for a long time, not execute it fully, is conceivable; but one would certainly expect to find the objects of the purpose all along treated in a manner con gruous to the purpose, and giving promise of ultimate fulfilment.

Secondly, from the adoption of the method of election for realising the universal design, it may be inferred that the pagan religions, on examination, will show traces of marked inferiority, as compared with the religion of the elect people. If it turned out to be otherwise, we should justly doubt whether the election was either real or requisite. The contrast ought to be apparent even at the outset, and it should become more marked with the progress of time. The method of election implies that religion cannot be left to look after itself, but needs special providential care; that without such care right thoughts of God, such as even pagans may attain to, are in danger of being lost, or remaining unfruitful. The plant of religion may at first be a good vine, but without special divine tending it must be prone to degenerate and to bring forth wild grapes. This is what theory leads us to expect, and it is what impartial study of ethnic religions tends to verify. It is characteristic of these religions, not so much to be without all true knowledge of God, as to be unable to retain that knowledge, and to make the most of it, and to go on from lower degrees of light to higher. Heathenism may be denned as religion that has made a good start, but is arrested in its free development and progress to perfection, and so has become retrograde. Having one source with the religion of the elect people, it does not, like it, flow on in ever-increasing volume, but loses itself in the sand.

Thirdly, the election being designed not merely to bestow on the elect people the great boon of the true religion, but to qualify it for communicating that blessing to the world, we should expect to discover in universal history traces of a twofold line of preparation—on the one hand, of the chosen people for giving to the pagan nations the benefit of the true religion; on the other, of these nations for receiving the benefit. The double process, to serve its purpose, would need to be a very comprehensive one, including within its scope not merely religion, but all other departments of human affairs—philosophy, science, art, war, commerce, politics. The larger process of preparation among the Gentiles is quite as necessary to the realisation of the divine end in election as the smaller one among the elect

<hr>

[1] Ewald, *Revelation: its Nature and Record*, pp. 203, 204. This work is a translation of the first part of Ewald's great work, *Die Lehre der Bibel vom Gott*. *Vide* list of books at the beginning of this chapter.

people. And its moral import is vast and varied. It means that God was never the God of the Jews only. It means that even by their very errors and failures God was bringing the Gentiles by a roundabout road to Christ. It means that there is no reason to take a despairing view of the spiritual state or future prospects of pagans on account of their comparative ignorance of the true God. That ignorance, as missionaries know, is often deep enough, but, however deep, it is a hasty judgment which pronounces it incompatible with salvation. This judgment at bottom rests on a mistaken view of the nature, purpose, and con sequences of election, a relative, temporary, and economic preference being mistaken for an absolute, eternal, and intrinsic one. The elect race is not the exclusive sphere of salvation. The elect are themselves saviours. To save is their very vocation. And the God of the elect is caring for others in the very act of electing them.

Some light even for pagans; heathenism nevertheless, on the whole, a failure ; its very failure a preparation for receiving the true religion—such are the inferences sug-gested by the method of election. If the facts verify these *a priori* inferences, the election will be at once shown to be a reality, and cleared of all liability to objection on the score of partiality.

At the close of this chapter it may fitly be pointed out how clearly the whole course of Israel's history shows that the supreme care of Providence was for the interests of the true religion, and not merely for the wellbeing of a pet people. If the supreme divine aim in calling Israel was to found a national theocratic kingdom, it was a failure; if it was to give to the world the true religion, it suc-ceeded. God took little pains to preserve the unity and peace of the people He called His own. He suffered it to be broken up into two rival kingdoms. He permitted the larger kingdom to be blotted out of existence, and the smaller, a century afterwards, to be carried captive to Babylon, to return after a season to its own land no longer a nation, but a petty church. The church in turn resolved itself into rival sects, presenting a ridiculous caricature of the ideal kingdom of priests and holy nation. And how fared it with the true religion throughout these sad centuries? Amid national disasters the light of prophecy shone. The post - exilian · Church produced the Psalter.[1] And when at length the Jewish State was on the brink of final ruin, He appeared who was to be the Light of the world. The elect nation was replaced by the Elect Man.

CHAPTER IV.

MOSAISM.

LITERATURE. — Ewald, *Geschichte des Volkes Israel*, Band II.; Wellhausen, *History of Israel;* Stade, *Geschichte des Volkes Israel;* Kuenen, *The Religion of Israel* (translation); Renan *Histoire du peuple d'Israel;* Schultz, *Alttestamentliche Theologie;* Riehm, *Alt. Theol.;* Koenig, *Die Haupt-Probleme der alt-Israelitischen Geschichte* (translated by T. & T. Clark); Robertson, *The Early Religion of Israel;* Geerhardus Vos, *The Mosaic Origin of the Pentateuchal Codes,* with an Intro duction by Professor W. H. Green of Princeton.

It was to be expected that the epoch of the Exodus should be associated with a new departure in revelation. Each of the three great stages in the evolution of Israel's religion was connected with a providential crisis in Israel's history; Mosaism with the escape from Egyptian bondage, Prophetism with the rise of the great Eastern monarchies, and Judaism with the Babylonish exile. None of these crises was greater than the first. The Exodus brought to a close a sojourn centuries long in a land of peculiar cus-

---

[1] This is not stated dogmatically, but as a critical hypothesis which an apologist has no reason to fear. On the apologetic significance of the Psalter viewed as of post-exilic origin, *vide* chap. vii. of this book.

toms and most peculiar religion, well called "the religion of mystery";[1] it meant deliverance from the oppressive yoke of Egyptian taskmasters long endured by the so-journers, and it would be remembered as a deliverance achieved by a series of remarkable events culminating in the way made through the sea that the bondslaves might for ever escape from their oppressors, who "sank as lead in the mighty waters," and feel, when they stood on the further shore, that they were a free people. No combina tion of circumstances can be conceived more fitted to produce an intense national self-consciousness, to awaken new religious thought, and to make a deep and indelible impression on character. The prophetic genius of a people that has had such an experience will have something to say of God and duty worth hearing, and not likely to be forgotten. It is therefore a violation of all historical probability to minimise the significance of Mosaism in deference to a naturalistic theory of evolution, which demands that the early stage in a religious development shall be sufficiently rudimentary to allow the whole sub sequent course of things to present the appearance of steady onward progress.

The grand outstanding, imperishable monument of Moses and his prophetic work is the DECALOGUE. We cannot, however, proceed to estimate the significance of that preg nant summary of duty without reckoning with the views of some modern critics, who doubt or deny the Mosaic origin of the Ten Words, while admitting that they reflect the spirit of Mosaic religion. The best way to do this is to show the intrinsic credibility of the Decalogue as a Mosaic utterance : how naturally it fits into and arises out of the position of Israel as an emancipated people, more especially in the first table, which embodies the religious idea of the legislator. The key to the situation is to be found in the preface, which, whether written on stone or not, was certainly written on the hearts of the

[1] So Hegel in his *Religions-Philosophie.*

emancipated people. " I am Jehovah thy God, who have
brought thee out of the land of Egypt, out of the house of
bondage." These words not only set forth Jehovah's
claim, but are a clue to the idea of God entertained by
the people of Israel or its representatives at the period of
the Exodus. The name for Israel's God is Jehovah, or
more correctly, *Jahveh*. It is in all probability not an
absolutely new name, but an old tribal name revived and
pronounced with new emphasis, and charged with deeper
significance. The origin and import of the name are
obscure, and therefore no inference, certain and reliable,
can be drawn from it as to the nature of the Being who
bore it. A surer index is given in what Jehovah has done
for Israel. He has brought her out of a land which has
been for her a land of long-lasting, intolerable oppression.
What educative virtue lay in that fact looked at on all sides !

Consider, first, the natural effect of a state of bondage in
producing a deep invincible dislike to all Egyptian ways
in religion. Nothing less probable than that Israel will
carry away from the land of bondage the religious customs
and ideas of her oppressors ; rather may it be expected
that she will studiously avoid them in all directions. It
may be assumed that, though living on the outskirts of the
land in which they are strangers, the Beni-Israel had
opportunities of becoming acquainted with local customs.
Moses, at least, there is reason to believe, knew these
intimately. And he knew only to abhor and shun ;
whence flow several important inferences. Thus: Egypt
was a land of many gods. It may therefore be expected
that redeemed Israel will eschew polytheism, and that a
fundamental article of her religious creed will be : Besides
Jehovah there is no God—a real practical monotheism, if
not a theoretical and speculative. This gives us the first
commandment in the Decalogue : " Thou shalt have no
other gods before me," to be understood as enjoining not
merely the worship of only one national God, but con
tempt of other gods. Again, Egypt was a land of images :

statues of the gods were to be seen everywhere ; not with
out artistic merit, noble in outline, though lacking indi
viduality. How natural that the children of the Exodus
should be proof against the fascinations of these divinities
in stone, and that it should become an article in their
creed that God is not to be worshipped by images. True,
they are represented as worshipping a golden calf at the
very foot of Sinai, which seems to show that their anti-
Egyptian prejudices were not so strong as might have
been expected. But it may be assumed that the indigna
tion of Moses at the sight was intensified by the thought
that the act of idolatry was a relapse into the heathenish
ways of Israel's oppressors. From him, true patriot as he
was, a prohibition against image-worship, such as we find
in the second commandment, was to be looked for. Once
more in the land of bondage there was in all probability
no resting-day for the poor, overtasked slaves. All days of
the week, if the week was known, were alike, a monotonous,
unbroken continuity of toil. How welcome then to the
ear of the emancipated the injunction of the Hebrew
legislator, " Remember the Sabbath day to keep it holy,"
whether we take it as creating a new institution, or as
reviving an old Hebrew custom compulsorily neglected in
the time of enslavement.

The Mosaicity of the first table of the Decalogue thus
appears to be intrinsically credible in the light of Israel's
past experience. The doubts of critics have been especially
directed against the second commandment, whose Mosaic
origin seems to them incompatible with the alleged pre
valence in after centuries of the use of images, even in
connection with the worship of Jehovah. The calves of
Jeroboam are pointed to in proof; for what, it is asked,
was the religion established by the first king of the ten
tribes but the worship of Jehovah under the image of an
ox ? And that this worship was not an innovation con
trary to previous custom, is argued from the manifest
impolicy of outraging popular feeling, and from the absence

from the records of any indications that the prophet Elijah disapproved of the State-worship established at Dan and Bethel. The first note of condemnation of the association of Jehovah-worship with the image of an ox was uttered, we are told, by the prophets of the eighth century, and in their case the prohibition is connected with new views as to the nature of God. It denotes, in short, the transition from a physical to an ethical conception of deity. The ox of the old sanctuaries was doomed by the men who gave to the world ethical monotheism; till then it had been a legitimate feature of Jehovah-worship. Two questions arise here: What are the facts, and how are they to be construed? Assuming the facts to be as stated by the critics, that at the various sanctuaries of Israel, from time immemorial, the ox had been associated with Jehovah-worship; that Jeroboam, in setting up the calves at Dan and Bethel, was not introducing new gods, but only estab lishing an old worship in new places; and that men of God like Elijah had no fault to find with him,—it becomes certainly less easy to believe in the Mosaic origin of the second commandment. One is tempted to think of it as a later insertion into an earlier form of the Decalogue in which it was wanting. But this serves no purpose, unless we get rid of other features of the Decalogue which show that the Jehovah of the Ten Words is no physical deity like the gods of Egypt, but an ethical being like the Jehovah believed in by the prophets of the eighth century.

To prove this, we have only to consider more fully what is implied in the preface. I am Jehovah, who have brought *thee* out of the land of Egypt. Consider the subject of redemption, and the means by which redemption is achieved. "Thee," Israel, a poor oppressed race, what a glimpse this affords into the nature of Jehovah! He is the Friend of the weak against the strong, of the oppressed against the oppressor; He loves justice, hates wrong, and has pity on its helpless victims. Many centuries later, a Psalmist, mindful of God's acts unto the children of Israel, sang of

Him as One who "executeth righteousness and judgment for all that are oppressed." [1] That this was Jehovah's character would be as clear to Moses as it was to the Psalmist, and it is quite credible that it is to him we owe the description of Jehovah as "merciful and gracious, longsuffering, and abundant in goodness and truth." [2]

And by what means does Jehovah deliver His oppressed people? The object of His love is no mighty nation with powerful armies at its command. If He be merely a national God, He is as weak as the people He befriends. But He has other forces than armed men, horses, and chariots at His disposal. Seas, winds, hailstorms obey Him; pestilential disease is at His service; all living creatures, even frogs, flies, lice, co-operate to accomplish His will. So it appears from the records; so His ransomed people believe, and, believing this, what can they think but that Jehovah, their Redeemer, is not merely their tribal God, but God over all? Put these two things together,—Jehovah the just and merciful, and Jehovah the Lord of the world,—and what have we but ethical mono theism?

We get the same result when we turn from the preface of the Decalogue to the Decalogue itself, and regard it as a whole. What at once arrests attention is the universal character of the code of morals it contains. There is nothing in the sum of duty local or national; all is human and valid for all mankind. That fact with reference to the contents of the second table, implies that ethical monotheism underlies the first. This inference is allowed by critics, and used as an argument against the Mosaic origin of the Decalogue. Thus among the reasons advanced by Wellhausen against its authenticity are these: "The essentially and necessarily national character of the older phases of the religion of Jehovah completely disappears in the quite universal code of morals which is given in the Decalogue as the fundamental law of Israel; but the entire series of

[1] Ps. ciii. 6. [2] Ex. xxxiv. 6.

religious personalities throughout the period of the Judges and
the Kings—from Deborah, who praised Jael's treacherous
act of murder, to David, who treated his prisoners of war
with the utmost cruelty—make it very difficult to believe
that the religion of Israel was, from the outset, one of a
specifically moral character. The true spirit of the old
religion may be gathered much more truly from Judg. v.
than from Ex. xx." Then again : " It is extremely doubtful whether the actual monotheism, which is undoubtedly
presupposed in the universal moral precepts of the
Decalogue, could have formed the foundation of a national
religion."[1] The most valuable feature in these extracts is
the admission they contain that the morality of the
Pentateuch is universal, and that the universal morality
implies monotheistic religion. The reasoning against the
authenticity of the Ten Words is not very formidable.
We are asked to doubt the lofty morality of Moses on
account of the low morality of later personalities. The
assumption is, that the moral growth of a nation must show
a steady advance ; there must be no lapsing from a higher
level, no tide-like movement ; the earlier stage must always
be the ruder. As if the moral ideal of Christ did not
tower above the actual morality of Christendom, as an
Alpine range of mountains rises above the plains ! Then
we are told that a monotheism as old as Moses could not
form the foundation of a national religion. Why not, if
the national religion happened to have for its peculiarity
among the religions of the world, monotheism, the belief
that there is only one true God ?

We may rest, then, in the conclusion that the Decalogue
is the work of Moses. It is impossible to assign for its
composition a more worthy time and author. The attempts
to find for it a suitable place in later ages are not satis
factory. One suggests the reign of Manasseh, when
Micah gave his memorable answer to the question, What
doth God require of man—an answer so like the Decalogue,

[1] *History of Israel*, pp. 439, 440.

in its eloquent silence as to cultus, that one might be tempted to conjecture that to Micah rather than to Moses the world owes the Ten Words.[1] But if the later prophet had done anything so great, there would surely have been a record of the fact in the book of his prophecies. Another suggestion is that the Decalogue originated at a time when prophetic protests first began to be raised against the traditional use of images in the worship of Jehovah.[2] One can imagine the addition at such a crisis to an already existing compendium of duty, of a new commandment directed against the use of images; but it is hardly likely that the first sketch of the code would have so late an origin. As little can we believe that so important a phenomenon would make its appearance in the world with so little noise. There was a finding of the book when the Deuteronomic code came into existence. The services of Ezra the scribe, in reducing to written form "the law of Moses," are duly chronicled. And the grandest part of that law, the very essence and kernel of Israel's religion, steals into existence without a father and without a date!

The original form of the Decalogue can only be conjectured. The two versions of it given in Ex. xx. and Deut. v. vary in several particulars, and the probability is that both are expansions of a more primitive version written in the lapidary style suitable to inscriptions on stone. Ewald reproduces the original thus:—

I am Jehovah thy God, who brought thee out of the land of Egypt, out of the house of bondage.

[1] Wellhausen, *History of Israel*, p. 486. "Perhaps to this period the Decalogue also, which is so eloquently silent in regard to cultus, is to be assigned." The period is that to which Micah vi. 1-vii. 6 belongs, which Wellhausen assigns to Manasseh's time. He does not suggest that the author of this passage composed the Decalogue, but one reading this passage naturally asks, Might not the prophetic oracle and the Decalogue proceed from the same hand?

[2] Schultz, *Alttestamentliche Theologie*, p. 199.

I.

1. Thou shalt have no other god before me.
2. Thou shalt not make unto thee any image (Steinbild).
3. Thou shalt not take the name of Jehovah thy God in vain.
4. Thou shalt remember the Sabbath day to sanctify it.
5. Thou shalt honour thy father and thy mother.

II.

1. Thou shalt not kill.
2. Thou shalt not commit adultery.
3. Thou shalt not steal.
4. Thou shalt bear no false witness against thy neighbour.
5. Thou shalt not covet thy neighbour's house.[1]

In what characters was the Decalogue written? The Hebrew alphabet, as we know it, was not then in existence, but that did not make writing for Hebrews impossible. Moses was doubtless acquainted with the hieroglyphic symbols of Egypt, one of the most characteristic features of the religion of mystery. There was also at his command the cuneiform syllabary of Babylon, which recent discoveries at Tel-el-Amarna show to have been in common use at the period.[2] It is even possible that he employed an alphabet current in the Minæan kingdom long anterior to the discovery of the Phœnician alphabet, and supposed by some scholars to be the source of the latter.[3]

The foregoing discussion of the authenticity of the Decalogue has anticipated much of what might be said in

[1] Ewald, *Geschichte des Volkes Israel*, Band II. p. 231. Vatke in his *Einleitung*, 1886, gives a scheme which varies from Ewald's in two particulars. He turns the preface into a commandment = I am Jehovah thy God, and omits the command against images. *Vide* p. 338.

[2] Clay tablets have been found there with inscriptions in cuneiform characters of date 1500 B.C., probably earlier than the Exodus. From these inscriptions it is inferred that at that period there was free literary intercourse between Egypt, Palestine, and Babylon, in the Babylonian language and syllabary.

[3] The Minæan empire is one of the most recent discoveries of Oriental archæology. It occupied the Arabian peninsula at a very ancient date. Archæologists describe the Minæans as a literary people, with an alphabetic

a positive statement concerning its import. It proclaims, as we have seen, a spiritual God, who loves justice and mercy, and rules over all, and it teaches a pure universal morality implying a monotheistic religious basis. But there are one or two other features which must be pointed out in order to make our estimate of its significance complete.

Foremost among these is the exclusion from the funda mental law of Israel—basis of the covenant between her and God—of everything of a merely ritual character, such as circumcision. In this respect there is a striking contrast between the religion of Israel as formulated by Moses, and the religion of Egypt as reflected in the ritual of the dead. In the trial of the soul after death therein described there is a grotesque mixture of merely ritual with moral offences. The tried one protests that he has not been guilty of uncleanness, perjury, injustice, inhumanity; and also that he has not neglected religious ceremonies, extinguished the perpetual lamp, driven off the sacred cattle, netted sacred birds, or robbed the gods of their offered haunches.[1] The fancied protest of the dead reveals the thoughts of the living, and shows that the ancient Egyptians failed to realise the vast gulf which divides moral duties from technical breaches of religious ceremonial. The Decalogue is a proof that Israel, or at least Moses, had mastered the grand distinction. Renan has remarked that the Decalogue is very analogous to the negative confession of the dead in the Egyptian religion.[2] What ought to strike one is not the resemblance, but the contrast. It is one of the points at which we are forced to recognise the wide difference between the religion of nature and the religion of revelation. That God had not left Himself without a

system of writing whence the Phœnician was derived. If this be verified, we shall have to regard Arabia as the primitive home of our modern alphabets. *Vide* article by Professor Sayce in *Contemporary Review*, 1st December 1889.

[1] *The Funereal Ritual*, translated by Dr. Birch, vol. v. of Bunsen's *Egypt's Place in Universal History*, pp. 252, 253.

[2] *Histoire du Peuple d'Israel*, p. 122, vol. i. of the English translation.

witness in the Egyptian conscience, the trial of the dead clearly shows. But that the light within was not unmixed with darkness, the confusion of the moral and the ritual in the same scene not less clearly evinces. In the Decalogue the supremacy of the moral shines with the brightness of the day. The fact of the contrast is patent, explain it as we may.[1]

The purely ethical character of the Decalogue has an important bearing on the question as to the relation of Moses to the ritual legislation recorded in the Pentateuch. In the previous paragraph we were concerned with a contrast between the religion of Israel and that of Egypt. What now invites our attention is a contrast between two different phases of the same religion: Mosaism and Judaism. In whatever relation Moses stood to the Levitical law, it is evident, the Decalogue being witness, that in his view it was of quite secondary importance. The motto of Mosaism was, to obey—moral fidelity—is better than sacrifice. With Judaism, what we may call *neo-Mosaism*, it was otherwise. The secondary with it became primary—or at least co-ordinate. The ritual took its place beside the moral. Not, indeed, that it became an end in itself. The leading aim of Ezra was the same as that of Moses, to make Israel faithful to her God. Ritual was intended to be a hedge to the true religion, to the worship of Jehovah, protecting it against the reinvasion of pagan idolatries. But the prominence given to it with this

---

[1] Critics discover in Ex. xxxiv. 14-26 another Decalogue, also the basis of a covenant, and try to reconstruct it in its original form. Thus Stade (*Geschichte des Volkes Israel*, p. 510) offers the following table :—1. Thou shalt worship no other god ; 2. Thou shalt make no molten image ; 3. Thou shalt keep the feast of unleavened bread ; 4. All the first-born are mine ; 5. Thou shalt keep the Sabbath ; 6. Thou shalt keep the feast of Weeks and Ingathering ; 7. Thou shalt not offer the blood of sacrifice with leavened bread ; 8. Of the Passover offering shall nothing remain till the morning ; 9. Bring firstlings of fruit to the house of Jehovah ; 10. Seethe not a kid in the milk of his mother. A curious mixture ! *Vide* Driver's *Introduction*, p. 37, where Wellhausen's reconstruction is given. The section containing this "Decalogue" belongs to the Jehovistic document.

view involved the risk of its becoming more important than the thing it guarded—a risk which the subsequent career of scribism shows to have been far from imaginary.

In assigning the sovereign place to the ethical, Moses showed himself to be well entitled to the designation of *prophet* conferred upon him by Hosea.[1] He was in spirit the forerunner of the prophets of the eighth century B.C., whose watchword was, not ritual, but righteousness. In this sense we may understand the statement of Jeremiah : "I spake not unto your fathers, nor commanded them in the day that I brought them out of the land of Egypt, concerning burnt offerings or sacrifices: but this thing commanded I them, saying, Obey my voice, and I will be your God, and ye shall be my people."[2] Some take this to mean that the whole Levitical law was post-Mosaic, that no such directions regarding sacrifices and kindred topics as are recorded in the middle books of the Pen tateuch emanated from Moses. This may be too wide an inference, and possibly the prophet's assertion may be only a strong way of saying that ritual had a very subordinate place in the Mosaic legislation, that the thing insisted on was Obedience, in the sense of heart loyalty to Jehovah and fidelity in all relative duties—in other words, compliance with the behests of the Decalogue. So much, however, it must mean if it is not to be robbed of all point and force. Whether, even when so modified, the statement of Jeremiah be compatible with Moses having anything like as much to do with the ritualistic Torah as is implied in the Pentateuchal narrative, is a question not to be lightly put aside. It does seem as if, in order to make the great truth, Obedience before sacrifice, valid, to impress upon a rude people a lesson which even highly civilised peoples are slow to learn,—that morality is of more worth than

[1] Hos. xii. 13 : "By a prophet Jehovah brought Israel out of Egypt." Moses is not named, but just on that account the designation of him as a prophet gains in emphasis.

[2] Jer. vii. 22, 23.

formal compliance with religious rules,—it would be necessary for a man occupying the position of Moses to keep himself aloof from matters of ritual as if they were not in his line, to be almost ostentatiously careless about them, to leave them to be attended to by other and smaller men, priests by profession. One can conceive how it might not be very difficult to pursue such a policy. Priestly ritual, at whatever period reduced to writing, was doubtless in the main of great antiquity. Probably the rules of worship were to a large extent old customs going back into the dim centuries before Moses.[1] In that case there would be no need for new legislation. It would be enough to let well alone, to endorse or countenance existing usage.

This we can conceive Moses doing either cumulatively or in detail, without prejudice to his grand function of prophetic legislator within the sphere of moral law. We can view the principles common to the various law-books, as having the stamp of Mosaic sanction, without assigning to them a place in the proper work of Moses, or raising them to the dignity of being an integral part of Mosaism. We may even go the length of discovering in the Decalogue itself a tacit recognition of ritual. If anywhere, that must be found in the Fourth Commandment, "Remember the Sabbath day." Without doubt, the first thing in the legislator's intention, in connection with the hallowing of that day, is *rest*. That appears plainly in both the versions of the Decalogue. God would have Israelites rest from toil on the seventh day, and above all see to it that all dependent on them had full enjoyment of their rest, reminding them of the time of Egyptian bondage when no resting-day came round, that they might be more considerately humane. It is this kindly provision for the need of the

---

[1] Schultz, *Alttestamentliche Theologie*, p. 461, says: "We will not err if we hold the material out of which the fabric of the ceremonial law is formed—most of the individual customs and usages—as of great antiquity, much older than the Old Testament religion."

labouring million that raises the Fourth Commandment to
the dignity of a moral law. But while rest is the thing
chiefly in view, worship need not be thought of as out of
sight. For right-minded Israelites resting-days will be
worshipping-days, when they will appear before the Lord
with thankful hearts, rejoicing in His goodness and giving
expression to their gladness by such acts as custom pre
scribes. And the "Remember" with which the Sabbath
law begins, may be conceived of as covering the whole
sphere of worship with all its relative usages. In that
case it would follow that Moses recognised the indispensableness of worship institutions for the wellbeing of the
state; and, on the other hand, the slight reserved manner
in which the recognition is made is significant as to the
subordinate relation in which Mosaism places acts of wor
ship to the discharge of moral duty.[1]

From the foregoing observations it will appear that the
question as to the relation of Moses to ritual is not one
which concerns the *existence* of ritual in the time of Moses,
but only the place to be assigned to it in the Mosaic
system. So viewed, it may be discussed with calmness.
The hypothesis that the Deuteronomic and priestly codes
are post-Mosaic, does not necessarily mean that their true
authors *invented* their contents and imputed them to Moses.
It only means that religious customs, mostly ancient, though
in some particulars new, were then reduced to written form
and ascribed to Moses not so much as author, but rather
as authority.[2] But the question, though thus restricted in
scope, is one of great importance for the right understand
ing of the place of Moses in the history of Israel's religion.
We must on no account conceive of that great man as a

---

[1] Riehm, *Alttestamentliche Theologie*, p. 74.

[2] Riehm *Alttestamentliche Theologie*, p. 81, says: "The Mosaic tradi-
s in reference to cultus were preserved by the priests at Shiloh. Written
codes prepared by the priests helped to make these traditions prevail
These codes they ascribed to Moses, but only their spirit and main features
are Mosaic; special features were added by the priests, partly in their own
interest, and many of them remained mere postulates."

person of priestly spirit, or even as belonging to the genus scribe, whereof Ezra is the most respectable representative. We must ever think of him as in vocation and spirit *the Prophet*. And to vindicate for him that character we must strenuously insist that the Decalogue, not the ritual law, is his characteristic contribution.[1] Moses did for his country men two things of quite incomparable value. First, he pointed the lesson of the Exodus, and all that led up to it concerning God. It is not affirmed that he introduced a theoretically new idea of God, but only that prophet-like he improved the occasion, and took out of the events all the instruction they were fitted to convey concerning the nature and character of God. God's self-revelation recorded in Scripture is not doctrinaire, consisting in abstract theological propositions. God revealed Himself in the Egyptian drama of Israel's history, and Moses understood the true import of what had happened, and conveyed it to his people. Next, he taught his people the supreme value of the great fundamental laws of conduct. He did not discover these laws, he did not need to discover them, or to have them for the first time revealed to him on Sinai: they were written on the hearts of all men, Egyptian and Israelite alike. What he learnt for himself and taught Israel was the sovereign importance of these laws. By writing them on stone tablets by themselves he said: thes

---

[1] Vatke (*Die Religion des A. T.*, p. 218) argues against the Mosaic origin of the cultus on the ground that the stiff mechanism of form is never the immediate, that is, cannot belong to the first stage of a religious development. This is a philosophic reason which may have its truth. But the ground on which I lay stress is the ethical or prophetic character o the work of Moses. Just because I agree with those who (like Professor Robertson in his Baird Lectures) argue against the naturalistic school for the ethical character of the Mosaic idea of God, I find it difficult to believe that Moses was the author of the elaborate system of ritual in the middle books of Pentateuch. Modern criticism helps us here by enabling us to form a thoroughly consistent conception of the character of Moses as a prophet and to assign to his work as an originator a simplicity analogous o the simplicity of Christ. Professor Robertson's reasoning from the ethicalism of the prophets to the ethicalism of Moses seems to me conclusive. When h applies his argument to ritual I cannot follow him.

are the things by which nations live and die. Do these
and it shall go well with thee, neglect them and thou shalt
perish. Through these two supreme services: the lesson
on God embodied in the first table of the Decalogue, and
the lesson on duty embodied in the second, Moses laid the
foundations of Israel's national life deep and strong. In
proportion as Israel shared the convictions of her great
hero, she had the consciousness of being a nation; in
proportion as she remained faithful to him would her
national existence be prolonged and her prosperity be
promoted.[1]

Enough has been said to place before the eye in general
outline the nature and value of Mosaism. For this purpose
use has been made of two contrasts: one between the
Decalogue and the Egyptian ritual of the dead, and another
between Moses and Ezra in relation to Leviticalism. To
make the picture complete, it may be well to advert briefly
to a third contrast, that between the Jehovah of the Deca
logue and the Baal of pagan Semitic religions. Jehovah
has no other gods beside Him or before His face, neither
male deities nor *female*. The Baal divinities of pagan
Semitic peoples, Babylonians, Phœnicians, Canaanites, have
all their female companions. Sexuality is a radical characteristic of deity as conceived by these peoples. That
means sensuality introduced into religion, sexual prostitu
tion erected into an act of worship, whereby Semitic
paganism becomes stamped with an exceptional vileness.
What a contrast is here in the idea of God, and what

---

[1] After quoting Kuenen's view that the great merit of Moses was that he
placed the service of Jehovah on a moral footing, Canon Cheyne, in a review of
Canon Driver's "Introduction" in the *Expositor* of February 1892, remarks :
"This surely ought to satisfy the needs of *essential orthodoxy*. For what
conservatives want, or ought to want, is not so much to prove the veracity
of Israelitish priests, when they ascribed certain ordinances to Moses, as to
show that Moses had high intuitions of God and of morality. In a word,
they want, or they ought to want, to contradict the view that the religion of
Israel, at any rate between Moses and Amos, in no essential respect differed
from that of Moab, Ammon, and Edom, Israel's nearest kinsfolk and
neighbours."

diverse fruit it must bear in social life, on one side severe
purity, on the other revolting, unmentionable vice! Whence
this vast difference between Israel and peoples to which she
is close of kin in blood and language? It is a fact con
firmatory of the hypothesis of election, tending to show that
the election of a people to be the recipient and vehicle of
the true religion, was at once very necessary and very
re: '

One thing is conspicuous by its absence in Mosaism : all
refer ice to the state after death. The fact has o ten been
commented on and explanations of it have been attempted
One thing is certain, the omission cannot be due ωο ωω
dea of a life beyond the grave not having been present to
the mind. No one could have lived in Egypt even for a
short time without hearing of the underworld with ωω
states of bliss and woe, and becoming familiar w ι the arts
of embalming by which the Egyptians, in a fu l , child....
battle with corruption, sought to endow even the body with
immortality, and to put the soul of the deceased in th
same position as if death had not taken place.   ero(
gives to the Egyptians the credit of being the first to teach
the doctrine that the soul is immortal,[1] and the mummies
found in the most ancient monuments show that the ʰ
was older than the time of Moses. Why, then, had the
Hebrew legislator nothing to say on the subject .   ro
bably just because the Egyptians had so much. He   em l
it better to have no doctrine of a hereafter at all than such a
loc ne as prevailed in the land of bondage. That gloomy
underworld presided over by a dead div   y, l
bidding judgment scene in the hall of ——   two truths that
"smal dogma of the transmigration of souls, that ghas'ˡʸ
practice of embalming—these were all things it were
b tte to get banished from the mind. The religion of
E ypt has been appropriately called the religion of death.
Fror such a religion the healthy Hebrew nature would
instinctively recoil Hence the expressive silence as to

: *Historia*, ii. 123.

the state beyond in the religion of Moses, which may with equal propriety be called the religion of life. Instead of a dead divinity judge of men after dissolution, it places a living divinity, who has done great things for Israel in grace and mercy, in the forefront of the law which seeks to regulate life on earth. Instead of saying, Live well, for remember, Osiris will judge you, it says rather, Live well, for the Lord thy God brought thee out of the land of Egypt. Instead of promising a life of bliss in the next world, which is but a shadow of the life on earth, it pro mises rather as the reward of well-doing national prosperity in the present world. Fear God, said Moses in effect to Israel, " fear God, and do good, so shalt thou dwell in the land, and thou shalt be fed; and for the rest leave yourself in God's hands. When you die, commit your soul to Him who gave it, and leave your body not to the embalmers, but to friends to bury it in the dust."

It has been suggested that the Exodus was the finale of a great religious war between the Hebrews and the Egyp tians.[1] It may appear a hazardous conjecture, though the references in the Pentateuch to the gods of Egypt as involved in the judgments executed on the people, seem to offer some foundation for it.[2] But the two religions were certainly very antagonistic in spirit, and when peoples cherishing so entirely diverse ideas about God and man, and life and death, live together in the same land, rupture must come sooner or later. Each must go its own way, and the two ways lead in very different directions. The way of Israel leads to light and imperishable blessing for the world; the way of Egypt leads to decay and death everlasting.

---

[1] Ewald, *Geschichte des Volkes Israel*, Band II. p. 80.
[2] Ex. xv. 11 ; Num. iii. 4.

CHAPTER V.

PROPHETISM.

LITERATURE.—Ewald, *Die Propheten des Alten Bundes;* Tholuck *Die Propheten und ihre Weissagungen;* Kuenen, *Prophets and Prophecy in Israel;* Koenig, *der Offenbarungsbegriff des Alten Testaments;* Robertson Smith, *The Prophets of Israel;* Reuss, *La Bible (Les Prophetes);* Duhm *Die Theologie der Propheten;* Duff, *Old Testament Theology;* Darmesteter, *Les Prophetes d'Israel* (a series of reviews, the first of chief importance), 1892; Renan, *Histoire du Peuple d'Israel,* vol. iii.

Mosaism, as a distinct phase of Israel's religious history, may be regarded as extending from the Exodus to the eighth century B.C., covering a period of some 600 years. During that long stretch of time Mosaic ideas worked ᴜᴋᴄ a ferment among the chosen people, ever tending to make them in thought and conduct a people answering to the divine purpose in calling them. It is needless to say that throughout these centuries, and especially those immediately following the conquest of Canaan, the Mosaic programme —Israel a holy nation in covenant with Jehovah, the one true righteous God—remained to a large extent an un realised ideal. The realisation, even approximately, of lofty ideals is never the work of a day. It was to be expected that the height of inspiration reached by a prophetic mind, at a great crisis like the Exodus, would not be sustained. Lapse to a lower moral and religious level was inevitable. It would not surprise us to find the "holy nation of Gods purpose scarce conscious of being a nation, far from holiness, and very unmindful of the Jehovah who brought their fathers out of the land of Egypt. Such were the facts regarding Israel during the period of the "Judges. I ᵛ was an obscure time of rude beginnings, of which the book of Judges gives a graphic and, in general outline if not in all details, true life-like picture. It is an interesting and hopeful story, in spite of its barbarisms, political, moral, and religious; for it is the story not of a corrupt effete nation drawing nigh to its end, but of a young people in the act of forming itself into a nation; abounding in the virtues and also in the faults of youth; too independent to tolerate a central authority; ever ready to fight with the old occupants of Canaan, yet only too accessible to the fascinations of their evil religious customs; capable of great moral excesses, yet not without a certain robustness of conscience that can be roused into indignation and swift vengeance by a crime which outrages natural feeling.

At the close of this dark age of beginnings appeared a faithful representative of Mosaism, under whose influence and guidance the fortunes of the chosen people took a new turn. Samuel did two things for Israel. He recalled her to her allegiance to Jehovah, and he made her feel as she had never done before that she was one people. The sense of national unity took practical shape in the desire for a king, and for a hundred years the twelve tribes enjoyed the happy, proud consciousness of forming a strong united kingdom under the reigns of Saul, David, and Solomon. But experience proved that it was as difficult to find a perfectly just wise king ruling in the fear of God and for the general good, as to be a holy nation. Bonds recently cemented are easily broken, and unjust partial government provokes rebellion. So it came to pass that national unity was soon disrupted, and two rival kingdoms took the place of one. The true religion, or indeed anything good, was not likely to flourish under such circumstances. Of the years which followed the rupture we know little, and what is recorded is far from satisfactory. The first bright event relieving the gloom of an evil time is the appearance of the heroic prophetic figure of Elijah the Tishbite, in the reign of Ahab, King of Israel. His task was to affirm with tremendous emphasis the truth: Jehovah the one God in Israel, against the king, who, having married a Tyrian princess, thought good to associate with Jehovah,

as an object of worship, the Tyrian divinity Baal. To
king and people this act might seem nothing more than a
courteous compliance with custom towards the gods of a
friendly nation, which could not well be avoided if Israel
was not to be entirely isolated. But Elijah cared nothing
for state courtesies and expediencies. He was jealous for
Jehovah's honour, and believed and taught that Jehovah
was a jealous God who would brook no rival, so doing his
best to bring his countrymen back to the Mosaic ideal:
"Thou shalt have no other gods before me."

Elijah's zeal would have been much ado about nothing
if the Jehovah he championed had been a mere physical
deity like the gods of the pagan Semites. It would then
have been a question between him and Ahab whether one
or two divinities of the same sort were to be worshipped
in the land. Elijah might in that case have been the
better patriot, more faithful than Ahab to the national
spirit and traditions, but no moral interest would have
been involved in the quarrel. The question between the
prophet and the king was of vital moment only if Jehovah,
as the former conceived Him, was a different kind of god
from Baal; not a mere national god, but a God with a
definite moral character, to whom righteousness was the
supreme interest. If such was the God Elijah believed in,
he did well to resist the introduction of other deities in
his jealousy for Jehovah. To place Baal beside Jehovah
was to rob Jehovah of His distinctive character, and to
degrade Him to the level of a merely national deity.
Jealousy is a just feeling in the worshippers of an ethical
god as it is an appropriate attribute of the god they
worship. To say of God that He is jealous is to affirm
that moral distinctions are real for Him, and to impute
jealousy to His worshippers is to say in effect that the
ethical interest in religion is the thing of supreme concern
to them. So we must understand the zeal of Elijah. It
was not the zeal of a patriot merely; it was the zeal of a
man who cared above all things for justice and purity and

all the moral interests covered by the Decalogue. The key to his character and public conduct may be found in his denunciation of the wickedness of Ahab in taking forcible possession of Naboth's vineyard. There we see what all along he has been aiming at in his uncompromis ing opposition to Baal. He will have Israel worship alone that God who loves right and hates ill, and suffers no iniquity to go unpunished, even though it be perpetrated by powerful rulers against defenceless subjects.

Can it be, as critics allege, that this man tolerated the worship of Jehovah by images? If he did, it must have been because the supposed existing practice in that respect did not appear to him as compromising the moral character of Jehovah. The question is not of vital im portance, unless it be assumed that the worship of Jehovah under the form of an ox necessarily implies that Jehovah was conceived of as a physical divinity like Baal. We are not, however, shut up to this position. The ox might be simply a symbol like the cherubim, and symbolism in religion, whatever its dangers, is not incompatible with the spirituality of the object of worship. But take the case at its worst. Grant that, as a matter of fact, the ox was to be seen in the days of Elijah in the provincial sanctuaries devoted to the worship of Jehovah, and that its presence there was contrary to the spirit of Mosaism as expressed in the Decalogue, and not without peril to the pure wor ship of Israel's God, and that Elijah looked on and said nothing. What then? Does it follow that he altogether approved? No, but only that his attention was absorbed by a far greater evil. First get rid of Baal, the foul divinity of Tyre, then there may be time to attend to the minor abuse of images in the sanctuaries of Jehovah.[1]

Elijah's protest produced important immediate results, but

[1] Professor Robertson, advocating this view of Elijah's conduct, and comparing his action with that of the later prophets who waged war with images, illustrates the situation by a historic parallel. "The two crises are very much like those which Europe passed through in its religious history—first the struggle as to whether the Crescent or the Cross should be the recognised

it wrought no permanent deliverance. The kings and people of Israel went on in their evil way, so that after the lapse of a century it was becoming evident to observing minds that the nation was ripening for judgment just when Providence was preparing in the East the instrument of her punishment. The situation offered a splendid oppor tunity for the reaffirmation of the principles of Mosaism, with fresh inspiration, and with new developments adapted to the novel circumstances. Such was the service rendered by the prophets of the eighth century B.C.

We must be careful neither to overestimate nor to underestimate the achievement of these remarkable men, with whose general religious ideas we have already made ourselves acquainted. On the one hand, it is an exaggera tion to say that the prophets converted Jehovah from a physical into an ethical deity. It is, of course, a postulate of naturalism that the objects of worship must be first physical and only at a later stage in the evolution of religion become ethical personalities, and it must be ad mitted that there is much in the history of religion to justify the assumption. In the case of Greece, *e.g.*, the gods worshipped at Dodona and Olympus in the ancient Pelasgic period—Zeus, Apollo, and Pallas—were simply objects of nature personified. By the time of Homer these and other physical divinities of the primitive time had become humanised and more or less transformed into august beings endowed with moral characteristics. Zeus, originally the blue heaven, had become the father of gods and men, the ruler over all, the god of moral order. It is not improbable that the nomadic ancestors of Israel in prehistoric times were, like the Aryan races, nature-wor shippers, and that spiritual conceptions of godhead were a later acquisition. What is contended for is that the trans-

symbol of superiority, and then the Reformation of religion from its own abuses in the sixteenth century."—*Early Religion of Israel*, pp. 226, 227. Duhm points out that Hosea was the first to condemn worship of Jehovah by images. *Vide Die Theologie der Propheten*, p. 101.

formation was not reserved for the eighth century B.C. It came much earlier, at least as early as the time of Moses. The ideality of God, that He is spirit, that He possesses a definite moral character, was an article in the Mosaic creed, and this faith, more or less clearly apprehended, formed an element in the religious consciousness of the best minds in Israel from the days of Moses onwards,[1] though doubtless it had to maintain an incessant struggle for recognition against lower and cruder views. In proclaiming an ethically-conceived Jehovah, therefore, the great prophets were not discoverers of an absolutely new truth : they were only reaffirmers with new emphasis of the hereditary faith of Israel, the beneficent source of all that was good in her history since the time of the Exodus.

"Reaffirmers," but certainly with new emphasis, and with an intensity of conviction and a width of comprehension which made the old faith practically a new revelation. The prophets of the eighth century are not to be conceived of as mere echoes or tame, servile interpreters of Moses. They were the recipients of fresh inspiration, and delivered their message, whether in substance new or old, as if the truth they announced had never been heard of before. Their thoughts were always subjectively original, even when objectively familiar. Compared with Mosaism their doctrine was, to a considerable extent, even objectively distinctive. The difference corresponds to diversity of situation. Moses, standing at the beginning of Israel's history, was naturally concerned about making his people a nation with Jehovah for their own covenant God. Hence he laid emphasis, not on Jehovah's universal relations to the world, but rather on His special relation to the chosen race. Not "Jehovah who chose you is the God of all," but "the God of all, Jehovah, chose you," was his message to the men whom he brought out of the land of bondage.

---

[1] Vatke maintains that the ideality of God, at least in abstract or germinal form, was an element of Mosaism. *Vide Die Religion des Alten Testaments*, p. 230.

That Jehovah was the God over all was shown by the marvellous events through which the redemption of Israel was accomplished; yet these events only tended to give prominence to the national aspect of Jehovah's character. Through them He punished the Egyptians for wrongs inflicted on His oppressed people. The prophets, on the other hand, in their situation, quite as naturally gave prominence to the universal aspect. The whole known world was astir with movements of which Israel was the centre. In the political life of the nations they saw one Mind and Will at work, and the thought was borne in upon them with irresistible force, "Jehovah is God over all." Then what did the events that were happening or impending mean? Not Jehovah judging the nations for Israel's sake, but Jehovah using the nations to punish Israel for her sins. On this side also the universal aspect rather than the special comes to the front.

Thus far of the contrast between Mosaism and Prophetism in reference to the idea of God. There is also a contrast between them in their respective relations to ethical interests. Moses in his position naturally became a prophetic legislator. It was his task to codify duty for the guidance of an infant nation. The prophets, coming on the scene far down in the history of the same people, had to perform the part of moral critics. While Moses set before the Israel of the Exodus the moral ideal, the prophets told the Israel of six centuries later how far short she came of realising the ideal. The prophetic era was not the time for framing a Decalogue: that is the proper work of the initial epoch; it was rather the time for testing conduct by a recognised moral standard, a function which the prophets performed with an unswerving fidelity and a burning moral enthusiasm that show how brightly the moral ideal shone before their spiritual eye.

It is to this latter aspect of the prophetic vocation that we are now more particularly to direct our attention. We are to make ourselves acquainted with the characteristics of the prophets viewed as moral critics of their time.

1. The first grand fundamental feature to be noted in this connection is the *passion for righteousness* with which all the prophets were consumed as if by a divine fire burning in their hearts. In most men the moral sense is so feeble that it is difficult for them to understand or sympathise with this feature of the prophetic character. Hence prophetic men, since the world began, have never been understood or appreciated in their own time. They have been deemed fools, madmen, revolutionists, impious miscreants; anything but what they were: the wisest, the noblest, the truest in their generation. Against such there has ever been a law of convention and moral mediocrity, which condemns the unusually good with not less severity and confidence than the unusually evil. Happily the world slowly wakens up to the fact that a few unusually good, wise, and earnest men now and then appear, and recognises them as such after they are dead, though it cannot endure them when living. To this "goodly fellowship" belonged the Hebrew prophets; and that they were of this type and temper is the first fact to be laid to heart concerning them if we would understand their character, vocation, and life-work. There have been men of the same type and temper in other lands, in all ages; such men exist in the world still; it would be a wretched world without them, for they are the very salt of the earth. But the Hebrew prophets are the first and best of their kind: men of absolutely unparalleled moral earnestness.

2. To this subjective disposition the prophets united a congruous faith in an objective moral order, in a power not themselves making for righteousness, in a living God who was at least as earnest as themselves in loving right and hating wrong, and wielding His power for the advancement of the one and the repression of the other. This morally earnest God, they believed, exercised a just benign rule over all peoples dwelling on the face of the earth.

Hence they did not, as moral critics, confine their attention to the conduct of Israel, though for obvious reasons that was the most frequent subject of their animadversions. They had a word of God for all the nations in turn. Their prophetic messages did not actually reach the nations con cerned. They were really intended for the ear of Israel, as moral lessons in the grand doctrine of an absolutely universal, impartial moral order, enforced by the just will of Jehovah. The judgments on Babylon, Egypt, Tyre, etc., were a concrete way of saying to their countrymen: God is just; He will not suffer wrong permanently to prosper; therefore fear ye and sin not. The chief interest to us, as to those to whom these prophecies of doom were first spoken, lies in the breadth and power with which God's moral government is asserted. Not in the accuracy with which the fate of the nations was predicted, revealing a miracle of prophetic foresight, lies the abiding value of these oracles, but in the fact that all nations are brought within the sweep of the divine moral order. That the fate predicted did overtake the nations is satisfactory evidence that the prophetic faith in that order was not mistaken.[1]

3. It was to be expected that men possessed with a passion for righteousness would place morality above religious ritual, and have for their watchword not holiness but righteousness. Such was the fact in the case of all the prophets, distinctive characteristics notwithstanding. It has been remarked that, while in Amos the ethical element is supreme, in Hosea the religious element is in the ascendant.[2] The statement has its relative truth, but

---

[1] The predictive aspect of prophecy almost exclusively occupied the attention of the older apologists. Predictions marvellously fulfilled, even to the minutest details, supplied for them welcome evidence that the pro phets were the divinely accredited messengers of a doctrinal revelation. This view is now allowed to retire into the background, and the best evidence that God spoke through the prophets is found in the high ethical character of their teaching. Vide on this *The Chief End of Revelation*, chap. v.

[2] So Duhm in *Die Theologie der Propheten*, p. 127.

not in a sense implying that Hosea placed ritual above righteousness. It is Hosea that says: " I desired mercy, and not sacrifice ; and the knowledge of God more than burnt offerings." [1] In few words this expresses the com mon attitude of the prophets. Nothing is more frequent and more familiar in the prophetic writings than con temptuous reference to careful performance of religious duties by a people far from God and righteousness in heart and life.

This anti-ritualistic polemic of the prophets is not decisive as to the non-Mosaicity of the Levitical law. Even if the priestly code, as we find it in the middle books of the Pentateuch, had been an exact record of Mosaic legislation for the regulation of worship, and recognised as such by the prophets, and the religious services of their contemporaries had been down to the minutest detail in scrupulous accordance with the rubric, their verdict would have been the same. When Amos, in God's name says: " I hate, I despise your fast days, and I will not smell in your solemn assemblies. Though ye offer me burnt offerings and your meat offerings, I will not accept them : neither will I regard the peace offerings of your fat beasts," [2] he does not necessarily mean to characterise these acts as mere will-worship, an unauthorised and therefore unacceptable system of religious ceremonial. The question put in a subsequent verse : " Did ye bring unto me sacrifices and offerings in the wilderness forty years, O house of Israel? " [3] does seem to point that way, and, with the similar statement of Jeremiah,[4] must be taken into account by those who contend for the Mosaic origin of the Levitical ritual. The point insisted on here is that the denuncia tions hurled by the prophets at the religion of their con temporaries is not a conclusive argument on the negative side of that question. However orthodox or regular it might be, they would have spoken of it in the same scornful

---

[1] Hos. vi. 6.   [2] Amos v. 21, 22.
[3] Amos v. 25.   [4] Jer. vii. 22, 23.

style, so long as it was associated with an unrighteous life. Their animadversions were not directed against a self-invented worship in the interest of worship according to rule, but against all religion, orthodox or heterodox, divorced from right conduct. If the ritual was in itself legitimate, so much the more pronounced does their zeal for the ethical *versus* the religious element appear. And we must not hesitate to credit them with the courage to assert their great principle,—the supremacy of the moral,—even at the risk of their seeming to be guilty of irreverence. They claimed unrestricted liberty of prophesying. They did not hold themselves bound by each other's opinions. The prophets of one generation might modify or cancel the oracles of those of a preceding generation. If Elijah tolerated images in the worship of Jehovah, that was no reason why Hosea should not denounce the calves. If Isaiah's watchword was the inviolability of Zion, that was no reason why Jeremiah should not utter the word of doom against the temple. Like Christ, the prophets could dare on due occasion even to criticise Moses: witness their reversal of the adage concerning the fathers eating sour grapes, in contradiction to the traditional and pre sumably Mosaic doctrine that the sins of fathers are visited on their children to the third and fourth generations.[1] They recognised no standard of unchangeable orthodoxy : the one law they owned was that of loyally following the present light vouchsafed by heaven to their own souls.

Nothing is more remarkable in the prophetic character than an exquisite sensitiveness to everything savouring of insincerity. It revealed itself in the abhorrence, justly com mented on, of all religion divorced from right conduct. It showed itself equally in a careful avoidance of whatever approached untruthfulness in religious language. The prophets considered it a sin to echo current opinion even when true. Jeremiah stigmatises the practice as stealing God's word every one from his neighbour.[2] He

---

[1] Ex. xxxiv. 7.   [2] Jer. xxiii. 30.

held, and all the prophets held, that a prophet ought to speak at first hand; not what had come to his ear through hearsay, but what God had revealed to his own heart. To repeat the thought of another, and say, He saith, was a practical lie: it was giving out as a personal conviction what had been slavishly accepted on authority. For a similar reason the prophets, Jeremiah again being witness, regarded with loathing the continued use of pious phrases which had ceased to represent conviction. "The burden of the Lord" is the instance given. What that phrase ought to mean! what it did mean to the genuine prophet, as when he had to foretell the approaching ruin of his country! And yet how lightly the burden lay on many to whom the next prophetic oracle was only a matter of idle curiosity. No wonder the sorrow-laden man of God uttered his stern interdict against the further use of a cant phrase, saying, "The burden of the Lord shall ye mention no more."[1]

Two remarks more may be added before passing from the present topic. One is that in putting morality above ritual the prophets were true to the spirit of Mosaism, whose grand monument is the Decalogue, wherein ritual has no place. With Moses, as with the prophets, morality was primary, ritual secondary. In taking up this position both Moses and the prophets rose far above the level of heathenism, to which a breach of ritual has ever appeared at least as serious as a departure from the laws of justice and mercy. It was a great step onwards and upwards in the moral development of humanity, when differentiation of the two kinds of action began to take place, and it was recognised that it was a worse thing to kill, or steal, or lie, than to make a slight mistake in religious ceremonial. That first step was taken by Moses, and the prophets only followed his lead when they strove by unwearied iteration to indoctrinate their countrymen in the great truth that justice and mercy are better than sacrifice. It is the

[1] Jer. xxiii. 36.

lesson of the Scriptures from beginning to end, yet Chris tendom, accepting them as the rule of faith and practice, is far even now from having thoroughly learned it.

The other observation has reference to the question, How far had the literary prophets a hand in bringing about changes in religious practice, such as the abolition of pro vincial sanctuaries and the concentration of worship in the one central sanctuary? The question is mixed up with debateable matters of criticism into which I cannot enter. The point I desire to make is that whatever line of action the prophets may have pursued in connection with religious reform, it would have for its guiding motive regard to ethical interests. They would strike into the movement because they saw that grievous moral abuses were con nected with the existing customs. This remark applies even to Hosea. The sin he denounces is not idolatry in the abstract, but idolatry associated with the moral licence of Canaanitish and pagan Semitic worship. "Whoredom and wine and new wine take away the heart;"[1] how suggestive these words of Dionysiac orgies, accompanied with drunken excesses and shameless sacred prostitution! Who, duly concerned for temperance and purity, would not wish these "holy fairs" put down?

4. It is important to note that the moral ideal of the prophets, while high, is thoroughly healthy and genial. Two features are specially noteworthy—the spirit of com passion which breathes through all prophetic utterances, and the entire absence from them of any trace of asceticism. The prophets are the champions of the poor and needy against the powerful and the proud, and yet while sternly demanding, even from kings, the practice of justice and mercy, they have nothing to say against a man enjoying life according to his station. The classic utterance here is that of Micah: To the man who inquires what God requires of him, imagining that some terrible sacrifices are included among the divine demands, the prophet replies:

[1] Hos. iv. 11.

" He hath shewed thee, O man, what is good; and what doth the Lord require of thee, but to do justly, and to love mercy, and to walk humbly with thy God ? "[1] Not less significant is the language addressed to a luxurious selfish monarch by the prophet Jeremiah : " Shalt thou reign, because thou closest thyself in cedar ? Did not thy father eat and drink, and do judgment and justice, and then it was well with him ? He judged the cause of the poor and needy ; then it was well with him. Was not this to know me ? saith the Lord." [2] Do justly and love mercy, and for the rest enjoy life within the limits of wise moderation, what a thoroughly reasonable scheme of conduct ! The prophets anticipated modern altruism, and understood that the service of others and the enjoyment of personal happiness are perfectly compatible. It never entered into their minds that ascetic renunciations and self-tortures, such as were practised both before and after their time in India, could benefit any one. How much healthier the Hebrew moral ideal than that of the Brahmans and the Buddhists.

5. For men of such moral intensity as characterised the prophets, trials of their faith in the righteous government of God were inevitable. For the moral order of the world is slow, if sure, in its action, and while just on the whole seems far from just in many particular instances. Such trials are appointed for all earnest believers in God, and they fell upon the prophets in the most acute form just because they were so tremendously in earnest in believing that Jehovah was righteous in all His ways. Moses, the first of the prophets, was no exception to this statement. At the period of the Exodus, indeed, Providence appeared to be at his bidding. Said, done, was the order of the day. There was hardly time to pray before needed aid came. " Wherefore criest thou unto me ? speak unto the children of Israel, that they go forward." [3] The hour of deliverance had come, and Providence was wide awake. But a long dreary period of oppression had gone before,

[1] Micah vi. 8.   [2].Jer. xxii. 15, 16.   [3] Ex. xiv. 15.

when the God of Israel seemed asleep, or indifferent, or
impotent.   That was for Moses a time of patient waiting
in the Arabian desert, nursing patriotic hope and watching
for the dawn.   Such waiting on God is a notable feature
in the experience of all men destined to leave their mark
on the world's history.   The men of the Bible knew it
well.   Prophets and psalmists often speak of it in language
thrilling with emotion, teaching that we have to wait on
God, and that it is worth our while to wait.   " I will wait
upon Jehovah, that hideth His face from the house of
Jacob," [1] writes Isaiah, pointing to good for Israel fervently
desired, but for a season withheld.   " Blessed are all they
that wait for Him," [2] writes the same prophet in a later
prophecy, conveying the confident assurance that God
will not permanently disappoint the expectation of those
who trust Him.   To these utterances all Old Testament
prophecy says Amen.

    Nothing is more admirable than the perfect candour with
which the prophets lay bare their hearts, and reveal the
struggle going on there between faith and doubt occasioned
by the absence of a perfect correspondence between conduct
and lot.   Two prophets of the Chaldean period, Jeremiah
and Habakkuk, are conspicuous in this respect.   Jeremiah
writes : " Righteous art Thou, O Lord, when I plead with
Thee.   Yet let me talk with Thee of Thy judgments :
Wherefore doth the way of the wicked prosper ? wherefore
are all they happy that deal very treacherously ?   Thou
hast planted them, yea, they have taken root : they grow,
yea, they bring forth fruit.   Thou art near in their mouth,
and far from their reins.   But Thou, O Lord, knowest me :
Thou hast seen me, and tried mine heart towards Thee." [3]
In the same spirit Habakkuk complains : " Art Thou not
from everlasting, O Lord my God, mine Holy One ?   We
shall not die.   O Lord, Thou hast ordained them for
judgment ; and, O mighty God, Thou hast established them
for correction.   Thou art of purer eyes than to behold

---

[1] Isa. viii. 17.   [2] Isa. xxx. 18. .   [3] Jer. xii. 1–3.

evil, and canst not look on iniquity: wherefore lookest
Thou upon them that deal treacherously, and holdest Thy
tongue when the wicked devoureth the man that is more
righteous than he?"[1] Jeremiah's perplexity arises from
the contrast between the prosperity of evil men within
Israel and the tribulations which have overtaken himself,
a man conscious of entire devotion to God's service. What
Habakkuk wonders at is that a nation like the Chaldeans
is permitted to crush a people like Israel, with all her
faults greatly superior to her oppressor, and containing
many persons faithful to God and to righteousness. In
both cases the problem is more or less distinctly one of
individual experience. Both prophets virtually ask, Why
should I, and others like me, fare so ill at the hands of
godless men, fellow-countrymen or foreigners, who seem to
have the power to do whatever they please? It was
about the time of Jeremiah that the problem began to
assume the individual form, a fact which may be used as
a canon of criticism for fixing the dates of the book of
Job, and of many of the Psalms in which the puzzling
questions of human life are looked at from the individual
point of view. It is when thus viewed that these questions
become most perplexing. It is never very difficult to
answer the question, Why does a nation suffer? There is
always seen in the best nation a sufficient amount of
misconduct to lend at least plausibility to the suggestion
that she suffers for her sins. But when great calamity
falls on a man like Job, described as " perfect and upright,
one that feared God and eschewed evil," or like Jeremiah,
able to call God to bear witness to his moral fidelity, the
sense of disharmony between character and lot becomes
very acute, and the need for a theodicy very pressing.
We cannot claim for the prophets and psalmists, or for the
unknown author of the book of Job, that they give us a
perfect solution of the problem, though here and there
hints of the true solution are traceable. But we may

[1] Hab. i. 12, 13.

Q

claim for them that they have adequately stated the difficulty, not merely by what they say, but by what they were. They were noble, leal-hearted, morally faithful men, with a lofty, exacting ideal of life, to which amid all temptation they remained true; perfect in the scriptural sense of being single-minded, while not free from defects and infirmities. Yet, one and all, they had a poor time of it in this world, from a eudæmonistic point of view. "So persecuted they the prophets." What does it all mean? that is the question they handed on to Christ for answer.

6. It is by their passion for righteousness, and their invincible faith in a righteous Ruler of the world, that the prophets are a living witness to the reality of a divine revelation given to Israel; by these, and by their magnifi cent optimism, to be considered in the next chapter. The apologetic value of Hebrew prophecy does not lie in predictions of future events capable of being used as miraculous buttresses to the Christian faith. Prediction is a feature of prophecy, could not fail to be; for what could men who with their whole soul believed in a moral order of the world do but declare that if sin was persisted in punishment would certainly follow? But prediction is, nevertheless, a subordinate feature of prophecy, and the prophets did not predict in order to supply apologists with arguments in support of a supernatural revelation. The prophets were before all things inspired witnesses to the reality of a divine kingdom. They were witnesses to their own time, each man speaking to his own generation, in language suggested by, and suitable to, the existing circum stances. The value of their witness lies in its perfect adaptation to the times. They did not speak before their message was needed, before their heart was made to burn by the moral situation to which they addressed themselves; and hence they spoke with freshness, with fervour, and with poetic felicity. We have, therefore, no interest in taking the conservative side on such a question as that relating to the date and authorship of the second part of

the book of Isaiah. Our interest lies rather in the opposite direction. These marvellous utterances have far more value when viewed as proceeding from an unknown prophet of the exile speaking to his fellow-captives by the rivers of Babylon of the mercies of God in store for Israel. We lose, doubtless, a miracle of foresight in the form of a prediction of deliverance through Cyrus, but we gain a moral miracle of faith and hope amid circumstances tempting to despair. Isaiah of Jerusalem foretelling the advent of Cyrus two centuries or thereby before the time would be a wonderful *vaticinator ;* but an unknown prophet of the exile speaking comfortably to Jerusalem in her desola tion is a moral hero, who, by the strength of his spirit, the depth of his sympathy, and the greatness of his expecta tion is a convincing proof that better days are in store for Israel, and for the world. His value lies in what he is, in what God by His illuminating Spirit enables him to be, not in what he says about Cyrus or anybody else.

The impression made by the oracles of Hebrew prophets as assertors of the moral government of God, is not weakened by comparison with the utterances of kindred spirits among other peoples, such as the Persians, the Chinese, and the Greeks. Zarathustra taught his country men to believe in a kingdom of righteousness, presided over by the wise spirit, Ahura-Mazda, whom it was the highest duty and blessedness of men to serve. The Chinese book of Odes contains many poems teaching the reality of a divine government, and not a few dealing with the dark, mysterious side of Providence in a manner which reminds one of those passages in Old Testament literature, wherein prophets and psalmists wrestle with doubts as to the justice of God, occasioned by the prosperity of the wicked and the evil lot of good men. The extant writings of the Greek tragedians abound in powerful affirmations of an all-pervasive moral order. In all three cases there is enough light to show that God had not left Himself with- out a witness to His righteousness. But compared with the light which shone in Israel, that vouchsafed to the three peoples named in the wisest sayings of their sages is dim. To save the goodness of Ahura-Mazda, Zarathustra found it necessary to invent an anti-god, Angri-mainyus, who should be responsible for all the evil in the world. There is no dualism in Hebrew prophecy ; in the unknown prophet of the exile there is an express repudiation of it, as if with conscious reference to the creed of the Persians: " I form the light, and create darkness ; I make peace, and create evil." [1] The Chinese poets do their best to vindicate the divine character against all suspicions of unrighteousness or indifference, arising out of untoward appearances. But they come far short of the Hebrew prophets, both in their perception of the mysteriousness of the problem and in their solution. In their easy, shallow theodicy they resemble Job's friends, who thought the clearing of God's character a very simple affair, rather than Job himself, who was profoundly conscious that God's way was in the sea. The following stanza may serve as a sample :—[2]

> "How great is God, who ruleth men below !
>   In awful terrors now arrayed.
> His dealings seem a recklessness to show,
>   From which we, shuddering, shrink dismayed.
> But men at first from Heaven their being drew,
>   With nature liable to change.
> All hearts in infancy are good and true,
>   But time and things those hearts derange."

God being thus cleared, the poet goes on to lay the blame of existing calamity on the king and his ministers. In another poem a famine is represented as a judgment on the king for employing worthless characters as ministers : [3]

> "'Twas merit once that riches gained ;
>   The case how different now.
> Troubles through all our time have reigned,
>   And greater still they grow

---

[1] Isa. xlv. 7.

[2] Taken from the *She-King ; or, The Book of Poetry*, translated into English by Dr. Legge. *Vide Chinese Classics*, iii. 321.

[3] *She-King*, p. 349.

> Like grain unhulled, those men in place,
> Like fine rice those who find no grace.
> Ye villains of yourselves retire,
> Why thus prolong my grief and ire."

Æschylus, Sophocles, and Euripides grandly proclaimed the doctrine of Nemesis, teaching their countrymen in their own dialect that God resisteth the proud, and giveth grace unto the lowly.[1] But in the background of their picture of human life is the dark figure of fate, a blind force exercising sway over both gods and men, without regard to character or moral interests. This pagan conception has nothing answering to it in Hebrew prophecy.

CHAPTER VI.

PROPHETIC OPTIMISM.

LITERATURE.—Principal Fairbairn (of Glasgow), *Prophecy;* Matthew Arnold, *Literature and Dogma;* Adeney, *The Hebrew Utopia;* Orelli, *Die Alttestamentliche Weissagung von der Vollendung des Gottesreichs* (translated by T. & T. Clark); Riehm, *Die Messianische Weissagung,* 2nd ed. (translated); Briggs, *Messianic Prophecy;* Delitzsch, *Messianische Weissagungen in Geschichtlichen Folge* (translated). *Vide* also Duhm's work; and Oehler, *Die Theologie des ATs.;* and Schultz, *Alttest. Th ol.*

Not less conspicuous in the character of the prophets than their passion for righteousness is the buoyant hopefulness with which they contemplate the future. Their writings are pervaded by the spirit of *optimism.* They believe, in spite of all present appearances to the contrary, that great good is in store for Israel and the world.

Either of these characteristics by itself would have

---

[1] English readers may easily form a good general idea of the moral and religious attitude of the Greek tragedians by perusing Professor D'Arcy Thomson's *Sales Attici,* in which extracts in Greek are given on one page and English translations on the page opposite.

sufficed to make the prophets outstanding men in the history of the human race. The passion for righteousness and the passion of hope are so far from being common, that those in whom either of them appears in a high degree must ever take rank among the world's remarkable men. But it is the combination of the two that makes the figure of the Hebrew prophet unique. The surprise is that a man of such moral intensity, so severe a critic of his time, should also be optimistic in his view of the future. It comes so natural to the moral critic to be gloomy and pessimistic that we wonder when we observe that these men who made the most exacting demands from their contemporaries, and pronounced on them the most unsparing condemnation for failing to comply therewith, give the most glowing, enthusiastic pictures to be met with in the world's literature of a golden age to come, when the loftiest ideals of goodness and happiness should be fully realised.

If these two sides of the prophetic character appear incongruous, not less so appear the objects to which the two ruling passions were directed. The passion for righteousness revealed to the prophet's eye an evil present; the passion of hope opened up to his view a perfect future. The two things are not in one line, they seem antagonistic, they present an apparently hopeless antinomy. If genera tion after generation the present be always evil, what reason is there to expect that any coming generation will be much better, not to say really good? Have we not here two irreconcilable products of prophetic thought, influ enced by two contrary moods strangely meeting together in minds of rare type? It is no small part of the im perishable merit of the prophets that they made no attempt to conceal the antinomy. There the two things stand side by side in their writings: black pictures of moral short coming, bright pictures of the future character of the same people. "Ah, sinful nation—a people laden with iniquity." "Thy people also shall be all righteous." It is a com- panion antinomy to the one pointed out in the last chapter, that, viz. between the ideal of God's moral government and the moral confusions of real life. The prophets had at their command no philosophy offering a complete solution in either case. They simply acknowledged frankly both terms of the antinomy, and for the rest walked by faith. Not that hints of solution did not suggest themselves. Men could not feel, as the prophets did, the heavy pressure of the contradiction without seeking, and to a certain extent finding, a way of escape. A most instructive instance of light springing out of collision, like a spark struck by a flint out of steel, is supplied in Jeremiah's oracle of the New Covenant. The prophet contemplates the return of the exiles to their own land, and their dwelling there in righteousness and peace. But the thought occurs to him : to what purpose return to Judæa if the old weary round of transgression is to be repeated, and what hope does the past history of Israel give of anything better ? How bridge over the gulf between the bygone centuries of disobedience and the hoped-for future of fidelity to God ? After long brooding, the answer comes at last in the visions of the night. What if the law written on stone tablets were written on the heart ? No wonder the prophet, on awaking in the morning, after the great revelation, found that his sleep had been sweet.

Let us consider the *source* of prophetic optimism, the *expression* of it, and its *value*.

1. The source was not the mere temperament or disposition of the prophet. The prophet as such is not characteristically hopeful ; his temptation rather is to be querulous, morose, gloomy, desponding. Taking moral intensity to be the fundamental feature in the prophetic character, the tendency unquestionably is to be so overwhelmed with a sense of the evil of the present as to be unable to hope for improvement. The prophet's eye is apt to descry on the horizon of the future only judgment. The Baptist's preaching was all of the coming wrath, the hewing axe, the winnowing fan, the unquenchable fire.

Shall we say then that the bright future was an ideal which the prophet created as a solace to relieve the gloom of the present? Hardly. A modern poet might write a bright poem to charm away melancholy, conscious that the verses he indited were only an artistic creation, with no pretensions to truth. But a Hebrew prophet was not a mere poet or sentimental dreamer: he was a man of serious spirit and practical mind, in dead earnest in all he said and did. If his prophecies of the future were poetic creations, they were creations in which he believed with all his heart. As he conceived the future, so he believed it would be.

To account for the hopefulness of the prophet we must fall back on his religious faith. It arose directly and immediately out of his faith in the election of Israel. If God chose Israel for a certain purpose, then that purpose must stand: that was self-evident, axiomatically certain, to him. With Paul he believed that the gifts and calling of God are without repentance. God's purpose in Israel's election might be variously conceived, and according to the conception would be the idea formed of the eventual fulfilment. If the purpose was to make Israel a holy state, then the future would present itself as that of a nation doing righteousness. If the purpose was to use Israel as a vehicle for conveying to the world the true religion, then the vision of the future might not involve prosperity for the chosen people, or even the preservation of her existence; but it would certainly exhibit to the seer's eye a world filled with the knowledge of the true God. The one thing sure was that the divine aim would be realised.

But this does not go to the root of the matter. Election is an act of will. The great question is, What is the character of the electing will? In other words, the ulti mate source of prophetic optimism must be found in the prophetic idea of God.

Now, the great broad fact here is that in the prophetic conception of the divine character mercy, grace occupies a very prominent place. God is nowhere conceived of as sustaining a merely legal relation to men, making certain demands on them which it lies with them to comply with, and administering rewards and punishments according as His behests are obeyed or disobeyed. The "covenant of works" is a theological abstraction representing an element in God's relations with men, but not a distinct substantive reality. At no crisis of human history, whether in the garden of Eden or out of it, was the element of grace, according to the biblical representation, wanting. God appears evermore as more than a moral Governor, even as a Redeemer, a Saviour; not only as an objective Power working on the side of righteousness, but as a gracious Power helping men to be righteous. The gracious aspect of the divine character is set in the forefront even of the Decalogue, the preface of which recalls to remembrance the deliverance from bondage. In that great event God's grace showed itself in outward providence working for Israel's redemption. Still therein God appears doing for Israel what she could not do for herself, in "love and pity" redeeming a helpless, enslaved race from a state of bondage; not rewarding for work done, but benignantly conferring benefit unmerited. In the same external, pro vidential sense God showed His grace to Israel all through her long history: as when He saved Jerusalem from Sen nacherib's army, and brought the exiles back from Babylon. But divine grace is not conceived of as limited to the external sphere. It is thought of also, especially in the later prophets, as a beneficent power working within men, enabling them to fulfil the divine will. Thus viewed, God is not merely a Being who sets before men a lofty moral ideal, but One who helps them to realise it; not simply a transcendent Majesty who says "thou shalt" under penalties, but an immanent spirit, conveying inspiration and strength to the soul. "The ideal without is also the power within."[1] This is the thought underlying Jeremiah's great prophecy of the law written on the heart.

[1] Jones, *Browning as a Philosophical and Religious Teacher*, p. 305.

God's grace in biblical representations works ordinarily within the sphere of the covenant and for the benefit of the elect people. But it is not restricted to Israel, as if Jehovah, while loving, kind, and good to Israel, her Husband, Father, Redeemer, were utterly regardless of the rest of mankind. A god so conceived would be only a national god, which, as we have seen, was not the kind of deity the prophets believed in. No barbaric divinity is Jehovah, gracious to His favoured race, ferocious towards all other races; but one who is good to all, and whose tender mercies are over all His works.[1] Him all lands may be invited to serve with gladness, because He is good, and His mercy is ever lasting.[2] To Him all the ends of the earth are bid look for salvation, as the one God over all, and alike gracious to all.[3]

With such an idea of God, prophetic optimism becomes easily intelligible. There is no limit to what may be expected from Almighty Love: "With Him is plenteous redemption,"[4] in all senses, and in all spheres, external or internal, and in all parts of the world. The things con nected with sin may be too strong for us to cope with, but they are not too strong for God.[5] He can pardon the most aggravated guilt, subdue the power of evil habit, extricate from the chains of punitive consequences. The prophets speak as men who believed this with all their hearts, and cherished boundless expectations from God's beneficent will. The style in which they express them selves on this theme is magnificent. Listen to Micah: "Who is a God like unto Thee, that pardoneth iniquity, and passeth by the transgression of the remnant of His heritage? He retaineth not His anger for ever, because He delighteth in mercy. He will turn again, He will have compassion upon us; He will subdue our iniquities; and Thou wilt cast all their sins into the depths of the sea."[6] Or to Hosea: "I will heal their backsliding, I will love

---

[1] Ps. cxlv. 9. [2] Ps. c. 5. [3] Isa. xlv. 22.
[4] Ps. cxxx. 7. [5] Ps. lxv. 3. [6] Micah vii. 18, 19.

them freely; I will be as the dew unto Israel: he shall grow as the lily, and cast forth his roots as Lebanon."[1] God a Physician, a magnanimous Friend, who overcomes evil with good, a springtide of hope and beauty and shooting life: what may not be expected from Him for Israel and for the world?

It is by keeping in mind the idea of God cherished by the prophets that we can understand not merely why they hoped so greatly, but why hope characterises them so markedly in contrast to the sages of pagan peoples. For the heathen poet the golden age lies in the past; for the Hebrew prophet it lies in the future. Whence this difference? Its ultimate source is diversity in their respective conceptions of God. The prophet believed, as no heathen poet or philosopher ever did, in the goodness of God. He discovered traces of that goodness in the whole history of his own people, and from the favour shown to her in the past inferred for her a great future destiny. More and more he opened his mind to the thought that from the same divine goodness would flow unimaginable benefit to the whole human race: that the latter days would give birth to a new heavens and a new earth wherein should dwell righteousness. For lack of this bright, inspiring faith in a good God heathen sages were not able to be so hopeful. Their measure of the possible was the actual, and the actual is so full of confusion, uncertainty, and chance, that pessimism for one who looks not higher seems inevitable.

2. The hope of Hebrew prophecy found very varied expression. An exhaustive account of the diverse forms under which the future good is presented is not here aimed at; it will suffice to indicate one or two of the leading types. The ideal is sometimes *political*. The picture presented is that of a nation delivered from the power of its foes, enjoying material prosperity under a just, wise government, and minded to shun the offences which had

[1] Hos. xiv. 4, 5.

brought upon it the calamities from which it is now happily
rid. Several of the earlier prophetic books offer a tableau
of this kind. Thus at the close of the book of Amos we
read :

" In that day will I raise up the tabernacle of David that
is fallen, and close up the breaches thereof ; and I will raise
up his ruins, and I will build it as in the days of old : that
they may possess the remnant of Edom, and of all the
heathen, which are called by my name, saith the Lord that
doeth this. Behold, the days come, saith the Lord, that the
plowman shall overtake the reaper, and the treader of grapes
him that soweth seed ; and the mountains shall drop sweet
wine, and all the hills shall melt. And I will bring again
the captivity of my people of Israel, and they shall build
the waste cities, and inhabit them ; and they shall plant
vineyards, and drink the wine thereof. They shall also make
gardens, and eat the fruit of them ; and I will plant them
upon their land, and they shall no more be pulled up out of
their land which I have given them." [1]

The prophet, it will be observed, goes back for his ideal
state of national felicity to the time of David. Israel, as
it was then, with as good a king, with as much internal
concord, and with similar outward wellbeing, and fearing
no foe : that will suffice for an ideal of the future good.
In some of the prophetic programmes of this type much
stress is laid upon the king who is to reign in the good
time coming, as if given a king of the right stamp all must
go well. In such prophecies the character of the king is
highly idealised. Thus Isaiah describes the model king as
one filled with the spirit of wisdom and understanding and
the fear of God, who shall administer justice with dis
crimination and impartiality, and shall show himself the
friend of the poor and the stern foe of all iniquity.[2] He
represents him as bearing, as the vicegerent of God, divine
titles : " Wonderful, Counsellor, Mighty God, Everlasting
Father, Prince of Peace." [3] It is to such prophecies of an
ideal king that the title " Messianic " properly applies.

[1] Amos ix. 11-15.   [2] Isa. xi. 1-5.   [3] Isa. ix. 6.

Isaiah's conception of the good time coming belongs to the political type. His ideal is a nation well governed, and enjoying in rich measure the blessings of abundance and peace. It is an ideal such as a wise, high-minded states-man might project, and which might conceivably be realised under the natural conditions of human society. To later prophets such an ideal no longer appeared attainable, or, if attained, the best possible; and accordingly in their writings the *summum bonum* undergoes perceptible transformation. The political gives place to the *ethical*, a reformed state to a regenerated people. So in Jeremiah's famous oracle of the new covenant. To this prophet Isaiah's ideal, even if attained, seemed a comparatively poor thing. Of what great avail were good government and plenty to eat, if the people were not individually righteous? The consummation devoutly to be wished were a people with God's law written on their heart. But how is this end to be reached? It seems something supernatural, not attainable under ordinary conditions. So Jeremiah felt; hence his remarkable idea of a new covenant. He despaired of obtaining any result of great and permanent value under the original Mosaic covenant or constitution. Herein he differed from his brother-prophet Isaiah. Isaiah stood on the old covenant, and aimed at a state in a sound healthy condition, such as any wise statesman might desire. Jeremiah gave the old covenant up as hopeless. He demanded, not reform, but revolution, a new constitution for a new people consisting of men and women whose hearts were right with God. He still conceives of regenerated Israel as a nation, and, like the older prophets, attaches great importance to the person of the king. "Behold, the days come, saith the Lord, that I will raise unto David a righteous Branch, and a King shall reign and prosper, and shall execute justice in the earth. In His days Judah shall be saved, and Israel shall dwell safely."[1] And, like Isaiah, he invests the king with divine titles.

[1] Jer. xxiii. 5, 6.

But there is a noteworthy change in the character of the attributions. Isaiah's titles are titles of majesty and dignity; with Jeremiah the ethical comes to the front. "This is the name whereby He shall be called, *the Lord our righteousness.*" [1] It is not legitimate exegesis to extract from this name, as Jeremiah used it, the Pauline system of theology; but it is legitimate to remark that the name is in sympathy with that prophet's great thought: the law written on the heart. If Jehovah is to write His law on regenerated Israel's heart, then He is the source of Israel's righteousness, and the king who reigns over regenerated Israel may well bear a name that bears witness to this truth.

Ezekiel seems to be in sympathy with Jeremiah in his conception of the good in store for Israel. He represents Jehovah as making this promise to His people returned from captivity: "A new heart also will I give you, and a new spirit will I put within you: and I will take away the stony heart out of your flesh, and I will give you an heart of flesh." [2] It has, indeed, been maintained that the re generation he speaks of is not moral, but ritual, and that his whole tendency leads on to Talmudism. [3] That is a question which cannot here be discussed. It must certainly be admitted that the spirit of Ezekiel is in many respects different from that of Jeremiah, and that he is a priest quite as much as he is a prophet. [4] Nevertheless, it remains true that there is essential agreement between the two prophets in their point of view. Both desiderate regeneration as necessary to the realisation of the ideal. If they differ, it is as to the means of regeneration, or as to the kind of laws to be written on the heart.

---

[1] Jer. xxiii. 6.   [2] Ezek. xxxvi. 26.

[3] Duhm, *Die Theologie der Propheten*, pp. 258, 263.

[4] Jeremiah also was a priest officially, but not in spirit. Darmestete truly says: "The priest in him was the servant and instrument of the prophet; in him, as in Isaiah, it is the prophet that dominates, that is to say, the reformer of the moral life, of the social life, of the political life."– *Les Prophètes d'Israel*, p. 69.

In the oracles of the great prophet of the exile we meet with an ideal of a third type, which may be distinguished as the *religious*. Here the model king disappears from view, and with him the nation, and Israel becomes a prophet or missionary fulfilling the high vocation of teaching the nations the true religion. "I will also give Thee for a light to the Gentiles, that Thou mayest be my salvation unto the end of the earth." Salvation consists in the knowledge of the true God, and Israel's honourable function is to be to communicate that knowledge as the inspired apostle of the faith. The golden age shall have come, and the ideal been realised, when the earth is filled with the knowledge of God. Under this view the highest good is a boon, not for the elect race merely, but for the world: her peculiar reward is the honour of being the instrument for achieving so great a result. "It is a light thing that Thou shouldest be my servant to raise up the tribes of Jacob, and to restore the preserved of Israel: I will *also* give Thee for a light to the Gentiles." Israel becomes great among the nations by becoming a servant to the nations in their highest interests, by acting as their religious teacher. Her glory is that she gives to the world the true idea of God.

High vocations bring not only renown but tribulations. The missionary of the true God must be a great sufferer. "Who hath believed our report? and to whom is the arm of the Lord revealed?"[2] "He is despised and rejected of men; a man of sorrows, and acquainted with grief."[3] This is the darkest phase in the sombre picture of human life, supplying a choice theme for the pessimist—the fact that those who have the faculty and the will to do the world most good usually receive the worst treatment at the world's hands. But there is another side to the picture, as bright as the other is dark. The suffering of the wise and the good is never in vain: it benefits the very men who are the cause of the suffering. "By His knowledge shall my

[1] Isa. xlix. 6.　　[2] Isa. liii. 1.　　[3] Isa. liii. 3.

righteous servant justify many; for He shall bear their iniquities."[1] Here is the answer to the riddle propounded in the book of Job: why do the righteous suffer? Here the optimism of the Hebrew prophets reaches its culmina tion and its vindication. That optimism does not consist in shutting the eyes to the evil that is in the world. On the contrary, it knows how to take that evil into the ideal as one of its constitutive elements, and transmute it into the highest good. The wise and the good suffer because the world does not know them, and by their patience they conquer their foes, and "divide the spoil with the strong." The fifty-third chapter of Isaiah is the last and highest word of Hebrew prophecy concerning the *summum bonum*. It sets forth the ideal as power reached through weakness, honour through shame, healing through pain, righteousness through wrong; reached not merely for the one who endures the weakness, the shame, the pain, and the wrong, but through him for the many.

3. When we inquire what is the value of prophetic optimism, we mean how far does it possess objective and permanent significance. That it possessed subjective value for the prophets themselves is a matter of course. It consoled them amidst the tribulations and calamities and iniquities of the present; it made life worth living; it gave the weary spirit the wings of a dove, on which it could fly away to a dream-world and be at rest. But what amount of truth is in these prophetic forecasts of the future, to what extent has history realised prophetic ideals?

Now it is a commonplace in the interpretation of pro phecy that all prophecies have not been fulfilled, and that some of them, in the precise form in which they are given, never will or can be fulfilled. The world has never yet seen Isaiah's model state, and there is little likelihood that it ever will. His conception of a great world-monarchy, embracing Egypt, Assyria, and Palestine, is now simply a monument to his genius. Jeremiah's noble thought of a

[1] Isa. liii. 11.

regenerated Israel is also destined to remain an unrealised ideal. The model king of Davidic type never came. There were some good kings, such as Hezekiah and Josiah, but they came far short of the prophetic ideal, and most of the kings were such as would break a prophet's heart. But it does not follow that prophetic ideals were idle dreams containing not even a kernel of truth.

In the first place, if there was any reality in the election of Israel, then the thought which underlies all Messianic prophecy, so-called, must be true, viz. that a great good is coming. When Jehovah chose Israel, He had a purpose in view which must be fulfilled, He commenced a process which must reach its consummation, He planted a vine which must bear its fruit. If no good is coming, then God's election of Israel is a failure, or rather it never took place; it is simply a notion of the Hebrew people having nothing answering to it in the realm of reality. What form the coming good is to take may be beforehand very uncertain; of its nature the prophets themselves may have had but a vague idea largely coloured in the case of each prophet by the circumstances of his own time. In consequence of the vagueness of their delineations, it may not be easy for us afterhand to detect a very striking or convincing correspondence between their pictures of the good that was coming and the good that came through Jesus Christ. It is certainly not so easy as many people imagine. But this at least ought to be true, that the prophets were not mistaken in believing that the best was yet to be.

This at least, and more. For if Israel was indeed an elect people, elect for the world's good, as well as for her own, the prophets were surely elect men who had something to say concerning the nature of the good, not merely to contemporary Israelites, but to men of all time. This being a reasonable and consistent view to take of them, we may with confidence extract from their writings some general outlines of the good that was to be. We may expect to find in their "Messianic" oracles at least an irreducible minimum of didactic significance.

One legitimate inference is the vast importance that may attach to a single individual as an instrument for the realisation of God's purpose in the vocation of Israel. This thought is suggested by the stress laid by the prophets upon the ideal king. "Behold, a king shall reign in righteousness!"[1] They speak as if the *summum bonum* might come through one man. It is characteristic of them to attach importance to the influence of the individual. They are hero-worshippers: the history of the world for them is the history of great men. The great man, the man in high place and worthy of his place, can do wonders. He "shall be as an hiding-place from the wind, and a covert from the tempest; as rivers of water in a dry place, as the shadow of a great rock in a weary land."[2] If this be true of any great man, of any noble-minded prince among men, how much more of the greatest, the ideal King, the Prince of princes! The value thus set in Hebrew prophecy on the moral hero prepares us for finding that the final result of the long historical development in Israel is one supreme man, the Light of the world. That the evolution of the divine purpose should issue in this may at first seem strange and disappointing. We began with the idea of a nation, a holy state in which all the people should be righteous, and after fourteen centuries we get what? A single unique man, of ideal worth, springing like a root out of a very dry ground. We may seek to reconcile ourselves to this result, not merely as in itself of inestimable value, but as the legitimate product of a process of development, by various lines of thought. From the point of view of comparative religion, it has

---

[1] Isa. xxxii. 1.

[2] Isa. xxxii. 2. Cheyne translates: "A great man shall be as an hiding-place from the wind;" and adds the comment, "Strictly any one (king or prince) who belongs to the class of great men." *The Prophecies of Isaiah*, *in loc.* On the idea of the passage, *vide* G. A. Smith's work on Isaiah, vol. i. chap. xv., with the suggestive heading, "A MAN."

been observed [1] that there comes a time in the religious development of nations which have been in a position to develop their intellectual life in purity and tranquillity through a long period of time, when the centre of gravity of all higher interests shifts from without to within. With this change comes a new form of spiritual fellow ship. In place of the nation there arises the school, the society, or the holy order. The centre of influence in such fellowships is an individual teacher of commanding personality. Illustrative examples are supplied in Socrates, Buddha, and Christ. There may be something worth noting in this. But for one who believes in a special revelation of God to Israel, it is more helpful to reflect that all Hebrew prophecy points to the individual as the source of salvation. I say not to *the Messiah*, as if they had all one definite personality in view, specially revealed to them as the final bringer in of the golden age. The thing here insisted on is the prominence given to the principle of individuality, and the inference suggested that the ultimate fulfilment of God's gracious purpose will come through one man. We may not be on so sure ground when we attempt to determine the manner of the man by aid of prophetic delineations. Historic exegesis may not justify us in treating Isaiah's list of wondrous attributes as personal characteristics, and so arriving at the conclusion that the Saviour of the latter days is to be not merely a great man, but God Almighty.[2] But it will justify us at least in expecting Him to be an Anointed One, divinely

---

[1] Oldenberg, *Buddha: His Life, His Doctrine, His Order*, pp. 3, 4.

[2] Professor Robertson Smith remarks (*The Prophets of Israel*, p. 307): "The prophet does not say that the king *is* the mighty God and the everlasting Father, but that His *name* is divine and eternal, that is, that the divine might and everlasting fatherhood of Jehovah are displayed in His rule." Ewald (*Die Propheten des Alten Bundes*) says: "We must look on it as the name which a new king assumed to be placed on his shield, banner, or arms; it could not be allowed more than a limited space upon the shield, and therefore had to be condensed.

Arranged thus { Wonderful-Counsellor, Hero-God,
{ Everlasting Father, Prince of Peace."

endowed with right kingly qualities of wisdom, justice, and benignity.

The ethical ideal of Jeremiah suggests another inference as to the nature of the good that is to be. His conception of a regenerated nation contains an element which goes beyond the limits of the ideal as he conceived it. He thought of a regenerated Israel, all her citizens having God's law written on their hearts. But why should regeneration be national? If you keep to externals, to such matters as language, race, land, and custom, you properly limit your ideal to a nation. But the moral law written on the heart has nothing merely national about it: it is the affair of humanity.

Consciously or unconsciously, therefore, Jeremiah gives us the great idea of a kingdom of God independent of nationality, including among its citizens all the pure in heart.

A royal man, and a divine kingdom: these are two of the goods that are to come in the era of consummation. But how are they to be connected? Let the prophet of the exile answer. The ideal man will make himself the king of hearts by wisdom and by suffering. He will show to teachable spirits the true God, and they will gladly take his yoke upon them; he will suffer at the hands of the unrighteous, and will conquer his enemies by meek endurance.

These three things, the highest boons of God to men: a moral Hero, a kingdom of the good, and the moral Hero making Himself the king of that kingdom by spiritual insight and self-sacrifice, as the suffering servant of God, are the chief fruitage of that remarkable group of prophecies usually called Messianic, which embody the optimistic ideals of Hebrew seers. They are not extracted from stray texts, or based on remarkable special predictions like that of the virgin conceiving, but represent the main drift of Messianic oracles. "The rod out of the stem of Jesse," the law written on the heart, and the "man of sorrows and acquainted with grief," are the foreground of the prophetic delineation of the future, the kernel of the *summum bonum* as conceived by the prophetic imagination, as the prophecies containing them are among the highest products of prophetic genius. They follow each other in the natural order of succession: first the king sketched by Isaiah of Jerusalem, then the regenerate people the lovely dream of Jeremiah, then the suffering servant of Jehovah presented to our view in all his tragic dignity by the prophet of the exile; prophetic insight becoming clearer and deeper with the course of time and the progress of events.

In Jesus Christ these three ideals meet. He is the Royal Man. He brings in the kingdom of grace. He is the man of sorrow who conquers human hearts by suffering love. Is this historic realisation of prophetic ideals an accident or a God-appointed fulfilment?

CHAPTER VII.

JUDAISM.

LITERATURE.—Ewald, *Geschichte des Volkes Israel*, B. iv.; Wellhausen, *Prolegomena;* Stade, *Geschichte des Volkes Israel;* W. Robertson Smith, *The Old Testament in the Jewish Church* (1st ed. 1881, 2nd ed. much enlarged, 1892); Schultz, *Alttestamentliche Theologie*, 4te Aufl.; Toy, *Judaism and Christianity;* Sack, *Die Altjudische Religion;* W. R. Smith, article on the "Psalter" in *Encyclopædia Britannica* (the main conclusions of this article are embodied in the new edition of *The Old Testament in the Jewish Church*); Cheyne, *The Origin of the Psalter* (Bampton Lectures).

In passing from Prophetism to Judaism as introduced by Ezra, we seem to make a great descent. As we study the relative literature, the thought suggests itself, what a fall is here! Reading first Isaiah, Jeremiah, and the prophet of the exile, then taking up Ezra and Nehemiah, we feel as if we were making a sudden plunge from poetry to prose, from inspiration to legalism, from a religion of faith to a religion of self-righteousness. The very prayers of Nehemiah seem to breathe a new spirit : " Remember me, O my God, concerning this, and wipe not out my good deeds that I have done for the house of my God, and for the offices thereof."[1] " Remember me, O my God, for good."[2]

Reverence for Scripture makes one hesitate to trust himself in forming such a judgment. And yet such hesitation is mistaken. Judaism may be a natural and legitimate step in the onward progress of the religion of Israel. God may be in it, using it as a preparation for the final stage, a harbinger of Christ. But that is quite compatible with its being in comparison with something going before inferior and weak, as even the advocates of traditional views as to the course of revelation will allow when they remember that the law came after the promise, to which nevertheless it was but a humble handmaid. The first thing needful, therefore, to a right understanding of the present phase of Israel's religion, is to grasp firmly the fact that it is a distinct thing from anything going before, and a decidedly inferior thing.

Judaism, apart altogether from critical questions, was distinct from Mosaism. The distinguishing feature of Mosaism, as we have seen, was that it asserted the supremacy of the moral, as compared with ritual. This fundamental principle the prophets reasserted with new emphasis and widened range of application, so showing themselves to be the true sons of Moses. On the other hand, the distinctive characteristic of Judaism was that it put ritual on a level with morality, treated Levitical rules as of equal importance with the Decalogue, making no distinction between one part of the law and another, but demanding compliance with the prescribed ceremonial of worship as not less necessary to good relations with God than a righteous life. This was a new thing in Israel;

---

[1] Neh. xiii. 14.   [2] Neh. xiii. 31.

and it was a great downcome : a descent from liberty to bondage, from evangelic to legal relations with God, from the spirit to the letter. It was so great a downcome that the difficulty is to see how God could have any hand in it. How could the Jehovah that inspired the Hebrew legislator and the prophets, giving to them those great, broad, free thoughts which still possess the highest spiritual value, be a party to the inbringing of an elaborate system of religious formalism ? Can we imagine Him inspiring Ezra the scribe as he plies his task of putting into written form the Levitical legislation as it lies before us now in the middle books of the Pentateuch ? Is not this new type of functionary, the *scribe*, the very antipodes of the prophet, and as antipathetic to the very idea of inspiration as the latter is in sympathy with it ? And what is the effect of Ezra's work ? Is it not a reversion to that confusion of morality with ritual characteristic of pagan conceptions of right conduct, as exemplified in the Egyptian trial of the dead ? It was the merit of Moses and the prophets, we saw, that they differentiated between the two kinds of action, as of altogether different value. What then, one naturally asks, is this Ezra movement but a cancelling of their beneficent work, and a lapse from the high moral level reached by them to the low level of heathenism ? [1]

Such is the difficulty we have to face. It has been observed that Levitical ordinances, whether they existed before the exile or no, were not yet God's word to Israel at that time.[2] The question is, Could they be God's word after the exile ? Is it not more easy to conceive them being God's word at the beginning than so late in the day, after He had given to Israel a far higher word ? Do these ordinances, coming in at so late a period, not look very

---

[1] Wellhausen, in his *Prolegomena to the History of Israel*, p. 422, says, " The cultus is the heathen element in the Israelite religion."

[2] Professor Robertson Smith, *The Old Testament in the Jewish Church*, 2nd ed. p. 310.

like a degeneracy such as is wont to occur in the religions of the pagans, whose first thoughts of God are often better than their last ; such as took place, *e.g.*, in the Persian religion, which as reformed by Zarathustra seems to have been a comparatively pure thing, but in after times became more and more an elaborate system of ceremonialism ? What if during the exile the captives had taken lessons from their masters ?

The attempt to show that the introduction of Leviticalism, viewed as happening after the exile, might be a legitimate step in the onward march of the religion of revelation, does seem very discouraging. And yet there is another side to the matter. Leviticalism, Judaism, may be conceived of as a husk to protect the kernel of ethical monotheism. Ezra and his companions, just because they were faithful disciples of the prophets, zealous for the honour of Jehovah, the God of Israel, might regard the enforcement of a carefully prepared scheme of religious ritual as the best means of protecting that honour from violation. It is significant, as an indication that this was really their point of view, that in the earlier period of the captivity the prophet Ezekiel began to occupy himself with the preparation of such a scheme. We must not try to minimise the significance of this fact by laying stress on the circumstance that Ezekiel was a priest. It is more to the purpose to note that the priest was also a prophet, and that in his whole way of thinking he was a link of connection between Prophetism and Judaism. The last eight chapters of Ezekiel's book of prophecy appear to be a first sketch of a Levitical system, prepared by one who believed that it would serve the end which all the prophets had at heart. These chapters, so viewed, are one of the strongest proofs that the priestly legislation of the Penta teuch was not Mosaic. If it had been, why should Ezekiel have occupied himself with the preparation of a fancy programme ? It is difficult on that view to regard that programme as serious, as anything more than a pastime to while away the weary days of the captivity. But this by

the way. The point insisted on here is that Ezekiel the ,
prophet takes also a great interest in ritual, and that this .
fact may fairly be adduced as a proof that to men setting .
a high value on the prophetic idea of God, the careful
regulation of religious ritual might, in the light of past)
experience, appear a matter of importance.

From this point of view we can see how Judaism, though ,
wearing a suspicious resemblance to heathenism, in attach
ing so much importance to ritual, nevertheless stands on a '
different footing. The promoters of the new movement .
did not really put ritual on a level with morality, as of
equal importance in the sight of God. They simply
regarded it as a very important means towards the great
end of keeping the people of Israel faithful in heart and
life to God. And it is not difficult to imagine how they
could arrive at this conclusion. We have but to make a
little effort to get inside the minds of the exiles. By the
rivers of Babylon they sat down and wept. But they did
more than weep; they thought much, earnestly, and sadly
on the past history of their people. In the clear light of X,
experience they saw that Israel's misfortunes had come
upon her for her sins; for the one grand all-comprehending
sin of unfaithfulness to Jehovah. Out of this insight sprang
a purpose of amendment, and a disposition to consider
carefully the best means for guarding in future against
the errors which had entailed on the covenant people such
an inheritance of woe. This penitent, pensive mood may
have borne fruit in various directions. Possibly one result
was the compilation of the historical books, in which the
story of Israel is told from the time of the Judges to the
destruction of Jerusalem.[1] Literary activity is one of the

---

[1] To the period of the exile Professor Ryle refers, among other literary
labours, the combination of the Deuteronomic law with the book of Joshua,
and with the Jehovist-Elohist history of Israel's beginnings. The motives
of this literary activity he finds in " the reverence with which the pious Jew,
in his Babylonian exile, would regard the archives that recorded the begin
nings of his nation and the foundation of his faith." *Vide The Canon of
the Old Testament*, p. 69.

consolations of captives, prisoners, and exiles. Bunyan wrote the *Pilgrim s Progress* in Bedford gaol, Spencer's *Faery Queen* was composed mainly in an Irish wilderness, and was thus, as the author tells us, "the fruit of savage soil." With books written under such conditions none can compare for sweetness, beauty, and calm, solemn dignity. How much of the best Book do we owe to the exiles of Babylon: the oracles of Isaiah the second, for example! The fact, if it be a fact, has doubtless something to do with the exceptional worth of these writings. It is by deep sorrow God makes men wise.

The study of the past history of Israel, with which we may conceive the best of the exiles earnestly occupied, might very readily suggest that the worship of Jehovah wanted regulation. They could see how the old provincial sanctuary system, that had been in vogue till the time of Josiah's reformation, opened a wide door to Canaanite corruptions. They could see how for want of due pre cautions idolatrous abuses crept into even the temple worship. From the whole survey they would get the impression that the religious life of their fathers had been too free, and that the only effectual way to exclude idolatrous practices in future, should God in His mercy restore them to their own land, would be to have the service of the sanctuary regulated down to the minutest particulars, with purity of worship as the guiding principle in the process of reconstruction. For the same general purpose of shutting out the impure influence of heathenism they would perceive the need of a carefully elaborated system of rules for securing holiness in the outer conduct, that the whole life of Israel might be clean in God's sight. The outcome of the reforming spirit would naturally be a body of rules like the priestly code, a very fully developed corpus of sacrificial and ceremonial law.

The promoters of this reforming movement might very well have the feeling that they were true to the spirit of Moses, and doing their best to preserve intact the Mosaic religion. The logic of their position might be thus put: One God, one sanctuary, and at the one sanctuary a care fully regulated service offered by a people scrupulously guarded against all uncleanness in all relations and actions of their lives. They might claim that this was the logic of history, each link in the chain of argument being established one after the other in Israel's experience. One God, said Moses, "Thou shalt have no other gods before me." Whatever more he said, Israel acted for long as if he had said no more. There were many sanctuaries in the land, and the worship carried on there was to a large extent spontaneous, and too often degraded by imitations of vile Canaanitish custom. Then at length it was seen that one God demanded one sanctuary, and the Deuteronomic law came into force. But even this reform did not secure for Israel's one true God His due honour. Jeremiah had to complain of his contemporaries that they burned incense unto Baal, and walked after other gods, and made the temple a den of robbers;[1] and Ezekiel, looking back on what went on there before the captivity, speaks of the defilement of the holy place by the "whoredom" of idolatrous worship, and by its sacred precincts being turned into places of sepulture for the kings.[2] Thus men zealous for God's honour were forced on to the final stage in the logical process: one uniform, carefully constructed, strictly enforced system of worship. And in carrying out this programme they might regard themselves as simply putting the copestone on the work of Moses, and feel entitled to invest the new code with the authority of his name.

This statement helps us to understand how the priestly code, assuming it to be in form, and in many of its details, a new thing, the product of the reforming zeal of the exiles, might reasonably be represented as a faithful following out of the principles of Mosaism. And this, it will be remembered, is what we here are chiefly concerned with. The question for us is not the critical one whether the priestly code be post-

---

[1] Jer. vii. 11. [2] Ezek. xliii. 7.

exilic, but whether, assuming that it was, we can claim for it to be in the intention of its authors, and in its main drift, a legitimate and useful development of Israel's religion. It may, or it may not be, that Ezra the scribe was something more than a clerk preparing a clean copy of an old statute-book, or even than a servile redactor of ancient unwritten usage; an originator, rather than a transmitter, such as Confucius modestly claimed to be. It is certainly not unnatural to regard Ezra, freshly arrived from Persia, in Palestine, with the law of his God in his hand, as an epoch-making man, a kind of second Moses, a new legislator only assuming the old one's name. But, be that as it may, the main question is, Was the work done by Ezra good and wholesome, or the reverse?

Now it needs but a hasty and general survey of the priestly code to be satisfied that there was much in it that tended towards the realisation of the Mosaic ideal of a holy people faithful to Jehovah. One outstanding feature in it is the prominence given to the idea of *sin*. This has indeed been represented as a fault in the new post-exilic system, as compared with the old religion of Israel. In the good old times religion, we are told, was a part of common life, and an incident of festive occasions. Worship and feasting went hand in hand. The sacred times were associated with the seasons of the year, which are the natural occasions of rejoicing, such as the seasons of the wheat harvest and the vintage. The sacrifices had little reference to sin, but were of a joyous nature,—"a merry making before Jehovah with music and song, timbrels, flutes, and stringed instruments." How sad that all this innocent happiness should pass away and be replaced by the "monotonous seriousness" of Levitical worship![1] Just as sad as that the Sunday sports and the dancing round the May-pole of merry old England should be replaced by the seriousness of the Puritans. Mirth is good, but too much mirth is unsuitable to the world we

[1] Wellhausen, *Prolegomena*, p. 81.

live in, and even dangerous to morals. A nation given up to mirth is apt to be a nation given up to moral licence. So it proved in Israel. And therefore it was well, it was a real advance in moral culture, that the religious system should be so altered as to develop a deeper consciousness of sin. It tended to a more exalted view of the holiness of God, and to greater heedfulness in conduct.

It is not difficult to see that the ceremonial law, not less than the sacrificial, tended in the same direction. The prescriptions with regard to uncleanness may seem to us very irksome, but it is when we look at them in the light of pagan Semitic worship that we perceive their beneficent purpose. In detail, these prescriptions have much in common with the customs of other peoples, like the Egyptians and Persians, but in aim they stand alone, and in reference to the paganism nearest Israel they have all the effect of a studied antagonism. The contrast has been well described by Schultz. "The nature-worship of the Canaanites draws the divine down into the processes of nature, and is implicated with them. The ceremonial law will first sanctify and purify these in order to lift them up to God. Nature-worship seeks to honour the Godhead by unlimited self-surrender to nature with its impulses, powers, passions, and motions. Death and procreation are for it the secret centres of the religious contemplation of nature. The ceremonial law seeks to honour the Creator of life as exalted above nature, by devoting to Him all that is natural, and by destroying all that is out of harmony with the divine."[1] In the light of this contrast we can understand and sympathise with the laws relating to sexual intercourse, the rite of circumcision, the purification of a mother after child-birth. They all tended to purity, and to the fostering of a salutary abhorrence of the vileness of Baal-worship which made prostitution a religious service.

One other feature of the priestly code may here be

[1] *Alttestamentliche Theologie*, 4te Aufl. p. 462.

briefly adverted to. The centralisation of worship in a single sanctuary, and the commitment of the whole sacrifi cial service into the hands of a priestly class, if an innovation as regards Mosaism, had certainly a tendency to prepare men for the religion of the spirit which came in with Jesus. In old times, it would appear, killing for food and sacrifice were the same thing, and every man was his own priest. Sacrifice was a thing of daily occurrence, and an essential element of religion. The centralisation of worship changed all that. Sacrifice became an affair of stated seasons, public sacrifice for all Israel threw into the shade private sacrifice, and the offering of victims became the business of a professional class. But religion is not an affair for two or three seasons in the year, but for daily life. Therefore men had to find out for themselves means for the culture of piety independent of Levitical ritual. The need was felt in exile when the temple worship was perforce suspended, and it would continue to be felt when the second temple had been built and a new altar erected. The synagogue, with its prayers and its reading of the Scriptures, met the want, and educated men for a time when temple and sacrifice would finally disappear.

Thus far my aim has been to show that Neo-Mosaism, as I have ventured to call the movement initiated by Ezekiel and consummated by Ezra, was a thing in which God-inspired men might have part. But now, quite compatibly with that view, it may be frankly acknowledged that the new turn taken by Israel's religion involved its own peculiar risks. The danger was that scrupulous care in the regulation of worship and the guarding of life from impurity would end in formalism, in that righteousness of the scribes which was so mercilessly condemned by Jesus. Freedom had ended in moral religious licence. Judaism cured that by hedging the people in on every side by positive law, and the evil now to be apprehended was that the cure would breed a new and worse disease — dead, rotten-hearted legalism. It might even be affirmed with a measure of

truth that the sinister reign of legalism began the day that
Ezra appeared on Jewish soil with the law in his hand.

Yet we have the means of satisfying ourselves that the
evil latent in the new movement remained an undeveloped
germ in Ezra's time and even for a while after. One
important fact tending to prove this is that men of prophetic spirit were in sympathy with Ezra's work; Ezekiel
for example. In the writings of this prophet, the char
acteristic mark of the new departure—the mixing of morality
with ritual, righteousness with technical holiness, as if they
were on the same level—is everywhere apparent. So, for
instance, in his description of the just man in the discourse
in which he controverts the proverb concerning the fathers
eating sour grapes and the children's teeth set on edge.
Acts of very different quality and value are all classed
together there as if of the same importance.[1] This is
certainly a descent from the high level of prophetic teaching,
or even of Mosaism. But that is a criticism of Judaism
which has to be made once for all. The thing to be noted
here is that there is not the slightest trace in Ezekiel's
prophecies of the common tendency of ritualism to under
mine the ethical, and to weaken or pervert the moral
sentiments. He hates oppression and inhumanity and
greed as vigorously as Amos or Isaiah.

Similar remarks apply to the great prophet of the exile.
There are indications here and there in the later part of the
book of Isaiah that the writer was not uninfluenced by the
spirit of Judaism, as in the manner in which the observance
of the Sabbath is spoken of,[2] and the eating of swine's
flesh condemned.[3] But with this leaning to the positive in
religion there is combined a most refreshing sense of the
supreme importance of the great principles of morality, and
a withering contempt for religious service divorced from
right conduct. Is it, asks the prophet indignantly, "Is it
such a fast that I have chosen? a day for a man to afflict
his soul? is it to bow down his head as a bulrush, and to

[1] Ezek. xviii.   [2] Isa. lvi. 4; lviii. 13.   [3] Isa. lxv. 4; lxvi. 17.

spread sackcloth and ashes under him? wilt thou call this a fast, and an acceptable day to the Lord? Is not this the fast that I have chosen? to loose the bands of wickedness, to undo the heavy burdens, and to let the oppressed go free, and that ye break every yoke? Is it not to deal thy bread to the hungry, and that thou bring the poor that are cast out to thy house? when thou seest the naked, that thou cover him; and that thou hide not thyself from thine own flesh?"[1] We feel that this teaching is in thorough sympathy with the prophetic passion for righteous ness, and anticipates the doctrine of the Sermon on the Mount.

But the amplest evidence that Judaism in at least its earlier stage was of wholesome moral tendency, and knew how to keep ritual in its own place, as only a means, however important, to a higher end, is supplied in the *Psalter*, which recent criticism with increasing confidence regards as, in its contents, mainly of post-exilic origin, and, in its use, the song-book of the second temple. There is no conceivable ground for being jealous of this conclusion, though somehow, owing to the influence probably of the old traditional opinion, there is a lurking inclination in one's mind to regard all attempts to assign to any of the psalms late dates as a dangerous heresy. Slowly, however, it begins to dawn on us that in this case criticism, like a wise physician, heals itself. Critics tell us that the priestly code is post-exilic, and we are apt to see in it, so viewed, simply a religious declension in which the God of Moses and the prophets could have no part. But the other doctrine of the critics concerning the post-exilic origin of the Psalter comes in as the needful antidote to this sceptical mood. For if the Psalter be indeed of post-exilic origin, then it is certain that Judaism, or scribism if you will, in the earlier stage at least, cannot have been wholly the evil thing we thought it. It was not such as to drive the spirit of inspira- tion away from Israel. Prophecy after all did not quite

[1] Isa. lviii. 5-7.

cease with Malachi. If, as the critics think, not a few
psalms, such as the 30th, and the group 113th to 118th,
also the group 145th to 150th, belong to the Maccabæan
time, then the light of inspiration lingered in Israel for
some three centuries after Ezra appeared in Jerusalem with
the law in his hand. Why should we hesitate to believe
this? Should we not rather be thankful to know that God
did not altogether forsake His people during the dreary
winter night of legalism, but gave them the twinkling
starlight of sacred poetry to keep them in good heart?

Those songs of the night are not only very beautiful and
charming as poetry, but highly spiritual. Though contain
ing no new ideas in advance of the prophets, they rise to
the highest water-mark of prophetic religion. They show
that the prophetic religion flowed on and kept the land
from becoming a wilderness under the arid influence of the
scribes. Perhaps we ought to say: they show that that
influence was not so arid as we are apt to imagine. For
they express unfeigned delight in the temple and its
services and sacred seasons,[1] and not less in the law
wherein psalmists found not merely ceremonial rules, but
great principles of wisdom.[2] The true source of the delight
is that God is there, and that the law and the religious
ordinances are the means of a blessed communion between
God and the soul. And this communion psalmists know
how to maintain apart from the temple and its cultus,
while keenly missing the privileges connected therewith.
Witness the contrition for sin expressed *ex hypothesi* by a
psalmist of the exile,[3] the hope in God of another psalmist
far removed from the house of God,[4] the joy in God
as a sun and shield, and as the source of all good, of
a third, who envies the birds that flit about the temple
precincts.[5]

The psalms are not only eminently devotional, but
humane. Not a few of them, such as the 67th, the 87th,

[1] Ps. v., xxvii., xlii., lxxxiv., cxxii.   [2] Ps. xix., cxix.
[3] Ps. li.   [4] Ps. xlii.   [5] Ps. lxxxiv.

and the 100th, breathe the spirit of universalism. They are in sympathy with the great word of the last of the prophets, which, like the cuckoo note, is the harbinger of the summer of the Christian era: "From the rising of the sun even unto the going down of the same my name is great among the Gentiles; and in every place incense is offered unto my name, and a pure meat offering." [1] Such psalms may be regarded as a counterbalance to the possibly necessary but somewhat repulsive severity of the policy pursued by Ezra and Nehemiah towards foreigners in insisting on separation from heathen wives, and in refusing to the Samaritans a share in the work of rebuilding the walls of Jerusalem. Other psalms, it must be admitted, seem to be animated by the same exclusive spirit—the vindictive psalms we call them, which, viewed as the utterances of a private individual, present a hard problem to the Christian mind. What, we are apt to ask, can the Spirit of God have to do with a prayer like this: "Let them be confounded and put to shame that seek after my soul: let them be turned back and brought to confusion that devise my hurt. Let them be as chaff before the wind: and let the angel of the Lord chase them"? [2] Probably the true view to take of these psalms is to regard the writer as personating the chosen people, and as complaining of wrongs done to her by pagan oppressors. [3] It must be acknowledged that the tone of such psalms, even when so viewed, stands in marked contrast to the spirit of Deutero-Isaiah when he represents the servant of Jehovah as a light to the Gentiles. It is one of the dark shadows cast on the sacred page by the legal dispensation.

Another of these shadows may, perhaps, be found in certain psalms which complain of disaster coming upon Israel, notwithstanding her innocence of all unfaithfulness to God. "All this is come upon us; yet have we not

---

[1] Mal. i. 11. [2] Ps. xxxv. 4, 5.
[3] So Professor Robertson Smith in article on " Psalms " in *Encyclopædia Britannica*.

forgotten Thee." [1] Such national self-consciousness of rectitude seems more in keeping with the spirit of the scribes than with that of the prophets, and may plausibly be viewed as a forerunner of Pharisaism. But the inference, though natural, is not certain. In such psalms as the 49th and 73rd we meet with the same problem in reference to individual life. Psalmists conscious of moral integrity complain of suffering at the hands of evil men, and want to know what it all means. But prophets like Jeremiah, whom we do not suspect of self-righteousness, do the same thing. And we should regard it as one of the merits of these prophets, and of the author of the book of Job, that rising superior to all spurious humility they have the courage to propound the question, Why do righteous men suffer? Demure piety, sophisticated in its moral sentiments by an artificial and abstract theology, would be apt to say: No such case can happen, for there is none righteous; all who suffer, suffer for their sins. Such abject self-condemnation is much more akin to Pharisaism than the manly yet modest self-approval of a Jeremiah or a Job. But if a prophet might without morbid egotism pass a favourable judgment upon himself, surely a psalmist might with still less risk of Pharisaic complacency form a favourable estimate of the moral and religious condition of his fellow-countrymen, and say: On the whole they have been in the right path, yet behold how they suffer! [2]

The foregoing considerations may suffice to convince us that Judaism, whatever its defects and tendencies, was a legitimate phase of the religion of revelation. It remains to inquire how far the transposition of the law as it lies before us in the Pentateuch, from the time of Moses to the time of Ezra, affects New Testament verdicts on the legal economy. These are that the law was subordinate to the promise, and came in after it to prepare men for the reception of the promise; and that it was a failure as a

---

[1] Ps. xliv.; *vide* also Ps. lxxiv.
[2] On the defects of Old Testament piety *vide* chap. x. of this Book.

means of attaining righteousness and acceptance with God, not merely on account of man's sin, as Paul taught, but on account of its intrinsic weakness and unprofitableness, its sacrificial system being totally unfit to deal effectually with human guilt and to bring men near to God,—the doctrine of the Epistle to the Hebrews. Being a demonstrated failure, the old legal covenant, it was held, must pass away, and give place to the new covenant prophesied of by Jeremiah. These peremptory judgments were pronounced by the inspired teachers of the Christian faith on the traditional understanding that the whole law of the Penta teuch was Mosaic. It is only when we keep in view this fact that we can fully appreciate the moral courage required to assert these positions in presence of an idolatrous rever ence for religious customs believed to be of very ancient and divine origin. Had the apostles shared modern critical views they might have taken their stand on the late and human origin of the system, and said: Leviticalism is not of Moses or of God; it is the work of Ezra and other unknown priests in Babylon, therefore it has no great claims on our respect. A much easier thing to say than : it is of Moses and of God, nevertheless it has been proved to be worthless except as a means of preparing men for something better, therefore it must pass away.

The supposed late origin of the Levitical law as a written code does not in the least detract from the validity of these New Testament verdicts, but rather strengthens it. If they hold good as against a law emanating from Moses, *a fortiori* they hold good against a law which came into force nearly a millennium later, and at the Christian era might still be regarded as a comparative upstart. The important principle enunciated by Paul, that the law was subordinate to the promise and came in after it, and between it and the promise, obviously holds on the critical hypothesis. It receives under that hypothesis a double exemplification. The Mosaic legislation came in after the call of Abraham, and the Levitical legislation came in after the promise of a new covenant with its law written on the heart. And there were two experiments to be made. One was to try whether a model state could not be built up on the foundation of the Decalogue. That experiment went on till the time of Jeremiah, when it had become clear to his prophetic eye that it had ended in failure. On the footing of a law written on stone-tablets a righteous nation he saw was not to be looked for; what was wanted was a law written on the heart. But this was not to come all at once. Jeremiah was six centuries in advance of his time. Men were not going to accept his conclusion without a convincing proof that there was no other way of it. And so the exiles returned from Babylon not with a simple spiritual law written on their hearts, but with an elaborate sacrificial and ceremonial law written in a *book*. Ezra appears with the priestly code in his hand, the fruit of much toil carried on through years spent in compiling, redacting, editing, and supplementing the Torah relating to worship and kindred matters. On the basis of that Torah a new experiment was to be made. The first experiment aimed at a righteous nation, the second at a *holy Church*. The second experiment was a more ghastly failure than even the first. The result was Rabbinism and Pharisaism: a people technically and outwardly holy, really and inwardly altogether unholy. By a prophet that might have been foreseen from the first. But the foresight of the wise does not render superfluous the age-long experiments whereby truth is made patent to all the world. Rabbinism had to be evolved before men could perceive the full significance of Jeremiah's oracle of the law written on the heart.

This breaking up of the one experiment into two, far from making the apologetic problem of the justification of God's way in the ages of preparation harder, seems rather to simplify it. If the whole Pentateuchal law was Mosaic, in the sense not merely of being as old as Moses, but of being God's word to Israel through Moses, then Jeremiah's verdict on the Sinaitic covenant must be held to have been pronounced in view of a completed historical experiment of what the law in all its parts was worth. There was in that case no room or need for a new experiment. The new covenant was due, and should have come forthwith. But in what light, then, are we to regard the four or five centuries of Israel's history between Ezra and Christ? How are we to take them up into the unity of the divine plan? They seem left out in the cold, a godless unintel ligible tract of time, having no perceptible connection with the history of revelation. Take it, on the other hand, that Jeremiah's verdict is pronounced in view of a legal pro gramme in which the priestly code had no part, as a divinely appointed system, then all becomes plain. The past history of Israel had shown that on the basis of Mosaism it was impossible to construct a really righteous nation. But a new experiment remained to be made. It had to be shown that it was equally impossible by means of an elaborate ritual to produce a holy *ecclesia*. The originators of the new experiment could start on their career with heart and hope just because it was new, some thing hitherto untried. Till their hope had been demon strated to be vain, the new era of grace could not come.

CHAPTER VIII.

THE NIGHT OF LEGALISM.

LITERATURE.—Ewald, *Geschichte des Volkes Israel*, Band iv.; Kuenen, *The Religion of Israel;* Robertson Smith, *The Old Testament in the Jewish Church* (2nd edition); Wellhausen, *Die Pharisäer und die Sadducaer;* Montet, *Essai sur les Origines des Partes Sadduceen et Pharisien;* Schürer, *Ges chichte des Jüdischen Volkes* (translated by T. & T. Clark); Drummond, *Philo Judaeus;* Sack, *Die Altjudische Religion, im Uebergange vom Bibelthume zum Talmudismus;* Thomson, *On the Books which Influenced our Lord* (Apocalyptic Litera ture); Cheyne, *Bampton Lectures on the Psalter* (Lecture vii.

on the Influence of the Persian Religion on Judaism); Toy, *Judaism and Christianity.*

I use this title to describe the state of religion among the Jewish people during the long period of above four hundred years which elapsed between the time of the prophet Malachi and the beginning of the Christian era.

The name is in every respect appropriate; even in regard to the comparative scantiness of available informa tion. The remark applies especially to the first division of the period, that during which the Jews were under the dominion of the Persians. Of this time, covering nearly a century, we know next to nothing. The one event con nected with it of interest to the Bible student is the production of the books of *Chronicles,* which probably took place towards the close of the Persian period.[1] This work, in which the books of *Ezra* and *Nehemiah* seem to have been originally incorporated, affords an interesting glimpse into the way in which pious Jews at the time when it was written regarded the past history of their nation. It is, properly speaking, not a history of Israel, but of Jerusalem, or of the religion of Jerusalem; giving first a hasty sketch of ancient history to the time of David, who made Jeru salem the capital of the nation; then the history of the city under David and his successors till the Babylonish captivity; then in *Ezra* and *Nehemiah* the history of new Jerusalem; the whole regarded from the Levitical point of view.[2]

The period now to be considered was deprived of the f_prophecy. With Malachi the sun of Hebrew prophecy set, not to rise again till John the Baptist appeared. Psalmists living in that dark time uttered the complaint: "There is no more any prophet."[3] Psalmists were indeed the only thing approaching to prophets forth-

[1] Ewald thinks it may have been written about the time of the death of Alexander the Great, which occurred in 323 B.C. *Vide* his *Geschichte des Volkes Israel*, i. 251.

[2] So Ewald, *Geschichte*, i. 251.   [3] Ps. lxxiv. 9.

coming in those years. Their sacred odes were the glitter
ing starlight of the long winter night. What a calamity
this disappearance of prophetic inspiration to a people that
had once listened to the oracles of an Isaiah and a Jere
miah! It was all the greater a calamity if the later
generations did not know how much they had lost. This
appears to have been the actual fact. The age of the hier-
ocracy, when priests and scribes bore rule, not only failed
to produce new prophets, but became incapable of appre
ciating the old ones. Speaking broadly, the great prophets
were neglected during the night of legalism. Their
prophecies were indeed collected for preservation and
assigned a place among the sacred writings. But that
place was second, not first. The law alone was emphatically
Scripture; all else was of secondary moment. The spirit of
the age even in Palestine was out of sympathy with
prophetism, and for Alexandrian Judaism it had almost no
meaning.[1]

Why did no prophets appear in those centuries? Was
it merely an unhappy chance, or was it a divine judgment?
It was neither; it was rather the result to be expected at
the stage at which the development of Israel's religion had
arrived. There was nothing more to be said on Old Testa
ment lines. The next thing to be said was the word
spoken by Jesus to the woman of Samaria, that local,
national, and ritual worship must cease, and give place to
a universal worship of the spirit. But the hour for saying
that had not yet come. Prophets do not speak till they
must. They do not arise till they are sorely needed, and
then they come and give voice to the burden that is on the
heart of all like minded with themselves. Such a crisis
could only come after legalism had had full time to bear
its proper fruit. At first, like monasticism in the Christian
Church, it appeared altogether a good thing, and commended
itself to the general religious consciousness. Psalmists
longed for the return of the sacred seasons, and were glad

[1] *Vide* Riehm, *Alttestamentliche Theologie*, p. 408.

when these came round and summoned them to go up to
the house of Jehovah.[1] They sang the praises of the law,
declaring that it was perfect, converting the soul and giving
wisdom to the simple.[2] The Chronicler was heart and soul
interested in the temple service. He delighted especially
in the temple music, and lost no opportunity of referring
to it in his narrative. He took pains to give the Levites
all due honour. He so discharged the office of historian
that in his pages the Levitical law seems to be in full force
even in the old times of David and Solomon. Obviously
the time for pronouncing the law weak and unprofitable,
and the Levitical religion incapable of perfecting the
worshipper as to conscience, is not yet come. The priests
and the scribes are in the ascendant, and must do their best
and their worst.

The scribes had very varied and apparently very useful
work to do. One task obviously lying to their hand was
that of multiplying copies of the book of the law which
Ezra, the father of their order, had written out in Babylon
and brought with him to Jerusalem. The transcription,
collection, and editing of other valuable writings, such as
those containing the oracles of the prophets, may be
regarded as a natural and probable extension of their work.
In the book of Nehemiah reference is made to the prophets
in terms which very fully acknowledge their importance as
God's messengers to testify against the sin of Israel,[3] and
which may be assumed to imply acquaintance with their
writings. In the second book of Maccabees, indeed, Nehemiah himself is credited with the founding of a library in
which the prophetic writings were included.[4] There is
nothing improbable in the statement; neither is it im
probable that the Levites, into whose mouth the prayer
containing the reference to the prophets in the book of

---

[1] Ps. cxxii.   [2] Ps xix.   [3] Neh. ix. 30.
[4] Chap. ii. 13. The statement is that Nehemiah "founded a library and
collected the (books) concerning the kings and prophets, and the (books)
of David and letters of kings about sacred gifts."

Nehemiah is put, and the scribes, whose chief interest and occupation was about the law, set sufficient value on the utterances of the prophets to desire their preservation, and to take some trouble for that purpose. And so we may legitimately conceive of the guild of the scribes as not only copyists and editors of the law, but also as collectors and editors of books of religious value, deemed sacred, though by no means put on a level with the Pentateuch.

Another very necessary department of scribe-work was the interpretation of the law. The law of the Lord might, as the Psalmist said, be perfect, but it is not easy to construct a code of rules, however numerous and exactly expressed, that shall be so complete, unambiguous, and self-consistent throughout, as to make further legislation unnecessary and commentary superfluous. The law of the Pentateuch was certainly not of that character. It contained bodies of law, apparently of different ages, difficult to reconcile with each other, and though when added together the rules of conduct in all departments of life were multitudinous, they still proved to be insufficient for men's guidance in all particular instances. There was urgent need either for new legislation or for dexterous interpretation. The scribes did not dare to assume openly the *role* of legislators: they adopted the safer line of the interpreter, and manufactured new laws under cover of explaining the old. Hence arose the *oral law*, for which not less than for the written law Mosaic origin and authority was claimed. It was a thing of evil omen, destined to grow to portentous dimensions, and to bear pernicious fruit. And yet it could plead utility, not to say necessity. What was the oral law but a *hedge* to the written law, a means of protecting it from the possibility of transgression?[1] This business of hedging once begun

---

[1] In the Pirke-Aboth the men of the Great Synagogue are reported to have said three things : Be deliberate in judgment ; raise up many disciples ; make a hedge around the law. These sayings indicate the aim and spirit of scribism.

was a serious affair. The law itself, as reconstructed by
Ezra, was a hedge to the religion of Israel, as a people in
covenant with God. And now in turn it was discovered
that it too needed a hedge. And the second hedge
needed a third, and the third a fourth, and so on *ad
infinitum*, till there was nothing but a vast expanse of
hedges, and the thing for which all the hedging had
taken place, the true worship and service of God, had
somehow disappeared. The immense development of con
centric hedge-work found its historic monument in the
Talmud, that vast pyramid in which Judaism lies entombed.
It was that pyramid the scribes, without knowing it,
were busy building, stone upon stone, during the night of
legalism.

There is reason to believe that while under Persian
dominion the Jews came under Persian influence to some
extent in their religion. This was a thing likely to
happen. For the Persians, besides being a friendly people,
had a kindred religion. Their idea of God was similar
to that of the Hebrew prophets. They thought of the
Supreme Being as one to whom moral distinctions were
real and vital, who loved righteousness and hated unright
cousness. This ethically-conceived deity, called Ahura-
Mazda, was for them the one true God. They did indeed
set over against the good and wise Spirit another spirit,
whom they called Angra-Mainyu, the evil-minded, on which
account it has been customary to represent the ancient
Persians as believers in a dualism rather than as monotheists. But the Persian dualism was involuntary. The
prominence given in the Zend religion to the evil spirit,
source and maker of all evil things in the world, was the
result and proof of its earnest ethicalism. The Zoroas-
trians were so bent on maintaining the holiness and good
ness of God, that to save these from being compromised
they were willing to sacrifice or imperil His sovereignty by
setting beside Him a rival deity, a sort of anti-god who
should be held responsible for all the evil that was in the

universe.[1] They held it to be the duty of every man to
love and serve the good Spirit, and to hate the evil spirit
and all his works. Between the two spirits and the king
doms of light and darkness over which they preside there
is an incessant war, and all men must choose on which side
they are to be; and well for the man who chooses the
kingdom of Ahura-Mazda and his righteousness, and strives
to advance it by purity, truth, culture of the soil, and the
practice of family duties, and who fights against Angra-
Mainyu, hating lies, deceit, adultery, murder, killing noxious
beasts, and carefully preserving the lives of all useful
animals.

From a religion like this, with an exalted idea of God,
and a noble ideal of human life, the Jewish people would
not feel it necessary to hold aloof, as they had been com
pelled to hold aloof from the religion of their Canaanite
neighbours, that they might escape moral contamination.
They might even be not unwilling to learn some lessons in
religion from their Persian masters. The subjects in which
they may be supposed to have received instruction are
chiefly these : ceremonial rules of purification, Satan, angels,
and the resurrection of the dead. Now that there is a
striking resemblance in these respects, as in their respec
tive ideas of God, between the religions of the two peoples,
there can be no doubt. In the Persian, as in the Levitical
religion, uncleanness, arising from contact with the work
of the evil spirit, such as death, and the means of removing
it, occupy a prominent place. The Hebrew Satan answers
to the Persian Angra-Mainyu. The Zend religion is rich in
spirits good and evil. The Zend-Avesta swarms with spirits
of every description, with uncouth names and diverse func
tions : Yatus, Pairika, Druants, wizard spirits, spirits of
the air, storm fiends—evil spirits all ; and Yazatas and
Fravashis, tutelary spirits for the days of the month and

---

[1] Darmesteter says that in the Indo-Iranian religion there was "a latent
monotheism and an unconscious dualism." Translation of the Zend-Avesta,
Sacred Books of the East, vol. iv., Introduction, p. lvii.

for particular clans and neighbourhoods, and, highest of all, the Amesha Spentas, the seven "undying and well-doing ones." And it is noticeable that in the later books of the Old Testament, as in Zachariah and Daniel, angelic beings are more prominent than in the older books. Finally, the doctrine of the resurrection is common to the two religions, and the fact is all the more remarkable that it is only in those books of the Bible which critics believe to have been written in the Persian period, or still later, that the doctrine makes its appearance.

Is this correspondence due to borrowing? It is a ques tion to be discussed without prejudice, and yet to be answered with caution. We have no cause to be jealous of the influence of surrounding peoples on the religious opinions of the Jews. It is a mere question of fact. On the other hand, it must be carefully borne in mind that mere resemblance does not prove conscious imitation or borrowing on either side. Common features may be " de velopmental coincidences "[1] in religions of kindred nature. It is natural that an earnestly ethical religion which sees in the whole history of the world a struggle between good and evil should in the course of its historical development evolve a doctrine of resurrection and eternal judgment. In the same way Angra-Mainyu and Satan may be a case of developmental coincidence. Every kingdom has a head; what more natural than that a religion which sees in the world a struggle between two kingdoms of light and dark ness should provide for the latter kingdom as well as for the former a head, without needing to go to a foreign religion in quest of one? The resemblance between Satan and Angra-Mainyu is not the thing to be accounted for, but rather their difference; this, viz. that Satan and his kingdom are not independent as are Angra-Mainyu and his kingdom.

Yet withal there appear to be distinct traces of Persian

---

[1] This most suggestive expression is borrowed from Principal Fairbairn of Mansfield College, Oxford. *Vide* his *Studies in the Philosophy of Religion and of History*, p. 23.

influence on Jewish religious opinion, at least in the depart
ment of angelology. The very names of spirits which figure
in the later Jewish books are suggestive of this, as, e.g., Asmo-
deus in the book of Tobit, which is simply *aeshma daeva*
done into Greek. And it is not difficult to see how it
came about that the Jews were ready to welcome Persian
ideas on this subject. These fitted into the tendency of
later Judaism to a transcendent conception of God. That
tendency revealed itself from the first in Levitical worship,
as reshaped by Ezra. The God of the Levitical cultus is a
far-off God. He keeps Himself aloof from sinful men in
jealous guardianship of His holiness. He confines Himself
to a most holy place into which no one but the high priest
may enter, and he only once a year, and with careful
precautions, while ordinary mortals stand without waiting
the result of sacerdotal mediation. Aloofness from the
world is but an extension of this idea of a far-off God, and
angelic mediation between the Divine Being and the crea
tion is parallel to high priestly mediation between the Holy
One and sinful Israelites. In this connection the altered
version of the numbering of the people by David in the
book of Chronicles is very significant.[1] In the book of
Samuel it is Jehovah that tempts David;[2] in Chronicles it
is Satan.[3] The change does not prove that Satan is an
importation from Persia, or even that the person responsible
for the change, whether the Chronicler or the unknown
author of a source used by him, was consciously influenced
by Persian ways of thinking regarding God's relation to
men's sin. But it does prove that at the time when the
book of Chronicles was compiled, Jewish ideas concerning
God had undergone important modification. It was then
felt to be unseemly to bring the Divine Being into so close
contact with man's misconduct, and the readiest solution
was to assign the function of the tempter to Satan, as an
intermediary between Jehovah and David. It is a solution
which may not satisfy us, but it is at least interesting as

---

[1] 2 Sam. xxiv.; 1 Chron. xxi.   [2] 2 Sam. xxiv. 11.   [3] 1 Chron. xxi. 1.

supplying unmistakable evidence of the existence of the tendency above referred to as opening a door through which Persian beliefs about the spirit-world might find entrance into the Jewish mind. The God of Judaism, the Chronicler being witness, is a transcendent Deity, exalted by His holiness far above human sin, presumably exalted also in His essential being above the creation; incapable of having anything to do with the world except through mediators human or angelic. A tendency like this, once it sets in, goes on till it reaches its natural limit. By and by it will be deemed improper even to pronounce God's name as it had once been current in Israel, and held a mark of piety to call Him Elohim or Adonai rather than Jehovah. Even in Ecclesiastes, probably of later origin than Chronicles, this habit appears to have been begun. The name Jehovah does not once occur in that book, and consistently with this fact God is spoken of as " He that is higher,"[1] and set in contrast to men by the formula, " God is in heaven, and thou upon earth."[2] In Philo the new way of thought culminates in a conception of God as the unknowable and inexpressible, incapable of relations with the universe, except through angels and Powers, and *logoi* and the Logos, semipersonal beings who flit through the dim world like owls in the night.[3]

Thus far we have had no occasion to think of the Jews in the period now under review otherwise than as a united people striving with one mind and heart to make God's law the rule of their lives. It is a rare community that knows no divisions in religion. The Christian Church has

---

[1] Eccles. v. 8. [2] Eccles. v. 2.

[3] In the above paragraphs I may appear to treat the question of Persian influence unsympathetically, but I do not wish to be understood as restricting that influence to the one point of angels, or regarding it as on the whole sinister. I am quite open to the view advocated enthusiastically by Cheyne in his *Bampton Lectures on the Psalter* in these words : " If Talmudic eschatology borrowed something from the less noble parts of the Persian religion, must not the psalmists, with their finer spiritual tact, have welcomed the help of its nobler teaching? Yes, surely. The earlier revelation

had ample and sorrowful experience of strife and separation caused by diversity of opinion and practice. The post-exilian Jewish Church was not wholly exempt from similar evils. The existence of serious cleavage became apparent during the period of the Greek dominion, when the *Pharisees* and the *Sadducees* came upon the scene as rival parties in religious and political affairs. The origin of these parties and of their names is involved in obscurity; for it is night, with only moonlight at the best, in which all objects are seen but dimly. Practically, it was a cleavage between the scribes and the priests; and when we consider the occupations of these two classes, their respective spheres of influence, and the tendencies naturally arising out of these, we can imagine how, long before it came to an open rupture, they fell away from each other in opinion, feeling, and interest. The priest was the performer of routine religious rites, the scribe was a student and teacher of the law. The sphere of the priest's activity was the temple, that of the scribe's was the synagogue. Hence arose a difference in point of popularity; the priest met the people on rare occasions, when they came up to Jerusalem at the seasons of the great feasts; the scribe met them every week on Sabbath days, when they assembled to offer prayer and hear the Scriptures read. To this must be added that the priests were rulers as well as religious officials. The high priest was the prince of the community, holding in his hands the reins of power. Hence crept into priestly families and circles aristocratic feeling, and a more or less secular spirit. The scribes, on the other hand, became not less naturally the representatives of democratic and religious tendencies.

---

to Iranian thinkers of these high spiritual truths, the universal Lordship of God, and His never-ending relation to the individual, must have had some providential object beyond itself. And I think that we can now see what that object was. The appointed time for the blending of the Aryan and Semitic mind, which was to occupy so many centuries, had come," p. 401.

✕ Renan has little faith in the Persian influence. He says the Jew in Babylon went about with his eyes shut and learned nothing.—*Histoire du Peuple d'Israel*, iii. 440.

By this contrast others are explained. The aristocratic temper is conservative in matters of opinion. Hence we are not surprised to learn that the Sadducees, who were the outgrowth of priestly tendencies, held on to the written law, and kept aloof from the oral law and the novelties of the schools, and further that they shut their minds to the new dogmas concerning angels and the resurrection. On this side the priests might claim to be, in comparison with the scribes, the party of old orthodoxy adhering closely to the ways of the fathers. But, on another side, they were likely to appear to less advantage. Their secularity, arising out of the exercise of government, would incline them to follow foreign customs when it seemed advisable in the interest of the state. This accordingly was what happened under the Greek dominion. The priests were the leaders in the process of Hellenisation, while the scribes were the champions of Jewish law and custom.[1]

It was inevitable that the latent tendencies of the two parties should come to the surface under Greek rule. The ruler was near at hand, not far away as in the case of the preceding Persian dominion. The Greek was in the land, dwelling in newly-founded cities bearing Greek names, enjoying Greek government, and fostering within them Greek customs. And Greek social life was an aggressive, infectious thing appealing to the senses, attractive and fascinating to all lovers of pleasure. Greek culture, too, was bright, rich, and beautiful, standing in brilliant contrast to the poverty of the Semitic world in all that belonged to art, science, and philosophy. Here was a situation to which the Jewish people could not remain indifferent. They must make up their minds either to surrender to the new Western influence, or to harden themselves against it. Some took the one course, some the other; some Hellenised, some stood loyally by old Hebrew ways. In their philo-Greek enthusiasm men got their names translated from Hebrew

---

[1] On this whole subject Wellhausen's Essay, *Die Pharisäer und die Sadducaer*, is specially instructive.

into Greek, and did their best to obliterate the physical sign of their connection with the Jewish race. They sacri ficed to idols, profaned the Sabbath, and were not content till they had obtained permission from the government to found a gymnasium in Jerusalem. And in this wild, god less movement of apostacy the priests, to their shame, were the ringleaders.

Then came a turn in the tide through the madness of Antiochus Epiphanes. Perceiving how willing many of the Jews, including some of the most influential men of the nation, were to become Greeks, he was misled into thinking that the whole people were prepared for the wholesale obliteration of everything distinctively Jewish. Orders were issued accordingly, the execution of which created a great reaction. It turned out that not only the scribes and multitudes of the people, but not a few among the priests, were prepared to resist the process of de nationalisation to the death. The hero of the patriotic revolt was Judas Maccabæus, and the result the triumph of the faithful in Israel over their pagan foes. The war ended, the union brought about by the dire crisis between priests and scribes also came to an end. Each party once more followed its proper bent. Sadducees and Pharisees struggled for ascendency, fighting with each other not less violently than they had fought together against the common enemy. Neither could claim to be a worthy representa tive of the religion of Israel. Ambition played a large place among the ruling motives of their conduct. More or less corrupt in spirit to begin with, they produced in each other, by their party antagonism, ever-increasing moral deterioration; till at length, a century and a half after the time of Antiochus Epiphanes, they had become what we see them in the Gospels: utterly opposed to each other in belief and policy, yet alike ungodly in spirit, and entire aliens from that divine kingdom whose advent Jesus proclaimed.

In the judgment of many modern critics, the time of

trouble, which gave to the Jewish people a hero in the person of Judas Maccabæus, also enriched their sacred literature by the addition to it of the book of *Daniel*. If this view be correct, then that book is of the *apocalyptic type;* that is to say, it presents what is really history under the form of prophecy uttered by a personage of great name, who lived long before the actual author's time. As such, it belongs to a class of literature much inferior to the collection of oracles uttered by the great prophets, who ever spoke in their own name what God had revealed to their own spirit. But it is a great book, worthy of a place in the Hebrew canon, well fitted to serve the imme diate object of nerving a persecuted people to heroic endurance, and memorable and valuable for all time as the first attempt to grasp the history of the world as one great whole, "as a drama which moves onward at the will of the Eternal One."[1] It is the brightest light of the night of legalism, greatly superior in value, if one may make comparisons between canonical books, to two other late additions to the sacred collection, *Ecclesiastes* and *Esther;* the former of which rather serves to show how deep the darkness was growing than to throw any light on the problems of life, while the latter, as a literary reflection of a Judaism of the narrowest type, seems to lie on the outermost fringe of what rightfully belongs to the category of the canonical. And as for the other apocalyptic books that were kept out of the canon, they are not worthy to be mentioned alongside of Daniel. They are, it has been truly observed, "in the unfavourable sense of the word, works of art; they smell of the lamp; it is no living, animated conviction that speaks in them, and therefore they are altogether unfit to arouse enthusiasm."[2] When or by whom they were written is unknown; it has been suggested that they proceeded from the fraternity of ascetics that lived in retirement from the world by the shores of

---

[1] Kuenen, *The Religion of Israel*, iii. 111.
[2] *Ibid.* iii. 114.

the Dead Sea, known by the name of the *Essenes*.[1] Be this as it may, one thing is certain : such books cannot possibly have exercised a decisive influence on the religious thought of Jesus. No man now can read the book of Enoch, the best of the class, except as a task connected with some special line of study, and it was probably little less dreary reading at the beginning of our era. Jesus, at all events, drew His inspiration from a very different source. Isaiah, especially Isaiah the second, was more to His taste than these fantastic apocalypses. A stray phrase may have found its way into His vocabulary from that quarter, but beyond this an influence emanating thence is not discernible in the Gospels.

The apocalyptic literature revived after a fashion the Messianic hope, and for this, perhaps, we ought to be grateful. But when we study more closely the presentation therein given of the Messianic age, we are conscious only of a limited sense of indebtedness. In some respects, indeed, there appears to be an advance beyond the standpoint of the great prophets. The view, for example, is extended from the nation to the world. The individual also comes more to the front as the recipient of blessing, the boon promised being resurrection to everlasting life. On the other hand, the *summum bonum* becomes here transcendent; it is transferred to the world to come, and has no place among the realities of the present world. Finally, in the apocalyptic presentation of the Messianic hope we pass from the poetry of the prophets to the dull, dogmatic prose of the scribes.[2] Reading an apocalytic picture of the good time coming does not affect us like reading the sixtieth chapter of Isaiah. The latter thrills,

---

[1] So Thomson (*Books which Influenced our Lord and His Apostles*) after Hilgenfeld. The Essenes are, as Cheyne in his *Bampton Lectures on the Psalter* well expresses it, "twilight figures" (p. 421), and of their connection with the apocalyptic literature there is little or no evidence.

[2] On the Messianic hope of the period of the scribes compared with that of the prophets, *vide* especially Schürer, *The Jewish People in the Time of Jesus Christ*, Div. II. vol. ii. p. 130 ff.

consoles, moves to tears; the former makes us melancholy. Scholars may revive a professional interest in apocalyptic, and it is not to be denied that the exegete of the New Testament may learn something from their labours; but the great heart of humanity has only one duty to perform towards it, and that is to consign it to oblivion.

An account of the religion of Israel during the period now under review would not be complete without a brief reference to the Jews scattered abroad over the Gentile world. The *Diaspora*, or dispersion, covered a wide area from Babylon to Asia Minor, but its chief seat was the Greek city of Alexandria, in Egypt, wherein a large number of Jews found a home under the friendly reign of the Ptolemies. The phenomenon, therefore, which above all invites attention in this connection is *Hellenism;* that is, Jewish religious thought as coloured by Greek influence in that great centre of Greek culture. Two facts of outstanding importance are associated with the movement: the use of the Greek language as an instrument for the diffusion of Judaism, and the use of Greek philosophy as an instrument for its dissipation.

The Jews resident in Alexandria, as a natural result of their intercourse with the Greeks, soon became Greek-speaking. An inevitable consequence of this was that a demand soon arose among them for a translation of the Hebrew Scriptures into their adopted tongue. The result was the *Septuagint.* Marvellous tales came into circulation at a later date respecting the circumstances under which this famous version was executed. The truth seems to be that it was produced, not by the authority and under the patronage of kings or high priests, but by private enterprise, in response to the general wish of the Alexandrian Jews, and to meet their religious needs. It was a work of time, the translation of the law, as the most important part of Scripture, being first undertaken; that of other portions following in due course. The great work was begun probably about the middle of the third century B.C., and had reached completion by the year 132 B.C., as we learn from the son of Sirach, who visited Egypt at that time, and found there a Greek version of "the law, and the prophecies, and the rest of the books."[1] The end aimed at was primarily the edification of Greek-speaking Jews, but, doubtless, through the Greek Bible many Gentiles became acquainted with the religion of the remarkable people that had settled among them.

The Septuagint has been carefully searched for traces of the influence of Greek philosophy on the mind of the translators. What we do find is clear evidence that the translators were not uninfluenced by the change that had come over their countrymen in Palestine in their way of thinking concerning God. There is the same tendency that we have noted in Leviticalism, and in some of the later books of Scripture, to conceive of God as transcendent, far away above the world and human sin and infirmity. For Jehovah the translators substitute "the Lord," ὁ κύριος. All anthropopathisms and anthropomorphisms in the original they carefully soften down. "God repented" is rendered "God reflected";[2] the statement that the elders of Israel saw God is transformed into "saw the place where God stood,"[3] and the privilege of Moses to see God's form becomes a privilege to see His glory.[4]

With all its defects, the Greek version of the Hebrew Scriptures was an important service rendered to the religion of Israel. The employment of Greek philosophy as an instrument of thought and vehicle of the Jewish faith was of more doubtful value. A full account of this movement cannot here be given. We see it in the initial stage in the *Wisdom of Solomon,* in which God is represented as creating the world out of formless matter, as a previously existing datum,[5] and the body of man is spoken of as the seat of sin, pressing down the soul and hindering the free

---

[1] *Vide* Prologue to the *Wisdom of Sirach.*
[2] Gen. vi. 6.   [3] Ex. xxiv. 10.   [4] Num. xii. 8.
[5] ἐξ ἀμόρφου ὕλης, xi. 18.

exercise of thought.[1] It reached its consummation in
Philo, a contemporary of Jesus,[2] whose manner of conceiv
ing God has been already indicated.[3] Philo was a gifted
and cultured Jew spoiled by being transformed into a
second-rate Greek philosopher. As a thinker, he was a
Jew in form and a Greek in spirit. He was a cross
between Moses and Plato. He took his texts from Moses,
and delivered on them sermons full of Platonic ideas and
un-Platonic rhetoric. For what we find in his writings, is
Plato at second hand, and very degenerate. Between his
turgid discourses and Plato's exquisitely graceful dialogues
there is as great a difference as between Jewish apocalyptic
and Hebrew prophecy. There is no true originality and
inspiration in him. He is a brilliant yet barren writer,
who will found no school and communicate enthusiasm to
no susceptible reader. The time at which he was born,
and his considerable importance in the eyes of his con
temporaries, might suggest the question, Can this be he
who should come? But one has only to peruse a few
pages of his voluminous writings to be satisfied that who
ever was destined to put the crown on Israel's religious
development it was not Philo. No deliverance was to
come to the Jews or to the world from that quarter.

Philo and the scribes were very unlike each other, yet
there was one bond of connection between them. How
ever wide apart their respective ways and goals, they
had the same starting-point. They both ascribed divine
authority to the law, and professed to derive all they
taught from that sacred source. Out of it Philo educed
Greek philosophy; the scribe, the traditions of the elders.
It was possible to arrive at so diverse results through the
employment of different methods of interpretation. Philo's
method was the free use of allegory; the scribe's was a
mechanical, irrational literalism.[4] The two methods, both

---

[1] φθαρτον γαρ σωμα βαρυνει ψυχην, IX. 15.
[2] Born probably 10 B.C.   [3] *Vide* p. 287.
[4] The scribes strove to show that the whole of the traditional law could be

alike vicious, supply instructive examples of the fatal abuse of a sacred text-book, showing how what might have been a light to the feet became an *ignis fatuus,* and a rule of faith was perverted into a blind guide of the blind. From these instances we learn that no book, however excellent, can be a self-acting infallible guide, and that all depends on how it is used. The higher the authority ascribed to it the more it will mislead, if false reverence be allowed to extinguish the light of reason. It would have been better for the Alexandrian Jewish philosophers and Palestinian scribes to have discarded the Book, and to have taught on their own authority. Their doctrine would have been much the same as it was, and they would have been saner and honester men. Their reverence for Scripture was a new form of idolatry, which took possession of the Jewish people after they had finally conquered all other forms. It proved to be the deadliest of all. They searched the Scriptures, and the more they searched the further they erred from truth and God.

The foregoing sketch of the religion of Israel during the centuries intervening between the Old Testament and the New is very disenchanting. The voice of prophecy hushed; scribism in the ascendant; God, partly through foreign influence, become transcendent and far-off; the evil spirit of sectarianism making its appearance; artificial pseudo-prophetic compositions taking the place of genuine prophetic oracles, and vapid Alexandrian rhetoric superseding grave Hebrew eloquence; the people of the living word becoming the people of the Book and making of that Book a fetich. Truly a dark time, in which even the brightest mani festation of the Hebrew religious spirit was of very mixed moral worth, the Maccabæan patriotic movement being by no means an exhibition of pure devotion to the

deduced from the written law. The feat was accomplished by aid of seven rules of interpretation formulated by Hillel, which look very innocent, but as actually employed could be made to educe any conclusions out of any premises. *Vide* Farrar's *Bampton Lectures on the History of Interpreta·tion,* p. 18.

universal interest of eternal righteousness, but in part a semi-fanatical outburst of zeal for national customs of merely statutory value.[1] The whole picture in all its aspects is a trial to our faith in the religious vocation of Israel. If Israel's religion was of special concern to God how was it allowed to come to this? If the divine spirit was immanent in Israel's religious history, whence this tremendous degeneracy? The phenomenon has its parallel in the history of the Christian Church which presents, in ecclesiastical Christianity as compared with the Christianity of Christ, a contrast not less glaring than that between prophetism and scribism. Such declensions are facts with which faith must reconcile itself the best way it can. In the case of the earlier declension the feat is not impossible. The lapse served to make the inherent defect of the legal system signally apparent, and so prepared the way for Jesus.[2]

CHAPTER IX.

THE OLD TESTAMENT LITERATURE.

LITERATURE.—Butler, *Analogy* (Part II. Chapter iii.); Pécaut, *Le Christ et la Conscience;* Robertson Smith, *The Old Testament in the Jewish Church* (2nd edition); Simon, *The Bible an Outgrowth of Theocratic Literature;* Ladd, *The Doctrine of Sacred Scripture;* Gladden, *Who wrote the Bible?* Reuss, *Histoire du Canon des Saintes-Écritures* (translated); Buhl, *Kanon und Text des Alten Testamentes* (translated by

---

[1] On this fact Darmesteter rests his chief argument against Havet's theory of the origin of the prophetic writings in the Maccabæan period. The originality of the prophets, he says, "is precisely that they are not conservers or restorers of the past, as were the Maccabees; they are the creators of the future. They are the apostles of a new faith which goes to elevate the nation above the brutalities of the universe."—*Les Prophètes d'Israel*, p. 132. He also remarks truly that the conquerors referred to in the prophetic writings do not appear, like Antiochus Epiphanes, as tyrants over conscience, p. 130.

[2] *Vide* on this Riehm, *Alttestamentliche Theologie*, p. 371.

T. & T. Clark); Kirkpatrick, *The Divine Library of the Old Testament;* Driver, *Introduction to the Literature of the Old Testament;* Ryle, *The Canon of the Old Testament,* 1892.

To say that God gave a special revelation to Israel is not the same thing as to say that He gave to Israel a collec tion of sacred books. Revelation and the Bible are not synonyms. There was a revelation long before there was a Bible. God revealed Himself in history as the God of the whole earth, graciously choosing Israel to be in the first place the recipient of the supreme blessing of the knowledge of the true God, and to be eventually His instrument for communicating that knowledge to the whole world. He revealed Himself as a gracious electing God to the *consciousness* of Israel, through spiritual insight into the true significance of her history communicated to the prophets; first to Moses, and then, in later centuries, to the prophets whose oracles have been preserved in books bearing their names. The election, and the providential training of Israel, and the gradually attained insight into the fact and purpose of the election, would have been a most important self-revelation of God though a literature of revelation never had arisen; and it would have accom plished most important purposes, though, as Bishop Butler remarks, not all the purposes which a recorded revelation has answered, and in the same degree.[1] Great things were done by God in Israel before the Hebrew Bible came into existence. Nay, one might say that the best days of Israel were over before the sacred Book appeared; that Jehovah was more manifestly present among the chosen people when she was the people of the living Word, than when she became the people of the written Book. The people of the Book were a degenerate people; the emergence of the Book was coincident with the night of legalism; and the use made of it was to a large extent idolatrous, and such as tended to hide rather than reveal

---

[1] *Analogy,* Part II. chap. iii.

God; this, however, from no fault of the Book, but rather from the fault of its readers.

While all this is true, it is nevertheless also true that given a revelation such as God communicated to Israel, a literature of revelation, though not a matter of *a priori* necessity, was a highly probable consequence. Record of some sort might be pronounced, in a broad sense, indispensable. The record might, indeed, conceivably be merely oral. How far oral tradition would have been an adequate means of preserving the knowledge of God's self-manifestations, and the idea of God these embodied, is a question of subordinate importance. All that we are concerned to maintain at present is, that if God specially revealed Himself to Israel it was well that all should have knowledge of the fact and of the mode and measure of the revelation vouchsafed, and that a written record, if not the only means of communicating such knowledge, is at least a most valuable means. As to the former part of this thesis, its truth is recognised in the familiar words of the Psalter: "One generation shall praise Thy works to another, and shall declare Thy mighty acts. I will speak of the glorious honour of Thy majesty, and of Thy wondrous works. And men shall speak of the might of Thy terrible acts: and I will declare Thy greatness. They shall abundantly utter the memory of Thy great goodness, and shall sing of Thy righteousness."[1] As to the latter part of the thesis, the Westminster Confession expresses itself in these sober terms: "Therefore it pleased the Lord, at sundry times, and in divers manners, to reveal Himself, and to declare that His will unto His Church; and afterwards for the better preserving and propagating of the truth, and for the more sure establishment and comfort of the Church against the corruption of the flesh and the malice of Satan and of the world, to commit the same wholly unto writing, which maketh Holy Scripture to be most necessary, those former ways

[1] Ps. cxlv. 4-7.

of God's revealing His will unto His people being now ceased." [1]

This doctrine may be regarded as beyond question, if the words "most necessary" be taken as implying a very high degree of utility, amounting to a practical necessity. Only when they are so interpreted as to involve the dogma that without the knowledge of Scripture salvation is absolutely impossible, are they fitted to create a prejudice such as finds occasional expression in the sneers at the religion of Christendom as a Book revelation. It cannot be denied that believers in the incomparable value of the Scriptures of the Old and New Testaments as the authentic records of divine revelations, have not always been sufficiently careful to avoid giving occasion for this unhappy prejudice. It was the tendency of theologians in the scholastic period of Protestantism to connect the ideas of revelation and record so closely together as to convey a false impression as to the precise function of Scripture. The Bible was to them not only the record of revelation, but the revelation itself, and hence acquaintance with the record was deemed indispensable to participation in the benefit of revelation. Unless men knew the written record, God might as well never have revealed Himself so far as they were concerned. An interesting illustration of this tendency is supplied by Richard Baxter. Baxter and Dr. Owen were together members of a committee appointed by the Parliament which made Cromwell Protector to draw up a list of fundamentals. The list was intended to define the meaning of the words occurring in the instrument of government, "faith in God by Jesus Christ," it being laid down in that document that all who professed such faith should have liberty, or free exercise of their religion. The divines appointed to perform the momentous task of fixing the basis of religious toleration, very soon found, in Baxter's quaint language, "how ticklish a business the enumeration of fundamentals was." Among the points in

[1] Chap. i. section 1.

dispute, according to our informant, was this: whether the knowledge of Holy Scripture was absolutely necessary to salvation. Dr. Owen took the affirmative side, and wished to make a fundamental of the dogma, "that no man could know God to salvation by any other means," evidently desiring to use it as a means of excluding the papists from the benefits of toleration. Baxter, as one would expect, stoutly maintained the negative, contending that Dr. Owen's thesis was neither a fundamental nor a truth, and that if, among the papists or any others, a poor Christian should believe by the teaching of another with out ever knowing that there is a Scripture, he should be saved, because it is promised that whosoever believed should be saved.[1] The weakness of Owen's position is apparent, and its mischievousness not less so; not merely in unduly narrowing the limits of religious toleration to the disturbance of the peace of the commonwealth, but still more in exposing faith in the utility of Scripture to the bitter assaults of free thinkers like Rousseau, who found it an easy task to refute such a doctrine as that of Owen by the method of *reductio ad absurdum*. How different from this exaggerated and perilous way of speaking con cerning the Bible indulged in by the theologian of the seventeenth century, the sober, moderate, dignified state ment of the Apostle Paul, "All scripture given by in spiration is *profitable*,"[2] useful. He does not deem it necessary to lay down a negative position as to what can be done without Scripture. He is content to teach positively that the Scriptures are useful for the ends of religious edification. Whatever may befall the man who has not the felicity to enjoy the aid of this valuable means of grace, it is certain, in Paul's judgment, that the man who has the Scriptures in his hand, and makes a wise use of them, is in a fair way of becoming perfect, thoroughly furnished unto all good works.

The utility and value of the Hebrew Scriptures arise

[1] *Reliquiæ Baxterianæ*, p. 199.   [2] 2 Tim. iii. 16.

ultimately from_this, that they are a literature of revelation, that is to say a record and interpretation of the self-revelation of God to Israel. This has to be borne in mind in comparing these writings with other books of a highly edifying character. Leaving this fact out of sight, one may think himself justified in putting certain books on a level with the Bible, or even in some respects above it. The Bible, it may be said, is a very good book, profitable for edification without doubt; but then there are other books also remarkable for this quality, such as the Confessions of St. Augustine, and the golden treatise of À Kempis on the Imitation of Christ, not to speak of the Dialogues of Plato and the Meditations of Antoninus. "Think you," asks a French writer of the school of Theodore Parker, "I search not my edification in the Bible, that it has ceased to console me, to lead me to repentance, to turn me from evil, to excite me to good? Have I given up using it as my daily bread, and has it disappeared from my house? Assuredly not. All I say is that nothing in the impression I receive from that book resembles *authority*. Between the Confessions of St. Augustine, the Meditations of Bossuet, the Imitation of Jesus Christ, and the Bible, I see a difference of degree, not of nature." [1] The answer to this is that the Bible is not a mere book of devotion, and still less, of course, a mere book of general literature, the literary remains of the Hebrew people. Viewed from the merely devotional or literary point of view, the Bible in some parts may be inferior to other books that might be named. But in this respect it is unique, that it is a literature which providentially grew up around a historical revelation of God in Israel, and which performs for that revelation the function of an atmosphere, diffusing the sunlight, so that the knowledge of God is spread abroad over all the earth. And in virtue of this function it may in an intelligible sense be called an authoritative_book. There is no other book but the

---

[1] Pécaut, *Le Christ et la Conscience*, pp. 19, 20.

Bible which serves this precise end, and the authority it possesses on that account can be got rid of only by denying the reality of the revelation of which it is the record.

In the light of this function other attributes ascribed by theologians to Scripture are most easily understood and vindicated—*perfection*, for example, or *infallibility*. In view of the unique nature of the holy writings as the literature of revelation, it is possible to assign to these attributes an important meaning without advancing what might be regarded as extravagant or ill-founded claims. In this connection it is of the utmost moment to distinguish between what individual believers hold as matter of personal conviction, and what as believers in revelation we are bound to hold. One may believe that the Scriptures in general, and the Hebrew Scriptures in particular, are characterised by absolute immunity from error in fact or sentiment, and yet as an apologist be entitled to ask, Is this characteristic necessarily involved in the end which these writings were designed to subserve? It will be obvious that the maintenance of the affirmative on this question is somewhat perilous, when it is considered in what state we possess the Scriptures now. For the million the only means of knowing the sacred books is through translations, which, however faithfully executed on the whole, do nevertheless but imperfectly reflect the sense of the original. Then even for the learned the Hebrew and Greek texts do not exist in their original purity. Nay, the text of the Hebrew Bible, with which we are at present concerned, never existed as one whole, in absolute purity. The errorless autograph for which some so zealously contend is a theological figment. There may conceivably have been such a document for each part in succession, but there never was an errorless autograph of the collection as a whole. The Bible was produced piecemeal, and by the time the later portions were produced the earlier had lost their supposed immaculateness. And that we may see how necessary it is to be circumspect in our *a priori* demands of perfection and faultlessness, it is well to remember in what form the words of the Hebrew autographs were written. They were written with consonants only, the vowels being left to be supplied by the reader, the result being that no man but the writer could be perfectly sure in numerous cases what he intended to say, and not even the writer himself, in every case, after the lapse of time long enough to allow partial forgetfulness of his thought to occur. The Masoretic Hebrew text is thus only an approximately accurate translation by Jewish scholars of the vowelless original.[1] This defect of the Hebrew language as written is an awkward characteristic of a book bound to be absolutely accurate in all its statements under pain of being tossed aside as useless in case a single error great or small be detected in it. No wonder some of the most logically consistent dogmatists of the seven teenth century met the dilemma by boldly maintaining that the vowel points were inspired.[2] Unfortunately this course cannot now be followed even by the boldest dog matist, and the only way of escape is to cherish the hope that the Hebrew Bible can be useful, supremely useful, for the end for which it was given, without possessing all the imaginary virtues which self-constituted champions of its perfection claim for it. In accordance with that view the aim of the apologist must be to ascertain the minimum requirements necessary to accomplish that end.

In order to serve their end as the literature of revelation the Hebrew Scriptures would need to be a reliable record of Israel's history in its main outlines, and a trustworthy interpretation of the meaning of that history. The hypothesis of faith is that in the history of Israel God revealed Himself as the God of a gracious purpose, and from the literature of revelation, if it deserve the name,

---

[1] *Vide* on this Professor Robertson Smith's *Old Testament in the Jewish Church*, Lect. ii., and Professor Kirkpatrick's *Divine Library of the Old Testament*, Lect. iii.

[2] So the *Formula Consensus Helvetica*. *Vide* Heppe, *Die Dogmatik der Evangelisch Reformirten Kirche*, pp. 18, 19.

it ought to be possible to learn enough of that history to see the purpose unfolding itself, and to get guidance in the interpretation of the essential facts from men to whom has been fully opened up the secret of the Lord. It is not necessary that every particular historical statement should be correct, but the general impression made by the whole story of Israel, as that of a people in a peculiar manner related to God, ought to be true, and the religious conception of Israel's vocation, and of God's character in connection therewith, formed by the prophets and embodied in their writings, ought to be objectively valid. If we cannot rely on the history in its main outlines, as the history of an elect people, and on the prophetic reading of the history, then there is no evidence that a special revelation took place. If, on the other hand, we can rely on both these, the Hebrew Scriptures are sufficient for this end; perfect for the purpose for which they were given, and a sure guide to faith, no matter how many defects there may be in the historical record, whether in the form of *lacunæ*, or of individual facts not quite accurately represented.

At this point the question may naturally be raised, How is the religious value of the Old Testament affected by critical views as to the late origin of the Pentateuch and of the law as a written code? The question resolves into two: First, assuming the correctness of these critical views, what value have the relative parts of the Bible for the unlearned reader entirely ignorant of criticism: do they not seriously mislead him? Second, how far can these Scriptures retain their value as a religious guide for those who accept the results of critical inquiry?

The unlearned reader regards the Pentateuch as the work of Moses, and all the laws it contains as delivered by him to Israel in the name of Jehovah. With this view he accepts all the statements he finds in the five books with reference to Israel's early history, and the incidents of the forty years' sojourn in the wilderness as absolutely and

U

literally correct. If critical theories be well founded, this implicit confidence is to a certain extent misplaced. Certain laws, for example, are put into the mouth of Moses, which were in reality of much later date, if not as customs, at least as divine commands. The plain reader is thus occasionally misled as to matters of historical fact; the thing did not always so happen as he is led to imagine. But does he get a wrong religious impression by taking all that is stated concerning the origins of Israel in Genesis, and concerning the Sinaitic legislation in the following books, as literally and exactly true? Certainly not; on the contrary, he simply learns with added emphasis the lessons which, on any theory that accepts revelation as a fact the books in question were intended to convey: that Israel was a chosen people, and that God's covenant with Israel was formed through the mediation of Moses. The first of these truths is vividly set forth in the story of the patriarchs in Genesis. The critical student of the Bible may have misgivings as to the historical exactness of many particulars in that story, but if he be a believing man he will accept the general significance of the narrative, viz. that from the very first God was preparing a people that should stand in peculiar relations to Himself, and perform a very important function in the religious history of the world. The unlearned man takes from the story the same meaning, only with greatly enhanced impressiveness because of his implicit confidence in all the details. So likewise with regard to the law. For the critic the law is Mosaic, only in the sense that it is the result of a development out of historical Mosaism. The Mosaic legislation, for him, contained the Levitical code only in the sense in which the acorn contains the oak. The one God of the Decalogue led eventually to one sanctuary, and the one sanctuary led in turn to a definitely regulated worship. For the unlearned man the one sanctuary and the priestly code are Mosaic in the same sense as the Decalogue is. In his way of viewing the matter, the tree did not grow, but was created full grown; just as for the generations of men who lived before the doctrine of evolu tion came into vogue, the diverse species of living creatures were regarded as immediate creations, not as the slow product of a secular development. Historically and scien tifically he may be mistaken as to the genesis of the law, as our forefathers are believed to have been mistaken as to the genesis of species; but his very mistake only tends to strengthen what even the believing critic admits to be a true impression : that the law as found in the Pentateuch was Mosaic. The difference between him and the critic is this : The_critic_says the law grew out of Mosaism, the plain man says the law was given by Moses.

It cannot be denied that the unlearned reader of the Scriptures loses something through his ignorance of criti cism, assuming always that its conclusions are well founded. He does not understand the real course of Israel's religious history, and misses all the edification which an intelligent view of that history is fitted to yield. Then through lack of such insight many things in the historical records remain unexplained puzzles for him. If, *e.g.*, the law of the one sanctuary was as old as Moses, how came it to pass that, up to a certain date, nobody, not even prophets and pious kings, seemed to know of it, or to pay any heed to it ? And how is it that in certain books of the Pentateuch a careful distinction is made between priests and Levites, while in Deuteronomy they seem to be identified ? And why do the Levites always appear in the fifth book of the Penta teuch poor portionless men, while in the middle books we find careful legislative provision for their needs ?

The existence of such unsolved problems for the un learned reader doubtless tends to mar his edification. But the evil is not irremediable. Criticism can be popularised. The process indeed involves peril. There is a risk that old reverence may be lost while new knowledge is being acquired. But that risk, to which faith is exposed in all times of transition, must be run. It will not do to say :

leave the plain man alone to enjoy his Bible in his own fashion; surely he can get all the benefit the Bible was intended to convey to devout souls without being de pendent on scholars. The fact is not so. The plain man can get some good from the Bible, enough to save his soul, without the aid of critics; but not all the good that is possible. He is much indebted to biblical scholarship for even the benefit he does derive from an uncritically read Bible. Without the aid of scholars he could have had no access to the Bible. First, the Massoretes had to furnish the Hebrew texts with vowel-signs, to indicate how the words were to be read and eliminate all possible ambi guities. Then men learned in Hebrew and Greek had to render the Old and New Testaments from the original languages into the common tongues. More recently ex perts have had to revise translations, to make them more exact, and to bring the Bible in the vernacular into more perfect correspondence with the best text of the original. All this lies behind us. It is now the turn of the critics to do their best for the people. This is the task of the future.[1]

But suppose the work done, the question which next arises is, How far will a critically instructed public be able to retain its faith in the Bible as a God-given, sure religious guide? Now in this connection it is a very reassuring consideration, that on critical views of the late origin of the Levitical law all New Testament verdicts concerning the law's function and value remain not only unreversed, but greatly strengthened. This point need only be referred to here, as it has been already handled in a previous chapter.[2] But there is another matter which has to be looked into. It may be thought that the ascription of laws to Moses, which in the actual form they assume in

---

[1] The task is even now being performed by such books as those of Robert son Smith, Kirkpatrick, Sanday, Ryle, Gladden, referred to at the head of this chapter.

[2] Vide p. 275.

the Pentateuch were of much later date, is an act of bad
faith, a *pia fraus*, which makes it hard to believe in the
inspiration of those who were parties to it. Now without
constituting ourselves special pleaders for Ezra and his
associates, let it be frankly granted that their notions, the
notions of their age and people, regarding literary morality
were not the same as ours. If the critics are right, Hebrew
editors could do without hesitation what we should think
hardly compatible with literary honesty : mix up things
old and new, ancient laws with recent additions; report
sayings of the wise, with editorial comments not dis
tinguished as such; collect utterances of different sages
and prophets under one name ; weave different versions of
one and the same event into one continuous though not
always harmonious narrative, without giving the slightest
hint of what they were doing. But what then ? This may
be crude morality, but it is not immorality. For there is
a broad distinction between these two things. Immorality
means breaking a recognised moral law ; crude morality
means conforming to a low moral standard. The former
produces an evil conscience which may well be regarded
as exclusive of all true inspiration;[1] the latter is compatible
with a perfectly good conscience, and therefore with a state
of heart open to God's inspiring influence. Deborah was
a heroic woman, and a true inspired prophetess, but she
could write the words: "To every man a damsel or two,"[2]
without feeling that she was saying anything indelicate or
immoral. It was not immorality, as it would be to us, but
it was very crude, barbarous morality. We must beware
of laying down hard and fast abstract rules as to the
conditions under which inspiration is possible. We only
make difficulties for ourselves by so doing, and play into
the hands of unbelief. Free thinkers of the eighteenth
century objected to the Bible as a professed revelation,

[1] The case of Balaam raises the question whether even a good conscience
be an indispensable condition of inspiration.

[2] Judg. v. 30.

because they held that if God was to make a revelation He would use as His instruments more exemplary men than the outstanding characters of the Bible are. It is arguing in the same spirit to say that God could not inspire, or employ as His agents, men capable of what we now might feel tempted to call a *pia fraus*. It is a sample of the mischievous apriorism which it is so difficult to get rid of in connection with this class of questions. It is, it may be added, an instance of the common tendency of religious people to *patronise* God, that is to say, to be more solicitous for His honour and dignity than He is Himself. How much of this there has been in connection with the sacred writings! God must write Hebrew with vowel points, otherwise His meaning will be ambiguous. He must write good, Attic Greek, free from Hebraisms and Hellenistic barbarisms, otherwise His reputation as an author will be compromised. He must employ paragons of moral ex cellence as the instruments of revelation, lest His holiness be stained by human faults. What is to be said of all this, and more of the like sort, but that it is folly like that of Job's friends, who constituted themselves patrons and champions of divine righteousness, and maintained that no really good man ever was allowed to suffer as Job suffered. The proper answer to all such *a priori* theorising is an appeal to fact. The righteous *may* suffer, for I suffer, said Job, sturdily refusing to deny facts because they might upset pet theories. God may inspire men who commit what we deem literary sins, say we, for books of the Bible in which these so-called literary sins are committed bear all the marks of inspiration —the divine in us bearing witness to the divine in them.

The utility of the Scriptures as a literature of revelation naturally involves that great importance should be attached to the collection into one volume or library of all the writings regarded as coming legitimately under that cate gory. In theological language, the function of Scripture

demands a *canon* of Scripture.[1] Now the history of the
formation of the canon, in the case both of the Old and the
New Testaments, is very disappointing. The facts are by
no means such as we should naturally have anticipated.
If one firmly believing in a divine revelation, and alive to
the value of a written record and interpretation to insure
that such a revelation should not be made in vain, were to
set himself to sketch an *à priori* history of the Bible, the
result might be something like this : " As each new scene
in the drama of revelation was brought on the stage of
history, God by a very special providence saw to it that a
competent chronicler and interpreter should be at hand,
and should give a clear, correct, and full account of all
that had been done and said, and that when the writing
was finished it should be duly certified and laid up for
preservation in a safe place. Thus, for example, was pro
vided for the information of all after ages a thoroughly
reliable, absolutely accurate record of the history of God's
dealings with the chosen race from the time of Abraham's
call to the time of settlement in the promised land, written
by men whose names are attached to the sections of the
narrative of which they were the authors. In the same
way was provided for the use of the Christian Church a
full, accurate, self-consistent account of the life of Christ,
written by eye-witnesses and certified to be their work by
evidence not to be gainsaid. And when the drama of
revelation was complete then all the separate books were
gone over, and, being found duly attested, were put together
as one in the face of the world by a body of responsible
men who were unanimous in their judgment as to what
ought to enter into the sacred collection." How different
the actual state of the case from this fancy picture ! Not
a few of the books which make up the Bible are anonymous,
and it is not possible to ascertain with certainty when or
by whom they were written. In the case of a book like

---

[1] On the history and meaning of the term, *vide* Reuss, *Histoire du
Canon des Saintes-Écritures dans L'Église Chretienne*, chap. xii.

Job that does not greatly matter, as its religious value is to a large extent independent of time and authorship. But it is a more serious thing to be left in doubt as to the authorship and date of the Pentateuch. The five Books of Moses, as they are commonly called, would have a much higher historical value if it were certain that Moses was their author, than if there were reason to believe that not even a considerable part of the literary material contained in the books, not to speak of the documents as they now exist, proceeded from the hand of the hero of the Exodus. The view taken by modern critics on this grave question is well known. It is not necessary here to discuss the question, but simply to advert to the fact that there is a question, as one of the disappointing phenomena connected with the sacred writings which run quite contrary to antecedent expectation. The dubiety about the authorship of the Gospels, especially of the Fourth Gospel, is another fact of the same kind. And there are many more. If it were a mere matter of doubts started by modern critics regarding the authorship of particular books in either Testament, the devout student might contrive to bear it with equanimity, comforting himself with the reflection that the modern mind is impatient of the fetters of faith, and has indulged in sceptical speculations concerning the Bible to a licentious extent in a passionate desire to regain freedom. But even in the ancient believing ages there were doubts: doubts as to the books which ought to be included in the sacred collection, doubts, *e.g.*, in connection with the New Testament in reference to no less than seven of its books: the Book of Revelation, and the Epistles of James, Jude, 2nd Peter, 2nd and 3rd John, and the Epistle to the Hebrews. And there is reason to believe that similar doubts prevailed for a time in reference to certain Old Testament books, and that the Jewish Church, not less than the Christian, had its list of *antilegomena*.[1] It is true indeed that in both

---

[1] Those chiefly belonged to the third division of the Hebrew Bible, the *Kethubim*. *Vide* on this Ryle, *The Canon of the Old Testament*, chap. viii.

cases these doubts were at length overcome. But how much more comfortable it would have been to know that there never had been any doubts, or room for them; as one cannot but feel that where there has been doubt once there may be doubt again, and that the hesitations of the Jewish and Christian Churches really signify that on the subject of the canon one can never get beyond probabilities.

The foregoing facts suggest certain reflections. The first is that it was manifestly not God's will to provide for the formation of a canon about which there could be no dispute, by a miraculous providence. It is conceivable that He might have done so, just as it is conceivable that He might have preserved the text of Scripture absolutely incorrupt. But neither in the one case nor in the other, nor indeed in anything relating to the Bible, has it pleased God to proceed in the way which we, looking at the matter theoretically, might think the best. But because there was no miraculous providence connected with the production of the Bible, it does not follow that God exercised over it no care whatever. We ought surely to apply to the Bible Origen's maxim that no good and useful thing comes to men without the providence of God. A book so supremely good as the Bible is not here *sine numine*. In this view men of all schools—Grotius,[1] Myers,[2] Gaussen[3]—concur.

A second reflection suggested by the facts above stated is, that a certain amount of dubiety concerning the history of the literature of revelation must be compatible with the realisation of the end for which, *ex hypothesi*, the Scriptures exist—to be a guide to religious faith. It seems due to the facts that doubts have existed even among believing men, regarding the authenticity of certain books of Scripture, and the canonicity of others, that we should abstain from exaggerated views as to the indispensableness of certainty on such questions. Such views would not be wise either

---

[1] *De Veritate Religionis Christianæ*, lib. iii. chap. ix.
[2] *Catholic Thoughts on the Bible and Theology*, p. 61.
[3] *The Canon of the Holy Scriptures*, p. 431.

in respect of our own comfort as individual believers, or in respect of the public interest of the faith. It is not a wise policy to offer to men the alternatives : all or nothing, either the whole Bible as it stands an unquestionable revelation from God, or give up the idea of a revelation altogether ; either an absolutely certain canon, or give up the notion of a divine purpose in connection with a col lection of writings recording and illustrating revelation. Rather let us admit, what is notoriously the fact, that it is possible for a man to be a sincere and sound believer and exemplary Christian, and yet have doubts, even ill-grounded and unreasonable doubts, respecting particular books of Scripture ; in other words, let us admit that the end of the Scriptures as a whole, the edification of men in faith and holiness, may be realised while uncertainty prevails in reference to particular books of Scripture. The possibility of this is well illustrated by the case of Luther, who was a most orthodox believer, and a noble Christian man, well furnished for every good work, and specially for rendering the Hebrew and Greek Scriptures into good idiomatic German, yet gravely doubted, nay strenuously denied, the canonicity of the Epistle of James, because it seemed to contradict the doctrine of justification by faith, his very orthodoxy being thus the source of his doubt.

Orthodoxy and piety being indubitably, as matter of fact, compatible with doubts concerning the canonicity of certain parts of Scripture, the question naturally suggests itself, How may this compatibility be made evident as a matter of theory ? We may employ for this purpose the idea of an *organism*. The Bible may be conceived as an organic body of writings, in which every particular book has its proper place and function. But in every living organism some organs are vital and some are not. There are parts of the body which to lose is to die ; there are others which we may lose without dying, or even materially suffering in health. "Some members of the body," writes Dr. Hodge, "are more important than others, and some books of the

Bible could be better spared than others. There may be as great a difference between John's Gospel and the book of Chronicles as between a man's brain and the hair of his head; nevertheless the life of the body is as truly in the hair as in the brain." [1] Dr. Hodge's point is that even unimportant books may be inspired. But the observation quoted serves our purpose equally well, which is to show that there may be doubts about certain books of the Bible without vital consequence to faith ensuing. The hair of the head is a part of the body, yet a man can live com fortably enough without it. In like manner it may happen to a man to be in doubt about this or the other book of Scripture, yet he may derive from the sacred writings the benefit they were designed to confer. It is not insinuated that all the books of the Bible whose canonicity has been doubted are as unimportant to the organism of Scripture as the hair of the head is to the body. Who would say this of the Epistle to the Hebrews, concerning which the early Church for a season stood in doubt? The purpose is merely to throw out a general reflection that may be help ful in perplexity, not to pronounce invidious judgments on individual books.

The history of the formation of the Hebrew canon is involved in deep obscurity. According to modern critics it was the work of the exile and post-exile period. The foundation was laid by the compilation of the Pentateuch by or under the direction of Ezra, whereon was gradually built up the superstructure of the Prophets and the Psalms. To the Psalter were finally added other books, mostly of late origin, the whole forming a group called in the Hebrew Bible *Kethubim,* and in the Septuagint *Hagiographa.*[2] This

---

[1] *Systematic Theology,* i. 164.

[2] Scholars distinguish three canons in the Hebrew Scriptures : 1. The *Law,* completed before 432 B.C. ; 2. The Law with the *Prophets* added, com pleted about 200 B.C. ; 3. The full canon of the Law, the Prophets, and *the Writings,* completed about 100 A.D., but virtually settled 100 B.C. *Vide* Ryle, *The Canon of the Old Testament,* for a full account of all that relates to these three canons.

miscellaneous group is, as has been remarked, " the region of the Old Testament *antilegomena*" various books, such as Chronicles, Esther, Canticles, and Ecclesiastes, having, apparently, been the subject of dispute in the Jewish schools. On this view of the post-exilic origin of the Hebrew Bible one cannot but have an uncomfortable feeling that the scribes had more to do with the collecting of the sacred writings than a Christian can regard as at all desirable. For to the scribe the law was supreme, and everything else, prophecy and sacred song, of quite sub ordinate importance. But the very fact that the Prophets and the Psalms found a place in the Hebrew Scriptures beside the Law shows that other influences were at work. For these portions of the Bible we are indebted, probably, far more to the piety of the Jewish people, than to the care of their legal instructors. They survive because the godly in Israel valued them as helpful to their spiritual life. All that the scribes had to do, when late in the day they turned their attention to the subject of the canon, was to recognise the verdict already pronounced by the voice of God's people.[1]

The law of the survival of the fittest may appear to some minds a very insecure basis on which to build the doctrine of the canon. It is common in matters of religion to demand more certainty than it is possible to obtain. To people of this temper the old view as to the formation of the Hebrew canon commends itself. It was founded on Jewish traditions of comparatively late origin. These traditions accredited Ezra, Nehemiah, and the Great Syna gogue, as it was called, with a very important *role* in con nection with the collection of the sacred books. The legend assumed two forms—one very extravagant, the other more rational. According to the tale told in the fourth book of Ezra, an apocryphal writing belonging to the close of the first century B.C., the holy books having been destroyed at

---

[1] *Vide* on this Professor Robertson Smith's *Old Testament in the Jewish Church*, 2nd ed. p. 163.

the time of the captivity, Ezra restored them miraculously through divine inspiration. The soberer form of the tradition found in the Talmud ascribes to Ezra, Nehemiah, and the men of the Great Synagogue only the work of completing the canon, the earlier writings being ascribed to other authors: the Pentateuch to Moses, the Psalms to David, and so on. The men of the Great Synagogue reduced to writing only the books contained in the mnemonic word Kandag; Ezekiel, the twelve minor prophets, Daniel, and Esther.[1] This tradition was afterwards modified so as to assign to Ezra a more important function. According to the later version, Ezra and the Great Synagogue collected into one volume the previously dispersed books, distributing them under the three heads of the Law, the Prophets, and the Kethubim.

This tradition has been very variously regarded. Formerly it was received implicitly as true, and the opinion held that the canon of the Old Testament was *simul et semel* settled through divine inspiration by Ezra and the Great Synagogue. In more recent times it has been treated with little respect. Some scholars regard the Great Synagogue as a pure myth, and its work on the canon as imaginary. Others, such as Ewald, hold that the "Great Synagogue," though surrounded with legendary elements, was not altogether mythical. We must be content to let it remain a dim shadowy object in the night of legalism.

Of much greater value than Talmudic traditions of late origin, regarding the collecting of the sacred writings, were a single positive statement in a book of pre-Christian date, indicating that at the time when it was written a collection actually existed. Such a statement occurs in *Ecclesiasticus*, or the *Wisdom of Jesus the Son of Sirach*, the probable date of which is about 130 B.C. In the prologue of that work there is explicit reference to a collection consisting of three divisions: the *Law*, the *Prophets*, and *the other national books*. The reference occurs in such a connection as to show that

---

[1] *Vide* Oehler on the Canon in Herzog.

the collection had been in existence long enough to be a subject of study to the writer's grandfather, and to give rise to a demand for translation into the Greek tongue. By 150 B.C., or thereby, the Hebrew Bible, if not complete as we have it, contained at least books in all the three cate gories contained in the Old Testament canon. If any books were wanting at that time, they would belong to the last of the categories: "the other books," "the writings." If the critical view as to its late origin be correct, *Daniel* might be among the missing books. *Daniel* itself bears clear witness to the existence of a collection of the *prophets*, in the words: "I Daniel understood by the books," [1] the books being those in which Jeremiah's prophecies were included.

As the Son of Sirach is the first known witness to the existence of a Hebrew canon, complete at least in its divisions, so another well-known Jewish writer, *Josephus*, is an important witness to the contents of the canon at the date when he wrote, about the close of the first Christian century. He refers to the subject in his work against Apion, in connection with an attempt to show the reliable ness of Hebrew history as compared with that of the Greeks. It may be well to quote what he says at length :

"Therefore with us there is not an innumerable multitude of books contradicting each other, but only twenty-two, embracing the history of the whole past time, and deservedly regarded as divine. Of these, five are by Moses, which contain the law and the series of events from the creation of man to his death. And this space of time covers almost three thousand years. But from the death of Moses to the reign of Artaxerxes, who after Xerxes ruled over the Persians the prophets who succeeded recorded the events of their time in thirteen books. The four remaining books contain hymns in praise of God and precepts most useful for the life of man. But from the reign of Artaxerxes to our time the events which have occurred have been preserved in writing but the records have not been deemed worthy of the same credit, because there was no exact succession of prophets.

---

[1] Dan. ix. 2.

But what faith we place in our Scriptures is seen from our conduct. No one has dared to add to them, or to take away from them, or to alter them. It is implanted in the mind of all Jews from their birth to regard them as the commands of God, and to abide in them, and if need be gladly die for them." [1]

The question has been much discussed how the contents of the Hebrew canon as it now stands can be grouped so as to bring out the number twenty-two, the interest of the problem lying in the wish to ascertain whether all the books in our Hebrew Bible were included in Josephus' list. The only book about which there has been any doubt is Esther. On the whole, it may be accepted as certain that the list of Josephus coincided with that of the canon of the Old Testament. [2] Another point of interest in the foregoing passage is the distinction drawn between the sacred writings and other Jewish books, and the ground of it : because there was no exact succession of prophets. By the time of Josephus the Jews had come to have a strong sense of the difference between canonical and non-canonical writings, and likewise a cut and dried theory as to the reason of the difference. A canonical book was a book written by a recognised prophet. Other books, however good, were refused a place in the canon, because they were not written under prophetic inspiration.

This theory of Josephus raises an important question : What is the test of canonicity ? It has been answered variously. One view is that that is canonical which the Church has declared to be such—which simply raises a previous question, What guided the Church in her judgment ? Another view is : that is canonical, in the case of the Old Testament, which had a prophet for its author, and in the case of the new, an apostle ; but this assumes certain knowledge of the authors of the books and of their standing, which in many cases is not forthcoming. Calvin, perceiving the unsatisfactoriness of these solutions, pro-

[1] *Contra Apionem*, i. 8.
[2] Such is the view of Ryle. *Vide The Canon, etc.*, chap. vii.

posed this test : the Spirit of God in the Scripture witness
ing to our spirit, and giving us a sure sense of its inspiration
and divinity, and so making us independent both of the
authority of the Church, and of all external questions as to
authorship.   A very good test applied to the Scriptures as
a whole, but one which fails us just when we most need
help, viz. in reference to certain books whose canonicity
has been disputed or seems intrinsically disputable.   The
witness of the Spirit may help us through our difficulties
about the Gospel of John and the Epistle to the Hebrews,
but what of Esther, Canticles, and Ecclesiastes ?   One
more suggestion is possible.   Find out the main drift of
Holy Writ, and then in reference to any particular book
that may be called in question ask, is its teaching in
harmony therewith ?   In other words, a useful test of
canonicity, if not the one test, is *organic function.*   Does
the particular book serve any purpose in the literature of
revelation, is it in harmony with its design and outstanding
doctrine ?   This was virtually Luther's method.   In his
hands it yielded some unsatisfactory conclusions, because
he had too narrow a conception of the scope of the Bible,
which he took to be the inculcation of the doctrine of
justification by faith.   That idea strictly applied would
reduce the Bible to very small dimensions.   If, however,
our conception of the *raison d'etre* of Scripture be sufficiently
comprehensive it will help us through most canonical pro
blems.   We shall have no difficulty in seeing that the Fourth
Gospel is an integral member in the organism of the New
Testament, even though in doubt as to its authorship, and as
little difficulty in deciding for the canonicity of the Epistle
to the Hebrews, though perfectly certain that it was not
written by Paul or any other apostle.   The problems that
remain unsolved, and leave us in permanent doubt, will be
found to be connected with books of minor importance.[1]

---

[1] The book of *Job* by the test of canonical function has a right to its
place, because it deals with the inevitable problem of the relation of God's
righteousness as Moral Governor to individual experience.   It does not

CHAPTER X.

THE DEFECTS OF THE OLD TESTAMENT RELIGION AND ITS LITERATURE.

LITERATURE. — Mozley, *Ruling Ideas in Ancient Ages;* Ewald, *Die Lehre der Bibel von Gott* (Band I., English trans lation by T. & T. Clark, *Revelation: its Nature and Record);* Schultz, *Alttestamentliche Theologie* (English translation T & T. Clark, 1892); Bruce, *The Chief End of Revelation*, chap. iii.; Driver, *Introduction to the Literature of the Old Testament.*

The remarks on the test of canonicity with which the last chapter closes may be held to imply that the canon is an open question. So in the abstract it is. It never can be anything else on the principles of Protestantism, which forbid us to accept the decisions of Church Councils, whether ancient or modern, as final. But, practically, the question of the canon is closed. Few have any disposition to go back on questions relating to the right of certain books to a place in the sacred collection. There is a general willingness to acquiesce in the judgments of the ancient Jewish and Christian Churches, even on the part of those who are most fully alive to the fact that there was a certain amount of haphazard in these judgments, and that they proceeded on principles which will not always stand close examination. As to the methods on which Old Testament canonical problems were disposed of we are very much in the dark. When, by whom, and why this or that particular book was admitted to the collection, and indeed solve the problem, but it negatives superficial solutions, and keeps the question open. The *Song of Solomon, literally interpreted as a story of true love proof against the blandishments of the royal harem,* is also right fully in the canon as a buttress to the true religion ; for whatever made for rity in the relations of the sexes made for the worship of Jehovah Baal- worship and impurity being closely associated. *Ruth* is a witness for tho universality of God's gracious purpose, and an antidote to the tendency of the elect people to hate foreigners. The same may be said of *Jonah,* whether taken as a history or as a parable.

X

another was excluded, we know not. But we do know
something of the grounds on which the judgments of the
Christian Church respecting New Testament books rested,
and we know that in some instances they were very
precarious. The most notable instance of a true judgment
being arrived at on false or uncertain grounds is presented
in the Epistle to the Hebrews. The Western Church long
doubted as to the right of that Epistle to a place in
the canon, and the doubt was connected with the question
of authorship. In the East, where Paul was believed to be
directly or indirectly the author, it was accepted without
hesitation as canonical; the Westerus, on the other hand,
hesitated as to admitting its claims just because the Pauline
authorship was not believed in. When at length a general
vote was given in favour of the Epistle, it was on the
understanding that it was one of Paul's. The principle of
judgment in such matters in those days was that canonicity
and apostolic authorship stand and fall together. That it
was a false principle is now generally admitted. Few
believe that Paul wrote the Epistle, yet as few doubt that,
tested by the principle of canonical function, it has as good
a right to a place in the New Testament as any book in
the collection.

What happened in the case of the New Testament
canon may also have happened in connection with the Old
for anything we know. We have no right to assume that
the Hebrew canon was settled under more special divine
guidance than that vouchsafed to the fathers of the
Christian Church in the performance of a similar task.
The presumption is all the other way. The adjustment of
the Hebrew canon took place in the night of legalism;
when the canon of the New Testament was fixed the
Church was largely filled by the spirit of Christ. The
possibility of wrong decisions, as, *e.g.*, in the case of the book
of Esther, must therefore be admitted.

Yet, in view of all this, every one is conscious of a
strong reluctance to reopen the question, and of a decided

inclination to accept the verdict of the Jewish Church as
final.   And acting on these feelings cannot involve any
risk to religious interests, provided we understand our
privilege and duty as Christians to read the Old Testament
with a discriminating eye.   This may seem a startling
statement, but it is one which admits of vindication not
only with reference to books of minor value and compara
tively doubtful canonicity, such as Chronicles and Esther,
but with reference to the whole Old Testament literature.
For it is axiomatic that that literature, as the literature of
the earlier stages of revelation, must share the defects of
the revelation which it records and interprets.   And if the
revelation of the final stage has done its proper work in us,
it has enabled us to see the defects of the revelation of the
earlier stages, and of the relative literature.   The word
which God in the end of the days spoke by One having the
standing of a Son, must enable us, if we give sufficient heed
to it, to read with discrimination the multiform and
fragmentary oracles spoken to the Jewish fathers by the
prophets, and to see clearly how true of them was the
confession Paul made for himself, " We prophesy *in part.*"
We not only may, as men taught of Christ, so read the Old
Testament, but we must.   We cannot help ourselves, if we
are to be loyal to the best we know.   Nay, we cannot
help ourselves, if we are really to use the Bible as a whole
wisely, as our " rule of faith and practice."   For the Bible
is a rule of a very peculiar kind.   It is a rule that is
constantly improving on itself, and men who use it are
expected to take note of the fact, and to allow the later
editions of the rule to have their own effect in antiquating
the earlier.   Thus the prophets in succession present under
various aspects the good time coming.   Their presentations
cannot be pieced together so as to form one harmonious
picture.   They are rather like the successive stages of an
organism, each of which in turn supersedes the one going
before.[1]   Thus again Levitical religion for the Old Testa-

---

[1] *Vide* on this, Riehm, *Messianic Prophecy*, pp. 135, etc.

ment saint was a source of delight; the author of the books of Chronicles writes as if the world existed for the sake of the tribe of Levi, and the performance of its sacred functions in the temple at Jerusalem. But the writer of the Epistle to the Hebrews, having listened to the voice of *the Son*, pronounces the whole Levitical system weak and unprofitable.[1] It was so, in his judgment, inherently and all along, even when the books of Chronicles were written. Can we, children of the new era of the better hope, read those books without feeling that more is made of the then prevailing system than it was all worth, and that the *Philo-Levitical* spirit of the writer is a religious defect, if not a moral fault?

The Christian revelation, with its relative literature, enables, justifies, compels us to criticise the earlier revela tion and its relative literature—such is the great principle under law to which we must use the Old Testament as part of the rule of faith. The question may not unnatur ally be raised, whether a guide in faith and conduct which thus changes, and requires us to judge earlier utterances by later, should be called a "rule." The word "rule" is suggestive of mechanical guidance, such as a man receives when he is told in definite precise terms what to do, and no room or need is left for the exercise of his own judgment. The Bible is certainly not a rule in this sense. The man who so thinks of it will come to it in a legal spirit, and will get from it, not guidance, but fatal mis guidance. Rabbinism is what results from using the Bible as a mechanical rule, a warning to all time how not to use the sacred book. The right use of the Bible requires much judgment, much spiritual insight, the power of appreciating its general scope, and of bringing the drift of the whole to bear on the interpretation of the parts. But the point more particularly to be insisted on is that the right use of the Old Testament requires that we be filled with the spirit of the New, and be able to judge

[1] Heb. vii. 18.

all that is written in the more ancient book in the light of
its teaching. This amounts to saying that the Bible,
instead of being a dead rule to be used mechanically, with
equal value set on all its parts, is rather a living organism,
which, like the butterfly, passes through various transforma
tions before arriving at its highest and final form.
Therefore the final stage is the standard by which all is to
be judged. This truth has two sides. It means, on the one
hand, that we should find Christ in the Old Testament, as
we find the butterfly in the caterpillar, and man, the crown
of the universe, in the fiery cloud. But it means also, on
the other hand, that we should see that the Old Testament
is defective in so far as it comes short of Christ, as we see
that the caterpillar is defective inasmuch as it is not yet
a butterfly, and that the universe is an incomplete and
comparatively meaningless thing till the evolutionary
process has culminated in man. Hitherto the Church has
has done ampler justice to the former aspect of the truth
than to the latter. It has been much more alive to
Christ's presence in the Old Testament than to His
absence. It has, indeed, so emphatically asserted the
presence as almost to obliterate the traces of absence. It
has so read Christ into the Old Testament, that the
caterpillar becomes a butterfly before the time, and all
sense of development, progress, growth in revelation is
destroyed. The remark applies especially to prophecy,
which, historically interpreted, is as a beautiful moonlight
in the night, but in the hand of interpreters too anxious to
put into prophetic oracles a specifically Christian meaning
becomes like the moon in the daytime : pale, dim, and useless.
But the remark also applies to the moral sentiments and
religious temper of Old Testament saints as reflected in
their writings. These are not allowed to appear defective,
as they occasionally were, but are apologised for, justified,
transfigured, under an impression that any other mode of
procedure would be incompatible with the reverence due
to the word of God. Run up to its logical conclusion,

this really amounts to denying the New Testament doctrine of the rudimentary nature of the earlier dispensation. Paul compares the law to a system of tutors and governors under which the heir of the promise was placed during the period of minority. Should it surprise us to find that the child's thoughts were like the system under which he lived ; in other words, that there are traces of the legal spirit in the piety of the men to whom we owe the Old Testament ? Why hesitate to recognise phenomena which simply serve to justify the judgment of the New Testament on the epoch of preparation ? Strongly impressed with the impolicy of such a course, I proceed to note some of the more out standing defects of Old Testament religion as reflected in the Hebrew Scriptures.[1]

1. The prophets and many of the psalms exhibit the highest water-mark of the Old Testament religion. We have but to recall such sunny lyrics as, " Although the fig-tree shall not blossom," " Thy mercy, O Lord, is in the heavens," " Whom have I in heaven," " The Lord God is a sun and shield," " They that wait upon the Lord shall renew their strength," to be impressed with the evangelic spirit of the writers, and to feel that whatever shadows of legalism may rest on the pages of the Hebrew Scriptures, the joy of sonship, the religion of trust in a heavenly Father's love is not unknown. Nevertheless, the spirit of sonship is not perfected even in those who, like the prophets, came nearest to the tone of New Testament piety. There is noticeable now and then a tone of complaint, as of men who do not fully understand and trust the loving-kindness of God. Even in the case of the men who sang, " Although the fig-tree," and " Whom have I in heaven," the mood expressed in their song did not come easily to them. It was a victory gained in a severe struggle with far-reaching doubt. The prophet Habakkuk had despairingly asked how God could look on while

---

[1] In what follows I repeat in substance statements made in *The Chief End of Revelation* (pp. 150-7), and add some new features.

deeds of barbarous cruelty were being perpetrated by
wicked men against the just, and the Psalmist had been
tempted by similar experiences to doubt whether God were
good even to the pure in heart.   This *querulousness*, in
view of the dark mysteries of human experience, is the
weak side of prophetic piety.   It stands in most striking
contrast to the uniformly buoyant, invincibly triumphant
tone of the New Testament, where it is impossible in a
single sentence to find an echo of Jeremiah's wail, " Where
fore doth the way of the wicked prosper ? " [1]   On the
mount, Jesus bade His hearers rejoice in sharing the fate of
which the prophets complained : " Rejoice, and be exceeding
glad : for so persecuted they the prophets." [2]   The difference
is not due to any natural superiority in point of heroism
in the men of the New Testament over those of the earlier
dispensation.   It was due rather to a new way of
regarding life which came in with Jesus Christ, in virtue
of which the least in the kingdom of heaven became
greater than the greatest of the prophets.   The contrast
in temper marks a real advance in the religious education
of the world.   The onward step lay in what has been aptly
called the " method of inwardness."   The prophets (including among them psalmists) placed the good which marks
God's favour too much in outward condition.   That they
did not do this exclusively is manifest from Habakkuk's
song, " *Although* the fig-tree shall not blossom. . . . Yet
I will rejoice in the Lord."   Yet the method of outward
ness was that which came natural to the men of the Old
Testament.   The very ideal of the good time coming for
Isaiah was just wise government and plenty of food.   Nor
was this a personal idiosyncrasy of that prophet.   It arose
directly out of the nature of the Mosaic covenant, which
was a covenant of God with a nation, and therefore had
for its sphere of action the political and social life of the
people.   Moses, in God's name, promised long life to
children who honoured their parents, and national pro-

[1] Jer. xii. 1.   [2] Matt. v. 12.

sperity to Israel so long as she was faithful to Jehovah.
Therefore all pious Israelites under the old covenant were
more or less worldly in their conception of the *summum
bonum.* Wealth, large families, long life were for them
the appointed rewards of well-doing. For men with such
ideas of happiness, springing directly out of the Sinaitic
covenant, disappointments were inevitable, bringing in their
train gloom, perplexity, doubt, a complaining temper, and
even a mood approaching perilously near atheistic pessim
ism, as we see in *Ecclesiastes,* with its monotonous, dreary
refrain, " Vanity of vanities "—a mood to be shunned as
we shun poison. For the moral order of the world does
not, with the regularity of clock-work, secure a perfect
correspondence between lot and conduct in this world,
either in individual or in national experience. One who
thinks otherwise will be compelled, sooner or later, by the
logic of events, to doubt either his own righteousness or the
righteousness of God, or to oscillate in sickening restless
ness between the two kinds of doubt. Certain parts of
the Old Testament, such as the book of *Job,* exhibit this
doubt in all its length and breadth and tragic depth. It
is their very *raison d'être* to exhibit it. So viewed, they
are a very needful element in the literature of the earlier
revelation. In them the old covenant pronounces on
itself a verdict of failure. In this connection we can see
how fitting it is that even that gloomy pessimistic book,
Ecclesiastes, should have its place in the canon. It shows
what the method of outwardness comes to, it is the method
discredited by the process of *reductio ad absurdum.* No
man with an intelligent conception of the Old Testament
religion and its defects will quarrel with *Ecclesiastes* being
retained in the canon. The only good ground we could
have for doing so would be the supposition that we are
bound, if we leave it there, to sympathise with all its
sentiments. But this supposition, as already explained, is
a mistaken one with reference to the Old Testament in
general, and *a fortiori* with reference to that particular

book. So far are the sentiments of the preacher who personates Solomon from being normative and authorita tive, that his book is in the canon to show us rather how we ought *not* to feel. To go about the world wringing one's hands, and wearing a rueful face, and crying *vanitas vanitatum*, because the preacher said it, is to miss the great lesson it was given him to teach. That lesson was not so much that *all* is vanity, as that the old Sinaitic covenant was vanity—proved to be vanity by allowing a son of the covenant to get into so despairing a mood. Jeremiah's new covenant is sorely wanted when it has come to this.

A second defect in the Old Testament religion, even as professed by the prophets, was *vindictiveness.* "Let me see Thy vengeance on them," prays even the tender-hearted Jeremiah, with reference to his fellow - countrymen who persecuted him on account of his faithfulness;[1] and many similar utterances may be found in the prophetic litera ture and in the Psalter. It is not for us to condemn those who breathed what may appear to us so unhallowed peti tions, or to assume airs of superiority over them. It were a shame to the least in the kingdom of heaven, to any man living in the era of grace, if he were not better than the best of the Old Testament worthies in this respect. For a higher ideal of patience has been set before us by the precepts and example of Christ, and as Dr. Owen, com menting on the admitted shortcomings of Old Testament saints, remarks: "All our obedience, both in matter and manner, is to be suited to the discoveries and revelation of God to us."[2] The vindictiveness of prophets and psalmists was not immorality, but crude morality : it was not trans gression of a high standard, as the like spirit would be in us, but conformity with a low standard. The legal cove nant allowed and even fostered, *per accidens*, such a spirit. "Eye for eye, tooth for tooth, hand for hand, foot for foot,"[3] said the most ancient code of civil law given to

---

[1] Jer. xx. 12.   [2] *Vide* his treatise on the 130th Psalm.   [3] Ex. xxi. 24.

Israel.   Moreover, prayer for the punishment of adver
saries was made almost necessary by current conceptions
of the moral order of the world.   The theory was that God
rewarded every man according to his works.   Hence not
to punish an enemy was to pronounce a verdict in his
favour, and against the man he had wronged.   The prayer
was an appeal to the Judge of all the earth to decide
between the two, the wrong-doer and the wrong-sufferer.
The injured one might be good - natured enough not to
wish any harm to the man who had treated him unjustly,
but he could not afford to be put in the wrong before the
face of the world, and before the bar of his own conscience.
It would be an intolerable thing that events should so fall
out that he would be forced to draw the inference: God
thinks my enemy in the right and me in the wrong.
This, not private, vengeful passion, was the secret of the
vindictiveness of the Old Testament saint.   In many cases
private feelings are out of the question, the prayer for
vengeance being uttered really in the name of the whole
community of Israel.   This remark applies, probably, to
many of the so-called vindictive psalms.[1]

All this may truly be said by way of apology for the
vindictive element in Old Testament literature.   Neverthe
less there it is, as an undeniable fact; and while Christians
are not called on to sit in judgment on it in a spirit of
self-complacency, as little are they called on to deny its
existence, still less to approve and imitate it, or to cite it
as Scripture sanction for cherishing vindictive passions.
Such a use of Old Testament Scripture, not unexampled in
Christian times, is barbarous, disgraceful, and disloyal to
the Lord Jesus Christ.

Of the defects of the *Law*, as contained in the Penta
teuch, it is unnecessary to treat at length.   Christ has
said all that needs to be said on the crudity of the civil
legislation ascribed to Moses.   His criticism is given in
few words, but it cuts deep.   " Ye have heard that it hath

[1] *Vide* chap. vii. p. 274.

been said, An eye for an eye, and a tooth for a tooth : but I say unto you, That ye resist not evil." [1] By this one sentence He constituted Himself a critic of the Mosaic civil code, and made it appear a crude kind of justice adapted to a morally rude condition of society. What He implied in the Sermon on the Mount He expressly said on another occasion, pronouncing the Mosaic statute of divorce a law adapted to a hard inhuman heart.[2] One who has learned of Christ can apply the principle for himself, and see that much in Israel's statute-book was destined to abrogation when the new covenant came, bringing the renewed heart and the perfect law of love written on the heart.

The literature of the post-exilic period, when, according to the critics, the Levitical code first came into full operation, exhibits defects springing out of the system under which it arose, shadows cast on the sacred page by the *Judaism* inaugurated by Ezra. The literature referred to includes *Chronicles, Ezra, Nehemiah, Esther,* and some of the Psalms. Three defects may be noted here : *Philo - Leviticalism,* an *exclusive, hostile attitude towards foreigners,* and a *tendency to morbid self-consciousness,* or *self-righteousness.*

The first of these defects is conspicuous in the books of First and Second Chronicles. The Philo-Levitical spirit of the writer has already more than once been adverted to,[3] and it is not necessary to add much here to what has been said.   That the author of these books was devoted to the temple and its ritual must be manifest to every one who takes the trouble to read them with attention.   That in itself was the reverse of a fault.   What is to be specially noted is the excess or exclusiveness of the interest. David's sins are passed over in silence, and even his ser vices to his country as a warrior and a secular prince are hurriedly narrated, and he appears in these pages chiefly as a man occupied with preparations for building the temple, and the organisation of worship on the Levitical

[1] Matt. v. 38, 39.   [2] Matt. xix. 8 ; Mark x. 5.   [3] *Vide* pp. 279, 281.

model. The omissions and the foreshortening may be said
to be due to the point of view, but the thing to be
remarked is the point of view itself and what it implies.
Leviticalism fills the mind of the writer. Ritual is not
only co-ordinate with righteousness, but it almost seems to
be the one thing needful. Devotion to the temple service
is apparently the grand requirement. It is not to be
supposed, indeed, that the chronicler is indifferent to moral
interests, that he thinks and means to suggest that it does
not matter what sins a man commits, though, like David,
he be guilty of adultery and murder, provided always he
be duly attentive to the technical duties of religion. Such
an impious sentiment is not in all his thoughts. Yet, in
his zeal for religious interests, he presents a picture of
David's life from which such an inference might plausibly
be drawn. A prophet like Amos or Isaiah could not have
written Chronicles. They had such a passion for righteous
ness, such a keen sense of the worthlessness of religion
divorced from morality, that they could not have brought
themselves to write a sketch of David's career, in which all
the black features were left out and only his zeal for God's
worship eulogised. We are in a different atmosphere
here from that we breathe on the mountain heights of
Hebrew prophecy. It is the incense - laden air of the
sanctuary, not the bracing air which blows over the Alpine
heights of duty.[1]

Traces of a proud national self-consciousness, combined
with exclusiveness towards foreigners, have been discovered
by critics in most of the books belonging to the post-exilic
period. Before referring to texts cited in proof of this, it
may be proper to point out that this defect in the reli
gious temper of the Jews after the time of Ezra is not to
be confounded with the vindictiveness already mentioned.

[1] The question has been discussed whether the chronicler followed a tradi
tion, wrote under the spontaneous influence of the contemporary spirit of
religion modifying history, or was guided by a conscious didactic aim.
Schultz decides for the third alternative. *Vide Alttestamentliche Theologie,*
p. 70.

That feeling is a desire for redress for wrong done, and as such it may be cherished against Israelites as well as non-Israelites. The feeling now to be considered is one of aversion to non-Israelites as such, simply as "aliens from the commonwealth of Israel, and strangers from the cove nants of promise." It might proceed either from pride or from fear. In the days of our Lord it certainly sprang mainly from pride. The religious Jews of that time, proudly conscious of their covenant relation to God, regarded the heathen world with haughty disdain. This was what came of election, misunderstood to mean a monopoly of God's favour : a sullen, proud, narrow-hearted hatred of the human race. The question is, Can any trace of this vice be discovered in the period covered by the latest canonical books, or of any feeling akin to it, or capable of being developed into it ? Not certainly, it may be said in the first place, in the action of Ezra and Nehemiah in insisting on separation from heathen wives, and in refusing to have fellowship with the Samaritans. These might be measures of mistaken severity, but they were prompted not by pride, but by fear of contamination. Further, aversion to foreigners, from whatever cause pro ceeding, is certainly not the sole prevailing tone of the post - exilic literature. As pointed out in a previous chapter, there is a hearty ring of universalism in some of the Psalms ; [1] and if the critics are right in assigning a late date to the books of *Ruth* and *Jonah*, these also are wit- nesses to the existence among the Jews after the captivity of a genial kindly feeling towards the outside peoples.[2] A third remark may be hazarded, viz. that if even so much as a germ of the Pharisaic feeling towards the Gentile world can be detected in the later books, it would not present itself to the consciousness of the writer as it may

---

[1] *Vide* chap. vii. pp. 273, 274.

[2] Schultz suggests that possibly we should see in *Jonah* and *Ruth* a reaction against the spirit which dictated Ezra's reform. *Alttestamentliche Theologie*, p. 417.

appear to us in the light of the New Testament. He did not wish to express proud contempt or abhorrence of heathendom, but only a thankful sense of privilege and distinction, not to be boasted of, but to be gratefully acknowledged to the praise of divine grace. The limitation of spirit is there, but it is a defect arising out of the legal system which wholly tended in the direction of isolation; not a vice of nature, or an unworthy passion of an unloving, selfish heart.

Traces of national self-consciousness as against a godless heathen world have been discovered by such comparatively circumspect writers as Schultz in most of the books assigned to the post-exilic literature. In certain of the Psalms, *e.g.* the 74th, in which Israel is called God's turtle dove, and the heathen are described as a foolish people.[1] In *Daniel*, where the land of Israel is frequently called "the glorious land,"[2] and the people of Israel are designated as "the saints of the Most High."[3] In *Chronicles*, where even the kingdom of the ten tribes seems to be treated as a heathen country, and as such all but ignored as not worthy of a place in the history of God's people; and where the misfortunes of kings of Judah, as of Jehoshaphat in connection with his shipping enterprise, are traced to alliances with heretical kings of Israel.[4] In *Esther* above all, where the vindictive spirit against heathen foes reaches a ferocity difficult to account for otherwise than by regarding it as an outbreak of unrestrained natural passion against persons who, as belonging to the *goim*, were not supposed to have any claims to humane treatment.[5]

In the Pharisaic character a proud self-consciousness as

---

[1] Verses 18 and 19. 　　　　　　[2] Chap. viii. 9, xi. 16, 41.
[3] Chap. vii. 18, 21, 25, 27.
[4] 2 Chron. xx. 35. The explanation of the disaster given by the writer is all the more remarkable that in the corresponding narrative in 1 Kings xxii. 49 Ahaziah asks permission to join in the venture, and Jehoshaphat *refuses.*
[5] *Vide* on all these and other texts, Schultz, pp. 415–419. With reference

towards the heathen world was accompanied with an equally proud self-consciousness as towards God. Is there any trace of the latter feeling in the later literature of the Hebrew canon? We should not be surprised if there were; for *Judaism*, laying so much stress on ritual, did tend to develop that outward formal type of righteousness with which self-satisfaction is apt to be associated. The appearance of such traces in canonical books of the Judaistic period would only serve to advertise the fact that Israel's religion had entered on a phase which involved certain spiritual perils, and to prepare us for the state of matters with which the Gospels make us acquainted. Now as to the question of fact, it would seem that, while there is no trace of *inculcation* of self-righteousness, there are some unconscious manifestations of what wears a suspicious resemblance to it, in the characters of the men who come under our notice at this period. I have already had occasion to remark on the peculiar tone of Nehemiah's prayers, a phenomenon which attracted my attention many years ago, when I should hardly have felt at liberty to pursue such a line of thought as that which occupies us in the present chapter. Those ejaculatory petitions, "Remember me, O my God, for good," struck me then as they strike me now, as something novel, something needing explanation, something not quite in keeping with Pauline ideas of justification. I have also alluded to the consciousness of perfect national rectitude expressed in the 44th Psalm, in the words, "All this is come upon us; yet have we not forgotten Thee, neither have we dealt falsely in Thy covenant. Our heart is not turned back, neither have our steps declined from Thy way."[1] This is not necessarily self-righteousness, for there

---

to *Esther*, Driver (*Introduction*, p. 457) remarks: "It must be admitted that the spirit of Esther is not that which prevails generally in the Old Testament; but we have no right to demand upon à priori grounds, that in every part of the biblical record the human interests of the narrator should in the same degree be subordinated to the spirit of God."

[1] Verses 17, 18.

is such a thing as suffering for righteousness' sake in national as in individual experience. Yet the utterance stands in striking contrast to the prophetic habit of thought, and it is possible that the Psalmist speaks out of the consciousness of a time when holiness was placed too much in compliance with sacrificial rites and ceremonial rules, and not enough in doing justice, loving mercy, and walking humbly with God.[1]

These and other defects [2] of Old Testament piety present no stumbling-block to intelligent Christian faith. They only help to make it evident that God, who in many parts and many modes had spoken to Israel by prophets and psalmists, had not yet uttered His final, because perfect, word. They show that the Hebrew Scriptures, while a true light from heaven, were but a light shining in a dark place until the dawn of day.

[1] In this passage, as also in Ps. vii. 9, 10, xvii. 2–5, xxvi. 1–5, Cheyne (*Bampton Lectures on the Psalter*, p. 369) finds "professions of innocence which are at variance with the normal Christian sentiment."

[2] The food of Daniel and his companions at the king's court has been supposed to indicate the ascetic spirit as an element in the Jewish religion at the time the book was written. In reference to the whole religious spirit of Judaism at this period, Schultz remarks: "Die Religion wird mehr zum Gesetze. Aus der Sittlichkeit wird das Vollbringen der Gesetzen-werke." He refers in proof to 1 Chron. v. 25, x. 10, xiii. 10, xxviii. 7, xxix. 19 ; Esther iv. 3, 16 (fasting, etc.) ; Ps. clxix. 164 (prayer seven times a day) ; Dan. i. 8–16 (ascetic abstinence), vi. 10 (methodised prayer).

BOOK III.

THE CHRISTIAN ORIGINS.

———◆———

CHAPTER I.

JESUS.

LITERATURE.—*The Lives of Jesus* by Farrar, Geikie, Keim, Weiss, Renan, etc.; Bruce, *The Kingdom of God*, 4th ed.; Dale, *The Living Christ and the Four Gospels;* Stearns, *The Evidence of Christian Experience* (the Ely Lectures for 1890); Herrmann, *Der Verkehr des Christen mit Gott*, 2te Aufl. 1892; Gore's *Bampton Lectures on the Incarnation*, Lecture VI.; T. H. Green, *Works*, vol. iii., Essay on "Christian Dogma"; Wendt, *The Teaching of Jesus* (T. & T. Clark, 1892).

Jesus of Nazareth is represented in the Gospels as the Christ, the Godlike King of Hebrew prophecy, the fulfiller of Israel's highest hopes and brightest ideals, the august Person in whom the history of the chosen people culminated, and the divine purpose in her election found its consummation and interpretation. And the Christian Church in every age has accepted this representation as true; that the man Jesus was all this is her firm faith. But if Jesus was the *Christ*, Christ was also *Jesus*, a man who lived in Palestine at a certain date, of very unique moral and religious character, and very welcome for His own sake, apart altogether from His relation to the previous history of the world in general, or of Israel in particular. And there are moods of mind in which one desires to look

Y

at the man apart from His official titles and dignities, just as one might go to Palestine desiring to see what the naked eye can see, forgetting for the time all the sacred historical memories connected with its hills, and valleys, and lakes, and streams. There are probably many in the present time who are in this mood. The title "Christ" sounds foreign and stale to their ear, and is suggestive only of religious delusion, the symbol of an extinct *Aberglaube*, or extra-belief. But the Jesus to whom it was applied still interests them. In spite of theological scepticism—nay, partly in consequence of it, the conviction remains, and gains in force, that the hero of the evangelic story is the sweetest, most winsome, and most powerful character in the whole history of humanity. They desire to become better acquainted with Him. They wish to know the real historical person called Jesus of Nazareth, being persuaded that the better He is known in the actual truth of His life the better He will be esteemed. They are impatient of the trappings with which faith has invested His person, the official robes and the aureole round his brow. Take these things away, they exclaim; we would see *Jesus*.

There need be no quarrel with this mood, or any un willingness to let it have its way. We are, of course, all aware that it is a very crude sort of Christianity that looks at Jesus apart from His connection with the antecedent history of His people. Marcionism, with its Jesus in the air, cannot be more than a stepping-stone to a higher and more abiding form of faith. But *that* it may be; that, for those in the mood described, it must be. You cannot make them Christians by the method of catechetical in- struction intended to fill the mind with orthodox opinions. Neither can you make them Christians by the method of evangelism, which, taking for granted conventional ortho- doxy, makes its appeal to the emotions. These methods have probably both been tried, and have failed. They must therefore be allowed to begin at the beginning, and to learn Christianity *de novo*, as the disciples of Jesus learned it; becoming acquainted first with the man, and then advancing gradually to higher views of His person and work. It is a slow process at the best, and there is a risk of its stopping short at the rudimentary stage ; but when it goes on to its consummation, it yields a far higher type of faith and discipleship than can be reached by any short and easy way. Let an inquirer first see the man Jesus, and love Him so seen, and then pass on to higher affirmations with full intelligence and perfect sincerity, and you shall find in him one who brings to the service of the kingdom of God, not opinion merely, or emotion, but the whole heart and mind: " all that is within " him.

This being so, it would seem as if the way of becoming a Christian just indicated were not only the way necessary to be taken in certain cases, but the desirable way in all cases. It is not, and never will be, the way of the majority, and yet it may be the better and the best way. That it is so, indeed, might be asserted with confidence on the authority of the Master. His method of dealing with men in quest of the highest good seems to have been in accord ance with that indicated as the ideally best. He did not come with all His claims and titles, and make recognition of these the first condition of discipleship. He was in no haste to get men to make correct religious affirmations concerning Himself, but rather took pains first to lay sound moral foundations of religious belief. He not only did not demand that candidates for discipleship should commence by calling Him Christ, Lord, God, Saviour, but He posi tively discouraged the use of all such titles till men had an approximately correct idea of their significance. At Cæsarea Philippi, when Peter made the confession, " Thou art the Christ," He charged His disciples that they should tell no man that He was the Christ.[1] That is, He wanted no man to call Him Christ who did not in some degree understand the true meaning of the title, but used it in a

[1] Matt. xvi. 20.

merely traditional sense. To the seeker after eternal life who accosted Him as "*Good* Master," He addressed the sharp interrogation, " Why callest thou me good ? " as if to say, make not goodness a matter of compliment ; call no man good till you know what goodness is, and whether the person to whom you apply the epithet deserves it.[1] Yet, while virtually advising this inquirer to suspend his judgment as to the applicability of the epithet "good" to Himself, Jesus, we note, invites him to immediate discipleship : " Go, sell that thou hast, and come, follow me." Had he complied with the invitation, he would gradually have learned the nature of true goodness, and that the Master he had chosen as his guide was indeed good. He would also have learned betimes to make important religious affirmations concerning the Master, such as that He was the Christ, or the Son of God. And these affirmations coming in due course would have had real value and life-giving power. It could bring no real benefit to him to call Jesus either good or God while he remained in ignorance of the spirit of Jesus, and was so far unacquainted with the nature of true goodness as to imagine, for example, that the Pharisees and the Rabbis were good. It can do no one good to call an unknown man God ; still less to apply that solemn designation to a man whose character and spirit are fatally misconceived. The virtue lies in the belief that God is like, yea is, the well-known man Jesus the Good.[2]

It thus appears that Christ's sanction might fairly be cited in support of the policy of postponing consideration of His higher claims, and making it the first business to become intimately and truly acquainted with the historical

[1] Mark x. 18. In the corresponding passage in Matthew Christ's question, according to the best reading, was : " Why askest thou me concerning the good ? " The discrepancy in the reports raises the question which version comes nearest to what Jesus actually said. I content myself with saying that the question put into Christ's mouth by Mark and Luke is very characteristic, true to Christ's whole manner of dealing with religious inquirers and aspirants to discipleship.

[2] *Vide* my *Kingdom of God*, 4th ed. chap. xv.

person so far as that is possible. The desire to know the Jesus of history, stripped bare of theological investiture, far from being an impiety, is a reversion to the method of the Author of our faith. This consideration may encourage men adrift on the sea of doubt to be thorough in their search for truth without fear of consequences. Haunting fears of eternal loss are a great hindrance to thoroughness in religion. What if I should die while the quest goes on, and truth is still not found? What if I should be launched into eternity when I have only reached the lowest stage of Christian belief, the sincere passionate conviction that Jesus of Nazareth was a *good man*, the one man I have known whom I could trust and love with all my heart? Must I not make myself safe by hastily patching up my sadly-tattered creed, and accepting in the slump all conventional, orthodox declarations concerning the Person of Jesus and the significance of His death? " Who is among you that feareth the Lord " and " walketh in darkness?" Let him trust in the name of the Lord, and abstain from kindling for himself fires in the night that shall blaze brightly for a while, then go out and leave him in deeper darkness. Let him be loyal to truth, and leave his soul in the hands of God. How foolish to think that one can save himself from the living God, searcher of hearts, by an orthodox system of theology hastily adopted for prudential reasons! And why entertain solicitudes to which Jesus was a stranger? He did not bid men hurry up and make haste to be orthodox, under pain of damnation if death overtook them while they were only on the way, and not at the goal. He acted as if He believed that men were in a saved condition when their face was turned in the right direction—toward God, truth, and righteousness, however far they might be from having attained the object of their quest. The prodigal had a far way to go to his father's house, but in the view of Jesus he was a new man from the moment he said, " I will arise, and go to my father."

But the question may be raised, Has the method of

learning Christianity recommended by Jesus not been
rendered difficult or impossible by the way in which His
first disciples have treated His life ?   The question con
cerns the historicity of the evangelic narratives.   It may be
said, it has recently been said with startling emphasis, that
none of the Gospels, not even those which are compara
tively trustworthy,—the Gospels of Matthew, Mark, and
Luke —are written in a historical spirit, by men whose
first concern was to ascertain facts and report them exactly,
but rather with the avowed purpose of verifying a religious
belief concerning the subject of the narrations.   The evan
gelists, it is held, were concerned supremely, not about the
facts, but about the religious significance of the facts.   And
they have taken no pains to keep the facts and their value
for faith apart, so that readers might have it in their
power to know intimately the man Jesus, before being
asked or expected to make any theological affirmations
concerning Him, such as that He was the *Christ*.

Now it must be admitted that there is a measure of
truth in this representation.   Fact and faith are blended
together in all the Gospels, and can only be separated by
a critical process ; and for one who handles the materials
in a purely scientific spirit without religious prepossessions,
it may in some instances remain doubtful how far the
statements of the evangelists can be accepted as historical.
But it is very possible to indulge in exaggeration here,
and it may confidently be affirmed that the sceptical or
agnostic temper has been carried to excess in connection
with the history of Jesus.   We are all apt to be uncon
sciously influenced by our bias.   If some are too ready to
receive with uncritical credence the things that are written
in the Gospels, others are far too suspicious, whether
biassed, as in the case of Mr. Huxley, by a severely
scientific habit of mind, or, as in the case of Dr. Martineau,
by a theory as to the inner light being the sole source of
revelation.   When a man happens to believe that he can
do without an objective light of the world, he can afford to

be very sceptical as to the existence of such a light,—
nay, if he be in a small minority in maintaining the
sufficiency of the inner light, he may be tempted to raise
a mist of doubt about the sun that no alternative may be
left but to trust in the guidance of the candle.

To open-minded men neither unduly dogmatic nor unduly
sceptical, a sufficient knowledge of the historical Jesus will
not seem unattainable. That such knowledge is possible is
a fair inference from the fact that so many have attempted
to write the Life of Jesus. Some indeed, such as Strauss,
have written in a predominantly sceptical spirit, having for
their leading aim to show that of the subject of the evan
gelic story little can be known. But others, such as Keim,
entirely free from orthodox prepossessions, and proceeding
on the principles of a naturalistic philosophy, have entered
on their task with the conviction that the Gospels contain
a large amount of genuinely historical material, and by the
literary result of their studies have succeeded in producing
a similar conviction in the minds of their readers. Even
without the aid of elaborate "Lives of Jesus," a candid
inquirer may attain a comfortable sense of the knowable-
ness of Jesus, by an unaided use of the Gospels. In
reading these memoirs you feel as one sometimes feels in
a picture gallery. Your eye alights on the portrait of a
person you do not know. You look at it intently for a
few moments, and then you remark to a companion, that
must be like the original, it is so real, so life-like. This
sense of verisimilitude has at least subjective if not ob
jective value. It stimulates to further inquiry, and creates
the needful hope and patience for its successful prosecution.

This feeling of reality may not be produced in the same
degree by all the four Gospels. It is indeed, as is well
known, in not a few instances confined to the Synoptical
Gospels, which by comparison with the Fourth have appeared
to many in a marked degree stamped with an aspect of
historicity. This prejudice against the Fourth Gospel, so
far as it is sympathised with by any one in quest of a veri-

table knowledge of Christ, may be provisionally utilised as a means of confirming his first impression regarding the other three. No candid man will allow the prejudice to settle down without further inquiry into a final judgment as to the claims of that Gospel to be a reliable source of knowledge concerning the work and teaching of Jesus. But till the Johannine problem is solved the inquirer may legitimately extract aid to a weak faith even from the diversity of the impressions made upon his mind by the different sources. Do the Synoptical Gospels seem to him to present a real unmistakably historical character, reserving doubts about details, in particular about the miraculous element connected with the birth, the public ministry, and the resurrection? On the other hand, does the Fourth Gospel, even in those portions in which no miraculous element is present, convey the impression of a personality noble but idealised? Let him use the contrast, not indeed as conclusively proving the ideality of the Johannine Christ, but as a means of strengthening his sense of the reality of the Synoptical Christ. The very consciousness of contrast is evidence that the critical spirit is at work, and that the impression of the verisimilitude of the Synoptical Christ is not a baseless caprice.

It is open to us to confirm our faith in the historicity of the Synoptical Jesus by another line of comparison. It is familiar to all readers of the New Testament how very few allusions to facts in the life of Jesus are contained in the Epistles of the Apostle Paul. By a careful search one might discover more than, after a hasty perusal, he expects; nevertheless the broad fact remains that Paul is nearly as sparing in his references to the Great Biography as he is to the scenery of the various countries he passed through on his missionary journeys. Two facts only in the history of Jesus seem to have interest for him: the crucifixion and the resurrection; and these possess interest to his mind not as mere facts, but on account of their momentous religious significance. He appears to care

nothing for what we call the Life of Jesus, but only for
the doctrine of Christ's atoning work and Divine Per
sonality. His interest in Christ is purely religious, not at
all biographical, and his presentation of Christ is dominated
throughout by theological ideas.

With the synoptical evangelists the case is far otherwise.
Their interest is by no means purely or even predominantly
dogmatic: they love to tell stories about Jesus which show
what manner of man He was, how He appeared from day
to day to His chosen companions. The materials collected
in their Gospels owe their origin to a different type of mind
from that of Paul. They bear witness to the existence
in the Palestine Church of a "simple healthy objectivity
which desired to know the facts about Christ, to ascertain
as far as possible what He said and did, to get a clear vivid
picture of His life and human personality."[1] If the companions of Jesus and those to whom they preached had
been as intensely subjective as Paul, and as preoccupied
with a few great ideas, these memoirs of the Lord would
never have come into existence. And that they were not
so preoccupied these memoirs sufficiently attest. For while
they do not possess the character of a colourless chronicle
uninfluenced by faith, they are certainly by comparison
with Paul's letters very lacking in what we may call the
theological interest. They contain little more than theo
logical germs, the mere rudiments of a doctrine of atone
ment, or of Christ's Person, or of the Church. From the
point of view of the dogmatic theologian this feature of
the Synoptical Gospels may be disappointing. Indeed, it
may be said with some measure of truth that the low
doctrinal position of these Gospels has led to their being
largely neglected in favour of the more theological writings
of the great apostle of the Gentiles: a neglect which has
brought upon the Church, especially on the Protestant
section of it, a serious penalty in the form of spiritual
impoverishment. But not to dwell on this, what I wish

[1] *The Kingdom of God*, 4th ed. p. 335.

now to point out is that that very feature of the Gospels which makes them disappointing to the dogmatist, is of great value to the apologist. Broadly put, the apologetic position is this : the less dogmatic presumably the more historical. Are the Synoptical Gospels deficient in materials for the construction of a system of Christian doctrines ? Then the fair inference is that the evangelists were not supremely concerned about theology, but had it for their chief desire to give a vivid true picture of Jesus as He appeared to the men who had been with Him.

On these grounds the earnest inquirer may with all con fidence trust his first impressions of the Synoptical Gospels, and come to them in good hope of acquiring a true knowledge of the historic Jesus. They will find there facts abund- antly sufficient for the exhibition of a character of unique moral and religious worth which is no invention, but one worked out on the stage of real life. The best thing they can do for their spiritual wellbeing is to go to the school of the evangelists and learn of Jesus. If they truly desire eternal life, this is their wise course. They will there learn at once the nature of true goodness, and what solid grounds there are for calling Jesus uniquely good. These are the first two lessons in the Christian religion, the foundation of all that follows, as our Lord declared by implication when He asked the aspirant, Why callest thou me good ? He did not, as some supposed, mean thereby to imply that He was conscious of moral defect. His aim rather was to give a first lesson in the way to eternal life. In effect the question meant : learn first of all what good ness is, and call no man good till you are sure that he deserves it. The practical way to work out this programme was to become a disciple of Jesus. In His company the inquirer would solve two problems at one stroke : discover the nature of the highest good, and perceive at the same time that the ideal of goodness was realised in the Master whom he followed.

The question, What is good ? is always one demanding

careful discriminating consideration. At no time is it safe to assume the accuracy of conventional notions on that subject. Least of all was it safe in the time of Jesus. There were two competing types of goodness in Judæa, then, between which men had to choose, that of Jesus and that of the scribes. What a difference! how utterly incompatible, how idle to call any man "good" until it was settled which of the two types was to be preferred! The thoughts and ways of Jesus, it is as certain as anything can be, differed radically from those of most of His Jewish contemporaries on all subjects pertaining to morals and religion. Righteousness, goodness, both theoretically and practically, was quite another thing for Him from what it was for them. The righteousness of the Rabbis consisted in observing innumerable minute rules regarding washing, fasting, tithe-paying, Sabbath-keeping, and the like, in being very self-complacent on account of their observances, and in thinking very meanly of all who were not as strict as themselves. Scrupulosity, vanity, and contempt made up the current type of goodness as embodied in the Pharisaic character. In the character of Jesus, as most realistically portrayed in the Gospels, we meet with a startling contrast. There is not only a total lack of conformity to the Pharisaic type, but a very pronounced antipathy to it. This indeed is the foremost feature in the new type of goodness, an intense detestation of counterfeit goodness. Jesus, as He appears in the Gospels, was gentle and charitable beyond expression; yet His abhorrence of spurious holiness amounted to a passion. What He detested He was not likely to imitate, and accordingly in no particular did His righteousness resemble that of the scribes and Pharisees. He was, for example, entirely free from religious scrupulosity, as we see from His mode of keeping the Sabbath, and from His neglect of the traditionary rules of the scribes respecting ablutions, fastings, etc. This free way of life was not, as many imagined, licentiousness, but a better way of serving God springing out of a different idea of God from that cherished by the scribes. The scribes had no real faith in the goodness or grace of God. They thought of God as a severe, exacting taskmaster, whose commands were not only high and difficult, but grievous. Hence they served Him in fear, lest by the most minute departure, even by inadvertence, from the bare letter of the law they should incur the divine displeasure with its attendant penalties. Jesus, on the contrary, had the most absolute faith in God's benignity. He loved God as a Father, and served Him as a Son, cheerfully, devotedly, and without dread, regarding His will as good and perfect and acceptable, and not doubting that He judged conduct reasonably, setting value not on outward conformity to mechanical rules, but on the inward spirit. The Rabbis feared that God would be angry if they did not pay their tithes with such scrupulous exactness as to include among the taxable articles garden herbs. To Jesus such fear appeared a foolish superstition and an injury to God. It was incredible to Him that God could be angry with men for such a reason. He believed that God's displeasure rested on selfishness, pride, cruelty, injustice, falsehood, not on petty breaches of man-made rules invented to be a hedge about the law.

Again, and above all, the goodness of Jesus was distinguished from the current type by its *humanity*. One of His chief grounds of quarrel with the traditional type of goodness was that it was inhuman, did not care for the people, but despised them as ignorant and profane, and contemplated their moral degradation with heartless apathy and even calm satisfaction. He, for His part, loved the people dearly, pitied them, sought their good by all means, taught them, healed them, kept company with them, took food in their houses, exposing Himself in so doing to suspicion, misunderstanding, and calumnious mispresentation ; regardless of the evil that might be thought or said about Himself, if only He might by such brotherliness comfort, gladden, and win to goodness the depressed, the unfriended, and the erring.

Once more Jesus stood in conspicuous contrast to the Pharisee by His *modesty*. This trait came out in the question, Why callest thou me good? expressive, not, indeed, of the sense of moral defect, but certainly of reverence for the august moral Ideal. What a shock of surprise the question must have given the young man familiar with the ways of the scribes! It was not their habit to decline titles of honour. They loved to be called "Rabbi." Vanity, ostentation, thirst for flattery were conspicuous vices of their religious character. Jesus testified of them that they did all their works to be seen of men, that they loved uppermost rooms at feasts, the chief seats in the synagogues, and greetings in the markets. His own way how different! He did not pray at the street corner but in the mountain solitude when men were asleep. He withdrew into the wilderness from popular applause. He said to His intimates, Tell no man that I am Christ. The Pharisees let their light shine so that it glorified themselves. Jesus let His light shine so that, while glorifying God and benefiting men, it brought to Himself reproach, blasphemy, crucifixion. Of a life having such issues a higher principle than vanity was the spring: the stern sense of duty, lowly self-suppressing love to men.

Here was a type of goodness worth admiring and imitating, set forth, not in theory, but in a living practice. Now we know what to say in answer to the question, Why callest thou Jesus Good? We call Jesus Good because, He abhorred counterfeit sanctity, served His Father with filial liberty and devotion, loved men even unto death, and shunned ostentation. We have good, solid, historical grounds for so thinking of Him. The evangelists had no inducement for exhibiting Him in this light except that the fact was so. On the contrary, the temptation of the Apostolic Church, as time went on, was to tone down the controversial aspect of Christ's character, and to exhibit His goodness apart from the shadows which bring its distinctive qualities into bright relief. The error and mis-

fortune of later ages has been to lose clear perceptions of
the real Jesus to the extent of well-nigh becoming insen
sible to the difference between His goodness and the
counterfeit presentation.   For this loss of true insight into
Christ's human character higher views of His Person cannot
compensate.   On the contrary, a faded humanity means
a divinity evacuated of its contents.   It is of no avail,
I must repeat, to call an unknown man, still less a
misconceived man, God.   God is a Spirit, not merely
ontologically but ethically, and of what quality His spirit
is the man Jesus declares.   God is love, and what divine
love means the ministry of Jesus in life and death shows.
God is good in the specific sense of being gracious, generous,
philanthropic, and the historic life of Jesus interprets for
us the philanthropy of God.   All we really know of God in
spirit and in very truth we know through Jesus; but only
on condition that we truly know Jesus Himself as revealed
to us in the pages of the evangelic history.   Knowledge of
the historical Jesus is the foundation at once of a sound
Christian theology and of a thoroughly healthy Christian life.[1]

Holding this view, I cannot regard with favour the
tendency visibly at work in the present time to make
Christianity as far as possible independent of history.   In
view of prevailing agnosticism, this tendency is very
natural.   When men are loudly and confidently saying : It
is impossible to know what the facts are as to the life of
Jesus, we cannot be sure of much more than that He
lived in Judæa at a certain time, and taught unpopular
views on morals and religion, and in consequence suffered
a violent death ; it is natural that believers should reply :
Our faith is independent of the uncertainties of the evan
gelic story ; we can get our Christianity by a short and
easy method, without troubling ourselves about what hap-

[1] On the need to go back to the consideration of the historical Jesus as an
antidote to the tendency of dogmatic decisions concerning the Person of
Christ to obscure His true image, *vide* Gore's *Bampton Lectures on the
Incarnation of the Son of God*, p. 144.

pened nineteen centuries ago, from the spirit of Christ living in the Church or from our own spiritual experience. Accordingly, the apologetic of the hour runs largely along these lines. Now that the Church can do nothing for a man in quest of faith, or that the "evidence of Christian experience" is without validity, I by no means assert. A species of Christianity might have been permanently propagated without any written record of the life of the Founder by the influence He exerted on His first disciples, and through them on their contemporaries, and through the first generation of Christians on the next, and so on till the world's end. Through word and act He moulds the men who are with Him, and makes them the heroes they afterwards appear, and so a certain definite type of religious thought and character is established. On this hypothesis Jesus would be simply the unknown cause of certain known effects, or a cause knowable only through the effects. Among these effects might fall to be reckoned the literary picture drawn by early Christians of Him whose name they bore : the acts ascribed to Him being such as they deemed congruous to His character, the words put into His mouth not actually uttered by Him, but expressive of thoughts which His spiritual influence enabled His disciples to conceive ; the Gospels, in short, a product not of memory, but of an inspired imagination. In proof that a religion might be successfully propagated under such conditions reference might be made to Buddhism, which has flourished for two thousand years, though concerning the history of the founder little or nothing can be definitely ascertained. A Christianity so originating and so perpetuated would be a purely natural product, entirely independent of all questions as to the present existence of Jesus or of the power of a " Living Christ " to exert supernatural influence on the minds of men.

Such a Christianity is better than nothing, but it surely leaves much to be desired ! For one thing it makes each successive generation very dependent on that which goes before. We receive our Christianity through the spirit of Christ living in the community into which we are born. But what if the spirit of Christ so-called be in great measure a spirit of anti-Christ? Is there no means by which we can protect ourselves from its baleful influence, no standard Christianity by which the actual can be tested, no ideal by which the real can be criticised? To this it may be replied: Yes, there is the evangelic presentation which by comparison is relatively perfect, the picture of the Master by those who were nearest Him, which, whether historic truth or poetic fiction, may be assumed to be in large measure true to His spirit. It is fortunate that there is such a picture to refer to—on naturalistic principles it might have been otherwise; and it may bring us nearer to the genuine image of Jesus than contemporary presenta tions. But it is not a matter of indifference whether it be truth or fiction. Its value, both as an instrument of criticism and as an aid to godly living, depends on the measure of its historicity. I want to be sure that the type of goodness portrayed in the Gospels was embodied in an actual life. If the Jesus of the Gospels really lived as there described, I have a right to condemn nonconformity to His image in others, and am under obligation to aim at conformity thereto in my own conduct. What He was we ought to be, what He was we can approximately be. But if the Jesus of the Gospels be a devout imagination then the right of reform and the obligation to conform cease. The fair Son of man belongs to the serene region of poetry; real life at the best must move on a much lower level.

Believers in the supernatural, in a Christ risen, ascended, and still living, may assert their independence of history in another way. They may make their own religious experi ence in conversion and sanctification their apologetic start- ing-point, and reason thus: Whatever difficulties may be raised about the earthly history of Christ we cannot doubt that He now lives in heaven, for we have experienced His spiritual power in our own hearts. We know therefrom not only that He lives, but what manner of being He is. The spiritual effects reveal the character of the Cause; through these we can form to ourselves a mental image of the exalted Lord. And by means of that image we can even verify the general truth of the picture of Jesus presented in His earthly history. The two likenesses correspond. There is in both the same holy abhorrence of sin, the same compassion for sinners, the same willingness and ability to save. This is in brief the form of an argument which admits of being indefinitely expanded and enforced with rhetorical power. And far be it from me to say that it is entirely illusory. But I do certainly think that it will not bear the strain which some seem inclined to put upon it.[1] In the first place, does not the experience which forms the foundation of the argument presuppose the faith which it is used to prove? The heavenly existence

Christ, and as much of His earthly life as we need to know, are deduced from an experience which is regarded as a purely objective and independent datum. Is it really an independent datum? Does it not depend for all its peculiar characteristics on preconceived ideas both of the heavenly and of the earthly Christ? Does not the ordinary convert take for granted the truth of what is said about Christ in gospels and epistles, and in the traditional teaching of the Church? Does not the quality of religious experience in general vary with the antecedent state of mind of its subject? Men living in heathen countries may their religious experiences, but they cannot have ically Christian experience while they remain ignorant Christ. Philosophers in Christian countries who have accepted the conclusions of negative criticism regarding the Gospels, can have a religious experience which they may think themselves entitled to call Christian, but it is one of a very different complexion from that of a convert t a revival meeting. It is such as results from the power f a few ethical ideas like that of dying unto self in order

[1] *Vide, e.g., The Living Christ and the Four Gospels,* by Dr. Dale.

to truly live.[1]   Theirs is indeed a Christianity independent of history, but it is not one likely to be accepted as ortho dox or legitimate by the patrons of the argument now under consideration.

That argument seems open to a second criticism—viz. that it puts the heavenly and the earthly Christ in the wrong order.   Its first inference from experience is the present Christ living in heaven, its second the past Christ who once lived on earth.   The Christ of history is honestly believed in, but faith in Him is not deemed necessary to the experience.   Experience does not arise out of but rather gives us that faith ; its sole and all-sufficient source is the heavenly Christ, and His spiritual powers.   This is a very precarious ground to stand on.   The earthly Christ is the source of the heavenly Christ's power.   The earthly Christ must first be in the mind as the lever on which the heavenly Christ works.   The heavenly Christ, or the Spirit who is His *alter ego*, takes of the things relating to the earthly Christ and uses them as means of moral renewal ; such is the account of the matter given by Jesus Himself as re ported in the Fourth Gospel.   Without these materials to work with the heavenly Christ would be impotent, or left in possession of only such power as He is able to exercise on such as never heard of His name.   If the Gospels were to be lost, or all faith in their truth to perish, Christianity as a distinctive type of religion would disappear from the world.[2]   It is essentially a historical religion.

In attaching such importance to intimate knowledge of the historic Jesus one may seem to lay himself open to the charge of clinging to a rudimentary religious intuition, with its inevitable limitations, instead of going on to perfection. The path leading thereto, we are told, is this : First comes the intuition of the man Jesus.   Then comes in due course

---

[1] *Vide* Works of T. H. Green, vol. iii.

[2] Stearns says : "There is no reason to believe that Christianity would for any long time continue to exist as an active power in the world were the Bible to be blotted out of existence."—*The Evidence of Christian Experience*, p. 314.

of development the dogma of the God-man, which invests
the historic Jesus with a divine nature, but in doing so
evacuates His humanity of its contents and reduces it to a
ghostly abstraction. Finally arrives the perfect stage of
the philosophic idea underlying the dogma : God manifesting
Himself in the world of nature and humanity.[1] Whether
this be a true account of the course Christianity had to run,
or not, need not be here discussed. Suffice it to say, that
if the choice lay between these three alternatives I should
prefer the intuition to either the dogma or the idea. If
the dogma did indeed imply the humanity of Jesus stripped
of all reality, it would cheat us out of the very boon sup
posed to be conferred by the Incarnation—God revealing
Himself through a human life. If the idea be the true
reality which makes us independent of empirical reality, we
gain, indeed, an imposing universal truth, but at the cost of
the inspiration which comes from firm faith in a perfect life
lived on this earth by a man in whom the Divine Spirit
was immanent in a unique measure. The need of the hour
is not philosophy, but restored intuition. Let us see Jesus
of Nazareth clearly, and, if need be, let the dogma be
reconstructed so that the vision shall remain in all its
vividness.[2]

[1] *Vide* Essay on "Christian Dogma" in Green's *Works*, vol. iii.

[2] The question discussed in the closing paragraphs of this chapter has
occupied the attention of German theologians. Among those who have con-
buted to its discussion in magazines and otherwise are Nosgen Haupt
d Koenig. Nosgen goes to an extreme in insisting on faith in the histori
city of the Gospels as essential. Haupt takes up a position similar to that of
Dr. Dale. The view of Nosgen is substantially that stated in the foregoing
pages. The most important work bearing on the question that I know is
Herrmann's *Verkehr des Christen mit Gott*, 1892. It is antipietistic in spirit
and in sympathy with Luther and with Ritschl's attitude in his *Geschichte
des Pietismus*, and insists on the supreme importance of knowing the historic
Christ. The risen Christ he regards, not as the source of faith, but rather
as the product of faith—a *Glaubens-gedanken*.

CHAPTER II.

JESUS AS THE CHRIST.

LITERATURE.—Stanley Leathes, *The Religion of the Christ* (Bampton Lectures for 1874): Matthew Arnold, *Literature and Dogma* (chap. vii.); Baur, *Geschichte der Christlichen Kirche*, 1er Band; Drummond, *The Jewish Messiah*, 1877; Stanton, *The Jewish and the Christian Messiah*, 1886; Baldensperger, *Das Selbstbewusstsein Jesu im Lichte der Messianischen Hoffnungen seiner Zeit*, 1888; Bornemann, *Unterricht im Christenthum*, 1891; Martineau, *Seat of Authority in Religion*, 1890.

Jesus, we have seen, was very welcome for His own sake, apart from His relation to the previous history of the world, or of Israel, and might on His own merits have for faith the highest religious value, as the revealer of God in the fulness of His grace and truth. And we can conceive of faith as expressing its sense of the absolute religious worth of Jesus in categories of thought current in the present time, rather than in those current in the long bygone ages and among other peoples, such as the *Christ* or the *Logos*. Faith has a perfect right to do so. Had the New Testament been written in this century and in Europe, the religious significance of Jesus might have been found set forth therein in terms not known in the first century, and in Palestine; and some of the terms used in the actual New Testament to express what Jesus is to faith, such as the Logos, might have been missing, though the truth thereby suggested— that Jesus has the highest value as the full self-communi cation of the living God, not merely for Israel, but for the Gentile world. for the whole human race—would not have failed to find recognition. It is the inalienable privilege of a living faith, and its instinctive impulse, to declare the treasure it finds in Jesus in its own way, and in words and ideas thrilling with its own fresh life. In poetry and in preaching it uses this liberty. In theology the privilege has been little taken advantage of, the tendency being to fall back on Scripture terms and categories as alone authorised, and as alone competent to express a true adequate doctrine concerning the person of Jesus.[1] Of these inspired terms the most valuable, and therefore most frequently to be used for the purposes of theology, are those which are most universal in their character, and most independent of local and temporary associations. Foremost among the titles of Jesus possessing this character are " Son of God " and " Son of man." The synthesis of these two titles expresses the eternal truth of Christianity as the universal absolute religion.

While all this is true, it is not unimportant for theology, and even for religious faith, to affirm of Jesus that He was the Christ. For we must not forget that Christianity is not merely a universal and absolute religion, but likewise a *historical* religion. In connection with this aspect of the Christian faith, that Jesus was the Christ is a very essential proposition. It implies in general that the Christian religion had its root in, and was the consummation of, the religion of Israel. We expect of the absolute religion that it shall be found on inquiry to be the crown and ripe fruit of the religious development of the world. This is the demand at once of faith and of philosophy. Neither can rest till it has been able to see in Jesus the Desire of all nations. That He was this so far as Israel was concerned is declared when we affirm that He was the Christ. The affirmation, if well founded, has apologetic value both for the religion of Israel and for the Christian religion. With reference to the former it implies that the religious history of Israel embodied a real self-revelation of God through a special gracious providence. With reference to the latter it implies•that in Jesus that revelation culmin ated, and that providence reached its goal. Each supports the claims of the other, and the two together constitute a harmonious, complete, historic movement.

. [1] *Vide* on this Bornemann. *Unterricht im Christenthum*, pp. 65, 66.

That Jesus is the Christ is therefore an important affirmation, if true. But on what grounds does the affirmation rest? Did Jesus claim to be the Christ, and was His claim valid? Let us look at the latter question first. Now it is important to have a clear understanding of what is implied in a valid claim, in other words what was the necessary and sufficient outfit for one who was to be a Christ. The question throws us back on Hebrew prophecy. For we may disregard in this connection the apocalyptic writings. Their bearing on the Messianic idea is of quite subordinate moment. It relates to the language rather than to the substance of the idea, so far as Jesus is concerned. These writings doubtless had a place in the religious development of Israel. But revelation is hardly responsible for them; for the most part they sink below the level of inspiration, and belong in spirit to the night of legalism. The question of vital importance is, What are the leading momenta in the Messianic idea as presented in the oracles of the Hebrew prophets? The question has already been answered by anticipation. In our study of the characteristics of Old Testament prophecy, and especially of its optimism, we found that the hopes of Israel centred around three things : a right Royal Man, a kingdom of the good with God's law written on their heart, and a suffering servant of God making Himself King of that kingdom by His spiritual insight and self-sacrifice. And at the close of that study it was affirmed that in Jesus these three ideals meet : that He is the Royal Man, the bringer in of the kingdom of grace, and the man of sorrow who conquers human hearts by suffering love.[1] That these ideals are the salient points of prophecy will probably be admitted by all competent students. That in Jesus they met will be not less frankly acknowledged by all who see in Him one very welcome for His own sake. For such Jesus is the one true proper Royal Man in all human history. His claim to be the wisest teacher and

[1] *Vide* Book II. chap. vi. p. 261.

the man of most tragic experience they readily own. His influence through wisdom and suffering their admiration and love confess. What more is needed to justify the assertion that Jesus is the Christ? To this ques tion one such as Mr. Arnold might reply—it is indeed the gist of what he has written on the subject in *Literature and Dogma:*—" Is not the correspondence between the prophetic ideals and the history of Jesus only an accidental coincidence ; very remarkable cer tainly, yet possessing no religious significance such as that assertion implies? When you say that Jesus is Christ, you mean that it was God's preannounced purpose that such a personage should come, and that in Jesus that purpose found its fulfilment. Might not the prophetic ideals be poetic dreams, and the correspondence between them and the life of Jesus, so far as real, only a curious historical phenomenon ? " Such scepticism is possible only to those who have no faith in a Living God who works out purposes in history. It is an attitude towards history analogous to that of the materialist towards the physical constitution of the universe. As the materialist regards the world as the product of a fortuitous concourse of atoms, so the man who, on the grounds indicated, doubts the Messianic claims of Jesus, regards history as a succession of events in which no trace of a Providence can be discovered. We must leave such a man to the enjoyment of his doubts. It is not to persons in such a state of mind we appeal when, having regard to the correspondence between prophetic ideals and gospel realities, we say, Jesus was the Christ.

If Jesus was the Christ He might know Himself to be such, and make public acknowledgment of the fact. Is there any good ground for believing that He did indeed advance Messianic pretensions ? With the Gospels in our hands it seems difficult to resist the conclusion that He did. Many sayings are recorded as uttered by Him which clearly imply a Messianic consciousness. Accordingly, that Jesus claimed to be, or allowed Himself to be called, the Messiah, is admitted by some of the most negative and sceptical critics of the evangelic history, as, *e.g.* by Dr. Ferdinand Baur, the famous founder of the Tubingen school of tendency - criticism. The concession, however, has little value, when those who make it conceive of Jesus as adopting or accepting the title simply from reasons of policy. Such was Baur's idea. His view of Christ's position is this: He was, and knew Himself to be, the founder of a new religion, ethical in spirit, and therefore universal in destination. To such a religion anything peculiar to the religion of Israel, and particularism of every description, was entirely foreign; its concern was with *man* and the essentially human. Jesus understood this quite well, and in His heart had entirely shaken off the narrow trammels of Judaism. But He could not entirely break away from these in His public action. In especial He could not disregard the national hope of Israel, the Messianic idea. He must bow to it as a great fact; as the inaugurator of the universal religion He must even Himself accept the title of Messiah, and play the corresponding *rôle* to the satisfaction of His countrymen, or, at least, of the most godly among them. To conquer the world, He must first get a foothold in Judæa, and that was possible only for one who respected and seemed able to fulfil the Messianic hope. This was the tribute which Jesus, however reluctantly, had to pay to the spirit of His time and people.[1]

It is so far satisfactory that the author of the Tubingen theory frankly acknowledges that Jesus, from whatever motives, did give Himself out as the Messiah. Yet even on this point, it must be confessed, his opinion is of less weight than it may seem entitled to in virtue of his great learning. For the truth is, it was Baur's interest to arrive at the conclusion that Jesus claimed to be the Christ. Only so could he secure the necessary conditions

---

[1] *Vide Geschichte der Christlichen Kirche*, Band I. pp. 36, 37.

for the dialectic process from which resulted, according to his theory, the old Catholic Church and its conception of Christianity. In Jesus, the initiator of the movement, must meet two things not absolutely irreconcilable, but certain to appear so to His followers. But lo! here are two things admirably fitted to serve the purpose of *Gegensätze* or antagonistic principles: the universal spirit of the new religion, and the particularistic form of the Jewish Messianic idea. They suit the purpose so well that it may be assumed without further trouble that they did both meet in the teaching of Jesus. And granting that they did both find a place in the doctrine of the Master, it is not difficult to conjecture what will follow. Some will place the emphasis of their faith on the one aspect of the doctrine, some on the other; whence will come first war, then efforts at reconciliation, then ultimate harmonious and stable peace. Such in a nutshell is the celebrated Tubingen theory of the origin of the Christianity of the old Catholic Church, as it made its appearance in the latter half of the second century.

If the alternatives were, Jesus calling Himself Messiah solely on grounds of policy, or totally ignoring the Messianic idea and hope, one could have no hesitation in preferring the latter. If we cannot have a Jesus who is the ripe fruit of Old Testament religion, let us at least have a Jesus who is sincere, unworldly, guileless—an absolutely true, pure-hearted, godly man; not a time-serving opportunist. We may not be able on these terms to hold fast the old faith in a revelation of God to Israel, but we shall at all events be able to think better and more hopefully of human nature. But there is another alternative besides the two indicated. Jesus might have a purified, trans-formed Messianic idea, and might with perfectly sincere conviction regard Himself as the realiser of that idea. It belongs to the theory that Jesus called Himself Messiah from motives of policy, that He should accept the Mes-

sianic idea pretty much as He found it. From all we
know of Him, this was intrinsically unlikely. As He
appears in the Gospels Jesus occupies an attitude of radical
dissent from the whole thought and spirit of His age. If
we are to understand Him thoroughly, we cannot attach
too much importance to this fact. His character and
historical position, as has been already pointed out in an
earlier part of this work,[1] are explained by two sets of
conditions, one positive and the other negative. The posi
tive conditions are : an elect people, a prophetic Messianic
forecast, and a sacred literature. To these three answer,
as a negative group, election misconceived and abused, a
degenerate corrupt Messianic hope, and Rabbinism, i.e.
enslavement to the letter of a Holy Book misinterpreted
and idolised. These three counterfeits went together, and
were naturally cause and effect of each other. To be out
of sympathy with any one of them was to be equally out
of sympathy with the others. That Jesus had no sym
pathy with Jewish exclusiveness, in its claim to a monopoly
of divine favour, is certain. That He had a passionate
aversion to Rabbinism and all its ways is, if possible, still
more certain. That the popular notion of Messiah had no
attraction for Him may be confidently inferred from these
two facts, not to speak of the concurrent evidence to this
effect supplied by the gospel records.

On the other hand, the solidarity of Jesus with the first
group of historical conditions was as pronounced as His
antipathy to their contemporary caricatures. He was,
like Paul, a Hebrew of the Hebrews. In his account of
the contents of Christianity as taught by Christ, Baur
represents Him as indebted to the Gentiles not less than
to the Jews: to Greek philosophy, as influenced by
Socrates, for His doctrine of the supreme value of man
as a moral subject; to the world-wide Empire of Rome,
for the universalist spirit of His teaching. But it is really
not necessary to go outside the Old Testament and the

---

[1] *Vide* Book I. p. 56.

Jewish people to understand and explain Jesus as far as that is possible. He believed with His whole heart in the divine calling of Israel; He loved the Scriptures; He especially delighted in the Psalms and the prophetic oracles, in the passion for righteousness to which they give eloquent expression, in the inspiring view which they present of the character of God, and in the glowing pictures they paint of the good time coming. If He had any favourites among the prophets, Isaiah, and, still more, the great unknown prophet whom critics call Deutero-Isaiah, had a foremost place amongst them; Jeremiah, too,— witness the allusion at the supper table to his oracle of the new covenant. The Gospels are full of echoes from the second half of the book which goes by Isaiah's name. With reference to the second Isaiah it has been beautifully remarked:—"As we enter the gospel history from the Old Testament, we feel at once that Isaiah is in the air. In the fair opening of the new year of the Lord, the harbinger notes of the book awaken about us on all sides, like the voices of birds come back with the spring."[1] It is open to any one to suggest that these references are due to the evangelists rather than to Jesus. But even if this were admitted, it would be a fair inference that their par tiality for Isaiah reflects a trait in the religious character of their Master.

From His favourite prophets Jesus doubtless drew His Messianic idea. It is from them mainly that we derive what we have found to be the cardinal elements of the Messianic hope — the Royal Man, the kingdom of the good, and the suffering servant of Jehovah. With these the mind of Jesus could be in perfect sympathy : their unworldliness, their lofty spirituality, would commend themselves to His pure, devout soul. For the advent of a man who, by his wisdom and patience, could found such a kingdom of the good with the law of God written on

---

[1] G. A. Smith, *The Book of Isaiah*, vol. ii. p. 282. *Vide* Matt. iii. 3-17, iv. 14-17, xii. 17-21 ; Luke iv. 18, 19.

their heart, in accordance with Jeremiah's oracle of the new covenant, He could sincerely and fervently pray. Nothing could be better for Israel and for the world than that such a man should come.

But could He imagine that He Himself was that man? There certainly never has been a man since the beginning of the world who more completely met the requirements. Suppose for a moment He was the very man, could He regard Himself as such? No, it has been replied, in effect, because such a Messianic self-consciousness is incompatible with the moral worth of One capable of being a Messiah. A self-conscious Messiah is, *ipso facto*, no Messiah; therefore all the words ascribed to Jesus which imply a Messianic consciousness must be regarded as an expression of the faith of the Apostolic Church, and not as genuine sayings of the Master.[1]

With the ethical postulate of this argument—that no utterances must be ascribed to Jesus incompatible with His meek and lowly spirit—we must all entirely agree. The problem of the reconciliation of Christ's Messianic consciousness with His humility is, I have for some time back perceived,[2] of greater importance than has been generally recognised, and Dr. Martineau deserves thanks for projecting it upon public attention with an emphasis which will insure that it shall not hereafter be overlooked. His view is that the problem is insoluble. In this view most certainly believers in Christ will not concur; nevertheless the argument advanced in its support will not be in vain if it compel believing men to see that there is a problem. We have been too much accustomed to talk about Christ's Messianic *claims*, without being sufficiently sensitive lest we should make Him appear to be animated by ambitious passions or by vain self-importance. We must be careful so to state His attitude towards His

---

[1] *Vide* Martineau, *Seat of Authority in Religion*, pp. 577-585.

[2] *Vide The Kingdom of God*, pp. 158-160; also *The Miraculous Element in the Gospels*, pp. 256-258.

Messianic vocation that these unholy elements shall be eliminated. This is possible by looking at the Messiahship ✓ on the side of duty rather than on the side of dignity, and by giving prominence to the suffering aspect of Messiah's career. It was in this way Jesus Himself contemplated His Messiahship. He thought of Himself as called to an arduous office, involving toil, humiliation, and sorrow. And therefore His attitude was not that of one making a claim, but rather that of loyal submission to the behest of divine Providence. "His coming forth as Messiah was not usurpation, but obedience; not free choice, but inevitable divine necessity."[1] The indignities of His earthly experience and the foreseen tragedy at the end of His career effectually guaranteed the purity of His motives. It is not the way of ambition to clutch at a position involving such experiences. No man taketh the honour of high priesthood to himself when the priest has to be also the victim. Neither is vanity or self-seeking likely to aspire to a Messiahship of which the outstanding feature is suffering.

Many of the utterances ascribed to Jesus, which involve a Messianic consciousness, plainly breathe the spirit of lowliness rather than that of arrogance or vain-glory. This holds true of the title *Son of man*, the favourite self-designation of Jesus. It expressed the Messianic consciousness of Jesus in three distinct directions by three distinct groups of texts. "It announced a Messiah appointed to suffer, richly endowed with human sympathy, and destined to pass through suffering to glory. In all three respects it pointed at a Messianic ideal contrary to popular notions. For that very reason Jesus loved the name, as expressing truth valid for Himself, as fitted to foster just conceptions in receptive minds, and as steering clear of current misapprehensions."[2] Even in those cases

---

[1] Baldensperger, *Das Selbstbewusstsein Jesu im Lichte der Messianischen Hoffnungen seiner Zeit*, p. 191.
[2] *Vide The Kingdom of God*, pp. 176, 177, and pp. 172-175 for the relative texts.

in which the title has an apocalyptic reference, the lowly mind shines through. The Son of man of the judgment programme is one who can say : I have been an hungered, thirsty, a stranger, naked, sick, in prison.

But there are certain words ascribed to Jesus in the Gospels which it is deemed impossible He could have uttered. Such are those in which He claims to be greater than Jonah, Solomon, and the Temple. These sayings do certainly express a sense of personal dignity, and we have only a choice between regarding them as on that account unauthentic, and discovering a way of harmonising a sense of dignity with the spirit of lowliness. Now there are two lines of thought which are available here. In the first place, it will be found that wherever Jesus appears in the Gospels in the act of self-assertion, it is always as against a spirit of scornful unbelief manifested in His environment. The most notable instance is that in which He claims to be the indispensable medium of the knowledge of the Father. When, according to the representation of the evangelist, did He utter those words beginning, No man knoweth the Son but the Father ? It was when He was confronted with the unbelief of the "wise and prudent." Did it not become even the meek and lowly One to draw Himself up to the full height of His dignity in such circumstances, even as it became Paul to assert His importance as the apostle of the Gentiles in opposition to Judaistic narrowness and intolerance ? If Judaists said to Paul, You are no apostle, that they might destroy His influence as the preacher of a universal Christianity, it became him, it was his positive duty, to say with emphasis: I am an apostle, not behind the chiefest apostles. To say this in such circumstances was not vain boasting, but proper jealousy for a great interest committed to his hands. Even so in the case of Jesus. If scribes and Pharisees, proud of their learning and sanctity, said : What can this Nazarene provincial have to say about God, or His kingdom, or His righteousness ? Jesus owed it to the truth that was in

Him to claim power to reveal the Father, and to proclaim His confident belief that, however despicable His present following might be, the future belonged to Him and the cause He represented.

The words in which Jesus asserted for Himself a greatness superior to that of Solomon, or Jonah, or the Temple are quite compatible with a lowly mind. They were all spoken in the same circumstances as those in which the claim to exclusive knowledge of the Father was advanced. And they were spoken in the same sense as that in which Jesus said of John the Baptist that even the least in the kingdom of God was greater than he. In personal terms Jesus expressed His sense of the greatness of the new era, His consciousness of belonging to a new world of values. Solomon represented material wealth and splendour, Jonah represented religious nationalism, the Temple represented a worship of outward sensuous ritual; Jesus represented the kingdom within, the religion of humanity, the worship of the Spirit; so did the meanest of His disciples. Therefore not only He, but the least in the kingdom of God, was greater than the men and things of greatest magnitude belonging to the old era. Thus understood, the sayings in question, which to a prejudiced critic wear an aspect of conceit, do but express, in a grand prophetic way, spiritual insight. The speaker was so remote from egotism, that He could afford to be indifferent to the superficial appearance of it in the form of expression, just as He was so remote from vice that He could afford to be the companion of the vicious, though in neither case without paying the penalty in an evil, misjudging world.

Thus far of one line of thought, which seems to supply real help towards the reconciliation of Christ's sense of Messianic dignity with His personal lowliness. The other remains to be briefly indicated. The problem of the reconciliation of dignity with humility is a general one in ethical psychology. If Jesus could not compatibly with His humility be conscious of His Messiahship, then it is impossible to combine humility with the consciousness of being a father, a chief magistrate, a judge, a minister of state, a king. The Messianic dignity is unique; still it belongs to a class. The grace of humility may be peculiarly hard to practise for the one man in history who can be the Christ; still the problem, if exceptionally delicate, is the same in principle for him as for all occupants of places of distinction. If an ordinary king can be humble, so can the Messianic King. If the leader of a great religious reform, like Luther or Knox, can be lowly, so can He who said, "Take my yoke upon you." And where is the difficulty in any case? Is the problem not constantly receiving solutions? Is it not among the great ones, great in position, responsibility, endowment, and influence, that true lowliness is found? Nay, is not God, the greatest, also the lowliest? "I dwell in the high and holy place, with him also that is of a contrite and humble spirit." Is this not the very truth involved in the incarnation—God humbling Himself to share and bear the sins and miseries of His own children?

Jesus was "He that should come." He was what was wanted—a man richly endowed with prophetic intuition, in spirit wholly opposed to Rabbinism, with the purity of heart needful to see God, and able to speak the last and highest word about God. He came when He was wanted, when Judaism had reached the lowest point of degeneracy, and the night of legalism was at its darkest. He understood the situation, and felt that it was His vocation to meet the pressing needs of the time, and did meet them with perfect fidelity and wisdom. By His public career He fulfilled God's purpose in the election of Israel, which took place for the sake of the true religion, not for the sake of its temporary vehicle. For the revelation of God and the moral renewal of the world one man turned out to be of incomparably more service than the whole nation of Israel, or the southern kingdom of Judah, or the post-exilian remnant. That was obvious to the first disciples

of Jesus, as it is to us. Therefore they called Him Christ.
Thereby they expressed the essential fact truly. In apply
ing to their Master that epithet, the apostles did not start
a false theory, or put upon Him "the first deforming mask,
the first robe of hopeless disguise, under which the real
personality of Jesus of Nazareth disappeared from sight."[1]
If, after they had believed in Him as the Christ, they
discovered minute correspondences between facts in His
history and prophetic texts, and delighted to point these
out, they did, to say the least, what was very natural and
innocent. If such correspondences were not fitted to pro
duce faith, they at least gave gratification to a faith already
existing, and in the main well grounded. The assertion
that the Messianic interpretation of the Old Testament in
the New Testament "has degraded the sublimest religious
literature of the ancient world into a book of magic and a
tissue of riddles"[2] will be endorsed only by those who
regard the Messianic hope as a fond delusion and romantic
dream.

CHAPTER III.

JESUS AS FOUNDER OF THE KINGDOM OF GOD.

LITERATURE.—Seeley, *Ecce Homo;* Strauss, *Das Leben Jesu,*
1835, *Das Leben Jesu für das Deutsche Volk,* 1864 ; Baur,
Geschichte der Christlichen Kirche; Keim, *Geschichte Jesu von
Nazara* (Band II. pp. 125–204 on the Miracles); Bernhard
Weiss, *Das Leben Jesu,* 1884 ; Havet, *Le Christianisme et
ses Origins,* vol. iv. ; Candlish, *The Kingdom of God Biblically
and Historically considered* (Cunningham Lectures, 1884);
Row, *The Supernatural in the New Testament,* and *Christian
Evidences viewed in relation to Modern Thought* (Bampton
Lectures for 1877) ; Fairbairn, *Studies in the Life of Christ;*
Bruce, *The Miraculous Element in the Gospels,* and *The King-*

---

[1] Martineau, *Seat of Authority in Religion,* p. 329.
[2] *Ibid.* p. 329.

dom of God ; Martineau, *The Seat of Authority in Religion* (Book V. chap. i. " The Veil taken away.")

The burden of Christ's preaching, according to the Synoptical Gospels, was the *Kingdom of God.* That they represent this as His great theme is one of many marks of their historic fidelity. For it was to be expected that the Christ, when He came, would make the kingdom the great subject of His discourse. The establishment of a holy state in which ideally perfect relations between God and man should be realised had been the aim of Jehovah and the hope of His people from the time of Israel's election. The attempts at realisation had been failures ; yet, still the hope lived on. At length Jesus came, and if He were indeed the Christ, what could He say but that now at last the kingdom was at hand ?

Being the Christ Jesus had more to do than to announce the advent of the kingdom. He was indeed, like John the Baptist, a prophet, but He was more. He was the King, and in that capacity He had to create the divine common wealth whose approach He, as a prophet, proclaimed. His creative activity had to assume two forms. He had not only to bring into existence the thing, but He had to originate the true idea of the thing. For the kingdom was as grossly misconceived by the common mind as was the Messiahship, so that when Jesus, at the commencement of His ministry, virtually intimated that through Him the kingdom was about to come, He thereby imposed on Him self the double task of making known the nature of the kingdom, and of giving to the kingdom truly conceived its place in history.

Two questions thus arise : What was Christ's idea of the kingdom ; and what means did He employ to bring it into existence ?

In the first chapter of this work it has been stated that two of the most outstanding characteristics of the kingdom, as Jesus conceived it, were *spirituality* and *uni-*

versality.[1] The two attributes imply each other. That which is ethical or spiritual is universal, and nothing in religion is universal but that which belongs to the spirit of man. Yet, while most students of the Gospels would be willing to concede the former of the two ascriptions, there has been much dispute concerning the latter. Some contend that the promise Jesus came to announce was purely national, and that everything in the Gospels pointing in the direction of a universal religion is part of the veil that must be taken away in order to see the true Jesus.[2] There is the strangest confusion of parties on the question, among those who deny the universalistic character of Christ's teaching being found so comparatively orthodox a theologian as Weiss, while Baur, as is well known, most strenuously maintained the affirmative. The opinion of Weiss, however, is no part of orthodoxy, it is only an instance of orthodoxy misled by an indiscriminate bias against Tubingen heterodoxy. For while the theory of Baur in regard to the origin of Christianity is in many respects radically false, and based upon a naturalistic philosophy, his view on the particular question now under consideration is well founded. That Jesus should be the conscious teacher of a universal religion was to be expected, not on the ground suggested by Baur, that the spirit of universalism was in the air, the result of the world-wide dominion of Rome, but simply because such a religion was the natural outcome of the religious development of Israel. The steady drift of Israel's history and of Hebrew prophecy, as has been made apparent in the foregoing book, was towards universalism. To say that Jesus came announcing the approach of a purely national theocratic kingdom, is to say that He did not understand the purpose of Israel's election, the prophetic doctrine of God, and the oracle of the new covenant. It is to suppose Him blind to the lessons taught by past failures to establish either a righteous

[1] *Vide* p. 3.
[2] So Martineau, *Seat of Authority in Religion*, pp. 585-587.

nation or a holy Church. The Jewish nation had been
wrecked, and the Jewish Church had ended in Rabbinism;
and now what remained but to try a new experiment, that of
forming a community based not on race or ritual, but on
spiritual receptivity to the love of God?

Universal elements do certainly enter into Christ's
teaching as reported even in the Synoptical Gospels; such
as the sayings concerning the coming into the kingdom of
strangers from all quarters of the earth,[1] and the preaching
of the gospel in the whole world,[2] and the parables of the
vinedressers, the great feast, and the prodigal son,[3] and the
programme of judgment.[4] The universalistic drift of
these texts and others of kindred character is for the
most part not denied; what is called in question is their
authenticity. The suggestion is that they express the views
of Christians of a later time when Gentile Christianity had
become a great fact, not the mind of Christ. Nothing that
an apologist can say can prevent such a suggestion being
made. But he can with reason affirm that it is gratuitous
and uncalled for; that there is no good ground for doubt
ing the authenticity of universalistic gospel texts; that
there is no presumption against Jesus being universalistic
in His spirit and tendency, if not in His outward activities;
that the presumption is indeed all the other way in refer
ence to one who had due insight into the meaning of His
country's history, and into His own position in the process
of its religious development. That the Gospels represent
Jesus as uttering words implying the near advent of a
religion of humanity is as strong a point in favour of their
historicity as that they represent the kingdom of God in
general as the main theme of His preaching. In both alike
Jesus was true to His antecedents, and to the needs, if not
to the spirit, of His time.

Before passing from this topic, let it simply be remarked

---

[1] Matt. viii. 11.   [2] Matt. xxvi. 13; Mark xiv. 9.
[3] Matt. xxi. 33-41; Luke xiv. 16-24; Luke xv. 11-32.
[4] Matt. xxv. 31-46.

in a sentence that this new idea of the kingdom, as spiritual and universal, not only found occasional expression in Christ's words, but was immanent in His conduct.   The interest He took in the common people was full of signficance as the sign of a new departure.   It proclaimed the importance of man, and it struck a death-blow at privilege. It was universalism in germ within the limits of the chosen race.

The attributes of spirituality and universality differen tiated the kingdom as Jesus conceived it from the kingdom of popular expectation ; which, while theocratic, was in other respects like any ordinary kingdom, outward and national.   To complete its definition, it is necessary to make use of yet another contrast.   The kingdom, as Christ presented it, was not a kingdom of *law*, but a kingdom of *grace*.   It was not a demand but a gift.   It was God as a Father, Christ's chosen name for the Divine Being, coming down to men to dwell among them as His children, merci fully forgiving their offences, and putting His Spirit within them that they might live worthily of their position as sons.   Such was the kingdom implied in Jeremiah's oracle of the new covenant, in contrast to that based on the old Sinaitic covenant with its law written on tables of stone. The contrast between the two kingdoms was indeed not absolute, but only relative, for as has been pointed out in another place, God's relation to men was never merely legal ; certainly was not so under the Decalogue, whose preface points to a work of redemption as the basis of Jehovah's claim to obedience.[1]   Still the contrast, though only relative, was sufficiently real to justify the broad statement in the Fourth Gospel : the law was given by Moses, grace came by Jesus Christ.[2]   Many things in the Gospels indicate that grace was the keynote of Christ's doctrine of the kingdom ; *e.g.*, the joyous spirit that ani mated His disciples in contrast to the gloom that brooded over the company gathered around the Baptist, the kind of

---

[1] *Vide* p. 249.   [2] John i. 17.

people who were chiefly invited to enter the kingdom, not
the righteous, but "sinners," and the eagerness with which
many of the class responded to the call.[1]

Thus did Jesus create a new idea of the kingdom of
God—new not in the sense that it had no roots in the Old
Testament, but in the sense of novel emphasis given to
germs of truth latent in Hebrew prophecy. We have now
to consider what means He employed to bring the kingdom
so conceived into existence.

Christ's means and methods were congruous to the nature
of the kingdom He came to found. It was a kingdom of
grace, and His main instrument was love. His outfit as
Messianic King consisted chiefly, and before all things, in
an unbounded sympathy with the sinful and miserable, an
"enthusiasm of humanity." The text He is reported to
have preached on in the synagogue of Nazareth gives the
key to His whole ministry. He was under an irresistible
impulse of the spirit of love to preach the gospel of the
kingdom to the poor, to heal the broken-hearted, to bring
deliverance to the captives, and recovery of sight to the
blind.[2] It was probably through this great tide of love
rolling through His heart that He became conscious of His
Messianic vocation; it was certainly by its mighty power
that He was carried triumphantly through all the arduous
tasks and trials of His public career. This love made
Him the "friend of publicans and sinners"; it also made
Him the marvellous healer of diseases. The former aspect
of His ministry drew upon Him the reproaches of con
temporaries; the latter aspect is the stumbling-block of
modern unbelief.

The miraculous element in the Gospels is a large subject
with many sides, demanding for its adequate treatment a
volume rather than a few paragraphs. It raises the ques
tion of the possibility of miracle, with reference to which
both philosophy and science are through many of their

---

[1] *Vide The Kingdom of God*, chap. i.
[2] Luke iv. 18, 19.

representatives in conflict with faith. This question cannot
be gone into here. A few observations, however, may be
helpful on two more special questions, viz. in what relation
does the miraculous element stand to the primitive tradition
of our Lord's ministry ; and in what relation does the same
element stand to that ministry itself as the outcome of
Christ's character and Messianic vocation ?

As to the former of these two questions, there seems to
be good reason to believe that miraculous or marvellous
acts of healing had a place in the original apostolic tradi
tion. The men who had been with Jesus had stirring
stories to tell of cures wrought on the bodies and minds
of the sick, on persons suffering from fever, leprosy, palsy,
demoniacal possession, blindness. Nine narratives of cures
of such diseases are found in the triple tradition which
forms the common basis of the Synoptical Gospels. The
primitive gospel, whether it was the *Logia* of Matthew or
the Gospel of Mark,[1] the report of Peter's preaching,
appears to have been to a greater or less extent a miracle
gospel.[2] This is, indeed, now very generally admitted, the
only question seriously debated being whether the cures
were in the strict sense miraculous, the naturalistic sug
gestion being that they were wrought by "moral therapeutics,"
or by hypnotism. But it is hard to conceive of leprosy or
of aggravated madness like that of the demoniac of Gadara
yielding to anything short of miraculous power. This is
virtually acknowledged by those who see in the story of
the leper not a case of cure, but simply a declaration that
the sufferer was already cured and clean, and in the story
of the Gadarene demoniac a " witty, in the literal sense,
impossible history."[3]

---

[1] On this topic, *vide* chap. viii. of this book.

[2] *Vide* on this topic, my *Miraculous Element in the Gospels*, chap. iii.

[3] So Keim in *Jesu von Nazara*. As Keim of all naturalistic theologians
goes furthest in recognising the general historicity of the gospel record, it may
be well to indicate here how he disposes of the miraculous element. He
accepts all narratives which do not necessarily involve miracle in the strict
sense. The rest he throws overboard as supernumerary (*überzahlig*). To

It was formerly maintained by Strauss and others that the gospel miracles were the product of faith in Jesus as the Christ. They were myths born of Old Testament precedents and prophecies setting forth the marvellous works Messiah must have wrought after Jesus had been accepted as the Messiah. There is good reason, however, to believe that these miracles were not the creations of faith, but rather an authentic element of the original gospel offered to faith. They were in part the ground of the belief that Jesus was the Christ among the first generation of disciples. How far can they render such service now ? This brings us to the second point we proposed to consider.

It must be confessed that miracles cannot be offered as evidences of Christianity now with the confidence with which they were employed for this purpose by the apologists of a past age. Men do not now believe in Christ because of His miracles : they rather believe in the miracles because they have first believed in Christ. For such believers Christ is His own witness, who accredits everything connected with Him : Scripture, prophecy, miracle. Those who are in this happy position need no help from apologists. But there are some who have not got the length of accepting miracles for Christ's sake, not because they are speculative unbelievers in the possibility of miracle,[1] but because they fail to see any congruity between miracles and Christ's personal character or His Messianic vocation. Now it is difficult to establish any such congruity when miracles are viewed in the abstract merely as products of supernatural power. Then they sink into mere external signs attached to Christ's proper work for evidential purposes, a mode of

---

the supernumerary class he relegates (1) duplicates, such as the second feeding ; (2) parables transformed into events, e.g. the cursing of the fig tree and the miraculous draught of fishes ; (3) picture histories, e.g. the Gadarene demoniac ; (4) imitation miracles after Old Testament patterns ; (5) the nature miracles (feeding, stilling of the storm, change of water into wine, etc.).

[1] For some remarks on the general subject of the miraculous, *vide* close of chapter v. of this book,

contemplating the subject which has ceased to have much value for many thoughtful minds.[1] It is otherwise, however, when the miracles of Christ are regarded, not primarily as acts of preternatural power, but as acts of unparalleled love. (The reference here, of course, is to the miracles of healing; the nature miracles must be left on one side to be dealt with as a special problem.[2]) Then there is no difficulty in perceiving how congruous the gospel miracles are both to the innermost spirit of Jesus and to His Messianic work. The constant desire of Jesus was to do good to the utter most extent of His power, and that was also His supreme duty as the Christ having for His vocation to establish the kingdom of grace. He healed men's bodies, as well as their souls, because He was able. Whence the power came, whether it was natural or supernatural, is a question of some scientific and theological interest, but not of vital religious importance. The thing to be chiefly noted is that, the acts of healing being witness, Jesus was a man who always did good to the full measure of His ability and opportunity. It is the divinity of His love, not the super-naturalness of His power, that commends Him to our faith, as a man, and as the Christ. The healing miracles played their part in the revelation of that love. They were not the whole of the revelation, or even the principal part of it. Preaching the gospel to the poor, and keeping company with people of evil repute, were even more significant

[1] On the old and the new ways of regarding the functions of prophecy and miracle in revelation, vide The Chief End of Revelation, chaps. iv. and v. The older apologists viewed prophecy and miracle as evidential adjuncts to a doctrinal revelation, and laid stress on their miraculousness as pointing to a supernatural agent. The modern apologist views them as integral parts of revelation, and lays stress on the ethical rather than on the supernatural aspect.

[2] On this group, vide The Miraculous Element in the Gospels, chaps. vi. and viii. The view there contended for is that the nature miracles are not, any more than the healing miracles, to be regarded as mere displays of power, thaumaturgic feats, but as serving a useful purpose in connection with Christ's work as the Herald and Founder of the kingdom of heaven. The nature miracles assert the supreme claims of the kingdom, and the certainty that its interests will be vindicated at all hazards.

manifestations of the ruling spirit of the Son of man. But all three should be taken together as belonging to the same category, and as integral parts of the Messianic ministry. That Jesus evangelised the poor, associated with the sinful, healed the sick, were each and all signs that He was the One who should come, the genuine Christ of a sin and sorrow-laden world.

The gospel miracles, supremely valuable as a self-revelation of the Worker, have also permanent didactic signifi cance as indicating that the kingdom of God is most comprehensive in scope, and covers all that relates to the well-being of man. Christ certainly cannot be charged with treating what we call spiritual interests as matters of subordinate importance. He was no mere social reformer, who thought all was well when the people had plenty of food and clothing, and when disease and care were rare visitants of their homes. He knew and taught that life was more than meat, or physical health or wealth. He constantly felt and showed a tender concern for the peace and health of human souls. But, on the other hand, that He was equally remote from the one-sidedness of an ultra-spiritualism the healing miracles conclusively prove. They are a protest by anticipation against all indifference to temporal interests as of no moment in comparison with eternal interests. They proclaim *social* salvation, however subordinate in value as compared with *soul* salvation, as nevertheless a part of the grand redemptive plan. They afford most satisfactory evidence of the entire healthiness of Christ's sympathies, the freedom of His religious char acter from all morbid elements, the sunny optimism of His spirit. What a contrast this Healer of disease and Preacher of pardon to the worst, to Buddha with his religion of despair! How incredible that the monk in his cowardly flight from the world is the true embodiment of Christ's ethical ideal! How manifest that the Christian as he ought to be, the true follower of Jesus, is a man who fights bravely and incessantly with every form of evil, whose passion is to leave the world better than he found it, and who makes no scrupulous distinction between saints and sinners, God's poor and other poor, in the exer cise of his benevolence, or between higher and lower interests in the measure of his zeal; but is ever thankful for opportunities of conferring benefit on any man, in any way, and to any extent!

As Creator of the kingdom of heaven, Jesus displayed not only unbounded benevolence, but consummate wisdom. This attribute was an indispensable instrument of love, without which, with the best intentions, it might have failed of its end. Accordingly, it occupies a prominent place in the prophetic picture of the Messianic King and Servant of Jehovah, in which He appears as one on whom the spirit of wisdom and understanding should rest, and to whom the isles should look for instruction.[1] The wisdom of Jesus showed itself conspicuously in the choice of men who "should be with Him," and in the whole training to which He subjected them. The materials relating to this subject may be reckoned among the most certainly historical in the gospel records. Only the most reckless scepticism could call in question either the choice or the training.[2] A man with such irresistible attractions, and having so much to teach, could not fail to gather around Him dis ciples; and that from among those who followed Him occasionally, He choose a limited number to be His constant companions is intrinsically probable. That He made the number *twelve* simply meant that in His mind the choice had an important connection with the interests of the king dom. And surely it had in reality! That miscellaneous activity among the people in evangelism and healing, how ever benevolent in spirit, would not by itself have amounted to much for the permanent fortunes of the kingdom. For

[1] Isa. xi. 2, xlii. 1-4.

[2] Havet, *Le Christianisme et ses Origins*, of recent writers the most sweep ing in his sceptical treatment of both Old and New Testaments, regards the call of the twelve as probably apocryphal; that there was a traitor among them he thinks also unlikely (vol. iv. pp. 38, 39).

all movements that are to be of lasting character, and to take their place in the general history of the world, the thorough instruction and discipline of the few is of greater moment than the transient emotional excitements of the many. Surely such an one as Jesus may be credited with fully understanding this! Therefore one cannot hesitate to believe that He chose men into whose ear He might speak the things which it would be their business after wards to speak from the house-top, as scribes well instructed in the mysteries of the kingdom. As little should we hesitate to find in the Gospels a generally faithful record of the sayings of the Master, as repeated and reported by the men who had been with Him.

Thus by the varied activities of His love and wisdom, Jesus did much for the founding of the kingdom during the years of His life spent in public ministry. But, strange as it may seem, He did even more for that end by His death. However it is to be explained, the fact is so. Had Jesus foreknowledge of the fact? According to the Gospels, He had. He is represented in the evangelic records as making mystic allusions to a tragic termination of His career from an early period, and some months before the close speaking to His disciples in plain, terribly realistic, terms of His approaching death. There is no good reason for regarding these representations as part of the veil that must be taken away in order to see the true Jesus. For the true Jesus, by common consent, was a man of exceptional, even unique, spiritual insight. Pure in heart, He saw God and the most recondite laws of the moral world clearly. He penetrated to the very heart of Old Testament prophecy, and grasped with unerring instinct its deepest essential meaning, as pointing to one God of grace over all and to a spiritual universal religion. Shall we doubt that His eye was caught and His heart set on fire by that most remarkable of Hebrew oracles concerning the suffering Servant of God? Is it credible that He failed to see, what even Plato under stood, that a perfectly righteous man must suffer for righteous-

ness' sake in this world, with His Hebrew Bible in His
hand, full of illustrative instances and of theoretic question
ings as to their *rationale?* On the contrary, that the
righteous man must suffer must have been a moral truism
to Him. He brought this conviction with Him from His
quiet home in Nazareth to His public ministry. And it
was not long before He began to get new insight into
it from personal experience. How could it be otherwise
with one so antipharisaical, living in a community utterly
given up to pharisaism? How soon the tender, sym
pathetic, loving spirit of Jesus would become aware of the
pitilessness of egoistic sanctity, and know that there was
nothing too dreadful to be feared from its conscientious
malevolence!

That Jesus understood from the first that the righteous
must suffer is not the thing to be wondered at. The
wonder lay in the construction He put upon the suffering of
righteousness. He regarded that, as everything else, with
cheerfulness and hope; not as an accident or a dismal fate,
but as the appointment of God, and the law of the moral
world, ordained for beneficent ends. Therein lay His
originality, His new contribution to the discussion of the
world-old question, Why do the righteous suffer? which for
Old Testament saints had been an insoluble problem.
Jesus solved the problem first for Himself, and then for all
who bear His name. He said: Not only I must die for
righteousness' sake, but my death will prove a signal
benefit for the kingdom of God.

The words reported in the Gospels as having been spoken
by Jesus, bearing on the significance of His death, are few.
Their genuineness has been disputed, but without reason.
It was to be expected that He would make some statements
on the subject, and those ascribed to Him are entirely suit
able to His situation, and to the initial stage in the develop
ment of Christian thought. They leave much to be desired
from the point of view of the dogmatic theologian, contain
ing only hints or suggestions of a doctrine rather than a

fully formulated doctrine ; nevertheless, they teach lessons
of real, rare value. Their general import is that Jesus died
for righteousness' sake in accordance with a law applicable
to all who are loyal to the divine interest in the world ;[1]
that His death should possess redemptive virtue for the
many ;[2] that He therefore died willingly in the spirit of
self-sacrifice ;[3] and that out of regard to His death, God
would freely forgive the sins of all citizens of the divine
kingdom.[4]

Sayings of Jesus bearing such meaning justify the great
importance attached to His death in the Apostolic Church.
Of this there are traces everywhere in the New Testament,
and not least in the four Gospels. These Gospels, by their
careful circumstantial narratives of the incidents connected
with the Crucifixion, sufficiently attest how central was
the place occupied by the death of the Lord Jesus in the
minds of believers. The story of the Passion, told with
such wondrous simplicity and pathos by all the evangelists,
is not theology, but it is something better. It is the product of a piety which saw in the cross and its accompani
ments a conflict between the sin of the world and the
patient love of God, and victory lying with the vanquished.
It is no indignant tale of foul wrong done to the innocent,
as it well might have been. The narrators have risen above
indignation into perfect tranquillity of spirit, because what
now chiefly occupies their thoughts is not man's iniquity
but Christ's meekness. They have not got the length of a
theory of atonement—at least, they state none ; but they see
on Calvary the fact of the Just One benignantly bearing
indignities heaped upon Him by the unjust, and graciously
forgiving His murderers. And what they see they say in
severely simple terms without sentiment or reflection, leav
ing the story to speak for itself. And it has spoken, and
continues to speak, with a power far beyond that of any
possible attempt at theological interpretation. Stand by

[1] Matt. xvi. 21–23.　　　　[2] Matt. xx. 28.
[3] Matt. xxvi. 13.　　　　[4] Matt. xxvi. 28.

the cross with Mary if you would feel the spell of the Crucified. Thence emanates an influence you will never be able to put fully into words. Theological formulæ may or may not satisfy the intellect, but it is the evangelic story of the Passion itself that moves the heart. Whatever formula we use must be filled with the story in order to become a vital religious force. Nowhere more than here have we occasion to note the unspeakable value of the Gospels to the Christian faith and life. "The love of Christ constraineth us," writes Paul. He means the love of Christ in dying for sinners. What a poor idea we should have had of that love had the history of the Passion been withheld; how little we should have known of its constraining power!

CHAPTER IV.

JESUS RISEN.

LITERATURE.—Strauss, *Das Leben Jesus für das Deutsche Volk;* Renan, *Les Apotres;* Weizsacker, *Untersuchungen über die Evang-Geschichte,* 1864; Keim, *Die Geschichte Jesu von Nazara,* Band III.; Holsten, *Zum Evangelium des Petrus und des Paulus;* Fairbairn, *Studies in the Life of Christ;* Milligan, *The Resurrection of our Lord* (Croall Lectures, 1881); Abbott, *Philochristus* and *Onesimus;* Wace, *The Gospel and its Witnesses,* 1883; Martineau, *The Seat of Authority in Religion,* pp. 358–378.

The Apostle Paul represents the resurrection of Jesus as a fact of fundamental moment to Christianity. "If Christ be not risen, then is our preaching vain, and your faith is also vain."[1] Modern unbelief regards the fact of the resurrection as of no importance, maintaining that it is the spirit or image of Jesus continuing to work in the world about which alone we need to care. Some, indeed, acknow-

[1] 1 Cor. xv. 14.

ledge that everything turns on the question as to the reality of the resurrection. Strauss speaks of that event as the point at which he must either admit the failure of the naturalistic and historical view of the life of Jesus, and retract all he has written, or pledge himself to show the possibility of the result of the evangelic accounts—that is, the origin of the *belief* in the resurrection without any corresponding miraculous fact.[1]

Whatever diversity of opinion may prevail as to the importance of the historic fact, there is entire agreement as to the vital importance of the *belief* in the fact entertained by the apostles and the Church founded by them. All admit both the existence of the belief and the essential service it rendered in establishing and advancing the Christian religion. Baur, *e.g.*, was fully aware that without that belief Christianity could not have got started on its marvellous world-conquering career. That being so, it is obviously incumbent on all who undertake to give a purely natural account of the origin of Christianity to explain the origin of the belief in the resurrection of Jesus. This, however, they find great difficulty in doing. Baur made no attempt at solving the problem; as Strauss remarked, he avoided the burning question, and, assuming the faith in the resurrection as a fact not to be disputed, however mysterious, contented himself with tracing its historical effects. This reserve may have been due in part to prudential considerations, but it was due also, doubtless, to a vivid sense of the unsatisfactoriness of all past attempts to account for the belief in Christ's rising from the dead on naturalistic principles. All theologians holding such principles have not been so discreet. Several have tried their hand at a solution of the hard problem, each in turn criticising his predecessor's theory, and all together, by their mutual criticisms, making the work of refuting sceptical views on the subject a comparatively easy task for the apologist.

[1] *Vide* his *New Life of Jesus.*

The hypotheses that have been suggested for explaining away the resurrection may be reduced to these five : —

1. That the whole affair was a matter of theft and false hood—falsehood on the part of Jesus, or His friends, or both combined, in collusion with one another, for the pur pose of propagating the belief that the Crucified One had risen again.

2. That Jesus was never really dead ; that after a temporary lapse of consciousness He revived, and was actually seen several times by some of His disciples ; that He lived long enough to be seen of Paul ; then, finally, died in some secret corner.

3. That the appearances of the so-called " risen " Christ were purely *subjective,* due to the excited state of mind in which the disciples found themselves after the death of their beloved Master. They, of course, longed to see the dead One again ; they thought they did see Him more than once ; their thought was perfectly honest, but it was, nevertheless, a hallucination. This is the *vision* theory.

4. That the appearances were not purely subjective, but had an objective cause, which, however, was not the veritable body of Christ risen from His grave, but the glorified Spirit of Christ producing visions of Himself for the comfort of His faithful ones, as if sending telegrams from heaven to let them know that all was well.

5. That there were no appearances to be accounted for, but only a strong way of speaking on the part of the disciples concerning the continued life of the Crucified, which gave rise to a misunderstanding in the Apostolic Church that embodied itself in the traditions of Christo-phanies recorded in the Gospels.

The first of these hypotheses, propounded by Reimarus and kindred spirits, is entirely out of date. Men of all schools in modern times would be ashamed to identify themselves with so base a suggestion ; we may therefore leave it to the oblivion it deserves, and confine our atten tion to the following four.

The second hypothesis, that of an apparent death or swoon, was in favour with the old rationalists represented by Dr. Paulus, and obtained for itself more respect than it deserves by the patronage of Schleiermacher. The explana tion offered by those who espouse this hypothesis is as follows :—Crucifixion, even when both feet and hands are pierced, causes little loss of blood, and kills only very slowly, by convulsions or by starvation. If then Jesus, believed to be dead, was taken down from the cross after some six hours, the supposed death may very well have been only a swoon, from which, after lying in the cool cavern covered with healing ointments and strongly-scented spices, He might readily recover. In support of the suggestion, reference is made to an account by Josephus of the recovery of one of three acquaintances of his own whom he found on the way crucified along with others, and whom he asked permission to take down from their crosses.

Admitting the abstract possibility of a recovery from swoon caused by pain and exhaustion, there is against this hypothesis the clear unanimous testimony of the evan gelists that Jesus was actually dead, not to speak of the statement in the Fourth Gospel that His side was pierced by the unerring spear of a Roman soldier. Another con-sideration fatal to the theory has been strongly put both by Strauss and by Keim. It is that a Jesus who had never been dead coming from His tomb wearing an exhausted, ghastly look could never have revived the hearts of the disciples, or led them to believe in a Christ who had been dead, and was alive again. Strauss states the objection thus—

" It is impossible that a being who had stolen half-dead out of the sepulchre, who crept about weak and ill, wanting medical treatment, who required bandaging, strengthening, and indulgence, and who still at last yielded to His suffer ings, could have given to the disciples the impression that He was a conqueror over death and the grave, the Prince of

Life, an impression which lay at the bottom of their future ministry. Such a resuscitation could only have weakened the impression which He had made upon them in life and in death; at the most, could only have given it an elegiac voice, but could by no possibility have changed their sorrow into enthusiasm, or have elevated their reverence into worship."[1]

The swoon hypothesis finds little support among recent writers. The larger number of votes is given to the *vision* theory. Among the ablest supporters of this theory are Renan and Strauss. It may be the easiest way of making ourselves acquainted with its bearings to hear what they have to say in its favour.

First, let us hear Renan—

"Enthusiasm and love know no situations without escape. They make sport of the impossible, and rather than renounce hope they do violence to reality. Many words spoken by the Master could be interpreted in the sense that He would come forth from the tomb. Such a belief was, moreover, so natural that the faith of the disciples would have sufficed to create it. The great prophets Enoch and Elias did not taste of death. That which happened to them must happen to Jesus. . . . Death is a thing so absurd when it strikes the man of genius or of a great heart, that people cannot believe in the possibility of such an error of nature. Heroes do not die. . . . That adored Master had filled the circle of which He was the centre with joy and hope—could they be content to let him rot in the tomb?"[2]

Resolved that Jesus should not remain among the dead, the believing company were in a fit state of mind for seeing the dead one alive again. The empty tomb—how emptied no one can tell—helped to make them more liable to hallucination. Mary Magdalene was the first to have a vision. She stood by the sepulchre weeping; she heard a light noise behind her. She turned; she saw a man standing; asked him where the body was; received for reply her own name, "Mary." It was the voice that

[1] *New Life*, i. 412.   [2] *Vide Les Apôtres*, pp. 2, 3.

so often made her tremble. It was the accent of Jesus. The miracle of love is accomplished. Mary has seen and heard Him. After one has seen Him, there will be no difficulty in others seeing Him; having visions will become infectious till it pass through the whole company of disciples.

Such is the Renan style of treatment—sentimental, theatrical, Parisian. The appearances of Jesus are the creation of excited nerves and ardent expectations. The slightest outward occasion acting on so susceptible subjects will produce an apparition. During a moment of silence some light air passes over the face of the assembled dis ciples. At such decisive hours, a current of air, a creaking window, a chance murmur decides the belief of centuries. Nothing easier than to see the risen One; nothing easier than to comprehend the hallucinations of those devoted ones.[1]

Strauss goes to work in a different way. He bases his argument on the fact that Paul classes the appearance of Jesus to himself with the earlier appearances to the dis ciples, and reasons thus: The visions recorded in the Gospels were the same in nature as that with which Paul was favoured. But Paul's vision was beyond question subjective, and Paul was a man predisposed to have such visions. He himself tells us that ecstatic conditions were of frequent occurrence with him.[2] His statement suggests attacks of convulsion, perhaps of epilepsy, as the physical cause of such experience, a suggestion confirmed by what he says elsewhere concerning the weakness of his body. A man with such a constitution was likely to have visions, in which were projected into space the thoughts and feel ings of his mind at a crisis of great excitement, like that of his conversion, when he was struggling against rising

---

[1] *Vide Les Apôtres*, p. 5 ff. Principal Fairbairn (*Studies in the Life of Christ*, p. 341) distinguishes Renan's theory as the *Phantasmal*. It is certainly phantastic enough.

[2] 2 Cor. xii. 1 ff.

convictions. And we can understand, in the light of his experience, how the disciples might have visions of Jesus after His death. That event was a great shock to their faith in Jesus as Messiah, and they must have felt a very strong impulse to overcome the contradiction somehow. Searching the Scriptures, they found passages which seemed to teach that it was appointed to Messiah to die, yet that death should not have power over Him. Hence they came at last, in the light of events, so to interpret the prophecies that they could include both death and resurrection in Messiah's experience. Jesus had died; it was now to be expected that He should rise again, according to the Scriptures. They did expect and long for so welcome an event, and out of their expectation came the visions which led them to believe that their Master was risen. "The heart thinks; the hour brings." Not all at once, not so soon as the Gospels represent, did the visions come; for time was needed to bring about a revulsion from the depression caused by the Crucifixion to the excitement out of which the visions sprang. The disciples retired to Galilee, and there, brooding on the Scriptures and visiting familiar haunts, they gradually got into the state of mind required for seeing visions.[1]

The vision hypothesis has been sharply criticised, and many weak points have been detected in it. Among these may be noted, in the first place, that, according to Strauss, the more rational advocate of the theory, time was needed to develop the state of mind demanded, whereas, according to the records, the Christophanies began within three days of the Crucifixion, and were all comprised within a space of little more than a month. It is a disadvantage to the theory that it should be obliged to depart so seriously from the evangelic tradition.

Assuming that the Christophanies began as early as represented in the Gospels, a second objection to the vision theory arises out of the fact that at the time the resur-

[1] *New Life of Jesus,* i. 430.

rection is reported to have taken taken place, and Jesus to
have showed Himself alive after His Passion, the disciples
were in so depressed a state of mind that subjective visions
were the last thing in the world likely to befall them.   All
the Gospels testify to the depressed, unexpectant mood of
the disciples at this period.   Matthew states that on the
occasion of Christ's meeting with His followers in Galilee
"some doubted."[1]   Mark relates that when the disciples
heard from Mary of Magdala that Jesus was alive, and
had been seen of her, "they believed not."[2]   Luke tells
that the reports of the women seemed to the disciples as
"idle tales."[3]   In place of general statements, John gives
an example of the incredulity of the disciples in the case
of Thomas.[4]   The women, too, appear not less unexpectant
than the eleven.   They set out towards the sepulchre on
the morning of the first day of the week with the intention
of embalming the dead body of Jesus.   Unexpectant of the
resurrection, the company of believers appear also in the
records equally sceptical as to the reality of the appearances
of the risen Lord.   The disciples doubt now the sub
stantiality, now the identity, of the person who appears to
them.   Their theory was that what they saw was a ghost
or mere phantom, just the theory of Renan and Strauss;
and the fact that they entertained that theory makes it
very difficult for us to receive it, and to believe with
Strauss that the faith in Jesus as the Christ, after receiving
through His death an apparently fatal shock, was sub
jectively restored by the instrumentality of the mind, the
power of imagination, and nervous excitement.

Besides the foregoing objections to the vision theory, others
have been urged with great force by Keim.   He rejects the
theory chiefly on these three grounds: (1) The simple,
earnest, almost cold unfamiliar character of the manifesta-

---

[1] Matt. xxviii. 17.

[2] Mark xvi. 11. This, however, belongs to the Appendix, which forms
no part of the original Gospel.

[3] Luke xxiv. 11.   [4] John xx. 24-29.

tions; (2) the speedy cessation of the appearances; (3) the entire change in the mood of the disciples within a short time, from the excited state which predisposes to visions to clear knowledge of Christ's Messianic dignity and energetic resolves to bear witness to the world for their risen and exalted Lord. In regard to the first Keim contends that the manifestations would not have possessed such a character had they been purely subjective in their origin. In illustration of the second, he observes that the mental excitement which makes optical hallucinations possible demands a certain breadth and width of time, as is seen in the case of Montanism which filled half a century with its multiform follies. With reference to the third, he points out that the sudden change of mood in the disciples is contrary to the usual course of such morbid conditions. The excitement which created the visions ought to have lasted a considerable time, to have cooled down gradually, and to have terminated not in illumination and energy, but in dulness, languor, and apathy.

These are forcible objections based on difficulties which the vision hypothesis cannot surmount. What then? Does Keim accept the faith of the Catholic Church that Christ rose from the dead with the body in which He died revivified and transfigured, and in that body showed Himself to His followers? He does not; and yet he admits that the Christophanies were not hallucinations, but had their origin in an objective cause. His idea is that Jesus, continuing still to live in His Spirit, produced the manifestations which the disciples took for *bonâ fide* bodily appearances of their risen Master, to give them assurance that He still lived, and that death had not extinguished His being. In His own words—

"Without the living Jesus the Messianic faith had been destroyed by the Crucifixion, and in the return of the apostles to the synagogue and to Judaism even the gold of Christ's teaching had been buried in the dust of oblivion. The greatest of men had passed away leaving no trace of Himself.

Galilee might for some time have related of Him truth and fiction, but His cause had produced no religious revolution, and no Paul. It lands in impossibilities to make the ordained of God so end, or to hand over His resurrection from the dead and for the dead to the uncertain play of visions. A sign of life from Jesus, a telegram from heaven was necessary, after the crushing overthrow of the Crucifixion, especially in the childhood of humanity. Even the Christianity of the present day owes to this telegram from heaven, first the Lord, and then itself. . . . The hope of immortality, otherwise a mere perhaps, has become through Christ's word, and visibly through His deed, a bright light and clear truth." [1]

This new *telegram* hypothesis, as it may be called, goes, it will be observed, beyond the limits of naturalism. This its author frankly admits. Science, he tells us, is nonplussed by the hard problem. History can take cognisance only of the faith of the disciples that the Master was risen, and of the marvellous effect of this faith—the founding of Christianity. But while science and history must stop there, faith can go further; that faith which ascends from the world to God, from the natural to the super natural, and can overstep the limits of sensible perception, and of the natural order to which science is bound down. In the exercise of this power it assures us not only that Jesus at death took His course to the world of spirits, but that it was He and no other who from that world gave to His disciples visions, and revealed Himself to His former companions. On this view the question of the resurrection as between Keim and the Catholic Church would seem to be a question of fact rather than one involving the theory of the universe. It is simply a question whether what was seen was the body that was laid in the tomb, or a vision bearing the likeness of that body, produced for the benefit of his disciples by the still living Spirit of Jesus.

While not a whit more acceptable to thoroughgoing naturalism than the Catholic view, Keim's theory has the disadvantage of being obliged to tamper with the gospel

[1] *Jesu von Nazara,* iii. 605.

narratives. He calls in question, for example, the statement that the grave was found empty. Why adopt a view which renders that necessary without any compensating advantage? Why not accept the view that the body seen was the body that had lain in the tomb? Is it because one cannot con ceive of a dead body coming to life again? Can one any better conceive of the appearance of a body produced in space by the power of Christ's will exerted from heaven? Surely the heavenly telegram which comes out at the earthly end as the image of a body is as much a wonder as the rising of a dead body from the grave!

One other observation may be made on this theory. It is open to the charge which is justly brought against the vision theory, that it makes the faith of the disciples rest on a hallucination. Christ sends a series of telegrams from heaven to let His disciples know that all is well. But what does the telegram say in every case? Not merely, My Spirit lives with God and cares for you; but, my body is risen from the grave. That was the meaning they put on the telegrams, and could not help putting. If that meaning was untrue to fact, how easy to have given another sort of sign! Why not emit a *voice* from heaven, saying: Be of good cheer, it is well with me, and I shall see to it that it shall be well with you till we meet ere long again. If the resurrection be an unreality, if the body that was nailed to the tree never came forth from the tomb, why send messages that were certain to produce an opposite impression? Why induce the apostles, and through them the whole Christian Church, to believe a lie? Truly this is a poor foundation to build Christendom upon, a bastard supernaturalism as objectionable to unbelievers as the true supernaturalism of the Catholic creed, and having the additional drawback that it offers to faith asking for bread a stone.

The foregoing hypotheses all go on the assumption that there was a real experience of the disciples demanding explanation. They saw the real body of Jesus who had not been actually dead, or they thought they saw the risen body of the dead Jesus and were mistaken, or they saw the real image of the body and were not mistaken. According to the most recent hypothesis there was no experience to explain. The Christophanies had no existence for the first disciples, but found a place only in the later traditions reported in the Gospels, so that what needs to be explained is simply the rise of the legend of the resurrection. Such is the view which, following hints from Weizsacker,[1] Dr. Martineau has espoused and advocated with his accustomed brilliancy. The fact basis of the legend in the experience of the disciples was, he thinks, simply this, that they believed that Jesus, the crucified, "*still lives*, and only waits the Father's time to fulfil the promises;" lives, not like ordinary mortals, in "the storehouse of souls in the underworld," but with exceptional spirits, like Enoch, Moses, and Elijah, in the home of angels. This faith came to them as their consolation after they had recovered from the awful shock of Calvary, just as there comes to all, after the first burst of passionate grief over bereavement, the consolatory thought that the dead one still lives in a better world. It came to them all the sooner, because of the commanding personality of Jesus. They could not believe that death could be the extinction of such an one as He. He must live still, like the great ones of the Old Testament (Renan's motto—"Heroes die not"—would seem after all to be the key to the situation). This faith that Jesus continued to live was the faith in the resurrection for the first disciples. They said, indeed, that they had *seen* Jesus. They could not avoid saying this in their preaching, for not otherwise could they convey to others the strong conviction

---

[1] *Vide* Weizsacker, *Das Apostolische Zeitalter*, p. 5. In his earlier work, *Untersuchungen über die Evangelische Geschichte*, Weizsacker expressed a view more akin to that of Keim. He remarks that what the disciples experienced proceeded from a continuous influence upon them by Jesus after His death. The Christophanies were not the product of the faith or phantasy of the disciples, but were given to them by a higher power. *Vide Untersuchungen*, pp. 572, 573.

of Christ's celestial life which in their own case was the fruit of personal intercourse with Him. But they meant no more than Paul meant when twenty-five years later he claimed to have seen the Lord at the time of his conver sion. Paul's vision, so far as we can gather from himself —the accounts in the Acts, we are warned, are not to be trusted—was purely spiritual. And we are reminded that Paul puts his vision on a level with those of the first disciples. If, therefore, his vision was spiritual, so was theirs. But how, then, we naturally inquire, did the legend of Christophanies of a more substantial character arise ? The answer is, through the craving of the Jew and Pagan for something better than subjective visions in proof that Christ still lived. Under the influence of this craving, hearers of apostolic testimony would be prone to convert spiritual visions into optical ones, and the apostles them selves would be tempted not to be very careful to correct misapprehension.[1]

The new theory, of which the above is a brief outline, raises two questions. Does it give a true account of the experience of the first disciples ; and does it give a probable explanation of the rise of the more materialistic legend of the resurrection ?

On the former score the theory is very open to attack. It imputes to the disciples a Pagan or Greek conception of the life beyond as purely spiritual. But the faith of the Jew was not in the immortality of the soul but in a re-incorporated life of the man, which, though lacking the grossness of the mortal body, was still perceptible by the senses. Then the statement concerning the nature of Paul's experience is far from indisputable. Great importance is justly attached to that experience. We are here in contact, not with hearsay or second - hand reports, but with the first-hand evidence of a witness of unimpeachable integrity and intelligence, telling us what happened to himself. Twice over in his First Epistle to the Corinthians he claims

[1] *The Seat of Authority in Religion,* pp. 363-377.

to have seen the Lord.[1] Did he mean thereby merely that he had realised vividly Christ's continued existence, or got a clear insight into the religious significance of his earthly history? That probably he did mean, but also more. We must remember Paul's position at this period. He was confronted with men who called in question his apostolic standing as a means of undermining his influence as a teacher. What right had he to have a peculiar way of interpreting the gospel; he who had no apostolic authority like the eleven with whom he was at variance? Conscious that he has this hostile attitude to reckon with, Paul says, among other things in self-defence, "I have seen the Lord." It was certainly his interest to mean more thereby than a mere subjective vision. For his antagonists might very readily suggest, What is a mere mental vision, a reflection of one's own moods and ideas, to a *bonâ fide* companionship such as the eleven enjoyed? It was to protect himself against such a suggestion that the apostle associated his own vision of the risen Christ with that of the first believers. Modern critics take advantage of the association to drag the visions of the disciples down to the supposed subjective level of the vision of Paul. But Paul's interest and intention in classing the two together was to level his own vision up to the objectivity of the earlier Christophanies. He believed that the eleven, that Peter, in particular, had seen the risen Saviour with the eye of the body, and he meant to claim for himself a vision of the same kind.[2]

The explanation given by the new theory of the rise of the legend of a physical resurrection is equally unsatis-

---

[1] 1 Cor. ix. 1: "Have I not seen Jesus Christ our Lord?" xv. 8: "Last of all he was seen of me also."

[2] That Paul believed in a corporeal resurrection is evident from the expression, "He rose again *the third day*" (1 Cor. xv. 4). Menegoz remarks: "The mention of the third day would have no sense if Paul had not accepted the belief of the community of Jerusalem that on the third day Jesus went forth alive from the tomb."—*Le Péché et la Redemption d'apres Saint Paul*, p. 261.

factory. It amounts to this, that the faith in the continued ·
spiritual existence of Jesus produced the later tradition of ₁
optical visions, not such visions the faith. It is a view
analogous to that of Strauss concerning the rise of miracle ·
myths, viz. that the faith that Jesus was the Messiah
produced these miracle legends. In both cases alike the '
true order of causality is inverted. Unless there had been ₁
wonderful works done by Jesus they would never have ᶦ
believed Him to be Messiah. The postulate of Strauss'
own theory is that it belongs to Messiah to do such works. ∕
That postulate did not take its place in men's minds for ᵢ
the first time after they had accepted Jesus as the Christ. ᶦ
In like manner it may be affirmed that without such ∧
visions as the Gospels report, the first disciples were not at '
all likely to have attained to firm faith that their deceased ∕
Master lived still. The element of truth in the older ∕
theories of Strauss and Keim is just this, that they both ∤
recognise that visions of some sort, subjective or objective, ∖
were necessary to produce in the minds of the disciples ·
the belief that their Master was risen.

Then observe what is implied in the assertion that the
later tradition of optical visions arose from the strong
manner in which the apostles expressed their faith that
their Master lived in heaven. They said they had seen
Jesus after His death, and their hearers understood them to
mean they had seen Him in the body. They had to say they
had seen, otherwise their hearers would not have believed
that Jesus lived on. Is this not very like the reinstatement
of pious fraud as a factor in the case, by reversion in part,
or in a refined form, to the long-abandoned theory of
Reimarus? The apostles could hardly be ignorant how
their statements were likely to be understood, and were in
fact understood.

The result of the foregoing inquiry is that all naturalistic ╻
attempts to explain away the resurrection, up to this date,
have turned out failures. The physical resurrection remains.
It remains, it need not be added, a great mystery. Much

that relates to this august event is enveloped in mystery. Not to speak of the discrepancy in the narratives, or the angelic agency, there is the fact that the resurrection body of Jesus appears even in the evangelic accounts a pneumatic body, and the further fact that according to the teaching of Paul, as well as the suggestions of reason, flesh and blood, a gross corruptible body, can have no place in the kingdom of God, or in the eternal world. In the resurrection of Jesus, two processes seem to have been combined into one: the revivification of the crucified body, and its transformation into a spiritual body endowed with an eternal form of existence; the first process being merely a means to an end, the actual, if not the indispensable, condition of the second.

CHAPTER V.

JESUS LORD.

LITERATURE. — Schleiermacher, *Der Christliche Glaube;* Ullmann, *Die Sundlosigkeit Jesu;* Wace, *Christianity and Morality* (Boyle Lectures, 1874–75); Abbott, *Onesimus;* Pfleiderer, *Paulinismus;* Menegoz, *Le Peche et la Redemption d'apres Saint Paul;* Herrmann, *Der Verkehr des Christen mit Gott;* Curteis, *The Scientific Obstacles to Christian Belief* (Boyle Lectures, 1884); Bruce, *The Miraculous Element in the Gospels* (Lectures IX. and X.); Bornemann, *Unterricht im Christentum. Lux Mundi* (Essay V.), Le Conte, *Evolution and its Relation to Religious Thought,* 2nd ed. (especially chap. viii.).

Jesus has for the Christian consciousness the religious value of God. He is the *Lord* Jesus, and as such the object of devoted attachment and reverent worship. What the metaphysical presuppositions of His divinity may be, and what the most fitting theological formulation of it, are questions on which different opinions have been and may continue to be entertained. It is even conceiv-

able that the Church of the future may decline to discuss
these questions, or to give them definite dogmatic answers,
and may regard with the reverse of satisfaction the answers
given in past ages. There is reason to believe that even
now there exists in many Christian minds a feeling of
coldness, not to say aversion, to the definition of Christ's
person handed down to us from ancient councils, as con
sisting of two distinct natures combined in the unity of a
single personality. This is not to be mistaken for a denial
of Christ's divinity. It may be a morbid mood, a phase of
that general aversion to precise theological determinations
which is an outstanding characteristic of the present time ;
but it is compatible with an attitude of heart towards Jesus
in full sympathy with the faith of the Catholic Church
concerning Him, even in the most orthodox generations.[1]

That Jesus had the religious value of God for, and was
worshipped by, the whole Apostolic Church is certain.
They called Him Lord, $K\nu\rho\iota o\varsigma$, the equivalent for Jehovah
in the Septuagint version of the Old Testament. With
out making too much of the fact, it may be held to
imply this, at least, that what Jehovah was to Israel,
that Jesus was to the religious consciousness of Christians, the object of that specific worship by which they
were distinguished from the rest of the world. There
is no difficulty in ascertaining the genesis of this faith of
the first disciples in Jesus as divine. It was not the
result of speculative thought, it need not even be regarded
as a direct revelation unmediated by any spiritual experi
ence. It sprang out of the impression made on their
minds by the facts of Christ's earthly history. Three

---

[1] Of this attitude the Ritschl school may be taken as representatives in
Germany, and the late Dr. Hatch (*vide* his *Hibbert Lectures*) in England.
On this anti-dogmatic tendency the late Professor Green remarks : " Proteus
will not be so bound. The individual, consciously or unconsciously, will
formulate the Christian experience, and left to himself will formulate it
inadequately. Released from the dogma of the Church, he will make a
dogma of his own, which will react upon and limit the experience."— *Works*,
vol. iii., Essay on " Christian Dogma," p. 182.

main sources of the faith can be specified: the holiness_of Jesus, His death, and His resurrection.

At the Capernaum crisis, when a disenchanted crowd deserted Jesus in disgust, Peter, according to the account in the Fourth Gospel, made in the name of the twelve the confession: "We believe and know that Thou art the Holy One of God."[1] This may be taken to be a faithful reflection of the feeling which arose in the minds of the disciples from the time they began to be closely associated with Jesus, and steadily grew in strength and vividness as their opportunities of observation increased. More and more it was borne in upon them that the Master they followed was exceptional, unique, in spirit and character. They were conscious that in wisdom and goodness He far surpassed themselves; and as they looked around they noticed a similar contrast between Him and all other men. Even the hostile attitude towards Him of the paragons of the righteousness in vogue tended to deepen their sense of His moral worth. It made them note more carefully the characteristics of His goodness, and become more fully aware how rare was the type of goodness He represented. It forced on their attention a remarkable moral pheno menon which, but for the glaring contrast and sharp conflict between their Master and the Pharisees, might have been treated as a thing of course. The contrast and conflict, doubtless, involved a keen trial of their faith and fidelity. In Christ's company they had to learn to bear isolation, and to become weaned from the common habit of taking current opinion, or the majority, as the guide in moral judgment. They were strongly tempted to think that the thousands on one side must be right, and the One on the other side must be wrong. They could not both be right, for the contrast was too glaring; but how hard to believe that so many men reputedly righteous and saintly were missing the mark, and that the "righteousness of the scribes and Pharisees" was of no value! Nothing will

---

[1] John vi. 69. ο αγιος του θιου is the readin in the best MSS.

help in such a case but personal spiritual discernment, and courage to follow our own moral instincts. These qualities the disciples possessed in sufficient strength to enable them to hold on to Jesus when the multitude deserted Him, and the wise and holy blasphemed Him. And their reward was a great discovery ; that in this forsaken and misjudged Man a new revelation of God was given. Whence this unexampled character, this wholly original way of thinking, feeling, and acting ? Obviously not from the spirit of the time whereof the Pharisees are the exponents, but from the Spirit of God. The unholy one, as men esteem Him, is just on that account the Holy One of God, and through Him we may know, as has never been known before, what Divine Holiness is.

The death of Jesus was a mighty factor in the exaltation of Him to the place of Lord in the hearts of believers. In the Crucifixion the two opposed judgments concerning Jesus found their culminating expression. For the false dying world of Judaism He became thereby the supremely unholy, profane, accursed ; for the new Christian world the supremely Just and Blessed. To the one Jesus was the abhorred criminal, to the other the revered martyr. But this is by no means the whole truth. For the company of disciples the Crucified was much more than the true faithful witness, worthy of profoundest veneration because He shrank not from the sacrifice of His life for the truth. He was the Saviour who died for the sin of the world; of His enemies, of those who believed in Him. How they came to regard the death of Jesus in this light need not here be discussed. It is enough to say that, beyond doubt, the members of the Apostolic Church with one consent did so regard it. The point now to be noted is, how powerfully and irresistibly the thought of Jesus dying as a Saviour led on to the worship of Him as Lord. With rapturous enthusiasm believers in the crucified Redeemer crowned Him their Divine King. " Unto Him that loved us, and washed us from our sins in His own blood, be glory and dominion for ever and ever."[1]

The doxology of the Apocalypse strikes the keynote of a strain which runs through the whole New Testament. Everywhere there is a close connection between Soteriology and Christology: Jesus Lord because Saviour. This is specially notable in the leading epistles of Paul, which, because of their all but unquestioned authenticity, and the exceptional significance of the religious personality of their author, are invaluable sources of information as to the genesis of the idea cherished by the Apostolic Church concerning the person of Jesus. The title Lord applied to Jesus, as Paul uses it, means "the One who by His death has earned the place of sovereign in my heart, and whom I feel constrained to worship and serve with all my powers." So, for example, in the text: "God forbid that I should glory, save in the cross of our Lord Jesus Christ, by whom the world is crucified to me, and I to the world;"[2] and in that other: "Being justified by faith, we have peace with God through our Lord Jesus Christ: by whom also we have access by faith into this grace wherein we stand."[3] In both the title "Lord" is used with conscious intention to acknowledge a debt of gratitude. Paul recognises Christ's worthiness to be called Lord because He died for man's salvation, and as the Lord to be preferred to the whole world, and all its possessions and enjoyments. In certain New Testament texts, God is represented as making the Crucified One "Lord," in compensation for indignities meekly endured, and as the reward of voluntary self-humiliation. In the above-cited utterances of Paul, we see Christian faith and love co-operating with God in the exaltation of the Redeemer.

The resurrection also, as was to be expected, greatly helped early disciples to rise to a lofty conception of Christ's person. A most interesting and instructive example of the manner in which it influenced Christian

---

[1] Rev. i. 5, 6.　　　[2] Gal. vi. 14.　　　[3] Rom. v. 1.

thought concerning the Founder of the faith is supplied in
the statement with which Paul commences his Epistle to
the Romans. He desires apparently, at the very outset, to
explain to the Roman Church his Christological position,
as it is obviously one of his principal aims in that writing
to indicate to that important Church how he conceives the
Christian faith in general. A statement made with such
an aim would be well weighed in every phrase and word,
and cannot be treated as an *obiter dictum*. Note, then,
what Paul says : The gospel he is commissioned to preach
is "concerning One who is God's Son, made of the seed of
David according to the flesh, and who was constituted
God's Son in power, according to the spirit of holiness from
the resurrection of the dead." The person so described is
then identified with Jesus Christ, who is finally denomi
nated "our Lord," the title given to Him in common by
all Christians.[1] Two points are specially noteworthy in
this passage,—the reference to the spirit of holiness, and
the function assigned to the resurrection of Jesus as an
event through which He was constituted the Son of God
"in power." Therefrom we learn that the holiness of
Jesus, and His rising from the dead, not less than His
redeeming death, played an important part in the develop
ment of the apostle's conception of Christ's person. The
three together were the elements out of which grew his
Christological idea. The holy life of Jesus evidently had no
small share in leading Paul to see in Him the Son of God
in a unique sense. The phrase "according to the spirit of
holiness" stands in manifest contrast with the phrase
"according to the flesh." It signifies that Christ, though
partaker of human flesh, was free from the moral taint
ordinarily associated with the $\sigma \acute{a} \rho \xi$. On the ground of
that moral purity, Paul ascribed to Jesus a Divine Sonship
involving at least ethical identity with God. But he
appears to attach still more importance to the resurrection
as a basis for the doctrine of Christ's Sonship. Son of

[1] Rom. i. 3, 4.

God, all through His earthly life, in virtue of His holiness,
Jesus, according to the apostle, was *constituted* God's Son in
an emphatic degree by the resurrection. "Constituted,"
for the rendering "declared" in the Authorised Version, and
retained in the Revised, does not do justice to the word
used by Paul. It points to something more than manifesta
tion, to a change in Christ's condition. Probably what the
apostle has in mind is the transformation of Christ's outer
physical nature, the replacement of the body of humiliation
by a spiritual glorious body, having as its result that the
risen One was henceforth altogether a spiritual being, the
pneumatic heavenly man, His very body radiant with
heaven's light as His Spirit was spotlessly pure. The idea
is that, previous to the resurrection, Jesus was the Son of
God on the inner side of His being (that is assumed, not
negatived, by ὁρισθέντος), but after the resurrection became
Son of God both on the inner and on the outer side, the
verb having its full force in the sense of "to constitute" in
reference to the latter. The expression "in power" (ἐν
δυνάμει), in harmony with this view, must be taken as
meaning—fully, out and out, altogether, without qualifica
tion, implying that the resurrection was the actual intro
duction of Christ into the full possession of Divine Sonship
so far as thereto belonged, not only the inner of a holy
spiritual essence, but also the outer of an existence in
power and heavenly glory.[1]

Such were the feelings and trains of thought through
which Paul and other believers in the apostolic age were
led on to faith in the divine significance of Jesus. They
point out the road along which all must travel to the same
goal, if their faith is to have any true value and virtue.
A ready-made dogma concerning the divinity of Christ
accepted as an ecclesiastical tradition can be of little service
to us. It may very easily be of serious disservice, acting
as a veil to hide the true Jesus from the eye of the soul.
The only faith concerning Jesus as the Divine Lord worth

---

[1] So Pfleiderer, *Paulinismus*, p. 129.

possessing is that which springs out of spiritual insight into its historical basis, and is charged with ethical significance.[1] Such a faith calls Jesus Lord by the Holy Ghost, and is legitimate, wholesome, and fruitful in beneficent effects. What more legitimate and wholesome than to think of Jesus, the uniquely good, as the very Son of God, absolutely one with God in mind, will, and spirit? Then we are assured that Jesus is a veritable revelation of the Father. The Son hath declared Him. And the revelation is welcome. If God be like Jesus, the world has cause to be glad. The worship of Jesus as God is the worship of a goodness which inspires trust and hope in every human breast. What more legitimate and wholesome, again, than the worship of the Crucified? It means that self-sacrificing love is placed on the throne of the universe, that God does not keep aloof from the world in frigid majesty, but enters into it freely as a burden-bearer, stooping to conquer His own rebellious children. On the metaphysical side the doctrine may be encompassed with difficulty, but ethically it is worthy of all acceptation.

The foregoing account of the genesis of apostolic faith in the divinity of Jesus may create the impression that the title Lord given to Him was merely the exaggerated expression of admiration for His character and of gratitude for His redeeming love. It would be a mistake, however, to suppose that the person of Jesus was not a subject of theological reflection for the first generation of believers. There are distinct traces of this in the epistles of Paul; for example, in the statement in the Epistle to the Romans, "For this Christ died and rose that He might exercise lordship over both dead and living,"[2] in which the divine right of Jesus to rule over the affections and destinies of all men living or dead is proclaimed in a theoretical connection of

---

[1] Herrmann (*Der Verkehr des Christen mit Gott*, p. 113, 2te Aufl.) remarks: "The right confession of the Godhead of Jesus depends on experience of the work which God performs through Jesus on the human soul."

[2] Rom. xiv. 9.

thought. A still more decided example may be found in the eighth chapter of 1st Corinthians, where the apostle speaks of Christ's place in the universe in a connection of thought which gives to his statement great doctrinal value.[1] With reference to the practice of eating meat offered in sacrifice to idols, he has strongly asserted the truth of the Jewish monotheistic creed: "There is no God, except one." One wonders what after this he will say concerning Jesus. He gratifies our curiosity by going on immediately after to make this statement: "For while it may be the case that there are gods so called, whether in heaven or in earth, as there be gods many and lords many, yet for us (Christians) there is one God the Father from whom are all things and we for Him, and one Lord Jesus Christ through, or on account of,[2] whom are all things, and we (in particular, as a spiritual creation) through Him." Here we, as it were, surprise Paul in the act of solving a delicate problem. As becomes a Jew he treats as nullities the gods and lords of the Gentiles, regarding them as gods only in name ($\theta \epsilon o \grave{\iota}$ $\lambda \epsilon \gamma \acute{o} \mu \epsilon \nu o \iota$), and over against these nullities he sets one real $\Theta \epsilon \acute{o} \varsigma$ and one real $K \acute{u} \rho \iota o \varsigma$. His faith in the one he has inherited from his Jewish fathers, his faith in the other has sprung out of his belief in Jesus as his Redeemer. How are the two faiths to be combined, how are their objects to be conceived as related to each other? The question involves, apparently, a dilemma for one by birth a Jew, and by conversion a Christian. Either he must hold fast by the abstract monotheism of Judaism and, in deference thereto, negative the worship of Christ under the title of $K \acute{u} \rho \iota o \varsigma$ as an idolatry, or he must give full effect to his Christian consciousness and worship Jesus as a Divine Lord, and modify his conception of deity so far as to make the divine unity compatible with plurality. The title "Father" appended to the Divine name in the text above quoted indicates that the apostle's mind gravitated in the direction of the latter alternative, and adopted as the solution of the

---

[1] 1 Cor. viii. 4-6.   [2] The reading varies. Codex B. has $\delta \iota' o \nu$.

theological problem: Jesus Christ my Lord, the Son of
the one true God the Father.

The *resurrection* could not but stimulate an active mind,
such as that of Paul, to theological reflection. To its
influence, probably, may be traced the theorem of the pre-
existence of Christ enunciated more or less clearly in some
Pauline texts—*e.g.* in Gal. iv. 4, " God *sent forth* His Son ; "
and in 2 Cor. viii. 9, " Ye know the grace of our Lord Jesus,
that being rich He became poor." [1] The pre-existence may
be viewed as the pendant and complement of the resurrec
tion. Through the resurrection and exaltation Jesus in a
sense, according to Paul, *became* divine. He was thereby,
as we learned from a notable Pauline text, constituted the
Son of God in power. But divinity in the proper sense, as
distinct from *apotheosis,* cannot begin to be. The divine
is eternal. Therefore He who was man, and thereafter was
exalted to God's right hand, must have been with God
before He came into the world. So the apostle seems to
have reasoned, if we may view the pre-existence theorem
as the product of reasoning rather than as a direct re
velation.[2]

It does not appear that the *sinlessness* of Jesus raised in
Paul's mind any questions as to the manner of His coming
into the world. That he earnestly believed Jesus to be
sinless he has put beyond doubt by describing Him in a

---

[1] Some render ἰπτώχευσιν "was poor," supposing the reference to be to
Christ's habitual condition on earth. While the verb by itself might bear
this sense, the aorist excludes it, as implying an act completed at a given
point of time.

[2] Bornemann says : "The thought of the pre-existence was not communi
cated supernaturally to the apostles, or originated by Paul, or unfamiliar in
that age. It was simply the natural application to Jesus of an attribute
already ascribed to Messiah in Jewish theology. Strange, new, and peculiar
as the idea seems to us, it was current then to express the higher, God-
derived, universal significance and superhuman perennial worth of certain
persons and things. It was applied, *e.g.*, to Moses, Enoch, Adam, the taber
nacle, the temple, the tables of the law." He remarks that the category
strictly applied involves some peril to the real humanity of Jesus. *Vide
Unterricht im Christentum,* p. 93.

well-known text as "Him who knew no sin."[1]   But no
where in his epistles can we find any clear reference to an
immaculate ⹁conception or ⹁ supernatural birth.   The contrary view, that Jesus came into the world in the ordinary
way, has been supposed to be indicated by the words "made
of the seed of David according to the flesh;"[2] but the
utmost that can be said is that we might naturally put
that construction on them in absence of information to the
contrary.   The expression is quite reconcilable with the
miraculous birth.   To the latter we might even with plausi
bility discover a positive allusion in the peculiar phrase
used by the apostle in his Epistle to the Galatians concern
ing Christ's birth, "made (or born) of a woman";[3] but it
is doubtful if, without the Gospels in our hands, it would
have suggested to our minds birth from a virgin.

It does not follow from the absence of express allusions
to the topic that Paul's mind was not exercised on it, any
more than it follows from the absence of allusion in his
epistles to many of the most memorable facts in Christ's
life that he was in ignorance concerning them.[4]   Still less
should we be justified in drawing the more sweeping infer
ence that, for the whole generation to which Paul belonged,
the problem of the manner of Christ's birth had no exist
ence.   The best evidence that Christians were thinking on
the subject is to be found in the narratives at the beginning
of the first and third Gospels.   The histories of the infancy
in Matthew and Luke do not belong to the original Synopti-

---

[1] 2 Cor. v. 21.

[2] Rom. i. 3.   So Pfleiderer.   [3] Gal. iv. 4.

[4] Menegoz thinks that Paul's mind was not occupied with the question,
and that it could have no doctrinal importance for him.   "The apostle did
not dream of making the holiness of Christ depend on the mode of His birth.
He had too much logic for that.   Whether the human nature of Christ pro
ceeded from a woman alone, or from the union of a man and a woman, it
would make no difference in Paul's ideas as to the heredity of sin.   In the
theology of the apostle the holiness of Christ is related to another origin than
to the mode of terrestrial conception.   He considered the birth of Christ in
every way supernatural.   The Incarnation was for Him a miraculous fact
whatever its mode."—Le Péché et la Redemption, p. 182.

cal tradition. They are a later addition prefixed to the
evangelic story of the public ministry and the final sufferings
of Jesus. They owe their presence in the latest redactions
of the memoirs of the Lord to the desire of disciples to
know all that could be known concerning Him from the
beginning of His earthly life. By the actual story they
tell concerning the birth of Jesus, they give a worthy and
acceptable account of the commencement of a life which
believers regarded as sinless. They embody the faith in
the sinlessness of Jesus in the form of a history of His birth
from a virgin through the power of the Holy Ghost. The
history is not the creation of the faith, a mere legendary
expression of the belief that the Lord of the Church was a
man altogether free from moral taint, but it came late in
the day when believers in a sinless Christ began to wonder
how such an one as He entered into human life. It was
welcome to them as a worthy account of the birth into
this time-world of the Holy One, of the congruous starting-
point of a life that knew no sin.

Some modern theologians, accepting the moral miracle of
sinlessness, reject the physical miracle, which, according to
the Gospels, was its actual, if not necessary, presupposition ; [1]
or at least treat it as a thing of no religious importance
so long as the moral miracle is believed in.[2] The element
of truth in these views is that the supernatural birth is not
an end in itself, but only a means to an end. It is the
symbol, the sinlessness being the substance. A sinless
Christ is the proper object of faith. Under what conditions
such a Christ is possible is a very important question, but
it belongs to theology rather than to religion.[3] Yet it has

[1] So Dr. Edwin Abbott. *Vide Onesimus*, Book III. par. 7.

[2] So Schleiermacher, *Der Christliche Glaube*, Bd. II. pp. 67, 84, 85.
Vide my *Miraculous Element in the Gospels*, pp. 352, 353.

[3] Bornemann remarks : "The discussion of the presuppositions of the person
and work of Christ is more the affair of theology than of the Christian
religion. Jesus did not appear that we men might scientifically solve the
mystery of His being, but that He might offer to us the solution of the
practical riddles of human life."—*Unterricht im Christentum*, p. 96.

to be remembered that faith is ever in a state of unstable equilibrium while the supernatural is dealt with eclectically; admitted in the moral and spiritual sphere, denied in the physical. With belief in the virgin birth is apt to go belief in the virgin life, as not less than the other a part of the veil that must be taken away that the true Jesus may be seen as He was—a morally defective man, better than most, but not perfectly good.[1]

That belief in the virgin life must go there can be little doubt, if we are to carry out to its utmost consequences a purely naturalistic theory of the universe. A sinless man is as much a miracle in the moral world as a virgin birth is a miracle in the physical world. If we are to hold a speculative view of the universe which absolutely excludes miracle, then we must be content with a Christianity which consists in duly appreciating a great but not perfect char acter, or cease to profess Christianity at all. If, on the other hand, to satisfy the demands of our religious nature we insist on retaining the moral miracle, then we must provide ourselves with a theory of the universe wide enough to make room for as much of the miraculous element as may appear to the wisdom of God necessary for realising His great end in creating and sustaining the universe. Such is the Christian theory of the universe, as expounded in an early chapter of this work.[2] It regards the kingdom of God as the supreme aim of God in creation and provi dence. Whether under this view miracle in the physical sphere shall actually come in, and to what extent, remains to be seen, but it certainly may. And though the scientific spirit indisposes all who come under its influence to believe that miracles actually happen, it has no right in the name of science to negative the possibility of their happening. It has been shown by a master both in science and in Christian philosophy how that possibility may be provided

---

[1] So Martineau, *Seat of Authority*, p. 651, in opposition to old orthodox Socinianism.
[2] Book I. chap. ii.

for without in the least disturbing the laws of the actual universe, viz. by finding the sphere within which the miraculous Power immediately works in the ultimate elements which for the actual universe remain unchanged, though not in themselves unchangeable.

Let us hear Lotze on this point [1]—

" The closed and hard circle of mechanical necessity is not immediately accessible to the miracle-working fiat, nor does it need to be, but the inner nature of that which obeys its laws is not determined by it but by the meaning (*Sinn*) of the world. This is the open place on which a power that commands in the name of this Meaning can exert its influ ence, and if under this command the inner condition of the elements, the magnitudes of their relation and their opposi tion to each other, become altered, the necessity of the mechanical course of the world must unfold this new state into a miraculous appearance, not through suspension but throu_h strict maintenance of its _eneral laws."

The bias_of faith in the present time is to make itself entirely independent_of the miraculous. But the thing is_ impossible. In this connection the position taken up by such writers as Schleiermacher and Dr. E. Abbott is peculiarly interesting, as showing what faith demands in the way of the miraculous, even in the case of those whose general attitude towards that element is one of scepticism and aversion. They must, at all hazards, have a sinless Christ, a man in whom God was immanent in a unique superlative degree, and this, as already remarked, is a moral miracle. Of course, one can understand how believing men, in sympathy with the anti-miraculous spirit of science, should endeavour to make this solitary phenomenon in the history of mankind appear as natural as possible. That means attempting to bring faith in an ideally-perfect man into line with the doctrine of evolution. Fruitful suggestions towards a solution of this problem must ever be welcome. One is to regard Christ, like all other great originators, as

[1] *Mikrokosmus*, Bd. II. p, 54, Eng. tr. p. 451.

a "sociological variation," the most remarkable of all, and as such unaccountable.[1] The most recent attempt to state "the relation of evolution to the idea of the Christ" is that of Professor Le Conte, whose line of thought is to this effect: "As organic evolution reached its goal and completion in *man*, so human evolution must reach its goal and comple tion in the *ideal man*, *i.e.* the Christ." To finding in Christ the goal of human evolution, the realisation of the human ideal, it cannot properly be objected that the goal, the ideal should appear at the end of the course of evolution. This holds good of animal evolution, but not of human evolution, and for this reason, that in the latter process a new factor comes into play, viz. "the conscious voluntary co-operation of the human spirit in the work of its own evolution." The method of this new factor consists in the formation, and especially in the voluntary pursuit, of ideals. Therefore the ideal in this case must come either in imagination or in fact, preferably in fact, in the course of the evolutionary process, and not at the end. "At the end the whole human race, drawn upward by this ideal, must reach the fulness of the stature of the Christ."[2]

This is an inviting train of reasoning, but not above criticism. Not to speak of the objections likely to be raised by a naturalistic philosophy to which it is an axiom, that the idea never realises itself in individuals, but only in the totality of individuals,[3] there is the more obvious objec tion anticipated by the author himself that all ideals are relative and temporary, that "ideals are but milestones which we put successively behind us while we press on to another." How then did it come about that the absolute moral ideal appeared in this world so long ago? It was a miracle. To this statement the author above referred to would not probably object. His theory provides for the

---

[1] *Vide* on this my *Miraculous Element in the Gospels*, pp. 348, 349, with the references to literature bearing on the subject.

[2] *Evolution and its Relation to Religious Thought*, 2nd ed. pp. 360–364.

[3] *Vide* Ullmann, *Die Sundlosigkeit Jesu*, p. 159.

miraculous. A goal in evolution, as he views it, is "not only a completion of one stage, but also the beginning of another and higher stage—on a higher plane of life with new and higher capacities and powers unimaginable from any lower plane." Applied to Christ this implies that He Himself was miraculous, and that with Him came into the world "new powers and properties unimaginable from the human point of view, and therefore to us seemingly super natural, *i.e. above our nature.*" [1]

CHAPTER VI.

PAUL.

LITERATURE.—Baur, *Paulus der Apostel Jesu Christi*; Renan, *Les Apotres* and *St. Paul*; Holsten, *Zum Evangelium des Petrus und des Paulus*; Pfleiderer, *Paulinismus*; Reuss, *Theologie Chretienne* (translated); Sabatier, *L. Apotre Paul* (translated); Farrar, *The Life and Work of St. Paul*; Matheson, *The Spiritual Development of St. Paul.*

The importance of the Apostle Paul to Christianity is universally acknowledged. The tendency, indeed, alike in orthodox and in heterodox schools of theology, has been rather to exaggerate than to under-estimate his significance. On the Tubingen theory, *e.g.*, Christianity would have been a failure but for Paul. From the point of view of Dr. Baur, while it was a vital condition of the new religion getting started on its career that faith in the resurrection of Jesus should somehow take possession of the minds of His dis ciples, yet that was not enough. Before Christianity could be said to be fairly on the march, it was necessary that the two opposite principles which met in the person of Jesus in immediate unity should find adequate representatives; that there should be some adopting as their watchword:

[1] *Evolution*, etc., p. 364. For an attempt to bring faith in the Incarnation into line with Evolution, *vide Lux Mundi*, Essay V.

Jesus the Christ promised to the fathers, and others who, while also believing Jesus to be the Christ, should inscribe on their banner the glorious principle—Christianity the universal religion. Given these the new religion was sure of a great future, in accordance with the historical law of development by antagonism. According to Dr. Baur there was no risk of the narrower, national view failing to find advocates numerous if not influential. It might be taken for granted that the average Jew believing Jesus to be the Messiah would be willing to change only as little as possible, would, in fact, remain as he had been, simply adding to his former beliefs and practices the conviction that in Jesus the Messiah had come, and fellowship with those who shared that conviction with himself. The difficulty and uncertainty would all be in the other direc tion : to find one or more worthy representatives of the universalistic spirit of Jesus. By the nature of the case they must be few; for they must be superior men, rising above the average level in genius, earnestness, force of mind and character, men belonging to the aristocracy of humanity, the number of which is always limited. What if such rare exceptional persons, capable of being vehicles of the universalistic idea, should not turn up ? The risk is as real as it would be fatal ; it will be well if the spirit of universalism shall find so much as one solitary effective representative. In absence of a living Providence, you cannot be quite sure that even one shall be forthcoming, though it is open to the naturalistic theologian to allay his anxiety on that score by the consoling reflection that at every world-crisis the needed hero does make his appear ance, not sent by God indeed, but produced by the uncon scious Forces at work in the great universe. Fortunately in the case of nascent Christianity the needed hero did appear in due time. And, of course, he was an epoch-making person, being nothing less than the man through whom the personal work of Jesus was saved from being an abortive attempt at the establishment of a new religion.

Such in substance is the view taken by the famous
founder of the Tubingen school of criticism as to the value
of Paul as a factor in the origination of historic Christianity.[1]
It errs on the side of exaggeration. Dr. Baur makes too
much of Paul. God could have done even without him,
and Christianity as a world-religion would have got started
on its career even though he had remained to the end of
his days a blasphemer and a persecutor. It is without
doubt a just view that a Christianity not universal in spirit
would have been an unfaithful reflection of the spirit of
Jesus, and that such a Christianity would have had no
chance of attaining to permanence and power. But it is
not the fact that Paul was the sole exponent of universalism. There is every reason to believe that there was a
party in the Palestine Church represented by such men as
Stephen and Barnabas, which, quite independently of Paul's
influence and antecedently to his conversion, understood
and sympathised with the humanistic tendency of Christ's
teaching.[2] And if we inquire into the source of this
Palestinian universalism, we cannot point to any more
likely origin than the preaching of the eleven. Why
should it be assumed that the original apostles were the
narrow Judaistic bigots it suits the exigencies of the
Tubingen theory to make them? It is only by straining
and special pleading that the New Testament literature
can be made to yield evidence in favour of such an
assumption.[3] The presumption is all the other way.
It was not in vain, surely, that Peter and John and
their companions had been with Jesus for years! If
the story of the *Acts* can be trusted at all, they had
imbibed during that time somewhat of the moral courage

Vide Baur's work, *Paulus der Apostel Jesu Christi*, and Bd. I. of his
Geschichte der Christlichen Kirche.

[2] *Vide* Weizsäcker, *Das Apostolische Zeitalter*, p. 437 (references are to
the first edition).

[3] The passage chiefly relied on for this purpose is Gal. ii. 11-21, which
tells of a collision between Paul and Peter at Antioch in reference to the
behaviour of the latter towards Gentile converts.

of their Master.[1] Why should we be incredulous as to their attaining also to some insight into and apprecia tion of His world-wide sympathies? In both respects they might come short of Paul; there is reason to believe they did. From all that we can learn their universalism was of a very mild type, compared with the passionate devotion of the apostle of the Gentiles to a gospel for all mankind on equal terms. But it was sufficient at least to help them to remember sayings of the Master of univer-salistic scope, and make them not disinclined to repeat these when communicating their reminiscences to the infant Church. Towards such sayings most of their audience might be like the wayside hearers of Christ's parable; but there were some, witness Stephen and Barnabas, who sup plied the good ground needful for bringing forth a univer salism of a more pronounced type than that even of the preachers.

The foregoing remarks are not, of course, to be taken as disparagement of Paul, but as a protest against a widespread tendency to make him the real author of Christianity.[2] While resolutely refusing him this honour, however, we must earnestly acknowledge his very great importance as the interpreter and eloquent preacher of what we believe to be the true mind of Jesus concerning the destination of the gospel. One cannot too much admire the providence of God which raised him up to be the apostle of Gentile Christianity, and the grace of God which prepared him for discharging the duties of that high voca tion with the greatest possible efficiency. He was, as we know from his own letters, beforehand a most unlikely instrument. A Pharisee of the Pharisees, a pupil of the Rabbis, an intense fanatical zealot for the Jewish law and traditions—how improbable that such a man would ever become a convert, not to speak of an enthusiastic preacher, of a religion which was in spirit and genius anti-pharisaic, anti-rabbinical, anti-legal! Likelier far that he will become

---

[1] Acts iv. 13. [2] So, for example, Pfleiderer in *Urchristenthum.*

the champion of the old religion of his fathers, the forlorn hope of Judaism, the Maccabæus of a new time waging an uncompromising life-long war against all defections from the national faith and customs. That, indeed, was the career he chose for himself, and had actually entered on. But God's plan for his life was different, and so Saul, the zealot for Jewish law and persecutor of Christians, became a preacher of the faith he once destroyed.

It was a great spiritual transformation, and one naturally asks how it came about. By what means was this Pharisaic zealot and bitter opponent of Christianity changed into a Christian, and *such* a Christian ; not merely believing that Jesus was the Christ, but espousing with all the enthusiasm of a passionate temperament, and all the logical consistency of a powerful intellect, the great idea of a gospel for the world ; treating the law, once everything to him, as nothing, and insisting that in Christ is no distinction of Jew and Gentile, but only a new humanity for which differences of race have no longer any meaning ? This is one of the hard problems for those who undertake to give a purely naturalistic account of the origins of Christianity. The attempts at solution which they have offered are based on the familiar axiom : extremes meet.[1] It is not at all surprising, we are told, that a man who has gone to one extreme should eventually, and it may be suddenly, swing round to the other extreme ; nor need we wonder if in connection with the excitement accompanying a very intense experience, such a man should see visions and hear voices corresponding to the nature of the change in con viction he is undergoing.

All attempts at explaining Paul's conversion without

---

[1] Baur contents himself with asserting in general terms the possibility of the great moral revolution coming about in a natural way. *Vide Der Apostel Paulus*, p. 86. Renan characteristically finds the problem quite simple, and explains the conversion of Paul on the same offhand jaunty method we have seen him apply to the resurrection of Jesus. *Vide Les Apôtres*, p. 182. The most elaborate attempt at a naturalistic explanation of the event is that of Holsten in *Zum Evangelium des Petrus und des Paulus.*

recognising the hand of God in it must be futile. In the last resort we are obliged to fall back on the apostle's own devout language and say, It pleased God to reveal His Son in him.[1] But it is not necessary to magnify the miracle of grace so as to make it appear a magical triumph over a psychological impossibility. In other words, we must not assume that it was in the highest degree improbable that one such as Paul had been before his conversion should become such as we know him to have been after his con version ; that so intense a Pharisee and legalist should ever become so eager an advocate of a religion utterly opposed to Pharisaism and legalism. On the surface the improb ability of such a change appears, as already indicated, very great. But looking below the surface one can see that the catastrophe was not so sudden or unprepared as it seems. The adage, extremes meet, does not explain everything, but it counts for something. The very intensity of Paul's Pharisaism tended to make him a Christian. With a little moral earnestness a man might remain a Pharisee all his days, but with a great consuming earnestness, a passion for righteousness, one is likely to go through to the other side of Pharisaism, into what Carlyle, speaking of Luther, called the more credible hypothesis of salvation by free grace.

That the great change in Paul's religious attitude was not without preparation, and in particular that his experi ences as a Pharisee contributed to bring it about, is not a matter of mere conjecture. His own letters contain some very significant autobiographical hints bearing on the point. Thus he tells us that while he was earnestly endeavouring to fulfil the requirements of the law, his attention was arrested at a certain stage by the tenth commandment of the Decalogue : Thou shalt not covet, and that through this prohibition, directed against inward disposition, as distinct from outward act, he attained to a new sense of moral shortcoming.[2] The fact is in various ways very instructive. It shows for one thing that even then Saul of Tarsus was

1 Gal. i. 15.   2 Rom. vii. 7.

no vulgar Pharisee, but a man of quite exceptional moral sensitiveness. The votaries of a religion of ostentation, who did all their works to be seen of men, did not trouble themselves about sins of thought and feeling, so long as all was seemly and fair without. Christ's indictment of His Pharisaic contemporaries turned largely on this very feature of their character. " Ye make clean," said He, " the out side of the cup." Their righteousness, in His view, was an affair of acting, hypocrisy. That could never have been said of Saul. He began, indeed, at the outside, and was careful to make all right there. But his oversight of evil within was due not to obtuseness of conscience, but chiefly to preoccupation. How tender and true his moral senti- ments were appeared from the serious view he took of the evil of selfish desires when he became aware of their presence in his heart.

As Saul differed from the ordinary Pharisee by his capacity of being distressed on account of sin within, so the actual distress evoked by the precept against coveting had much to do with his final abandonment of Pharisaism. When through that precept he became aware that there was a whole world of sin within of which he had hitherto remained unconscious, the beginning of the end had come. The suspicion could not but arise that righteousness on the method of legalism was impossible. That it did arise we know from another autobiographical hint in Paul's letters : " When the commandment came, sin revived, and I died." [1] " I died," that is, hope died ; hope of salvation on the Pharisaic programme of self-righteousness. This was not Christianity, it was only despair of Pharisaism ; but as such it was a decisive step onwards towards the new standing ground. It was the everlasting no of incipient unbelief in self-righteousness preparing for the everlasting yes of faith in salvation by grace. It is not to be supposed that the everlasting no was pronounced at once, frankly and unreluctantly. Pharisaism dies hard. Religious pride

[1] Rom. vii. 9.

is not easily broken ; only in noble truthful natures can it
be broken at all.   How sorely against the grain of human
nature it goes to renounce the boast of virtue, and to acknow
ledge that all one's painful, protracted, laborious efforts to
build up character, and quite successfully so far as reputa
tion is concerned, have been vain !   The wild colt will for
a time " kick against the pricks " before he is fairly broken
in.   The happy phrase put into Christ's mouth by the
historian of *the Acts*, in the third recital of the story of
Saul's conversion,[1] hits off exactly the situation.   There are
rising convictions destined to conquer, but meantime stub
bornly resisted.   The Pharisaic fanatic was kicking against
the pricks at the very time he was persecuting the followers
of Jesus ; for a man is never so violent against an opinion
as when he is half-convinced it is true, and yet is unwilling
to receive it.   And in passing it may be remarked that
Saul's exceeding madness against Christians, taken in con
nection with his waning faith in Pharisaism, implies that
Christianity appeared to him during the persecuting period
as the rival of legal righteousness.   Christianity, as he
viewed it in these days, must have been something more
than a variety of Judaism having for its distinctive tenet
the belief that Jesus was the Christ, and in all other
respects conforming to existing Jewish opinion and practice.
Had it been no more than this it would have been difficult
to understand what there could be in the Christian com
munity to provoke such bitter hostility in Paul's mind.
The fact that he persecuted the Church is the best proof
that in the bosom of that society a new religion had
appeared destined to alter much.   A sure instinct told the
ardent young Pharisee that there was something that boded
danger to the religion of the law, latent possibly as yet,
and only partially comprehended by the adherents of the
new sect, but certain to become operative more and more
in such a way as to show that the martyr Stephen had
truly divined the genius of the nascent faith.   But for this

[1] Acts xxvi. 14.

he would have let the Christians alone. That they believed '
a crucified man to be the Christ would not have provoked ,
his ire. At most he would have regarded their belief
simply as an absurd opinion. It was the spirit of the new ⟨
religion, its anti-legal undercurrent, which made it for him
at once a source of fascination and an object of fear and
hatred.

When a crisis occurs in a life of great moral intensity
the issues involved are wont to be very radical. That Saul
of Tarsus, even with his new insight into sin and his
despair of attaining unto righteousness, should become a
Christian was not a matter of course; but that in case he
became a Christain his Christianity would be very thorough
going might be taken for granted. It is not difficult to
determine what the leading characteristics of his altered '
religious attitude would be. He would see clearly that the
seat of true righteousness was in the heart, and not in the
outward act. There would be a great change in his way of
regarding the Jewish law. The veneration for it he had
learned in his father's house, and in the Rabbinical schools,
would give place to a feeling that might easily be mistaken
for contempt. The convert would say to himself: Whatever
that law is good for, and that it serves some good end I
must believe, for God is its author, it is not that way a
man can reach righteousness and salvation. Out of some
such feeling grew the doctrine concerning the law formu
lated in later years, that its real God-appointed function
was to provoke into activity the sinful principle in human
nature, so to give the knowledge of sin and prepare the
sinner for receiving God's grace in Jesus Christ. Along
with this contempt for the law as a way to righteousness
would go loss of respect for Jewish prerogative. Jewish
pride would pass away with that on which it fed. If by all
our efforts to keep the law we cannot commend ourselves
to God, why should we think that Jews are more to God
than Gentiles? That we have a God-given law is a poor
ground of boasting; the grand fact about us all, Jew and

Gentile alike, is that we are all *sinners* in God's sight.
Here was Pauline universalism in germ. Once more, the
new religious attitude would involve an altered view of
man's relation to God. According to the old view, the
relation was a purely legal one : God made demands with
which men were bound under heavy penalties to comply.
But with the great crisis would come insight into the
blessed truth that God's attitude towards men is not that
of One who simply makes demands, but before all things
that of One who *gives*. The idea of divine exaction would
retire into the background, and the idea of *divine grace*
would come to the front. It was not a novel idea. It was
as old as the prophets, as old one may say as Moses, though
the long dreary night of legalism had caused it to be almost
wholly forgotten. It only needed to be rediscovered, and
Saul in the time of his spiritual tribulation, when the
words, "Thou shalt not covet," were ringing in his ears,
was in a state of mind favourable for making the discovery.
God's grace was his only chance of salvation, his only
refuge from despair. How sweet to one in such a forlorn
condition Jeremiah's oracle of the new covenant with the
law written on the heart, or the new name for God, "Father,"
recently coined by Jesus and used by Him to proclaim a
gospel of divine mercy towards even "publicans and
sinners"! We need not doubt that both these aids to the
new yet most ancient way of thinking concerning God were
available to Saul in his time of need. Bunyan in his hour
of darkness searched the whole Scriptures in quest of texts
that might encourage even him to hope in God's mercy.
Why should Saul in despair of salvation by self-righteous
ness not be equally on the alert to discover texts like:
"There is forgiveness with Thee," and "I will put my law
in their inward parts"? And it is surely not a violent
supposition that some stray samples of the new Christian
dialect reached the ears of this remarkable pupil of the
Rabbis, and that some such words as those in which Jesus
thanked His Father that the things of the kingdom were

revealed to babes, while hid from the wise and understand
ing, brought comfort to his heart in the time of his distress !

The forementioned elements of the Christian conscious
ness of Paul are all fair deductions from what we know
from himself concerning his state of mind antecedent to his
conversion. They probably all entered into his new reli
gious attitude from the day he became a Christian, though
all their implications might not be immediately apparent to
his view. If the general characteristics of that attitude
have been correctly determined, it will be seen that Paul's
Christianity was essentially the same as that of Christ.
For him, as for the Great Master, it was the religion of
the spirit as opposed to ritualism, the religion of faith as
opposed to legalism, the religion of grace as opposed to
self-righteousness, and the religion of humanity as opposed
to Jewish exclusiveness. But Paul's Christianity was not
merely a religion like that of Christ : it was a religion of
which Christ was the central object. The most vital and
specific article of his creed was the doctrine of Christ's
atoning death and of justification through faith therein.
It does not come within the scope of an apologetic treatise
to enter into a detailed explanation or defence of that
doctrine. Its general import, which is all that here concerns us, is sufficiently clear. Paul, the Christian, believed
in a righteousness of God freely given to all who believed
in Jesus as crucified for their salvation. He put his conception in compact form when he spoke of the sinless Jesus
as made sin for us " that we might be made the righteous
ness of God in Him." [1] This righteousness of God in
Pauline dialect is a synonym for pardon. It does not
cover the whole ground of a sinner's spiritual need. What
of the heart righteousness which the quondam Pharisee had
discovered to be necessary ? A very important part of the
apologetic side of Paul's system of thought, as expounded
in his four great Epistles, is that which has for its object to
show that the ethical interest, or personal holiness, is not

[1] 2 Cor. v. 21.

compromised by his doctrine of justification. That end is accomplished by what has been not inaptly called his "faith-mysticism," that is to say, his conception of believers in a Christ who died for them, as also dying with Him and rising to a new life. The latter aspect is not less essential to Paul's theory than the former.

There are no autobiographical hints in Paul's letters as to the genesis of his doctrine of justification by faith in Christ's atoning death, such as those which help us to understand his loss of faith in justification by law. We are left to our own conjectures. Several possible sources of the great thought suggest themselves. Doubtless the faith of the first disciples that Jesus was the Christ though crucified would have its own influence. Then the Pharisee's despair of self-achieved righteousness would powerfully contribute to prepare his mind for the reception of the new idea. For though he had lost confidence in his own righteousness, he did not lose the craving for righteousness, or the urgent sense of its indispensableness. He felt all along that righteousness must be forthcoming somehow. From that feeling to faith in an objective "imputed" righteousness of God was indeed a long step, though it looked in that direction. It has been thought that the theology of the Jewish schools gave the anxious inquirer the hint out of which his doctrine of justification was developed. The Jews believed that the surplus merits of the fathers might be imputed to less holy men, and that the sufferings of the righteous could atone for the sins of the unrighteous. They did not, strange to say, apply the theory to the Messiah, in whose case one would expect it to be best exemplified. But the theory, once broached, might easily be extended in that direction. A suffering Christ, such as Christians believed in, was in harmony with Hebrew prophecy, if not with Rabbinical traditions. He, like others, might suffer unjustly, and His sufferings might atone for the sins of His people. One does not care to think of the great apostle as indebted to the Rabbis for any parts of his system, and yet it is not inconceivable that he may have "spoiled the Egyptians," and borrowed from his former masters ideas capable of being made serviceable to a faith which was to be the destruction of Rabbinism.[1]

With more confidence we may suppose that the resurrection of Jesus, boldly proclaimed by the first believers, and put beyond doubt for himself by the appearance of Jesus to him on the way to Damascus, powerfully helped Paul to grasp the thought of Christ's death as an atonement for sin and a source of righteousness. Twenty years after his conversion he wrote in one of his letters that Christ "was raised again for our justification." [2] From the day that he believed that Jesus rose from the dead he probably conceived of Him as being raised for His own justification in the first place. That is to say, for the new convert the resurrection of Jesus was conclusive proof that Jesus had not suffered for His own offences. The question inevitably arose, for whose then? for it was an axiom for Paul, as for the Jews in general, that death was the penalty of sin. The answer of faith, as formulated by the apostle in after years, was, He suffered for our offences, the Sinless One had been made sin for us to the effect of enduring sin's appointed penalty. This thought, like those previously enumerated, probably formed an element in Paul's Christian consciousness from the first, though no clear statement of it is to be found in his mission discourses reported in *Acts* or in his earliest Epistles.[3]

---

[1] *Vide* on this subject Pfleiderer's *Urchristenthum*, pp. 154–171, and for the views of the Jewish schools Weber's *System der Altsynagogalen Palästinischen Theologie.* That Paul's modes of reasoning betray the influence of early Rabbinical training is now pretty generally admitted. His arguments based on the use of the singular "seed" (Gal. iii. 16), the veil on the face of Moses (2 Cor. iii. 13), and the allegory of Hagar and Ishmael (Gal. iv. 24), may be referred to as instances. These things, in which Paul paid tribute to his age, only serve by contrast to enhance our sense of his insight into the great principles of Christianity. In this region what strikes one is not the resemblance but the contrast to Rabbinism.

[2] Rom. iv. 25.

[3] On Paul's earlier mode of presenting Christianity, as exhibited in his

On the whole, it may be said that the main source of Paul's theology was his experience. It was a theoretical solution of the problem of his own individual conscience, How shall a man be just before God? It may wear a technical aspect, due to the fact that it was formulated in connection with a great controversy concerning the meaning of the law and the destination of the gospel. But it is not scholastic in spirit, but thrills throughout with the fervour of intense religious emotion. To this cause it is due that Paul's attention is concentrated on two events in Christ's earthly history : His death and His resurrection. These were the events which met his most urgent spiritual necessities. This concentration is the secret of his lasting power. It enabled him to grasp the religious significance of the events referred to with a clearness of insight, and to express it with a vividness, which have given his state ments, apart from the deference paid to them as inspired, a permanent hold on the mind of Christendom. We can hardly think of the general religious truth that we are saved by grace, apart from Paul's special theological formu lation of it in his doctrine of justification.

But concentration brings limitations as well as power. Limitation is, indeed, a condition of power. Prophets pro‐ phesy in part, and they tell upon their time because they do so. Paul's prophetic intensity and onesidedness enabled him to assert the independence and universality of Chris tianity with an emphasis which put the matter for ever beyond controversy. It therefore does no dishonour to him to take in earnest his own words concerning the limited nature of all prophecy, and to say that he has not in his Epistles exhausted the significance of the earthly history of Jesus. He has not even presented in all its aspects the meaning of Christ's death. He has set forth with power the mystic solidarity of believers with a crucified and risen Saviour, but he has not taught with

discourses reported in Acts and 1 and 2 Thessalonians, *vide* Sabatier, *The Apostle Paul*, Book II.

breadth and emphasis the precious doctrine of Christ's temptations and priestly sympathy. For that we must go to the Epistle to the Hebrews. He has stated in the avail able categories of thought the theological importance of Christ's death, but he has not exhibited its ethical import as the result of the sufferer's fidelity to righteousness and to His Messianic vocation, which is the foundation of the theological superstructure. To learn this first and funda mental lesson we must go to the Gospels, where Christ's public ministry, as it unfolds itself, is seen to be an inces sant and deadly conflict with a counterfeit righteousness of which Paul himself was first the dupe and then the victim. And much more of great value to the Christian faith and life is to be learned from the same source, which is not to be got out of Paul. There we find the historical vouchers for the fierceness of the temptations and the depth of the sympathy whereof the author of the Epistle to the Hebrews delights to discourse. There we see that redeem ing gracious love to the sinful in daily exercise, which for Paul was God-commended by the supreme instance of the cross,—a love all the more impressive that it was shown toward objects neglected by the reputedly good, as past all hope of salvation. There the nature of true goodness is revealed by contrast with a spurious type, arrogant in its pretensions and intolerant of rivals. There the doctrine of God as the Father in heaven, and of man even at the worst as His son, is asserted with a breadth, simplicity, and emphasis unique in the history of religious literature. There we become acquainted with another mode of present- ing for man's acceptance the *summum bonum*, Christ's own chosen way, viz. as a kingdom of God. Paul's point of view is individual. Christ's is social. The righteousness of God is a boon offered to faith as the solution of the ' problem of the individual conscience. The kingdom of God . is a gift of divine love to men conceived of as related to God as sons and to each other as brethren, a gift which cannot be enjoyed except in connection with a social organism. The two aspects of the *summum bonum* are not incompatible or without important points of contact. The idea of social solidarity in reality underlies Paul's concep tion of the highest good. Believers are in mystic unity with Christ; they die, rise, and ascend to heaven with Him. They are a joint-stock company for good and evil, first in their common relation to the Head, and inferentially in relation to one another. Still what is present to the mind of one who regards the highest good under the Pauline aspect is the question, How am I as an individual man to become just before God ? It is a vital question, but it needs supplementing by the larger one, How am I to get into right relations with the whole moral world ; with God and with my fellowmen ? Christ's answer to the latter question may be found alternatively in His doctrine of God and man, or in His doctrine concerning Himself. Think of God as your gracious Father, and of all men, even the most degraded, as His sons, and let your life be dominated by this great ruling thought. Regard me as at once Son of God and Son of man, and in fellowship with me enter into possession of the same divine dignity, and the exercise of the same human sympathies. It is the business of theology to determine the affinities between the Galilean and the Pauline Gospels, but it is the privilege of religious faith to enter into life by the door which Jesus has opened without stopping to try whether Paul's key fits the lock. The words of Jesus are "words of eternal life," and no truth not spoken by Him can be essential to salvation, however helpful for upbuilding in faith. His teaching contains in the smallest measure a local and temporary element. Paul and the author of the Epistle to the Hebrews, as to the form of their thought and their modes of reasoning, spoke largely to the men of their own generation, having it for their task to reveal and commend the spirit of the new Christian era to minds wedded to the past. Jesus addressed Himself to humanity, and many of His sayings, even in their form, are as modern as if they had been uttered in the present century.

These observations may serve as a corrective to a tend
ency that has been more or less operative, especially in
the Protestant section of the Church, to discover the gospel
almost exclusively in Paul's writings, and to neglect the
Gospels as of little doctrinal value. In avoiding one extreme, however, we must beware of going to another, that
of neglecting Paul in our new love for the Gospels. This
tendency is not without its representatives, and it has found
a persuasive mouthpiece in Renan. In his work on St.
Paul this author writes: "After being for three hundred
years the Christian doctor *par excellence*, thanks to Protest
ant orthodoxy, Paul in our day is on the point of finishing
his reign. Jesus, on the contrary, is more living than ever.
It is no more the Epistle to the Romans that is the *resume*
of Christianity. It is the Sermon on the Mount. The true
Christianity which will remain eternally, comes from the
Gospels, not from the Epistles of Paul."[1] This is a superficial hasty verdict. A truer judgment will recognise that
the Christianity of Paul is essentially the same as that of
Jesus. Nor will a candid mind reckon it an unpardonable
sin that Paul's thoughts on the nature of the Christian
religion were cast in a controversial mould. That the
apostle was a controversialist is a fact, but it was his mis
fortune, not his fault. The great question regarding the
relation of Christianity to Judaism could not fail to arise
sooner or later. Conflict on this point, on which the whole
future of Christianity turned, was inevitable, and some one
must render the inestimable service to humanity of fighting
for the right in the momentous quarrel. Paul was the man
selected by Providence to perform this task, and instead of
blaming him for his destiny, let us rather be thankful that
he discerned and chose the right side, and fought for it with
incomparable skill and with heroic determination, as well
as with triumphant success.

[1] *St. Paul*, pp. 569, 570.

CHAPTER VII.

PRIMITIVE CHRISTIANITY.

LITERATURE. — Neander, *History of the Planting and Training of the Christian Church;* Baur, *Die Geschichte der Christlichen Kirche,* Band I., and *Paulus der Apostel;* Albrecht Ritschl, *Entstehung der Alt-Katholischen Kirche* (2te Aufl. 1857); Hausrath, *Neutestamentliche Zeitgeschichte* (translated); Reuss, *Geschichte der heiligen Schriften N.T's,* ote Aufl. 1874; Keim, *Aus dem Urchristenthum,* 1878; Holsten, *Das Evangelium des Paulus,* 1880; Bleek, *Introduction to the New Testament* (translation); B. Weiss, *Introduction to the New Testament* (translation, 1887); Weizsacker, *Das Apostolische Zeitalter,* 2te Aufl. 1891; Pfleiderer, *Urchristenthum.*

Christianity, as apprehended by Paul, was, we have seen, a universal religion. His mode of thought, when engaged in theological discussion, might be distinctively Jewish, and his method of using Scripture in proof of his positions might occasionally betray the influence of early training in the Rabbinical schools, but in all his Epistles he represented Christianity as a religion to be made known unto all the nations unto obedience of faith. From these same Epistles, especially from those written to the Galatian and Corinthian Churches, it is evident that his view did not command unanimous assent, but was bitterly opposed by a section of the Christian community. That diversity of opinion as to the relation of Christianity to Judaism prevailed in the early Church appears likewise from the Epistle to the Hebrews. The author of that Epistle is evidently in sympathy with Paul, but he writes to a body of Christians, apparently Hebrews in race, who had little insight into the genius of Christianity and little inclination to regard it, as he did, as the absolute religion entitled to supersede the old Jewish covenant and Levitical worship.

Such divergencies of view within the bosom of the

Church naturally raise the wider question, Through what phases did Christianity pass in the formative period of its history, and in what relation did these stand to Christ and to Paul: the great Master and His greatest disciple? On this question great difference of opinion prevails among theologians. The whole subject of primitive Christianity, as it was taught by Jesus, and as it manifested itself in the period antecedent to the formation of the old Catholic Church, is the battle-ground of contending parties, and the whole truth as to the matters in debate is by no means on either side of the controversy, whether orthodox or heterodox.

Four distinct theories concerning the tendencies at work in early Christianity have found advocates among modern critics.[1]

1. The first of these theories is that of Dr. Ferdinand Christian Baur. According to Baur, Christ not less than Paul was universalistic in spirit. He taught a religion purely ethical in its nature, equally adapted for all climes, and destined in His intention to become the religion of humanity. But His disciples failed to apprehend the drift of His teaching, so that, after His death, among all the men bearing the title of an apostle, Paul was the only one who entered with intelligence and enthusiasm into the spirit of the Master. Hence arose, in course of time, a great controversy as to the relation between Christianity and Judaism, in which Paul was on one side, and all the eleven original apostles on the other; Paul contending for the right of Christianity to be an independent religion, and to go on its world-conquering career untrammelled by the uncongenial restrictions of Jewish law and custom; the eleven striving to keep the new religion in a state of pupilage to the old. The history of Christianity from the

---

[1] For the sake of definiteness in statement, I connect these theories with as many individual names. It will be understood that each name repre sents more or less a school. For a sufficiently full account of the critical literature bearing on the subject, *vide* Weiss, *Introduction to the New Testament*, Introduction.

apostolic age to the rise of the old Catholic Church in the middle of the second century was the history of this con troversy in its various stages of (1) unmitigated antagonism between the two opposed tendencies; (2) incipient and progressive reconciliation; (3) consummated reconciliation and completed union and unity. The books of the New Testament all relate to one or other of these stages, and their dates may be approximately fixed by the tendencies they respectively represent. A book which belongs to the first stage, and advocates either pure Paulinism or a purely Judaistic view of Christianity, is therefore early and apostolic; on the other hand, a book which belongs to the final stage, and presents a view of Christianity rising entirely above early antagonisms, must be of late date, and cannot have had an apostle for its author.

2. The most thoroughgoing opponent of the Tubingen theory is Dr. Bernhard Weiss. This author, whose con tributions to New Testament criticism possess much value, is animated by an undue desire to negative Baur's con clusions all along the line. On this account a large deduction must be made from the weight to be attached to his statements on the questions at issue. It is not the fact that the Tubingen school is always wrong, and it is a very questionable service to the Christian faith that is rendered by an apologetic going on that assumption. Briefly put, the view of Weiss is that neither in the case of Jesus nor in the case of Paul was Christianity, as originally conceived, universalistic. The aim of Jesus was simply to establish a theocratic national kingdom in Israel. He never dreamt of calling in question the perpetual obligation of the Mosaic law; and the idea of making dis- ciples among the Gentiles arose in His mind only at a late period in His career, when He began to despair of winning His countrymen to righteousness. Somewhat similar, according to this author, was the experience of Paul. His universalism was not the immediate outcome of the spiritual crisis which issued in his conversion; it was an afterthought

suggested by outward events. He does, indeed, in his Epistle to the Galatians, connect his conversion with the divine intention to make him an apostle to the Gentiles, but we are not to suppose that this was clear to him from the beginning. He is simply reading the teleology of his conversion in the light of long subsequent history. What really first opened his mind to the great thought of a vocation to apostleship in the Gentile world was his experience of Jewish unbelief and Gentile receptivity on his mission tour through the cities of Asia Minor. That mission was not, in the intention of the Church at Antioch in Syria, a mission to the heathen, but only to the Jewish Diaspora, but it suggested the idea of a heathen mission to the susceptible mind of Paul. The results revealed to him a divine purpose to reject Israel and to call the Gentiles in their room.[1]

On this view there were no materials out of which a great controversy concerning the nature of Christianity could arise. There were not two ways of thinking on the subject. The contrast between Paulinism and the Judaistic Christianity of the eleven disappears. A universalism of conviction had no existence : all were Judaists to begin with, and the only universalism known to the Apostolic Church was of an opportunist character, and such as there was did not distinguish Paul from the original apostles, for all alike bowed to events and acknowledged that God had granted to the Gentiles eternal life.

3. More in sympathy with the views of Baur are those of Weizsäcker. He believes that the religious spirit both of Jesus and of Paul was pronouncedly universalistic. Far from doubting the claim of Jesus to this attribute, he is of opinion that His universalism was of a more decided character than even that of Paul. He differs from Baur chiefly in thinking that there was a universalistic tendency at work in the Palestine or Hebrew Church entirely independent of Paul; specifying as instances Stephen, Barnabas,

[1] *Introduction to the New Testament*, pp. 154, 164.

and Apollos. The original apostles he conceives to have sympathised with this tendency to a certain extent, though coming far short of the Gentile apostle in zeal for the great cause of a Christianity emancipated from the dominion of Jewish legalism.[1] This view, in itself intrinsically probable, has an important bearing on the history of early Christianity. It reduces the cleavage in the Church to less formidable dimensions. It leaves room still for controversy arising out of diversity of view as to the nature and destination of the Christian faith, but the war of conflicting opinion could not, on Weizsäcker's conception of the state of parties, be the tragic affair that it was bound to be according to the Tübingen scheme. For, in the first place, by his account all the leading men were practically on one side; whereas, according to Dr. Baur, the state of the case was Paul single-handed *versus* the pillars of the Church. Then, in the second place, the cleavage in the Church, on the Weizsäcker theory, was not one of race. Paul had warm friends and supporters, not only among Gentile converts, but also among Christians of Hebrew extraction. On these terms a controversy of an epoch-making character, and forming the great event of early Church history, could not possibly arise.

4. Pfleiderer, while believing that the teaching of Jesus contained the germs of universalism,[2] reserves for Paul the praise of being the first to proclaim with clear insight and impassioned emphasis the great doctrine of a gospel of grace for the world, and for all on equal terms, involving as a corollary the abrogation of the Jewish ceremonial law both for Jewish and for Gentile believers. The leading apostles, especially Peter, he conceives as sympathising to

---

[1] Weizsacker, *Das Apostolische Zeitalter*, p. 437.

[2] Among the historically reliable data going to prove that Jesus was animated by a "reforming free spirit," Pfleiderer includes the sayings concerning the new wine and old skins, the relativity of the Sabbath law (the Sabbath made for man), the worthlessness of the ceremonial law, and the destroying of the Temple and building of a spiritual temple. — *Urchristenthum*, p. 493.

a certain extent with Paul's position, but lacking a distinct understanding and firm grasp of the principles at stake, and on that account disqualified for rendering Paul effective service against his Judaistic opponents, and even exposed to the risk of being themselves mistaken for antagonists. In such circumstances misunderstanding, alienation, and controversy might easily arise. But in Pfleiderer's view the great fact of primitive Christianity was by no means the conflict between Paulinism and Judaism, but rather the development which Paulinism itself underwent. For this writer Paulinism is Christianity. It is the one thing we surely know in connection with the beginnings of the Christian religion, an island of firm historical ground surrounded by a sea of uncertainty. Its influence can be traced everywhere in the New Testament, in Gospels and in Epistles, and the movement of thought to which it gave rise is the one phenomenon of first-rate importance with which the student of Church history has to deal down to the middle of the second century. But what is Paulinism? It is, according to Pfleiderer, a complex system of ideas derived from different sources, lacking inner harmony, and liable therefore to part company in the course of time. The account he gives of the theological system of Paul is analogous to that given by Baur of the teaching of Jesus. In both cases two things are tied together, which, if not absolutely contradictory, are at least heterogeneous, and therefore sure to fall asunder in the course of development. In the case of Jesus, according to Baur, they were: a universalist religious spirit and a nationalistic form, the Jewish Messianic idea. In the case of Paul, according to Pfleiderer, they were two sets of ideas, the one borrowed from the theology of the Pharisaic schools, the other from Hellenistic philosophy, as represented by the Book of Wisdom. What he got from the former source we already know: it was mainly his doctrine of imputed righteousness.[1] What he got from the latter source it is not so easy

[1] *Vide* p. 425.

to make out; for at this point the theory of our author wears the aspect of an airy speculation with a very slender basis of fact. But so far as one can gather, the Hellenistic influence is traceable in Paul's ideas of the future life, in his anthropology, and, above all, in his doctoine of *imparted* righteousness. Paul, we know, was not content that the believer should have God's righteousness imputed to him on the ground of Christ's atoning death. He held it indispensable that the believer should be really personally righteous, and this he was persuaded all believers could become through mystic fellowship with Christ crucified and risen. In neither part of this composite doctrine of righteousness, according to Pfleiderer, was the apostle original. He derived the one half from the school of Gamaliel, the other from the school of Philo. His theory of imputed righteousness was, we are informed, " Christian ised Pharisaism," and his theory of real righteousness " Christianised Hellenism." [1] And what, we naturally ask, was the subsequent fortune of these two theories ? Not exactly to fall asunder into antagonism, and become the watchwords of fiercely contending parties. Rather this : the theory of imputed righteousness was too abstruse, peculiar, and Jewish to be understood by Gentile Chris tians ; therefore it was to a large extent ignored, and only the Hellenistic side of Pauline theology took root and grew with a vigorous and lasting vitality in the great Christian community of which Paul was the founder. So arose a new type of thought, Pauline in its origin, holding firmly the great principle of Christian universalism, but dis regarding Paul's controversial theology and rising above the antitheses of original Paulinism. This new catholic theo logy is, we are told, not to be regarded either as an external reconciliation of Paulinism and Judaistic Christianity, nor as a corruption of Paulinism through heathenish super ficiality and Greek world - wisdom, but rather as the legitimate development of Hellenism Christianised by

[1] *Urchristenthum,* p. 175.

Paul, and, as such, distinct both from Paulinism and from
Judaistic Christianity, a third thing beside and above
both.[1]

Of these hypothetical constructions, which seem to
exhaust the possibilities of the case,[2] that of Weizsäcker
possesses the highest measure of probability. His idea of
the religious attitude of Jesus, as more purely and absolutely
human and universal than that even of Paul, especially com
mends itself as thoroughly reasonable. Weiss has, indeed,
gained from Hartmann the praise of having given the truest
account of the Christianity of Christ.[3] It is a doubtful
compliment as coming from a man who thinks Christianity

---

[1] *Urchristenthum*, pp. 616, 617.

[2] If not absolutely, at least relatively to the assumption common to all the
four theories of the genuineness of the four great Pauline Epistles (*Galatians
Corinthians, Romans*). It might entirely alter the whole character and
course of primitive Christianity if there were grounds for regarding these as
spurious, and late products of a partisan pen in the second century. There
have not been wanting men bold enough to advocate this view. Thus quite
recently, Professor Steck of Bern, following Professor Loman of Amsterdam
(*Quæstiones Paulinæ*), has presented himself as its champion (*Der Galater-
brief nach seiner Echtheit untersucht*, 1888). The resulting conception of
primitive Christianity is to this effect : The opposition between the real
Pauline and the original apostolic tendency was not at first very marked ; it
rose to its height only gradually, and after the death of the Apostle Paul.
Originally the two tendencies were not so very far apart. Paul was, perhaps
a little freer than Peter, but that was all. Only after the death of
Paul did the antagonism become acute, and even the "Pauline" Epistles show
us the progressive development of one side of it. First, the Epistle to the
Romans quietly expounds the Gentile-Christian view ; then the two Epistles
to the Corinthians, assuming a livelier tone, glorify Paul as the minister of
the new covenant, and advocate a law-emancipated Paulinism ; finally
Galatians ventures to storm the citadel of legalism and to assume a defiant
tone towards the authority of the original apostles (pp. 372, 373). Steck
regards the *Acts of the Apostles* as an earlier writing than these four Epistles
and a much more reliable source of information as to the character and views
of Paul. On this new theory Paul assumes a quite subordinate place in the
history of nascent Christianity, and the Epistles bearing his name, which
have been supposed by modern critics to be the surest historical foundation
for their theoretical constructions, are degraded into clever fabrications of
some unknown writer of the second century.

[3] *Vide Die Selbstzersetzung des Christenthums und die Religion der Zu-
kunft*. p. 41.

is far gone in a process of self-dissolution, and who seems
bent on reducing the claims of Jesus on the gratitude of
mankind to a minimum.[1]   It has always appeared to me
that with all his critical acumen, Weiss lacks the power of
appreciating the character of Christ, and that the great sub
ject of the evangelic narratives as exhibited in his pages,
while a very important official personage, is nevertheless
a commonplace man.   It is hard to understand how any
one recognising the substantial historicity of the Gospels,
and studying them with unbiassed mind (but there lies the
difficulty!), can arrive at the conclusion that Jesus was as
national and narrow in His views and feelings and hopes
as the ordinary Jewish Christian of the apostolic age.   So
many things in the Gospels of unquestionable authenticity
point the other way ; that passionate abhorrence of Rabbinism, that loving, comrade-like relation to the outcasts,
that significant parabolic comparison of the religious move
ment He had inaugurated to new wine and a new garment.[2]
Jesus seems to have risen above legalism and Jewish par
ticularism without effort or struggle, as a bird rises from the
ground into the air, its native element.   Paul purchased his
spiritual freedom at a great price, but Jesus was free-born.
Regarding His early education we have no information ;
He may have been brought into contact in His boyhood
with the Rabbis, but no trace of Rabbinical influence can
be detected in the self-manifestations of His manhood.
The baleful spirit of legalism never seems to have touched
His virgin soul.   Paul's emancipation came through his
eventual insight into the inward nature of true righteous
ness.   That it came to him at all evinced his moral
superiority to the ordinary Pharisee ; but that it came to
him so late evinces with equal clearness decided short
coming from the ideal experience.   Why should it be

---

[1] *Vide Die Krisis des Christenthums in der Modernen Theologie.*

[2] Pfleiderer finds in these parable germs, whose historicity he thinks there
is no ground for questioning, the revelation of a clear energetic consciousness
on the part of Jesus of the essential newness of His ethico-religious spirit in
relation to Judaism.   *Vide Urchristenthum*, p. 365.

necessary to wait so long to be conscious of coveting, or to see that coveting was sin, or to learn that a man might be like a whited sepulchre, fair without, full of dead men's bones and of all uncleanness within ? Can we not imagine one seeing into all that intuitively ; and was not Jesus in His whole cast of mind and spirit just the one to have this instinctive insight and all that went along with it ?

Paul came far short of the ideal, and was much inferior every way to his Master, but he was not so dull and slow to learn as Weiss has represented him. Nothing could be more prosaic than this author's whole conception of the apostle's religious experience. His conversion was a pure and absolute miracle. It was a miracle wrought by an external cause, the appearance to him of the risen Christ on the way to Damascus. It was not prepared for or rendered probable by any antecedent spiritual experience ; it was an accident so far as any such experience was concerned. By his fanatical zeal against the Christians at the time it occurred, Saul was not kicking against the pricks of rising conviction, but simply seeking to win the favour of God by adding to his stock of merit. He might have gone on in this course indefinitely had not Christ happened to appear to him to stop his persecuting career.[1] Many years after his first conversion to Christianity he underwent a second conversion to Christian universalism, the cause this time also being external circumstances.[2] On this view Paul's experience loses all moral contents and his convictions all spiritual depth, and from being one of the few very great men of the human race, he sinks down to the level of a third-rate actor in one of the grand dramas of the world's religious history. One wonders how the greatest of the universal religions ever came to be, with such a dearth of insight and foresight and initiative in its originators. But the poverty is not in them, but in their modern interpreters.

For it may be confidently affirmed that not only Jesus

[1] Weiss, *Introduction to the New Testament* i 152
[2] *Ibid.* i. 154.

and Paul, but even men of the second magnitude, such as Stephen, Barnabas, and Apollos, had a prophetic presenti ment that their work concerned mankind. It is not credible, as Weiss alleges, that the fanatical rage of the Jews against the protomartyr had no more serious cause than the free exercise of the recognised prophetic right of denouncing unbelief and impenitence, and threatening with destruction a people persisting in evil courses.[1] The men who stoned him to death acted, doubtless, under the in fluence of a vague but overmastering feeling that his eloquence meant danger to Jewish privilege and preroga tive, and portended an incipent religious revolution. His doctrine was a fateful word, like that of Mahomet when he said, The idols are vanity. What manner of man Barnabas was sufficiently appears from the fact of his being sent as a deputy from the Church in Jerusalem to Antioch when the Greeks there began to receive the gospel.[2] The historian calls him "a good man."[3] His goodness consisted in a capacity for generous sympathy with a new departure, by which pusillanimous narrow-hearted men might have been scared. It was characteristic of him that on this occasion he went down to Tarsus to seek Saul.[4] He knew that Saul was the man for the work that had just commenced, and that it was the work for which he had been specially prepared. The two men were well-matched comrades as the agents selected by the Antioch Church for the first Gentile mission. We are told, indeed, that it is an entire mistake to suppose that it was a mission to the heathen that was then inaugurated: it was merely a mission to the Jewish Diaspora which by good luck led to conversions among Gentiles.[5] How the prosaic mind sucks all the

---

[1] Weiss, *Introduction*, i. 168, where we are informed that it is a thoroughly erroneous idea that Stephen appeared in the primitive Church as the forerunner of Paul.

[2] Acts xi. 22.

[3] Acts xi. 24, ἀνὴρ ἀγαθός; where the epithet ἀγαθός is to be taken as signifying magnanimous.

[4] Acts xi 25.

[5] Weiss, *Introduction*, i. 163.

romance out of history, and levels everything down to flat commonplace! If we are to regard the account given in *the Acts* as at all reliable, it is quite certain that something great, unusual, startlingly novel, and solemn, in view of its unforeseen possibilities, then took place. The brethren fasted, we are told, as men for whom fasting has not become an ascetic habit do only on very solemn occasions. The very terms in which the Holy Spirit is represented as suggesting a line of action to the brethren assembled imply that some thing extraordinary is in contemplation.[1] The untranslated and untranslatable Greek particle δή, of rare occurrence in the New Testament, is very significant. Scholars know how frequently it is used in Plato's dialogues, and what liveliness it communicates to the discussion. It is an emotional particle, and as used by a Greek must have been accompanied by appropriate gestures and uttered with a peculiar intonation. As employed by the sacred historian, it conveys the idea of a great new thought or purpose flashed with the vividness of lightning into the mind. A mission to the Diaspora would hardly answer to that description. Nor would there be any point in speaking of Barnabas and Saul as "called" to such a mission.[2] What special call or qualifications were needed, unless it were the power to resist temptations to home-sickness, which, as it turned out, John Mark did not possess?[3]

That Apollos shared Paul's universalistic attitude is sufficiently evident from the manner in which the apostle speaks of him in his First Epistle to the Corinthians. "He recognises his independence, and that he has his own way of teaching, and yet he is conscious of being at one with him in the main matter; the conception of the gospel, the principles on which they work, the universalism, are the same for both."[4]

---

[1] αφορίσατε δη μοι τον Βαρναβαν, etc.

[2] Acts xiii. 2.   [3] Acts xv. 38.

[4] Weizsäcker, *Das Apostolische Zeitalter*, p. 438. Weizsäcker points out that a similar position of independence and yet affinity in spirit and tend ency is assigned by the Apostle Paul to Andronicus and Junia in Rom. xvi. 7.

As already indicated, I do not think there is any solid foundation for the attempt to trace certain elements in Paul's theology to Hellenistic influence. In particular it seems futile to ascribe to such a source his very character- istic doctrine of mystic fellowship with Christ crucified and risen as the source of personal sanctity. It is quite unnecessary to seek for any explanation of this doctrine outside the exigencies of Paul's own spiritual life. As a religious man he felt the need for something more than objective righteousness, or pardon, and that something more he got by habitually realising his oneness with Christ, and so letting Christ's spiritual influence flow in upon him in full stream. As a theologian also he found this train of thought useful to him for apologetic purposes, especially as helping him to repel the suggestion that on his system men might continue in sin that grace might abound. He met the sinister insinuation by saying: Thus rather do we Christains view the matter; if One died for all, then all died with Him.[1]

While denying that this fertile thought came to Paul from any external source, I regard it as quite probable that many Christians of Gentile birth felt more drawn by the mystic side of Paul's doctrine of righteousness than by its legal aspect, as indeed is the case with many Christians in our own time. We must beware, however, of exaggerating the importance of the fact, as is certainly done both when it is regarded as the effect of a particular type of non-Christian thought influencing the minds of Christians, and when it is made the watchword of a school or party within the Church supposed to have played an important *role* in early ecclesiastical history.

From the foregoing statements some important inferences may be deduced.

(1) In view of what has been said respecting the per sonal religious attitude of our Lord, the authenticity of sayings universalistic in drift ascribed to Him in the

_____
[1] 2 Cor. v. 14.

Gospels is not to be hastily suspected, any more than their natural meaning is to be explained away. Special texts may give rise to critical doubts, but these must be dealt with individually, each on its own distinct merits, not summarily disposed of by sweeping general assumptions. The bearing of this remark will be illustrated in next chapter.

(2) In view of the evidence produced that there existed in the early Church a Christian universalism entirely in dependent of Paul, it is obvious that the presence of a universalistic element in any New Testament writing cannot by itself be regarded as a proof of Pauline influence. This observation applies very specially to the case of one of the most important books of the New Testament, *the Epistle to the Hebrews*, concerning the aim, authorship, and destination of which the most diverse opinions have been entertained. Dr. Baur's view of this writing is familiar to students of modern critical literature. He regarded it as a work of con ciliatory tendency, emanating from the Judaistic side of the great controversy, written by a man who had risen far above the narrowness of Judaism, and desired to raise others to the same level by exhibiting the ancient Hebrew cultus as a sub ordinate, rudimentary, and transient stage in the process of religious development, destined to be superseded by the ab solute eternal religion, Christianity. This conception of the aim of the Epistle of course involves the frankest recognition of its universalistic standpoint. The implied, though nowhere expressed thought of the author, according to Dr. Baur, is that the Hebrew religion, with its Levitical ritual, only needs to be reduced to its spiritual basis and generalised into its ideal import to become the religion of mankind.

According to Dr. Weiss, the Epistle is of Judaic Christian origin, and of course lacks the universalistic element. Dr. Pfleiderer, on the other hand, is in full accord with Dr. Baur and the great majority of interpreters, in recognising the broad humanity of the Epistle, but equally, as a matter of course, he attributes that feature to the influence of Paul. He places the book in the class of New Testament writings to which he gives the collective title of *Christian Hellenism* or *Deutero-Paulinism*, having for their character istic the combination of some of Paul's ideas, especially of his universalism, with elements of thought derived from the Alexandrian Jewish philosophy. The aim of this class of writings in general being, in his view, to counteract a tendency to religious syncretism manifesting itself not merely among Jewish Christians, but more especially among Gentile Christians who had formerly been Jewish pros elytes, he does not accept the traditional opinion that the Epistle was originally written for the benefit of a Hebrew community. The true source of his bias on the question as to the destination of the Epistle is obvious. Its alleged Deutero-Pauline character demands a later date than the eve of the destruction of the holy city, the most fitting occasion for an Epistle addressed to a Hebrew Church, and designed to warn them against apostasy and its fearful penalty.

There is no good reason for regarding the Epistle as Pauline, either at first or at second hand. Its universalism, indeed, must be apparent to every unprejudiced mind, but just on that account it may be pointed to as one more proof of the existence in the early Church of a Christian universalism independent of Paul. Who wrote it it is impossible to tell. It certainly was not written by Paul. With equal certainty it may be affirmed that it was not written by an immediate disciple of the apostle's, the whole style of thought being entirely different from that of his recognised Epistles. The name of Apollos, though unsupported by ancient testimony, satisfies better than any other suggestion the requirements of the case, which demands an author in sympathy with Paul in his general religious attitude, but differing from him in temperament, training, and spiritual experience, and consequently in his manner of conceiving and expressing the Christian faith. Of the aim of the Epistle no better account can be given than the traditional one, according to which it was designed to preserve a community of Hebrew Christians from apostasy at a time of special trial, arising partly from out ward tribulations, partly from lack of true insight into the genius and worth of the Christian religion. All other suggestions seem by comparison far-fetched and pointless.

(3) The views we have been led to adopt on the ques tions discussed in this chapter in a large measure take away the foundation for the imputation of theological tendency to the writers of the New Testament. The Tubingen school, as is well known, were great offenders here. In their cut-and-dried scheme, every book took its place under some controversial category, and every writer had to serve as a more or less conscious instrument in connection with some phase of the great dialectic process. Thus, the *Acts of the Apostles* was written at a time when men were weary of the long strife, and would be thankful to be assured that it was a mistake to suppose that the founders of the Church had been seriously at variance. The writer, sympathising with this feeling, set himself to promote union by composing a historical romance of the apostolic age. To create the desired impression he adopted the plan of making Peter, the hero of the first part of the work, act in the catholic spirit of Paul; and Paul, the hero of the second part, act in the accommodating spirit of Peter.

A theory of omnipresent tendency inevitably acts pre judicially on critical inquiry in two ways: by shaking confidence in the truth of narratives in professedly his torical books, and by imperiously determining the dates at which particular books were written. The more tendency the less fact, and given the tendency of a book its date is approximately fixed. Thus, to return to the book of *Acts*, its aim being to create a pleasant though false impression regarding the relations of the apostles, the writer had to invent his facts, real history supplying no such incidents as were necessary for his purpose. Before Baur's time Schneckenburger had propounded the theory of the apolo-

getic aim of *Acts*, and suggested that an irenical purpose
had guided the writer in selecting the incidents to be
recorded.   But Baur, in adopting the theory for his own use,
peremptorily negatived the idea of selection, and insisted
that *invention* alone would meet the exigencies of the case.
His contention, if not necessarily valid, at least illustrates
well how surely imputation of tendency gravitates toward
denial of historicity.   Then as for the date, the book of
Acts has assigned to it a late origin by the mere fact of
its being written to gratify the general desire for peace, the
second century being well begun before men had got into
that happy mood.

  If the state of opinion in the apostolic age was such as
now represented, this ingenious theory regarding the book
in question tumbles to pieces like a house of cards.   In
that case it would not be necessary for the historian of the
doings of the apostles to invent situations in which Peter
should appear as a man who shared the views of Paul as
to the universal destination of Christianity.   Why should
he not act in the spirit of universalism if Paul had not a
monopoly of that article?   And why impute to the his
torian any other aim than that of recording transactions
which he knew to be true and deemed important?   Grant
that he regarded these transactions with the eye of a
Paulinist, enthusiastically devoted to the cause of Gentile
Christianity ; his interest was not on that account neces
sarily theological or controversial, but might be simply
religious.   And what time would be more appropriate for
recording them than when they were comparatively recent,
and when their significance was only beginning to dawn
upon the mind of the Church ?   The suggestion does not
settle the question as to the date of composition, but it
indicates that an early date was at least possible, if not
probable.

  In the coarse form which it assumed in the hands of
Dr. Baur and his followers, the theory of tendency now
finds little favour.   But in a more refined form it still

lives, and is a fruitful source of bias in critical questions. Pfleiderer, *e.g.*, has developed a new *Tendenz-Kritik* in connection with his favourite hypothesis that the great phenomenon of primitive Christianity was Paulinism and its later developments. The one respect in which he improves upon the work of his predecessors is, that the tendency he ascribes to New Testament writers is not, on the whole, so conscious and deliberate as the Tubingen school represented it. The sentiments of a later age are, he thinks, occasionally ascribed to the founders of the Church involuntarily, rather than with any conscious intention, the writers being unable to conceive of Jesus and the eleven and Paul as thinking otherwise than according to the fashion of the time in which they themselves lived and wrote. But in some instances he imputes theological motive almost as broadly as Dr. Baur. Thus he represents Mark's Gospel, in his judgment the earliest of the three synoptics, as written in order to complete and ground the *Pauline Gospel* by a historical account of the life, teaching, and death of Jesus.[1] *Matthew*, on the other hand, the latest of the three, as he treats it, is little else than an endeavour to remodel the evangelic history in accordance with the principles of *Deutero-Paulinism*, after it had become the creed of the Catholic Church. Elimination of intention in this case is impossible, because the writer of the first canonical Gospel is supposed to have the second and third Gospels under his eye. The dates assigned to *Mark* and *Matthew* are in accordance with their supposed aims. The former is conceived to have been written not very long after Paul's death, the latter is relegated to the middle of the second century.

This new criticism of the Gospels is not less violently theoretical than the older type which it aspires to super sede, and it is certainly as little entitled to implicit credence.

[1] *Urchristenthum*, p. 415.

CHAPTER VIII.

THE SYNOPTICAL GOSPELS.

LITERATURE.—H. J. Holtzmann, *Die Synoptischen Evangelien*; Weiss, *Introduction to the New Testament, Das Matthäus Evangelium,* and *Das Markus Evangelium* (*vide* also Bleek's *Introduction to the New Testament,* which, though older than than of Weiss, is in some respects more satisfactory); Bruce, *The Kingdom of God;* Pfleiderer, *Urchristenthum* (*vide* also Martineau, *Seat of Authority in Religion,* in which he largely follows Pfleiderer's critical verdicts); Marshall, "The Aramaic Gospel" in *The Expositor,* 1891; J. Estlin Carpenter, *The Synoptic Gospels,* 1890.

There are important questions relating to these Gospels with which general Apologetic is not directly concerned. The problem, *e.g.,* presented by their verbal resemblances and differences, and the literary criticism connected therewith, lie outside our plan, and belong to Introduction. The apologist is chiefly interested in the question of historicity.

In this connection much weight must be attached to the ancient tradition. The two statements of Papias, reported by Eusebius, respecting the reputed authors of the first two Gospels, are specially entitled to serious attention. In the order in which they are given by the historian they are as follow : "Mark being the interpreter of Peter wrote carefully, though not in order, as he remembered them, the things spoken or done by Christ;" "Matthew wrote the *Logia* in the Hebrew language, and each one interpreted these as he could."[1] Till recent times it was universally taken for granted that the two evangelic writings referred to by Papias were our canonical Matthew and Mark, the first Gospel as we have it being Matthew's Hebrew original done into Greek. Modern critics for the

---

[1] Eusebii, *Historia Ecclesiastica,* lib. iii. c. 39.

most part dissent from the traditional view, but not to the extent of treating the statements of Papias as of no account. They believe that Matthew and Mark did write books relating to the ministry of Jesus as Papias declares. With reference to Mark critics are not agreed whether the book he wrote was our canonical Gospel bearing his name, or was related to it as a first sketch to a revised edition, the ground for the doubt being that the canonical Mark seems to be a somewhat onesided record of the things done by Jesus, rather than a balanced account both of things done and of things said.[1] With reference to Matthew, the prevailing opinion is that he did not write our first Gospel, but a book consisting chiefly of sayings of Jesus, furnished probably with brief historical introductions explaining the occasions on which they were uttered, though to what length the historical element extended is matter of dis putation.[2] These two writings, Mark's narrative and Matthew's *Logia*, critics regard as the two chief sources of the Synoptical Gospels, the former of the incidents common to the three, the latter of the sayings common to " Matthew " and " Luke." As such they form the solid foundation of the evangelic history, the guarantee that when two or three of the Synoptical Gospels agree in their report of what Jesus said or did we are in contact with fact, not fiction.

In the value thus assigned to the ancient tradition all men of sober unbiassed judgment will be disposed to acquiesce. They will read the Gospels with the comfort able assurance that for the words of Jesus common to the first and third they have one apostle as voucher, Matthew, and for the deeds of Jesus common to the three, another

---

[1] H. J. Holtzmann (*Die Synoptischen Evangelien*) is the leading advocate of an *Urmarkus*.

[2] Weiss strives to magnify the amount of the historical element in the Logia. Holtzmann, on the other hand, ascribes to the *Urmarkus* a larger amount of the didactic element than is contained in the canonical Mark. The question at issue between the two critics is which of the two writings referred to by Papias was the chief source for our Synoptical Gospels, Weiss claiming the distinction for Matthew's *Logia*, Holtzmann for Mark's document.

apostle's authority, that of Peter, of whose preaching, according to Papias, Mark's narrative was a digest. Criti cism which disregards, or treats as of little value, such precious morsels of information as those preserved by Eusebius is open to the suspicion of being under the in fluence of *a priori* bias. Such bias is very apparent when it is given as a reason for doubting the connection between Mark's narrative and Peter's preaching, that the former contains a number of " legendary and allegorical miracle-histories," or when, in defiance of the express statement of Papias that Matthew wrote a book of *Logia*, it is held to be altogether doubtful whether the first and third evan gelists drew any of their material from that source, and whether we do not rather owe their reports of supposed sayings of Jesus largely to their powers of literary invention.[1]

The naturalistic bias, which doubts the historicity of the miraculous element, one can understand ; but it seems pure wantonness to doubt the authenticity of sayings ascribed to Jesus by two evangelists, and intrinsically credible as utterances of the Master. Why, for example, hesitate to take the remarkable passage, beginning " I thank Thee, O Father,"[2] as a *bonâ fide* report of solemn words spoken by Jesus at some important crisis in His life ? Yet Pfleiderer invites us to see in this passage a hymn of victory invented by Luke, and borrowed from him by the author of the First Gospel ; a hymn in which the Pauline mission to the heathen is celebrated as the victory of Christ over Satan's dominion in the world, and Paul's cardinal doctrine of the knowledge of God and of His Son being hid from the wise and revealed to the unwise finds suitable recognition. This is tendency-criticism run mad, the tendency at work being to make Paulinism in one form or another the one great fact and factor in nascent Christianity.

Theoretic critics tell, each one in turn, their own story

---

[1] So Pfleiderer, *vide Urchristenthum,* pp. 414, 416.

[2] Matt. xi. 25 ; Luke x. 21.

very plausibly, but it helps to deliver simple readers from the spell of their enchantment, to compare the results at which they respectively arrive. Such a comparison does not inspire confidence in the methods and verdicts of *Tendenz-Kritik* as practised by the experts. This may be illustrated by placing side by side the views of Baur and Pfleiderer respecting the Synoptical Gospels. Take first the order in which these Gospels were written. Baur arranges them thus: Matthew, Luke, Mark; Pfleiderer simply reverses the order, so that it runs: Mark, Luke, Matthew. With reference to the historic value of the Gospels the two masters are equally divergent in opinion. In the esteem of the earlier critic Matthew is entitled to the highest measure of credit; for the later he possesses the least. Their judgments as to the tendencies dominant in the several Gospels are curiously discrepant. Baur thinks Mark is studiously neutral, neither universalistic nor Judaistic; Pfleiderer thinks he is out and out Pauline. Matthew for the former represents a Judaistic conception of Christianity irenically inclined towards Paulinism; for the latter it is the mouthpiece of a Catholic Church-con sciousness as remote from the narrowness of Judaism as the Fourth Gospel. In reference to Luke the two critics are more nearly at one, it being possible for two roads going in the most opposite direction to meet at a single point. In both critical systems Luke is a *Unions-Pauliner*, a Paulinist with most friendly feelings towards Judaists, and bent on seeing a good side in every party.

Such glaring contradictions tend to throw discredit on all criticism dominated by cut-and-dried theories, and might seem to justify total disregard of the arguments by which the theorists seek to establish their conflicting views. And if the aim of the apologist were merely controversial he might save himself trouble by leaving the advocates of rival critical schemes to refute each other. But his main purpose is to establish faith in the historical worth of the Gospels, and sometimes important aid towards the attainment of that end may be obtained through the study of unbelieving attacks, even though they may be far from formidable in their logic, and destined to exercise only a transient influence on opinion. On this ground it may be worth while to devote a little attention to recent critical developments.

The general reflection may here be premised that it is seldom difficult for the promoters of ambitious critical theories, even when these are directly antagonistic to each other, to adduce some facts in support of their views. It is, indeed, a poor theory that cannot find at least a few phenomena that lend plausibility to its leading positions. Baur showed great ingenuity in discovering features in the Gospels that seemed to bear out his reading of their theological tendencies, and in doing this he rendered permanent service by directing attention to characteristics which had previously been to a great extent overlooked. We need not grudge the same praise to the most recent worker in the same field. Pfleiderer has been as successful, for example, in pointing out traces of Paulinism in *Mark*, as Baur was, in his day, in demonstrating the prudential neutrality of the same Gospel. With an eye sharpened by the desire to find materials to justify inductively a foregone conclusion, he has detected in quite a number of instances more or less resemblance between words imputed by the evangelist to Jesus and well-known Pauline doctrines.

Thus in commencing His ministry Jesus says : " Repent and believe the gospel." Here, remarks the theoretical critic, as in Paul, faith in the God-given message of salvation is the first demand.[1] In the narrative of the first announcement of the passion several Pauline echoes are discovered. Thus when the evangelist remarks concerning the explicit character of the announcement that Jesus spake the *word* openly, he is supposed to have in mind Paul's " word of the cross." The terms in which Jesus rebukes Peter : " Thou mindest not the things of God but the things of men," are suggested by those in which Paul declares that his gospel, though it be

[1] *Urchristenthum*, p. 362.

the wisdom of God, is foolishness and an offence in the eyes of men. The demand of the Master, that all His disciples shall take up their cross and follow Him, is obviously an echo of the characteristically Pauline idea of the participa tion of the believer in the crucifixion of the Redeemer, all the more that before the event Jesus could not have ex pressed Himself in such language.[1] Once more, the incident of the two sons of Zebedee teems with Pauline allusions. Every word of Jesus on that memorable occasion recalls a Pauline utterance. "To sit on my right hand and on my left hand is not mine to give," echoes Paul's doctrine of election; "Whosoever of you will be the chiefest shall be servant of all," is a reminiscence of Paul's statement con cerning himself that though free from all men yet he had made himself servant unto all. And the great word con cerning the Son of man coming not to be ministered unto but to minister, and to give His life a ransom for many, corresponds so closely to Pauline expressions concerning the self-impoverishment, self-emptying, and self-humiliation of the heavenly Christ, that the co-operation at least of Pauline influence in the formation of the saying may legitimately be suspected.[2]

These instances suffice to exemplify the method of proof. Suppose we allow almost all that is contended for, and in doing so we should be going beyond the limits of truth, what does it amount to ? To this, that there are corre-spondences between the teaching of Jesus, as reported by the evangelists, and the teaching of Paul. But was not such correspondence intrinsically probable ? Was it not to be expected that men like Jesus and Paul should think alike on the great fundamental truths of religion, such as the vital significance of faith, the necessity of self-denial, and the connection between moral greatness and the humility of love ? Such truths are the great commonplaces of biblical religion, held and taught with one consent by all inspired men whose thoughts are preserved in the Scrip tures, and agreement in them is no proof of dependence of one upon another. And if in the cases of Jesus, as

[1] *Urchristenthum,* p. 384.   [2] *Ibid.* p. 395.

reported, and Paul, there be in some instances reason to suspect dependence, the question is always open, On which side is it? Is the evangelist's report of Christ's teaching coloured by Paulinism, or does Paul's teaching now and then betray traces of the influence of an acquaintance more or less extensive with the sayings of Jesus? The possibility of the former alternative is not denied, all that is here suggested is that a mere general correspondence does not settle the question either way.

It may be added that in none of the cases above cited is there the slightest ground for alleging Pauline influence, nor would any one that had not a theory to defend ever imagine that there was. Every one of the sayings possesses intrinsic probability as an utterance of Christ, not even excepting that concerning cross-bearing as the law of discipleship. Death by crucifixion did not begin with the case of Jesus. He had heard of it, possibly He had seen it before; He knew it to be the most ignominious, painful, and repulsive form in which to encounter the last enemy, and even though He had not been aware that He was to meet His own end in that way, He might have spoken as He did by way of expressing the general thought that the faithful disciple was he who, for truth's sake, was willing to endure a felon's fate.

The foregoing observations have their full force in reference to the so-called "Hymn of Victory": "I thank Thee, O Father." The genuineness of this utterance might be supposed to be sufficiently guaranteed by its being common to Matthew and Luke, and therefore presumably taken from the apostolic book of *Logia*. But not to insist on this, I simply dispute the conclusiveness of the proof that it is a free composition of the Pauline evangelists based on characteristic utterances of the apostle of the Gentiles, and on the signal success of his career. The affinity between this great word of Jesus and the teaching of Paul is fully admitted; it might be even more strongly asserted. It might be pointed out, for example, that from that word we may learn the nature of the spirit of adoption of which

Paul speaks, the characteristic marks of a true filial relation to God. Jesus the Son in the hour of trial unbosoms Himself to His Father, and in doing so reveals a spirit of submission, trust, and peaceful fellowship towards God, and of independence towards the world, perfected in His own case, and capable of being imparted to those who follow Him as their Master. The whole utterance is thoroughly in sympathy with Paul's teaching in Romans viii., but it is not Pauline in the sense of being a composition put into Christ's mouth by an evangelist whose mind was steeped in Pauline doctrine. It is, on the contrary, according to all indications, a true saying of the Lord Jesus. It is in keeping with all we know of His mind, and it perfectly suits the situation.

Jesus always spoke of God as Father, and of Himself as Son. He acted uniformly on the belief that disciples and citizens of the kingdom were to be got rather from among the ignorant, despised people of the land, than from among the men of the law. He always had faith in His own future, and believed that God's kingdom would come bringing a crown to His head. And He ever promised to His faithful ones participation in His own great fortunes: crowns, thrones, kingdoms, a full unstinted share in the privilege of sonship. As for the situation, it is probably more correctly indicated in Matthew than in Luke. In the former Gospel the word is represented by implication as spoken in an hour of trial, when Jesus is made very conscious of the contemptuous unbelief of the influential in Israel; in the latter, on the other hand, it appears as spoken in an hour of joy, viz. on the return of the seventy with their glowing reports of the signal success of their mission. The setting of the word in Luke, and the mission of the seventy, or at least the prominence given thereto, may be regarded as indications of the Paulinism of the third evangelist, who, while faithful in reporting Christ's sayings, seems to have exercised discretion to a certain extent in fixing their historical occasions. The devotional utterance of Jesus, while not unsuitable for a season of joy, is peculiarly suited to a time of trial, when the unbelief of the world makes Him fall back on the consolations of His per-

sonal relations to God, and provokes the assertion of His
importance as Mediator, and of His entire independence of
the patronage and favour of men priding themselves on
their wisdom.

The unceremonious manner in which so very important
a saying is taken away from Jesus and credited to the
evangelist, compels us to consider on what principles
criticism, not bent on proving a theory as to the course of
early Church history, is to proceed in deciding questions of
genuineness.   Now, one very obvious principle would seem
to be that it is to be presumed that an evangelist will not
lightly depart from his professed design in writing a
Gospel.   The good faith of the evangelists is now happily
admitted on all hands.   There is, and there is room for,
difference of opinion as to what is compatible with good
faith and good conscience.   That may vary according to the
custom of the time in which an author lives.   But if any
New Testament writer plainly intimates his intention to
proceed upon a plan, it may be taken for granted that he
will faithfully adhere to it to the best of his knowledge and
judgment.   Applying this remark to the synoptical evan
gelists, we find that Matthew and Mark do not admit us
into their secret, though their whole manner is that of men
stating what they believe to be facts.   Luke, however,
does, in his preface, take the reader into his confidence, and
carefully explains to him his aim and method as an author.
Without straining his words, we are entitled to infer from
that preface that Luke is going to tell us what can be
ascertained, from written sources or otherwise, concerning
the words and deeds of Jesus.   He alludes to the work of
predecessors as a help in his task, he refers to the twelve
as the original source of information, and he indicates it as
his desire to enable his readers to attain certain knowledge
in the matters of which he writes.   All this surely reveals
a purpose to write, as far as possible, history.

This is a most important conclusion, which carries much
along with it.

In the first place, it covers as with a shield the historicity of *Mark*. That Mark was one of Luke's sources is generally admitted by critics.[1] It is a point, indeed, on which any one can easily satisfy himself, for it requires only an attentive perusal of the two Gospels to perceive that Luke has reproduced in his pages the substance of Mark, and often in the same order. It follows from this that Luke regarded Mark as a good source, good in the sense of being a reliable report of the apostolic tradition, a faithful record of what had been learned from the eye witnesses and ministers of the word.

But the conclusion drawn from Luke's preface covers more than that portion of his Gospel which is identical with Mark. It covers also that which is over and above, the large amount of material, chiefly consisting of say ings of Jesus, found in Luke's pages, to which there is nothing corresponding in the Second Gospel, or even in the First. Luke's prefatory statement entitles us to hold that he had sources for these sayings, as well as for the deeds for which Mark was his chief voucher, and that he believed them to be true words of the Lord. In view of that statement, to say that the greater part of the material in Luke's Gospel, in excess of Mark, has no distinct his torical source, but is to be ascribed to the literary art of the author, is to trifle with his good name, and to magnify his intellect at the expense of his conscience. If we are to take the evangelist seriously, we must hold that he had a source for the "Hymn of Victory," and for the many beautiful words, such as the parable of the Prodigal Son, found only in his Gospel, as well as for the parable of the Sower, or for the feeding of the five thousand.

Luke's shield is broad enough to cover even the head of Matthew. When we can control the first evangelist, as in

---

[1] Pfleiderer, *Urchristenthum*, p. 416, says : That Mark was one of Luke's forerunners, whom he wished to surpass in completeness and orderly arrangement is certain, and is hardly doubted now by any one. The narrative and order of Mark form the groundwork and frame into which Luke interpolates his additional material. .

all matter common to him with Mark and Luke, or with Luke alone, we find that he gives substantially the same account. In these portions of his Gospel he obviously means to write history. He is not romancing or writing fiction for a purpose. This being the character he has earned when in company, he is entitled to the benefit of it when he is alone. Like Luke, he is sometimes alone, as in the gracious invitation, " Come unto me "; in the *logion* concerning the Church, " On this rock "; and in the repre sentation of the last judgment. We must refuse to believe that these are compositions of the evangelist, simply because when we have the means of testing him we find that he is not a man given to inventing, but to simple, honest, matter-of-fact narration.[1]

Yet, withal, it must be admitted that neither Matthew nor any of his brother evangelists is a mere chronicler. For the writers of the Gospels the religious interest is supreme. Their temper is that of the prophet rather than that of the scribe. They are truly inspired men, and as such their main concern is not to give scrupulously exact accounts of facts, but to make the moral and religious significance of the facts apparent. Hence a considerable amount of freedom in reporting may be noted even in Luke, who by his preface seems to lay himself under obligation to aim at exactitude in narration. It is not to be supposed that in execution he forgets, or is untrue to, his preconceived plan. We ought rather to regard it as part of his plan to relate the facts of Christ's ministry so that they shall be a true mirror to the spirit of Christ, and give readers a just and beneficent conception of His character.

---

[1] The *gracious invitation*, according to Pfleiderer, is a composition of the evangelist's, based on a passage in the *Wisdom of Sirach* (ii. 23); the *logion*, "On this rock," is simply the expression of the Catholic Church consciousness as it took shape about the middle of the second century; the judgment programme, in Matt. xxv., is a beautiful witness to the ethical humane way of thinking of the evangelist and of the age in which he lived, according to which the lack of Christian faith in the heathen is com pensated by Christlike love, and the dogmatic universalism of Paul is replaced by an ethical universalism. *Vide Urchristenthum*, pp. 513, 520, 532.

Hence omissions of narratives contained in his sources, which might be misunderstood, such as the story of the Syrophenician woman reported by Mark; also of duplicate narratives which might be regarded as superfluous, such as the second feeding of the multitude, also reported by Mark, to make room for new matter of a pronouncedly evangelic type, acts and words of grace, which to the evangelist appeared most characteristic of Jesus. Hence the toning down of the severer aspect of Christ's teaching, and especially a great reduction in the amount of the anti-Pharisaical element, as compared with Matthew. Hence, once more, a distinct colouring in the reports of Christ's sayings, so as to make the gracious evangelic drift of His doctrine more conspicuous.[1]

Such phenomena of the adaptation of facts to the service of mirroring the spirit, suggest the question, How far might this process be carried? Can we, for example, conceive of an evangelist stepping out of the actual into the possible, in order that he might have ampler scope for the embodiment of his conception of Jesus than the grudging data of reality supplied, especially in the case of a life of so short duration? With writings adopting this method of setting forth ideal truth we are very familiar in modern times, and it has been consecrated to the service of religion by

---

[1] On these phenomena of Luke's Gospel, *vide* introduction to my work, *The Kingdom of God.* In that introduction, as in the above remarks, it is assumed that the variations in Luke's reports of our Lord's words, as compared with Matthew's, are due to the religious idiosyncrasy of the writer, and his care for the edification of his readers. It has recently been attempted to explain many of the phenomena of variation by the hypothesis of an Aramaic source, in which many of the words were ambiguous and could be taken in different senses by persons consulting the source. *Vide* Professor Marshall's articles in *The Expositor*, 1891. This may solve some of the problems, but by no means all. Luke's variations have a common character. This could not be the result of accident; it brings in the element of *preference*, either in Luke or in the traditional reading he followed, or in both. The view given in the text further implies the secondary character of Luke's reports as compared with Matthew's. Pfleiderer labours to establish the contrary view, but he overlooks many of the facts bearing on the question. *Vide Das Urchristenthum*, pp. 478-543.

some well-known classics. Ancient literature likewise supplies some instances, such as the Dialogues of Plato, wherein is exhibited an ideal picture of Socrates, and the book of Job in the Hebrew canon. *A priori* it is not inconceivable that the method might be applied to Jesus. A disciple might say to himself: I desire to show my beloved Master as He appeared to me, and for this purpose I shall not only report what I saw Him do and heard Him say, but also indicate what He would have done and said in circumstances which might have occurred, but did not actually occur. Viewing the matter in the abstract, we are not perhaps entitled to negative dogmatically as inadmissible such use of ideal situations for evangelic pur poses. One thing we are entitled to insist on is that whatever method an evangelist employs for his purpose, he shall be faithful to the spirit. The only justification for the introduction of ideal elements would be that they enabled one holding up the mirror to Jesus to show His character more adequately on all possible sides. And in no case would inspiration be more needful than to enable an evangelist to use the ideal method wisely, so as to be absolutely faithful to the mind and spirit of Him whom he undertook to portray.

It is well known that in the judgment of some we have an actual instance of this method applied to the life of our Lord in the case of the *Fourth Gospel.* That view will fall to be considered hereafter. Meantime we have to inquire whether there be any reason for thinking that the synoptical evangelists, all or any of them, have used the ideal method to any extent.

As already indicated, it is not a question as to the legi- timacy of the method, but of the actual intention of any of the evangelists to use it. Now, viewing the matter in that light, it must be admitted that there is no trace of any such intention in the first three Gospels. The evidence all points in the opposite direction. The problem the synoptists set themselves was not: given a clear insight into the spirit of

Jesus to show it to others by a free use of incidents real or ideal, but given a sufficient collection of real facts so to set them in a continuous narrative that the thoughtful reader shall gradually attain a true insight into the spirit of Jesus. Their narratives are in their intention objectively historical; if any legendary element has found its way into their pages it is to be regarded as a tradition, not as an invention. This is the view naturally suggested by Luke's preface, and borne out by the whole character of these three Gospels.

There is one instance in Luke in which it might with plausibility be alleged that the ideal method has been resorted to: the story of the anointing in the house of Simon the Pharisee. This, it may be said, it has indeed often been said, is simply Luke's version of the story of Mary of Bethany related by Mark, so altered as to make it serve the purpose of showing in a signal instance the grace of Jesus towards the sinful, in all its touching tenderness and magical transforming power. And without doubt the serviceableness of the incident to this end constituted its attraction for Luke, and supplied the motive for its being introduced into his narrative. And equally without doubt the story as he gives it, whether a real or an ideal occurrence, is thoroughly true to the spirit of Jesus. Nothing was more characteristic of Jesus than His gentle, delicate sympathy with the disreputably sinful. If such a thing did happen as a fallen impure woman coming into a house where He sat at meat, and acting as she is reported to have done amid the frowns of Pharisaic guests, it may be taken for certain that He behaved towards her and spoke of her as Luke represented. And that primitive disciples, knowing the Master's way with sinners well, and valuing it duly, might in absence of a good illustrative instance invent one, or at least adapt an actual occurrence to the purpose, is not unimaginable. Only in that case we should have to regard Luke, in view of his preface, as the reporter of a congenial tradition, rather than as the inventor of a beautiful tale. But there are several things which are against the idea that the story is an invention either at first or at second hand. In the first place, the parable of the two debtors is an original element. There is nothing corresponding to it, or that might suggest it, in the story of the anointing in Bethany. Then the moral of that parable is equally original. It accredits itself as a saying of Jesus by its audacity and its liability to be misunderstood. The sentiment virtually taught is : " the greater the sinner the greater the saint." Who could invent such a bold thought, and put it into the mouth of the Master ? The average disciple would be more likely to shrink from it, with the result of its falling entirely out of the evangelic tradition. Then, finally, this sentiment has to be looked at in connec tion with others said to have been spoken by Jesus in defence of His bearing towards the disreputably sinful, as forming together with them His apology for an innovating love that treated with contempt conventional distinctions between man and man. That Jesus was assailed on this account is as certain as anything we know about Him ; that He would be ready with His answer may be taken for granted, and what better, more felicitous, more Jesus- like answers can be imagined than those ascribed to Him : The whole need not a physician ; he loves much who has sinned and been forgiven much ; there is a unique joy in finding things lost ? With all respect for the evangelists, I do not think they could invent anything so good as that. Therein Jesus was decidedly " over the heads of His reporters."

The section in Matthew's Gospel which most wears the aspect of an ideal history is that containing the great commission of the risen Christ to His disciples.[1] For critics who assume that the miraculous is impossible, the mere fact that this commission is represented as emanating from the risen Christ stamps it of course as unhistorical. But leaving that fact out of view, the terms in which the

[1] Chap. xxviii. 16-20.

commission is expressed are such as to arrest the attention even of believing students of the evangelic records. One notes therein the injunction to administer to disciples the rite of baptism nowhere else referred to in the Gospels, the full-blown universalism,[1] the Trinitarian formula,[2] and the promise of a perpetual spiritual presence ;[3] all more or less suggestive of a later time, and apparently expressive of the developed Christian consciousness of the Catholic Church, rather than of what was likely to proceed from the mouth of Jesus before He finally left the world.

Two ways of meeting the difficulty have been suggested. One is to regard the last three verses of the Gospel as an addition by a later hand, corresponding somewhat to the Appendix to Mark's Gospel,[4] and, like it, rounding off and worthily ending a narrative which, without the addendum, would have a very abrupt close.[5] This solution, however, is purely conjectural, without fact-basis in textual criticism.[6] The other mode of dealing with the question is to regard the words put into the mouth of Jesus as, in the intention of the evangelist, not a report of what the risen Jesus said to His disciples at a given time and place, but rather as a summary of what the Apostolic Church understood to be the will of the exalted Lord. On this view the commission to the eleven is not what Jesus said to them on a hill in Galilee, but what He spake to them in spirit from His heavenly throne. For this way of construing the passage

---

[1] Ver. 19, "Teach, make disciples of, all the nations."

[2] "Baptizing them in the name of the Father and the Son and the Holy Ghost."

[3] Ver. 20. "And, lo, I am with you always, even unto the end of the world."

[4] Mark xvi. 9-20.

[5] Mark's narrative closes with, "Neither said they anything to any man ; for they were afraid" ($\dot{\epsilon}\phi o\beta o\hat{v}\nu\tau o\ \gamma\acute{a}\rho$) ; Matthew's ex hypothesi would close with, "When they saw Him, they worshipped Him ; but some doubted" ($o\grave{\iota}\ o\grave{\iota}$ $\grave{\epsilon}\delta\acute{\iota}\sigma\tau a\sigma a\nu$).

[6] As is well known, Mark xvi. 9-20 is omitted in the most important MSS., such as א, B. Nothing corresponding to this occurs in connection with Matt. xxviii. 18-20.

there seems to be some justification in the introductory
words, wherein the speaker describes Himself as one having
all power in heaven and on earth. It is the style of one
no longer walking on the earth, but sharing in heaven the
world-wide power and providence of God.[1]

On this hypothesis the great commission is really an
idealised utterance of the Lord Jesus, and the only question
is, Is it faithful to His teaching? We cannot hesitate to
answer this question in the affirmative. A man of genius
characterising a preacher of a bygone generation said, His
meaning comes out in the sentence after the last. Apply
ing this to the subject in hand, we may say that the com
mission to the apostles is the sentence after the last in
relation to Christ's recorded utterances during the period of
His public ministry. The records do not indeed contain
any words relating to baptism, but it is not likely that the
custom of baptizing converts would ever have arisen unless
there had been some sanction for it in the apostolic tradition
of the teaching of the Master.[2] For all the other features
vouchers can easily be produced. The universalism of the
commission does not go much beyond the word concerning
the preaching of the gospel in the whole world spoken on
the occasion of the anointing in Bethany.[3] The Trinitarian
formula simply sums up in a single phrase the theology of
Jesus. He ever spake of God as Father, He called Himself God's Son, and in the few utterances concerning
the Holy Ghost recorded in the Synoptical Gospels He
represents Him as God communicating Himself in His
grace to receptive souls, the *summum bonum*. The Christian
faith in Christ's recorded teaching, as in the baptismal
formula, is faith in a Divine Father who sent Jesus His
Son into the world on a gracious errand, and who bestows
the spirit of light and purity on those who believe in the

---

[1] The above is the view adopted by Weiss. *Vide Das Matthaus-Evan-
gelium*, pp. 582 584.

[2] *Vide* on this point my work on *The Kingdom of God*, p. 257.

[3] Mark xiv. 9.

Father and the Son.[1] Finally, the promise of a perpetual
spiritual presence is but a legitimate development out of
germs contained in Christ's authentic sayings. A *spiritual*
presence, as distinct from an eschatological *parousia*, is not
unknown to the primitive tradition. It is found in the
words, "Where two or three are gathered together in my
name, there am I in the midst of them,"[2] whose authenticity
there is no good reason to doubt. Then the prolonged
Christian era implied in the promise, "Lo, I am with you
all the days," is, there is ground for believing, a real feature
of Christ's forecast of the future, as contrasted with that of
Paul and of the early Apostolic Church.[3] It was a feature
in which Jesus was "over the heads of His reporters," and
was not understood until events threw light on the signi
ficance of His sayings. The primitive Church slowly
learned that the world was to last longer than they at first
expected just by its lasting. The destruction of Jerusalem in
the year 70 A.D. did much to open their eyes. They had
thought that immediately after the tribulation of those
days the end would come and the Son of man arrive. The
end did not come, the world went on as if nothing had
happened. Then it began to dawn on them that many
days and years might pass before the final consummation
took place. The closing words of Matthew's Gospel reflect
this altered state of feeling. The fact is suggestive of a
date of composition subsequent to the great Jewish cata
strophe. The great apocalyptic discourse, as recorded in the
twenty-fourth chapter of the Gospel, on the other hand,
speaks for a date antecedent to the affliction of Israel, the
"end" being there connected more closely with the affliction
than was likely to be done by one writing *post eventum.*
The seeming discrepancy is one of the things that might be
adduced in support of the hypothesis that the great com
mission is an addition by a later hand.

---

[1] *Vide The Kingdom of God*, p. 258.
[2] Matt. xviii. 20.
[3] *Vide The Kingdom of God*, chap. xii.

The result of the whole foregoing inquiry is to confirm the first impression as to the historicity of the Synoptical Gospels, which, in the first chapter of this book, the student was encouraged to trust, in seeking through them to attain to a true knowledge of Jesus. The evangelists have told a story reliable in all its main features, which we may read with minds undisturbed by the confident assertions of critics bent on verifying adventurous theories.

CHAPTER IX.

THE FOURTH GOSPEL.

LITERATURE.—Sanday, *The Authorship and Historical Character of the Fourth Gospel*, 1872, *The Gospels in the Second Century*, 1876, Articles on the Present Position of the Johannean Question in *Expositor*, 1891–2 ; Salmon, *Introduc tion to the New Testament :* Westcott, *The Gospel according to St. John* (Introduction); Reynolds, "Introduction to John's Gospel" in *Pulpit Commentary ;* Reuss, *La Bible, Nouveau Testament,* 6me partie, *La Theologie Johannique ; The Fourth Gospel* (E. Abbott, A. P. Peabody, J. B. Lightfoot), 1892 ; Watkins, *Modern Criticism and the Fourth Gospel* (Bampton Lectures, 1890) ; Gloag, *Introduction to the Johannine Writ ings ·* Wendt, *Die Lehre Jesu* (two parts, of which second translated and published under the title *The Teaching of Jesus*) · Oscar Holtzmann, *Das Johannes-Evangelium unter- sucht und erklärt,* 1887 ; Weizsäcker, *Das Apostolische Zeitalter* , Paul Ewald, *Das Hauptproblem der Evangelien- frage* 1890. *Vide* also Articles in the *Contemporary Review* for September and October 1891, by Schürer and Sanday.

The Fourth Gospel presents the hardest apologetic pro blem connected with the origin of Christianity. The stress of the problem does not lie on the question as to Johannine authorship. A question of that kind can in no case be vital to the Christian faith. Questions as to the authorship of particular biblical books are questions of fact, not of faith. They may in some cases be very important to faith,

but hardly ever essential. In_the_present_ instance it is in
a_high degree the interest of faith to assert its independence
as far as _possible of_ the question of authenticity. For
while the doctrinal significance of the book is great, its
claim to have been written by the Apostle John does not
rise above a high degree of probability. And the faculty
of estimating the grounds on which the claim rests is
not at the command of all believers in any considerable
measure. It varies in different men, not only with theo
logical bias, but with knowledge, temperament, and the
power of historical imagination. Hence the most diverse
conclusions are arrived at from the same premises. Some
are confident that the Apostle John did not write the Gospel
which bears his name, others regard it as beyond all doubt
that he did, others again know not what to think, and
incline alternately now to this side and then to that ; some
think he wrote a part of the Gospel, a *Grundschrift*, while
others believe that he rather inspired the man who wrote
the Gospel than wrote it himself in part or in whole.
Possibly the question may never get beyond this unsatis
factory condition ; possibly it may be settled conclusively
by the discovery of some lost book such as the *Exposition
of the Oracles of the Lord*, by Papias. Meantime, pending
such happy discoveries, men will continue to form conflict
ing judgments according to their intellectual and religious
idiosyncrasies.[1]

The_really vital question is, Have we two_incompatible
Christs_in these evangelic memoirs, all professedly or appar
ently historic : one Christ_in the three synoptists, another in
the Fourth Gospel _by whomsoever written ? Have we here
not merely different material showing the same person per
forming new actions and uttering new sayings, but material
conveying a different general impression not reconcilable with
that made by the reports of brother evangelists ? That there

---

[1] Reuss says that for a long time to come the question of the origin of the
Fourth Gospel will be decided for most students by personal disposition.
Vide La Bible, 6me partie, p. 102.

should be a considerable amount of valuable material relating
to the public ministry of Jesus lying outside the limits of the
synoptical record, is nowise improbable. It is quite conceiv
able that our Synoptical Gospels represent a very one-sided
tradition, that they are not even the main stream, but only
a tributary of the broad river of evangelic story, and that
the stereotyping of this fragmentary representation as if it
were the whole, in those parts of the Apostolic Church in
which the three first Gospels arose, was due to the prestige
belonging to certain sources used in their construction ;
bearing apostolic names, therefore justly valued as docu
ments of first-class importance, yet actually far from com
plete as records of Christ's words and deeds. Matthew's
Logia, and Peter's reminiscences taken down by Mark,
neither pretending to be exhaustive, might thus together
become the innocent cause of an impoverished partial
evangelic tradition being taken for the whole, so making it
necessary that one who knew that there was much more of
not less value to relate should write such a book as the
Fourth Gospel.[1] But what if it should be found on inspec
tion that this supplementary Gospel was really not a
supplement but a substitute, a heterogeneous presentation
of a great Personage, bearing the same name, but exhibiting
a spirit, character, and claim foreign to the Jesus of Matthew,
Mark, and Luke ? In that case it would be difficult to
believe that one of the men who had been with Jesus wrote
the book. But that would be the smallest part of the per
plexity resulting. In the case supposed we should be
obliged to choose which of the two Christs we were to
believe in, that of the synoptists, or that of the Fourth Gospel.

The Church catholic has not felt itself to be placed in
any such painful predicament. It has found in the three
first Gospels on the one hand, and in the Fourth on the
other, views of Christ distinct, indeed, but not irreconcilable.
In the former it has recognised the picture of Jesus on I

---

[1] The above is substantially the view advocated by Dr. Paul Ewald in *Das
Hauptproblem der Evangalienfrage.*

human side, as the Son of man; in the latter the picture
of the same Jesus on the divine side, as the Son of God.
And it is the fact that in the Fourth Gospel the divine side
of Jesus is shown that has led many to regard the question
of its authorship as vital to faith. They wanted to be sure
that the doctrine of Christ's divinity rested on apostolic
authority, feeling that unless it was one of the men who
had been with Jesus that wrote the prologue, in which He
is called the Logos, His right to the title might rest on an
insecure foundation. One can fully respect this feeling,
and yet it is, to say the least, an exaggeration. Our accept.
ance of the high doctrine of the Logos must rest on the
inspiration of the evangelist, whoever he was, not on the
merely external fact of his being one of the twelve. The
doctrine of the Logos was no part of the personal teaching
of Christ. It does not belong to the evangelic history, but
to the philosophy or the theological construction of that
history. If it represent a true insight into the meaning of
Christ's history, it is an insight having its origin, not in
the witness of the physical eye or ear, but in a spiritual
illumination indispensable even to a John, and not unattain
able by any unknown disciple well instructed in the things
of the kingdom of heaven, though not privileged to be one
of the companions of the Lord. In this connection it is
important to remember what we have already had occasion
to note concerning the genesis of the faith of the first
disciples in Jesus as divine. That faith was not the result
of speculation, neither was it a direct revelation, either
from heaven or through the lips of Jesus unmediated by
religious experience. It was due rather to the impression
made on believing, loving hearts by the personal holiness,
the death, and the resurrection of Jesus.[1] Hence the
possibility of a fact which might otherwise seem surprising,
viz. that the highest views of Christ's person to be found in
the New Testament, outside the Fourth Gospel, are con
tained in the writings of men who had little or no first-

[1] *Vide* p. 400.

hand acquaintance with the teaching of Jesus, that is to say, in the Epistles of Paul and the Epistle to the Hebrews. The Christology of the proem to the latter book approaches very closely to that contained in the introduction to the Fourth Gospel, and its objective value to the Church depends not on any direct acquaintance of the author with what Jesus said or did,—for to that he expressly indicates he could lay no claim,[1]—but on the spiritual insight he possessed into the religious significance of Him through whom God had spoken His last word unto men.

The external evidence as to the Johannine authorship of the Fourth Gospel, on which experts pronounce such diverse judgments, cannot easily be summarised so as to put ordinary readers in a position to form an opinion of any value.[2] In view of the contradictions of men trained to estimate the worth of evidence, one may well distrust himself, and shrink from the task of arriving at even a juryman's judgment on the question at issue. One who feels himself incompetent to play the difficult part of a historical critic may reasonably take up the position of deferring to the patristic tradition, and to the opinion of such modern inquirers as think that the evidence for Johannine authorship amounts to little short of demonstra tion, though unable quite to rid himself of the uncomfort able haunting doubt that it is by no means so strong as sanguine reasoners assert.[3] The assumption of such an attitude is justified by the fact that as inquiry proceeds the question in debate is being steadily narrowed. The extreme views of the Tubingen school as to the late origin of the

---

[1] Heb. ii. 3. This text implies that the writer belonged to the generation which enjoyed the benefit of the preaching of the apostles. What the Lord had first spoken, he and his contemporaries had confirmed unto them by those that heard Him.

[2] For statements of the external evidence readers are referred to books dealing expressly with the subject. Sanday's *Gospels in the Second Century* (1876) and Watkin's *Bampton Lectures for* 1890 may be specially mentioned.

[3] Dr. Sanday, writing in *The Expositor* for December 1891, on the external evidence, says: "It can hardly prove that the Fourth Gospel was written by John in a strict sense of the word 'prove.'"

Gospel are now virtually antiquated, though still finding representatives in such writers as Pfleiderer and Martineau. By various lines of evidence the date has been steadily pushed back to a time which brings apostolic authorship within the range of possibility. The alternatives now may be said to lie between the Apostle John and a disciple of the apostle, belonging to the Ephesian school, acquainted with the traditions of his teaching and under his inspiring influence. The difference between these two hypotheses in the view of some is still serious, while to others it appears trivial ; but it is beyond all question that the theory of Johannine *inspiration,* as distinct from authorship, advocated by such a weighty writer as Weizsäcker, can be regarded with equanimity by even the most conservative, in comparison with a theory which relegates the Gospel to the middle of the second century, remote from apostolic influence, and regards it as the product of new religious tendencies and the child of an alien world.[1]

But, granting Johannine authorship, or, at least, inspiration, the problem of the Fourth Gospel is by no means solved, nor is the mind of the perplexed inquirer therewith set at rest. Rather the serious difficulty then begins. For the question comes to be, How is it possible that a Gospel so different in character from the first three Gospels, on good grounds regarded as substantially true to historic reality, could emanate directly or indirectly from the mind of one of the men who had been with Jesus ? Till this has been seen to be psychologically credible no rest to the doubter, or signal profit to the reader, is possible. It matters not what the amount of external evidence for Johannine authorship may be. Suppose it reached the certainty of mathematical demonstration, and not merely a fair degree of probability, it would do no more than compel

---

[1] In the article previously referred to Dr. Sanday says : " I am less sure that the conditions might not be sufficiently satisfied if the author were a disciple of John. There would then be no greater difficulty in accounting for the transference of his name to it than there is in accounting for the like transference in the case of St. Matthew."

sullen silence so long as the mind remained unconvinced of the inner harmony between the Fourth Gospel and the other three. And when I speak of external evidence in this connection, I have in view not merely such testimonies as can be gathered from the writings of the early fathers, such as Irenæus, Justin Martyr, and Hippolytus, but also all particulars that can be gathered from the book itself, not entering into the substance of its teaching, that point to, or are compatible with, Johannine authorship. For example, the numerous incidental references to places and customs, which show that the writer was a Jew intimately acquainted with the topography of Palestine and the manners of its people,[1] a fact obviously fitting into, if not proving, Johannine authorship. To the same category may be referred what may be called the external aspect even of some of the most characteristic didactic matter of the Gospel. Take, *e.g.*, the introductory section concerning the Logos. There are two questions that may be asked here. One is, Can the view of Christ embodied in the Logos-section be reconciled with the synoptical presentation of Christ's person ? the other is, Was it possible for one of the men who had been with Jesus to conceive of Him as the Logos, or rather could that conception arise *within the apostolic generation?* The former question belongs to the region of internal evidence, that, viz. which helps us to accept the Fourth Gospel as on the whole faithful to the historic personality of Jesus ; the latter comes under the category of external evidence, having for its aim to prove Johannine or apostolic authorship. Now, with reference to the external aspect of the Logos idea, it may be argued with much force that its appearance in the Fourth Gospel is perfectly compatible with the hypothesis that the Apostle John wrote it. Assuming that the idea originated with Philo, which, however, in the view of some is not a necessary assumption, there was plenty of time for it to

---

[1] For illustrations of this *vide* Bishop Lightfoot's contribution to *The Fourth Gospel, Evidence External and Internal of its Johannean Authorship*, 1892.

gain general currency, and to reach Ephesus, before the period at which the Gospel, according to the ancient tradi tion, was written, the last decade of the first century. And it is nowise incredible that a John, Jew though he was, might find the word useful as helping him to claim for the Lord Jesus a place in the Christian view of the universe analogous to that of the Logos in the Alexandrian philo- sophy.[1] Neither is it incredible that by the time the Gospel is reported to have been written, the Church's view of Christ's person had, even in the course of natural evolu tion, reached a point which made the new term needful and convenient. Think what a high view of Christ's position in the universe is expressed even in Paul's Epistles written in the fifth decade of the first century, not to speak of that set forth in the prologue of the Epistle to the Hebrews, whose date is disputed, but in all probability ought to be placed before the destruction of Jerusalem in the year 70.

Among the real or alleged phenomena of the Fourth Gospel there are others besides the presence in it of the Logos idea, which on due consideration the inquirer may be able to regard as not vital to the problem at issue. There is, for example, the free treatment of history ascribed to the writer by even the more circumspect of modern critics, who find in his narratives transparent allegories, theology disguised under a historical form.[2] It were unwise to affirm too dogmatically that such a "sovereign handling of the history"[3] is incompatible with Johannine authorship. As already stated,[4] it is *a priori* conceivable that one of the men who had been with Jesus might, to a greater or less extent, apply the ideal method to the biography of the Master. It is simply a question of what any particular evangelist intended to do. Now as to this we have no such explicit statement in the Fourth Gospel as is given in the prologue of the Third; our judgment as to the author's

---

[1] So Wendt, *Die Lehre Jesu*, Erster Theil, p. 310.

[2] So, *e.g.*, Weizsacker and Reuss.

[3] Harnack in *Dogmengeschichte*, i. 85.　　　[4] P. 460.

aim and plan must rest on an inspection of the contents. And there are some things that seem to indicate a purpose to keep in contact with the solid ground of fact, and not to move at will in the airy region of imagination. There is, e.g., the sober, lengthy narrative of the Passion, in the main a repetition of the synoptical story, while possessing its own special features. There is likewise the equally sober, briefer narrative of the feeding of the five thousand, again sub stantially a reproduction of the synoptical account. From the historical character of these sections of the Gospel, in which it is in company with the other three, it is natural to infer the historicity of other narratives in which it stands alone, as, e.g., in those relating to Nicodemus, the woman of Samaria, and the Greeks who would see Jesus.[1] Another circumstance cannot but strike the candid inquirer as curious. If the narratives, especially the miraculous nar ratives, be, as is alleged, allegories in disguise, how comes it that in the first sample of the kind, the story of the turn ing water into wine, the writer has not by a single word hinted at his method of teaching, and so furnished his readers with a key to the interpretation? That sober historical style at the end of the book, in the story of the crucifixion, and this quasi-historical style at the commence ment, which coolly invents facts as the vehicles of ideas and assumes that every one will understand what it is doing, taken together present a combination which, to say the least, is very odd and puzzling. The natural way of escape from perplexity is to assume that the writer intends to relate fact both at the beginning and at the end.

Yet, on the other hand, there are phenomena in this Gospel which seem plainly enough to indicate that through-

---

[1] Baur objects to this inference, in so far as the history of the Passion is concerned, on the ground that even in it the writer of the Fourth Gospel is influenced by a peculiar interest, the desire to illustrate the fundamental idea which dominates the whole book. He refers in proof to the manifest wish to excuse Pilate and throw all blame on the Jews, and to the section about blood and water which, he holds, cannot be history. *Vide Kritische Untersuchungen über die Kanonischen Evangelien*, p. 208.

out the narrative the predominant interest for the writer lies in the theological or spiritual import of the stories he tells. This is specially remarkable in connection with the incidents relating to Nicodemus, the woman of Samaria, and the Greeks who would see Jesus. In each of these cases the story is unfinished, the character is introduced to start a discourse of Jesus, and then allowed to drop out of sight. The evangelist seems to care nothing for what happened to the subordinate actors in the drama, and to be solely concerned about the words their brief appearance on the stage gave the principal actor occasion to speak. One may begin to wonder whether personages who are so summarily dismissed be indeed historic realities, and not merely dramatic creations designed to give a realistic setting to great thoughts of the Master. The incidents, however, possess intrinsic probability.

Another thing that may be regarded as compatible with Johannine authorship, and not vital to the apologetic problem, is free reporting of those very thoughts of Jesus about which there is reason to believe the writer of the Fourth Gospel was supremely concerned. That the words of our Lord have, as a matter of fact, been very freely reproduced in this Gospel is an opinion held by an increasing number of reverent and conservative scholars, who firmly believe in the Johannine authorship.[1] For those occupying this posi tion the question arises, How such free reproduction by one who had been with Jesus, an eye and ear witness of His personal ministry, is psychologically conceivable ? It is a question which they have doubtless for various reasons been tempted to shirk, but which some recent contributors to the discussion of the Johannine question have very fairly

---

[1] Westcott (*The Gospel according to St. John*, Introduction, p. lviii) admits that St. John has recorded the Lord's discourses with "freedom." Watkins (*Bampton Lectures*, p. 426) says, "The key to the Fourth Gospel lies in translation." Sanday (*The Authorship and Historical Character of the Fourth Gospel*, 1872) argues for a modification of Christ's words through the unconscious action of a strong intellect and personality. Still more decidedly in his recent articles in *The Expositor*.

and fully faced.[1] Various helpful lines of thought have been suggested. One, for example, lays stress on the free use of the *oratio directa* as not only sanctioned by the literary habit of the age,[2] but almost inevitable to one who, though writing in Greek, thought in Hebrew. In virtue of the peculiarity of the Hebrew tongue "that it has not developed what we call the indirect speech,"[3] it came to pass that a writer using that language, or having his mind dominated by its idiom, would be obliged to report the words of another as if he were giving the *ipsissima verba*, even when all he intended was to give their gist, effect, drift, or legitimate consequence. Under this method of writing, what seems a literal report might contain only the substance of what was said, or it might be impossible to tell where the words of the speaker ended, and where the comments of the reporter began. But obviously this theory will not account for all the phenomena. All the evangelists were Hebrews, but there are few who do not believe that the synoptical evangelists reproduce the words of Jesus with more exactness than the writer of the Fourth Gospel. Even in their reports, in those of Luke for example, critics think they can discover a certain measure of freedom in reporting, but with considerable unanimity they would say that in the Fourth Gospel a much larger measure of freedom is observable. The question thus arises, Whence this difference?

An explanation is naturally sought for in the circumstances and character of the writer. Stress may be laid on three things: age, intellectual and spiritual idiosyncrasy, and the religious environment. According to the patristic tradition, John wrote his Gospel at an advanced period of life, half a century or so after the time of his personal companionship with Jesus. No wonder, we are ready to say, if at

[1] Very specially Dr. Sanday in the articles referred to in previous note.

[2] *Vide* Gore, *The Incarnation of the Son of God* (Bampton Lectures, 1891). "The literary habit of the age allowed great freedom in the use of *oratio directa*," p. 71.

[3] Robertson, *The Early Religion of Israel*, p. 422.

so great a distance from the events the memory even of
Christ's never-to-be-forgotten words had grown dim, so as
to leave in the mind of the aged disciple only a general
though true impression, which in writing his Gospel he was
obliged to express in his own language, the exact words
employed by the Master being no longer at his command.
This suggestion, however, will not carry us very far, nor does
it seem as if we could justly lay much emphasis on lapse of
recollection, in view of the vividness and accuracy with
which in many cases the external situation of gospel in
cidents is reproduced down to the minutest detail. We
cannot but feel that one who could remember dates and
places, and even the very hour of the day at which parti
cular incidents occurred, could equally well recall words,
unless there were some other influence at work causing
them to disappear from consciousness. Such an influence
we may discover in the transmuting activity of the evangelist's mind acting upon the original data, the words of
the Lord Jesus. These were most liable to undergo trans
mutation. Dates, localities, festive seasons, journeys to
Jerusalem remain intractable to spiritual alchemy ; but
words provoke thought, they are seeds which develop into
trees ; and as the tree is potentially in the seed, so a devoted
disciple may feel that the whole system of thought, which
has grown up in his mind out of the germs of truth
deposited there by his Master may be, nay ought to be,
accredited to that Master. He may therefore deem it
quite unnecessary anxiously to distinguish between what
the Master actually said and what grew out of it. He
may even find it difficult or impossible to make the
distinction, the mental activity having been so long exer
cised, not in recollecting the *ipsissima verba* spoken by the
teacher, but in brooding meditation on their import. And
it is obvious that the stronger the mind of the pupil the
more likely this was to happen. The commonplace disciple
might be able many years after to recall almost exactly
what Jesus had spoken, just because in his case the seed

of truth had lain in his mind comparatively unfructified. But the disciple of original mind, mystic temper, and strong spiritual individuality might by comparison fail in recollec tion, just because he had been so prolific in reflection. In the one case the corn of wheat abode alone in its unim paired historic identity, because it had not fallen into a productive soil ; in the other it lost its separate existence and lived in the harvest of thought it had produced in a receptive spirit.

Environment also must count for something as a stimulus to the process of transmutation. The traditional seat of the evangelist when he wrote his Gospel was Ephesus. It was a great intellectual centre in which diverse religions and philosophic tendencies met, flowing in from all quarters, east, west, north, and south, Asia, Africa, Europe. Many minds were active there, many catch-words, such as the Logos, were current ; there was a Christian Church in the city full of its own peculiar life, yet not uninfluenced by its non-Christian surroundings, and obliged to reckon with the multifarious influences at work ; and the Apostle John, according to the tradition, was at its head, its ruler and spiritual guide. His position was one of great responsibility, and his ability, as one of the twelve to speak with authority about Jesus, would be the chief source of his power to meet the requirements of the situation. But the situation would also react upon him in his capacity as an evangelic witness. It might do so in two ways : First as a stimulus to that process of reflection on the words of Jesus already described, through which he gradually gained insight into the signifi cance of Christ's personal ministry ; next as creating a demand for a statement of the essential truths of the Christian faith in terms suited to present needs and modes of thinking. Under the former aspect its effect, in con junction with other causes, might be a process of mainly unconscious " translation " of Christ's teaching into a new dialect ; under the latter aspect it would act as a summons to a conscious deliberate adaptation of the Christian faith

to the religious demands of the hour. How far the modifi-
cations in the reports of our Lord's words in the Fourth
Gospel are spontaneous and unconscious, and how far
conscious and intentional, it may be impossible to deter
mine. But we may certainly see in the prologue an instance
of the evangelist deliberately setting himself to define the
attitude and claims of Christianity in reference to current
systems of religious philosophy aspiring to domination over
the minds of men. "They talk grandly of the Logos," says
the evangelist in effect, "let all earnest souls in quest of
truth find in Jesus the Logos they seek."

If we can conceive it possible for one of the men who
had been with Jesus to report his Master's words with such
freedom as is implied in the substitution of the developed fruit
for the original historic seed-corn, we shall find no difficulty
in regarding as a possible feature of his Gospel a certain
disregard of time or of the law of progress in his narrative
of the incidents connected with the personal ministry,
exemplified by the Baptist calling Jesus at the very be
ginning " the Lamb of God who taketh away the sin of the
world," and by the first disciples recognising in Jesus at the
outset the Christ, of whom Moses in the law, and the pro
phets did write, the Son of God, the King of Israel. The
alleged "foreshortening," or "anticipation," has been ascribed
partly to defect of memory, partly to the very activity and
strength of the evangelist's mind.[1]   Possibly it were better
to trace it to the action of a mystic temperament prone to
disregard distinctions of time, and to be indfferent to the
progress of historic development. A mind of this type
lives in the eternal, and sees all things *sub specie æternitatis*.
Eternal life, not a thing of the future, but a present good,
is the *summum bonum* brought to the world by Jesus, as
presented in the Fourth Gospel, and every topic treated of

---

[1] Sanday, article in *The Expositor*, January 1892, pp. 23, 24. The state
ment given in the foregoing part of this paragraph is little more than a free
reproduction of Dr. Sanday's views as contained in various passages in his
recent articles. *Vide* especially *The Expositor* for May 1892, p. 390.

is appropriately contemplated from the eternal point of
view.   The whole earthly life of Jesus is an episode in the
eternal life of the Logos.   Why carefully distinguish between now and then, to-day and to-morrow, in the details
of a life which as a whole is dominated by the category of
the eternal ?

After this lengthy statement it may be well to indicate
distinctly the relation in which an apologist stands to the
critical questions referred to.   He is not called on to
pronounce dogmatically on these questions, and to say
whether and to what extent free reporting of evangelic
incidents and speeches, and dislocation of historic order, are
actual characteristics of the Fourth Gospel.   It is enough
for him that a large and increasing number of experts say
that they are, to an extent greatly exceeding the measure
in which they are traceable in the Synoptical Gospels.
The question which concerns him is how far the alleged
phenomena affect the religious value of the Fourth Gospel
as a source for the knowledge of Christ.   The view here
contended for is, that they are not so vital as at first sight
they may seem.   The efforts of recent scholars go far to
prove that they are compatible with apostolic, that is to
say, with Johannean authorship.   But if an apostle wrote
the Gospel, then we can feel tolerably sure that with what
ever freedom the acts and words of Jesus have been
reproduced, the total effect of the picture is truth ; the
mirror held up to Him faithfully reflects His lineaments and
spirit.   We can be sure, for example, that whatever were
the actual words spoken by Jesus at the well of Sychar,
the discourse on the true worship put into His mouth, is in
the spirit of universalism which it breathes, a thoroughly
reliable representation of His real religious attitude.   If it
were not so, it would be seriously misleading, and further, it
could not be apostolic in its source.   If, on the other hand,
it be so, then we can not only regard the discourse as in
its general drift true to the spirit of Jesus, but for all
practical purposes of Christian instruction use it as through-

out an exact report of Christ's words, disregarding scruples arising out of critical considerations.[1]

But now at last we come to the heart of the question. Can we say that this Gospel as a whole, in its general drift and tendency, is indeed true to the spirit of Jesus, as we have become acquainted with it by aid of the first three Gospels ?

A striking phrase in the prologue awakens expectation. "Full of grace and truth":[2] the words create the hope that we are about to have the choice theme they suggest amply illustrated, and to be shown the glory of Jesus as the Friend of the sinful, and the Teacher of a rich varied system of moral and religious truth. Especially do we look for an exhibition of that side of Christ's character which earned for Him the honourable nickname of the Friend of publicans and sinners, all the more that the evangelist makes it evident by the repetition of the word "grace" how fully alive he is to the fact that beneficent benignant love occupied a prominent place in the public ministry of Jesus. "Of His fulness," he adds, "have all we received, and *grace for grace.*" Then, as if to apologise for the stress laid on that boon, as if it were the gift for which above all others Christians were indebted to their Lord, he goes on to point out that that which made the coming of Jesus Christ into the world an epoch-making event, worthy to form the commencement of a new era, was precisely that thereby grace and truth, as distinct from the law given by Moses, received a worthy satisfying realisation. But on reading further we gradually discover that

---

[1] May we regard John xvi. 12–14 as covering the principle that whatever the illuminating Spirit taught a disciple to see in the words of Jesus was a word of Jesus ? In favour of this is that in this Gospel the Holy Spirit is the *alter ego* of Jesus, John xiv. 16, 18. As with Paul, the Spirit is the Lord. If this interpretation be correct, then we have in the passage positive proof that the evangelist would not think it necessary to distinguish between the exact words of Jesus and what they had grown into in his mind, but might give all as a discourse of the Master.

[2] John i. 14.

to illustrate the theme, Jesus full of grace, cannot have been a leading aim of the evangelist. One would rather say that he regards it as a commonplace not needing illus tration for readers who are supposed to be persons who have already received an abundant supply of Christ's grace, as an object both of knowledge and of experience. For, in point of fact, there is in the Fourth Gospel very little of that sort of material which constitutes the specialty and glory of the synoptical histories, and justifies the claim of the gospel they contain to be called the gospel of pardon and hope for the sinful. There are no stories like those of Matthew's feast, the woman in the house of Simon the Pharisee, and Zacchæus the publican, illustrating Christ's tender sympathetic interest in the moral outcasts of Jewish society ; no apologies for loving reprobates like *the whole need not a physician, much forgiven much love, the joy of joys is to find things lost.* The nearest approach to these synoptical features may be found in the narratives of the woman of Samaria, and of the woman taken in adultery. But in neither case is the lesson directly taught the gracious attitude of Jesus towards the erring. From both one can learn by inference that the Jesus of the Fourth Gospel is the same Jesus of whom Pharisees complained : This man receiveth sinners, and eateth with them. But that is not the moral which the author of that Gospel, in these stories, makes it his business to inculcate. His lead ing motive in introducing the narrative of the Samaritan woman is to report the discourse of Jesus on the true worship, and in that of the woman taken in adultery it seems to be to show the desire of the Pharisees to bring Jesus into bad relations with the legal authorities. The mildness of Jesus towards the offender is a subordinate point.[1] The difference between the synoptical presentation and that of the Fourth Gospel is very apparent when we compare two narratives in other respects similar: the

---

[1] The genuineness of the *pericope adulteræ* is extremely doubtful, but of that we need not here take account.

healing of the palsied man on the one hand,[1] and the healing of the man who had an infirmity thirty and eight years on the other.[2] In the one we hear Jesus utter the character istic word of encouragement and sympathy, "Courage, child, thy sins be forgiven thee." In the other there is at first no word of sin or forgiveness, but only of a physical miracle which, being wrought on the Sabbath day, provoked the hostile comments of the Jews; and when afterwards sin is spoken of at a subsequent meeting between Jesus and the healed one, it is in a severe minatory manner.[3]

The fair conclusion from all these facts seems to be, that while the grace of Jesus Christ, in the sense of redeeming sympathy with the sinful, and its cardinal importance in the Christian faith, is fully recognised in this Gospel, it did not enter into the plan of the writer to enlarge upon it. One reason, if not the sole reason, for this probably was that the writer had in view, as his first readers, disciples supposed to be familiar with the gracious aspect of Christ's character and ministry.[4]

What then, we ask, was the leading aim of the writer? If it was not, as we at first thought, to exhibit the glory of Jesus in the fulness of His grace, what else could it be? Apparently it was to show the glory of the Incarnate Logos as divine; by a detailed narrative to let it be seen

[1] Matt. ix. 2-8.

[2] John v. 1-15. Oscar Holtzmann makes the general criticism that the chief defect of the Fourth Gospel lies in the absence of promises and demands in reference to the moral condition of men, *i.e.* words bearing on pardon and repentance.—*Das Johannes-Evangelium*, p. 92.

[3] John v. 14.

[4] The emphasis with which the evangelist speaks of the love of Jesus to His disciples, and the delight he takes in exhibiting the intimate fellowship of the Master with his companions during the closing hours of His life (chaps. xiii. xvii.), may suggest the question, Was this "grace," whereof mention is made in the prologue, Christ's love for "His own," the twelve, and all others who like them and through them believed in Him? Such seems to be the view of Mr. Barrow (*Regni Evangelium*, p. 49). "Where are the 'gracious words' of Him who drew and held the thronging crowds? They are reserved for the chosen few whom the Father has given into His hand."

how through the dense veil of the flesh the rays of a divinity that could not be hid still brightly shone. The Christ of the Fourth Gospel seems, in spite of all humiliat ing circumstances, to be a glorified Christ, a Son of man who all the while is in heaven. This view seems to be borne out by the miraculous narratives of this Gospel, as compared with those in the Synoptical Gospels. The dif ference has been broadly expressed by saying that while the synoptical miracles are in the main miracles of *humanity*, the Johannine miracles are miracles of *state*.[1] They appear to be wrought not for the benefit of others, but to glorify the worker. They are often, objectively viewed, acts of humanity; but from the narrator's point of view that seems to be an accident. It was an act of compassion to heal the impotent man at the pool of Bethesda, but he was one of many selected apparently to exhibit Jesus as a fellow-worker with the Father. In the Synoptical Gospels, on the other hand, how often do we read: "And He healed them *all*," the aim of the evangelists manifestly being to exhibit Jesus as intent on doing as much good to men as possible.

This characteristic of the "Johannean" miracles is a feature which must be looked at in any thorough attempt to estimate the religious value of the Fourth Gospel. It has lately been brought into great prominence by being made one of the main grounds of a partition theory as to the composition of the Gospel, according to which it con sists of a Johannine source, containing chiefly discourses of Jesus, with later additions, including many of the mira culous narratives, inserted by an editor who imperfectly understood the mind of Christ and the meaning of His actions. The underlying assumption is that an apostle could not so far have mistaken the aim of Christ's miraculous works as to regard them as mere thaumaturgic displays of power, *Ostentationswunder*[2] It is incumbent on those who believe at once in the unity and in the

---

[1] Bruce, *The Miraculous Element in the Gospels*, p. 151.
[2] *Vide* Wendt, *Die Lehre Jesu*, Erster Theil, p. 238.

apostolic authorship of the Gospel to do their best to break the force of this argument by presenting the miracles it reports in a more favourable light. For this purpose it might be pointed out that the glory which is represented as the aim of the miracles is not of the vulgar sort, but, in some instances at least, is rather what the world would call humiliation or shame. Thus the raising of Lazarus glorified the Son of God not merely by showing His divine power, but by causing His crucifixion. Then it might further be remarked that we are not to assume that the evangelist gives a full account of Christ's motives as a miracle worker, any more than of His miraculous works whereof He reports only a small selection. He might be aware of the humanity that manifested itself in Christ's miracles, and fully alive to its value, just as he knew and appreciated the grace of Christ's ministry, though he passes it over as a commonplace. Indeed, we may regard the overlooking of the humanitarian aspect of the miracles as a mere detail in the more comprehensive feature of the Gospel first remarked on, its omission of illustrative in stances under the category of *grace*, whose importance nevertheless it emphatically recognises in general terms.

Thus far, then, our answer to the grave question under discussion must be as follows: The Fourth Gospel does not ignore, deny, misconceive, or misrepresent the gracious spirit of Jesus as revealed to us in its loveliness in the synoptical presentation of His life. The writer knows that spirit, and assumes that his readers know it, and have received it and its blessing into their hearts. He says nothing in his Gospel which contradicts that view of Christ's character, or disparages it; on the contrary, he reports words and acts of Jesus in which it is implied and presupposed. But, on the other hand, he makes no special contribution to its illustration. He has another end in view, distinct, though not incompatible. He places the emphasis on another aspect of the incarnate life of the Son of God. His point is not that the Son of God was gracious, but that the grace manifested was that of a Divine Person, and in his zeal to make this apparent he allows the grace to retire into the background, and brings the power with which it was associated to the front. In his own theological way he does indeed set forth the love of Jesus to the sinful, as when through the lips of the Baptist he calls Him the Lamb of God, and through Christ's own lips he represents Him as giving His flesh for the life of the world, as the good Shepherd who giveth His life for the sheep, as lifted up that He might draw all men to Him. Yet it can hardly be said that this is the burden of the story as a whole, in the sense in which this can be affirmed of the other Gospels. How the fact ought to affect our practical estimate and use of the Fourth Gospel in relation to the other three, is a question to be hereafter considered. Meantime let us finish our comparison of the two presenta tions of Christ.

Christ's antipathy to Pharisaism, which, not less than His sympathy with "publicans and sinners," was a conspicuous feature of His religious character, according to the synopti cal presentation, is not accentuated in the Fourth Gospel. The two classes of society are indeed hardly distinguished, being merged in the one comprehensive category of "Jews," who in turn appear as a section of the great godless world. Minor shades of moral difference fade away before the one radical division of mankind into children of light and children of darkness. Yet the antagonistic attitude of Jesus towards the religion in vogue does find occasional recognition, as in the passage, instruc tive throughout, where He describes Himself as one who receives not honour from men, in contrast to those who receive honour one of another.[1] The whole matter is here in a nutshell. The Pharisee desires and obtains praise from his fellows. His is a religion of vanity, ostentation, and self-conscious goodness; it is all on the outside, and steadily tends to insincerity and hypocrisy. Jesus neither desires

[1] John v. 41, 44.

nor obtains the praise of men. His goal is duty, not applause. Self is suppressed. Ostentation is abhorrent to His lowly mind. His goodness is in the heart, not a thing for outward show; and He loves truth in the inward parts with a sacred passion. That the religion of Jesus was free from the scrupulosity of Pharisaism, not less than from its ostentation, is not shown with the amplitude of detail we find in the synoptists; but the fact is suffi ciently attested by Sabbatic miracles,[1] which give rise to altercations somewhat after the manner with which the first three Gospels make us familiar.

It is impossible here to go at length into the question how far the general view of the teaching of Christ pre sented in the Fourth Gospel corresponds to that given in the other three. It might fairly be contended that under an undoubted superficial diversity in form there is sub- stantial identity in import.[2] Yet, on the other hand, candour might demand the admission that such an identity cannot easily be made out without some toning down of distinctiveness on either side. One would certainly expect to find that the obliteration of the distinction between Pharisee and "sinner" was not without its effect on the Johannean presentation of Christ's doctrine concerning God and man. There is really a perceptible difference here. God is "the Father" in the Fourth Gospel as in the other three. But He is the Father chiefly in reference to the Divine Son, and under Him to those to whom the right is given to become children of God.[3] God has no prodigal sons.[4] All men are either sons of God or sons of the devil. There is no doctrine of the worth of man even at the lowest in virtue of his spiritual endowments or possibili-

---

[1] John v. 5-9, ix. 9-14.

[2] Such is the view which Wendt endeavours to establish in detail in his work on *The Teaching of Jesus.*

[3] John i. 12.

[4] In John iv. 21, 23 Jesus calls God "Father" in the hearing of the Samaritan woman, a representative of the prodigal class, but it is with reference to the "true worshippers."

ties. There are no pregnant sayings like that one: " How much is a man better than a sheep." All of this sort may be understood and taken for granted, though it is not said.[1]

In view of the foregoing comparative estimate the question arises, What is the proper place and use of the Fourth Gospel as a source of knowledge concerning the Lord Jesus?

Its proper place is second, not first. It is the second lesson-book of evangelic knowledge, not the primer. Whether in the intention of the author it was a supple ment to the synoptical account of the life of Jesus, sup posed to be familiar to his readers, it may be impossible to determine, but certainly its power to edify largely depends on its being used as a supplement. Some are of opinion that the Fourth Gospel was first written, and that the other three presuppose its existence.[2] It is a very improbable hypothesis, contrary at once to ancient tradition, to the all but unanimous opinion of modern critics, and to the internal evidence of theological development witnessing to a com paratively late origin. But even if the fact were so, the gospel, *ex hypothesi* first in the order of time, would have to be treated as second in the order of use. Apart from all doubtful questions of date, the Synoptical Gospels must be regarded as the " Propylæum of the Evangelic Sanctuary."[3]

The fact being so, how inconsiderate and mischievous must be all comparisons between the Fourth Gospel and the other three, which amount to disparagement, and encourage neglect, of the latter; as if the Christian disciple might leave them on one side, and, ignorant of all their rich and varied teaching, religious and ethical, rush at once to the second lesson-book. There has been too much of

[1] Wendt's treatment of the theme " God as the Father " is not satisfactory. Identity of view between the Fourth Gospel and the other three is brought out by an understatement of the synoptical doctrine of Fatherhood and Sonship. *Vide The Teaching of Jesus.*

[2] *Vide* Halcombe, *The Historic Relation of The Gospels.*

[3] So Reuss, *La Bible*, volume on *The Johannine Theology*, p. 107.

this ill-judged way of speaking. It began with Clement of Alexandria,[1] it was continued by Luther, it received too much countenance from Schleiermacher, and it is still echoed in a sequacious spirit by some writers on the Gospels. In the case of Schleiermacher disparagement of the synoptical presentation of Christ almost goes the length of contempt, and as showing what this tendency lands in, it may be well to reproduce his words. He writes:

" Nothing betrays less sense for the essence of Christianity and for the Person of Christ, as also historic sense and under standing of that through which great events come to pass, and how those must be constituted in whom these have their real ground, than the view which first quietly appeared maintaining that John had mixed much of his own with the sayings of Christ, but now, having grown strong in stillness and furnished itself with critical armour, ventures on the bolder position that John did not write the Gospel at all, but a later author invented this mystic Christ. But how a Jewish Rabbi with benevolent feelings, somewhat Socratic morals, some miracles, or what at least others took for such, and a talent for uttering apt maxims and parables (for nothing more remains, nay, some follies we have to pardon in him according to the other evangelists): how, I say, one like that could have brought forth such an effect as a new religion and church, a man who, if that was all that could be said of him, could not be compared to Moses and Mahomet, is not made clear to us."[2]

Few now will go as far as that. Still, in the writings of orthodox defenders of the authenticity of the Fourth Gospel comparisons are made to the effect that in the synoptics we read chiefly of the external life of Jesus— His intercourse with men and His discourses to the multi tude, whereas in *John* we see into Christ's inner nature

[1] Eusebius (*Hist. Eccl.*, lib. vi. 14) reports Clement as saying that John, seeing that the somatic aspects of Christ's ministry were shown in the Gospel, and exhorted by His companions, under divine inspiration wrote a spiritual (πνευματικόν) gospel. The work from which Eusebius quotes is lost.

[2] *Ueber die Religion*, p. 309.

and behold the very heart of Jesus disclosed.[1]   The inquirer who desires to know Jesus truly will do well to regard with a measure of suspicion such statements.   The fact is not as represented.   The heart of the man Jesus in its rich fulness of grace and spiritual truth is more ade quately shown in the first three Gospels than in the Fourth. The writer of that Gospel, as we have seen, did not even propose to exhibit in detail the fulness he speaks of in the prologue.   He writes for readers whom he assumes to have already received of that fulness, and by some means to have mastered the lesson we learn now through the Synoptical Gospels.[2]   Briefly put that lesson is: God in His righteousness and grace revealed through a holy loving human character.   That lesson the Fourth Gospel does not cancel, but throughout implies, and in some places teaches. But its superadded specific lesson is: God in the glory of His Majesty and Might revealed as it were behind a lowly humanity, the glory of the only begotten Son shining through the fleshly veil.   As teaching that lesson it may fitly supplement the synoptical presentation, but it cannot possibly supersede it.[3]

The Logos theorem need not deter from such supplement ary use.   It is not the key to the Gospel.   Instead of explaining everything, it is itself a riddle that needs to be

---

[1] *Vide* Gloag, *Introduction to the Johannine Writings*, p. 156.

[2] Reuss says: "The Gospel was written for intelligent disciples" (*La Bible, La Theologie Johannique*, p. 49).   Again: "The author has not wished to teach history, he supposes it known, and aims at Interpreting it," p. 13.

[3] Reuss, to quote him once more, remarks: "The idea of Christianity in the Fourth Gospel is not intelligible till the synoptical presentation has been assimilated.   To make the Johannean theology the starting-point is to mis take the intentions of the Master and the destination of the Church," p. 107. On the other hand, Weizsäcker thinks that the Johannean *Christusbild* is an indispensable supplement of the synoptical, and that only through it have we the explanation of the whole higher influence of Christ's personality. "The great charm of that picture, which the ancients expressed by saying that the other Gospels give the body, this the soul of the history, and which still exercises its power in a similar sense, rests on this that the whole subse quent effect of the life, and the results thereof for faith, are here introduced into the history itself."—*Das Apostolische Zeitalter*, p. 556.

explained. It is not explained by an offhand reference to
Philo. The term Logos may hail directly or indirectly
from Alexandria, but not the idea the evangelist associates
with it.[1] The Logos of Philo is an intermediary between
a transcendent, absolute deity, and a world with which
he can have no relations. God is not so conceived in this
Gospel. He is indeed described as One whom no man hath
seen at any time, and whom the only begotten Son declares,[2]
but He is also represented as loving the world and giving
His Son for its salvation,[3] and as raising the dead and
quickening them.[4] If He does not exercise the function of
judgment, it is not because it is beneath His dignity as the
Absolute, but because He deems it equitable that men
should be judged by one who is Himself a Son of man.[5]
The Son does not work instead of a Father too exalted to
do anything; He works with and as the Father.[6] It is not
the Son alone who dwells with the faithful, the Father also
is immanent in them.[7] The idea of God is distinctively
Christian. So is the idea of the highest good. There is
indeed frequent mention of the knowledge of truth as if
the *summum bonum* were gnostically conceived. But the
knowledge spoken of is attained through the doing of God's
will.[8] The ruling spirit of the Gospel is not gnostic or
speculative, but ethical. In that respect it is worthy to
have an apostle for its author. And in no respect does an
apostolic authorship seem incredible. It has indeed been
pronounced beyond belief that a companion of Jesus could
come to think of Him as the Incarnate Logos, or that any
power either of faith or of philosophy could so extinguish

---

[1] So Harnack, *Dogmengeschichte*, i. 85. For the extremist type of the
opposite view, *vide* Thoma, *Die Genesis des Johannes-Evangelium*, 1882.
For Thoma the Fourth Gospel is a life of Jesus after the type of Philo's
Vita Mosis, allegory everywhere, fact nowhere.

[2] John i. 18.   [3] John iii 16.   [4] John v 21.

[5] John v. 22, 27. According to Oscar Holtzmann the Logos idea has only
the value of a *Hilfsvorstellung* in the Gospel, because the transcendence of
God is not carried out. *Das Johannes-Evangelium untersucht und erklärt*,
p. 82.

[6] John v. 19, 20.   [7] John xiv. 23.   [8] John vii. 17.

the recollection of the real life and set in its place this wonderful image of a Divine Being.[1] If we have rightly regarded the Gospel as intended for the use of disciples assumed to be familiar with the primitive evangelic tradition, the writer must have conceived it possible for his readers to combine the two images. He could hardly have thought this possible for them unless he felt it to be possible for himself. Why then should it be possible for a scholar of John's who had got the human image from his lips, or from current tradition, or from the Synoptical Gospels, and impossible for John himself, who had got that image from personal intercourse with Jesus? It seems as if the capacity to effect the combination depended not on external circumstances, but upon spiritual idiosyncrasy. Given the mystic temperament already spoken of, the problem seems not insoluble. It becomes then simply another example of the habit of regarding all things *sub specie æternitatis*, with comparative indifference to historical sequence, the state of exaltation anticipated, at least in part, the Son of man even while on earth represented as in heaven.

CHAPTER X.

THE LIGHT OF THE WORLD.

LITERATURE.—Ladd, *The Doctrine of Sacred Scripture; Lux Mundi;* Martineau, *The Seat of Authority in Religion;* Stanton, *The Place of Authority in Religious Belief;* Gore, *Bampton Lectures on the Incarnation* (Lect. vii.); Herrmann, *Der Begriff der Offenbarung* (Vorträge der Theol. Konferenz zu Giessen); Clifford, *The Inspiration and the Authority of the Bible;* Briggs, *The Bible, the Church, and the Reason;* Leopold Monod, *Le Probleme de L'Autorité,* 1891.

To the burning question, Who or what is the seat of ultimate authority in religion? the most recent apologetic

[1] Weizsacker, *Das Apostolische Zeitalter,* p. 535.

answers, Christ: Christ, not other religious masters, not the individual reason, not the Church, not even the Bible.

The lordship of Christ over the conscience is a common place accepted by all Christians. But it is the fate of commonplaces, especially in religion, to be neglected in favour of propositions less fundamental, more doubtful, much controverted, and which, just because they are the subjects of controversy, excite exceptional interest and monopolise attention. So it happened that the great commandments of the Decalogue were made of none effect by Rabbinical traditions, the offspring of zeal for the keeping of the divinely-given law. A similar mischance has overtaken the authority of Jesus. For one section of Christendom the Church has taken His place as Lord, for another the Bible; in either case without intention, and for the most part without consciousness, of disloyalty. The question as to the seat of authority is sometimes formulated without reference to Christ, the only alternatives thought of being the Bible, the Church, or reason. In view of such facts, it is incumbent to resurrectionise the buried commonplace, and to reassert with emphasis that Jesus Christ is the Lord of Christendom, and the Light of the World.

Authority has been not only misplaced, but so grievously misrepresented in its nature that the very word, as employed in the sphere of religion, has become an offence to the friends of truth and freedom. It has been exercised in the name of God with brute force: sometimes in behalf of the false, creating a deep sense of wrong; sometimes in support of truth, creating against it a violent prejudice. It has been claimed for Scripture misconceived as a Book of Dogma, having for its *raison d'etre* to teach a system of doctrinal mysteries undiscoverable by reason, and incomprehensible by reason, with the result that revelation has been made to appear the antithesis of reason. The claim has been made to rest on the external evidence of miracles and prophecies conceived of as purely evidential adjuncts of a doctrinal revelation; evidence capable at most, when skilfully stated, of silencing opposition, but having no power to produce religious faith in a revelation not in itself acceptable or self-evidencing. In view of these abuses, which form a large chapter in the history of Christianity, it is of urgent importance to recall attention to the claims of Christ to be the Master, and to bid such as labour under the burden of doubt listen to His voice when He says, " Learn from me." So doing they shall escape, not only from doubt, but from every form of usurpation ; from all that savours of Rabbinism in religion, and from the irritation inflicted on reason and conscience by its galling yoke. For there is, indeed, in Jesus and His teaching a " sweet reasonableness." His yoke is easy ; His authority is gentle as the light of day. What He says about God and man and their relations needs no elaborate system of evidences to commend it. It is self-evidencing. It is rest-giving. Heart, conscience, reason rest in it. Men who have long wandered in darkness leap for joy when at last they come to the school of Jesus, and discover in Him the true Master of the spirit. Such was the experience of men in ancient times coming to Jesus from the schools of Greek philosophy ; such is the experience of many in our day who had despaired of attaining to religious certainty.

Christ is not the only claimant to lordship in religion. He divides the world with other masters. In view of the wide prevalence of Buddhism and Mahometanism, it may seem bold to call Christ the Light of the World, and as if modesty required us to be content with the ascription to Him of a merely provincial authority. But no Christian can acquiesce in this compromise. Faith demands for its Object a universal sway : that at the name of Jesus every knee should bow, and every tongue confess that He is Lord to the glory of God the Father. And, if necessary, faith will undertake to justify its demand by a comparison of Jesus with other religious initiators. Such a comparison, indeed, is not indispensable to legitimise the Christian's exclusive homage to Jesus, nor in discussions on the seat of authority in religion does it usually enter as an element. In these days, however, when the scientific study of religion on the comparative method is so much in vogue, it is well, both for confirmation of the faith of the individual Christian, and for the vindication of missionary enterprise, to be ready with an answer to those who ask us to show cause why Christianity should supersede all other religions. A course of study on "Christ and other Masters,"[1] if not an essential department of apologetics, would be at least a very helpful special discipline. It is a study which a believer in Christ has no temptation to shun. Christ gains by comparison. As in our studies in the second book of this work we found that occasional comparisons with contemporary religions served to evince the superiority of the religion of Israel, so we should find on placing Jesus side by side with Buddha, Confucius, Zoroaster, Mahomet, that He stood visibly higher than they. This line of inquiry cannot, of course, be gone into here; all that is possible is to indicate its utility, and to explain briefly the method of the argument.

The method is comparative. The argument goes to show that Jesus is wiser than other masters; that the Christian religion is superior to other religions in all important respects, and therefore, on the principle of the survival of the fittest, ought to supersede them. Such a mode of reasoning may appear unsatisfactory to an enthusiastic faith. Nothing will satisfy it but proof that Christianity is not only better than this or that religion, but the best possible, the absolute religion, and therefore destined eventually to become universally prevalent. By all means let such a proof be led if it can; yet let not the other less ambitious, more circuitous, line of argument be despised. Unsatisfactory as it may appear, it was the line of argument pursued by the author of the Epistle to the Hebrews

[1] This is the title of a work by Mr. Hardwick on the religions of the world.

in his endeavour to establish the claims of Christianity to be the perfect, and therefore the final religion. " The best possible," was his thesis, but his method of proof was " Christ better than prophets, better than angels, better than Moses, better than Aaron ; therefore listen to Him when He speaks, more attentively than to any other speaker in God's name." It cannot be amiss to follow His example, and, extending his argument beyond biblical limits, to say : Christ better than Buddha, better than Confucius, better than Mahomet, better than every name that has been held in reverent esteem ; therefore hear ye Him, all peoples that dwell upon the face of the earth. It were well if mission aries were able to issue modern versions of the Epistle to the Hebrews adapted to their respective spheres of labour, and furnished with wise citations of the facts which justify the demand they make for earnest heed to the voice of Jesus.

The comparative argument has the merit of simplicity. It can be understood and appreciated by all, learned or unlearned, black or white, savage or civilised. There is that in every man that makes him ascribe a certain authority to all wisdom and goodness. Every human being tends to bow before a saint or a sage. Every human being has further the power, more or less developed, to dis criminate between degrees of sanctity and wisdom, as he has the power to see that the light of the sun is greater than the light of the moon. "God made two great lights ; the greater light to rule the day, and the lesser light to rule the night."[1] How shall I know which of the two lights, the sun and the moon, is entitled to be regarded as the greater light ? It is a matter of eyesight, of the power to appreciate the difference between daylight and night-light. If the superiority of daylight is not evident to my eye, all the argument in the world will not convince me of it. But there never was a man, having the use of his eyes, who needed any such argument. Even so there is in the

[1] Gen. i. 16.

natural conscience a faculty to see that one light in the moral world is greater than another. Show a man, even in Africa, first the moon and then the sun, and he will see for himself that the sun is the greater light, to be welcomed, as men welcome the dawn of day.

The comparative argument has the great recommenda tion that it permits frank recognition of all the good that is in ethnic religions. To praise the sun it is not necessary to maintain that he is the only light. You can recognise the moon, and even wax eloquent on the weird beauty of her dim light, without compromising the claims of the ruler of the day. Still less difficult ought it to be for the Christian to acknowledge the minute lights of pagan night, and to say in thankfulness, not in scorn, " He made the stars also."

Among the rival claimants to be the seat of authority in religion is the individual reason. The light within the only, and the sufficient, source of revelation, and the test of all alleged revelations: such was the watchword of the deists, and there are those in modern times who re-echo the sentiment. In the case of the deists the thesis was asserted with a self-complacent and even contemptuous dis regard, not only of the light from above, but even of the aid derivable from the wisdom of the past, or from a care fully conducted education. The plain uninstructed man, even the savage, might know all that needs to be known of God as well as, nay even better than, the most learned philosopher. Modern rationalists have a more adequate sense of the weakness of the individual reason, of the need of extraneous aids, and of the vast extent to which every man is indebted to the religious history of the past, and to the inspirations of the present. The idea of the social organism has taken firm possession of the public mind, and all realise the truth of Paul's saying, " None of us liveth to himself." Nevertheless there are those who teach that human reason, or rather God immanent in human reason, is the seat of religious authority, that nothing can properly be described as revelation except such religious intuitions as come to us though the action of reason, and that all aid from without, from whatever quarter coming, must take the form of a stimulus " which wakes the echoes in ourselves, and is thereby instantly transferred from external attestation to self-evidence." [1]

In criticising this theory it is not necessary to take up the position of utter antagonism, and to pronounce it entirely false. There is much in it with which one can cordially sympathise. We can repudiate, for example, not less earnestly than Dr. Martineau and those who agree with him, the old-fashioned antithesis between reason and revelation as belonging to an exploded deistic conception of God's relation to the world as purely transcendent. The light from above must not be placed in abstract opposition to the light within, as if the two had nothing in common. The light from above is no light for me until it has become a light within shining in its own self-evidence. It is in vain that the sun shines if I have not an eye to see its beams. Then, so far as I am concerned, the light shineth in darkness, and the darkness comprehends it not. But the light may be there all the same, and it may be owing to some disability in me that it is not a light within as well as a light without. And this is one direction in which the rationalistic theory is at fault. It does not take suffi ciently into account the disabilities of reason. It assumes reason to be in a normal condition, whereas its eye may be dim through the influence of an abnormal moral condition. Dr. Martineau has much to say of the faith-woven veil that hides the face of the true Jesus. He has not suffi ciently borne in mind the veil that is on the face of the human soul, preventing it from seeing the light of God. Must that not be taken into account in order to understand the religious history of the world ? Whence comes it that men have been so backward in learning the knowledge of

[1] Martineau, *The Seat of Authority in Religion*, preface, p. vi.

God ? Why must the heathen religions, after the most generous allowances, be pronounced unsuccessful ? Why is it that the utterances of sages are often so disappointing and so contradictory, and that the wisest words of the wise have taken the form of a sigh for a surer word than any they have heard from others, or have themselves been able to speak ? It is on account of the moral evil that is in the world, and partly also on account of the physical evil that oppresses the life of man. By reason of the one the sense for the true and the good is blunted, by reason of the other men have not the courage to trust their spiritual intuitions, and are the victims of an incurable doubt of the goodwill of God. On both accounts there is room and need enough for a surer word, if any such might be forth coming.

This brings us to another defect of the theory under consideration, viz. its failure to recognise the possibility of some one appearing in the world possessing an altogether unique exceptional power of spiritual intuition, and of so speaking of God as to wake the " echoes in ourselves "— making us see things as we had not seen them before, or trust thoughts of our own hearts which had before seemed too good news to be true. It is not necessary that all men should be in the dark ; it is conceivable that there should be One in whom was the true life and the true light, whose mind was the express image and radiance of the mind of God. Such an one the Christian finds in Jesus. And it is because Jesus has for him this value that he recognises Him as an ultimate religious authority. It costs him no effort to do so. He is not conscious of any violence or humiliation done to his reason in bowing to the authority of Christ. For Christ speaks *with* authority just because He does not speak *by* authority, like the Rabbis citing the names of celebrated teachers in support of state ments possessing no intrinsic power to commend themselves to acceptance. He speaks as the spontaneous mouthpiece of God, of nature, of the forces of human nature working down in His soul. God reveals Himself to His spirit as a Father, and He constantly calls Him Father. The world in its beauty and sublimity unfolds itself to His eye, and He speaks with inimitable simplicity of the lilies, birds, and stormy winds. Almighty pity stirs His bosom as He witnesses the sin and misery of men, and He speaks to the fallen the message of pardon and regeneration. A vision of heavenly purity and goodness bursts on His view, and He discourses of the kingdom of heaven, and in golden sentences declares who are its citizens: Blessed the poor, the meek, the pure, the peaceable, the passionate lovers of righteous ness. The sweet reasonableness of all this is irresistible. It is the very reason of God, the universal reason, find ing normal, perfect, adequate expression, and correcting, strengthening, enlarging, in one word, "educating"[1] the reason of man. Truly the yoke of this Teacher is easy. His way of teaching, and the substance of His teaching, show at once the objective reality of revelation, and its intimate relation to reason. He says things not said before, or not so said as to be of use, yet recognisable at once when said, as true and worthy of all acceptation. Take the one instance of calling God *Father*. To all practical intents this was a new name for God, as Jesus used it. Yet the new name was recognisable at once by unsophisticated consciences as expressive of the deepest truth concerning God, and the most welcome. How strange that men should have been so long in finding out a truth so simple and so acceptable! The thought might easily suggest itself even to the most primitive men that God was to all men what a father is to his family. Nay, it had suggested itself to the early Indian Aryans, witness the name *Dyaus-pitar*, heaven-Father. But men had not the courage to trust their own spiritual intuitions. They could not seriously

---

[1] Mr. Gore well says: "All legitimate authority represents the higher reason, educating the development of the lower. Legitimate religious authority represents the reason of God educating the reason of man, and communicating itself to it."—*Bampton Lectures on the Incarnation*, p. 181.

believe anything so good concerning God. An evil conscience made that difficult, and also the manifold tragic experiences of life. And it is in this connection that the need and utility of an objective revelation be come very apparent. The function of revelation is not, as has been supposed, to reveal truths which the human mind is unable to conceive.[1] It is rather to convert conceivable possibilities into indubitable realities,[2] to turn, *e.g.*, the fancy or dream of God as a Father into a sober fact. Christ did that by Himself believing with all His heart in the Fatherhood of God, and by being Himself a heroically loyal Son. The revelation lay not in what He said so much as in His own personal religion and conduct. He realised the good in His own character, and He believed in spite of all temptations to the contrary that God wills the good, and by His almighty providence works incessantly and supremely for its realisation. And simply in virtue of being the one man in history who has done these two things perfectly, Jesus is a most veritable and valuable objective revelation, mightily helping us to be the sons of God, and to believe stedfastly in Him as our Father, and winning from those He helps joyful recognition as their authoritative Master.

Thus far all believers can go in acknowledging their indebtedness to Jesus. Some go much further and say, It is owing to Jesus that we really believe that there is a God at all. That is to say, they claim for Jesus not merely to have brought our spiritual intuitions out of a state of mere virtuality into conscious vigorous exercise, but to have given us that knowledge of God which men have striven to acquire by the methods of natural theology. Such thinkers disallow the ordinary proofs for the being and nature of God, drawn from the idea of God in the

---

[1] Such is the view of W. R. Greg in *The Creed of Christendom*, vol. ii. p. 172.

[2] *Vide* this view stated at greater length in *The Chief End of Revelation*, pp. 27-31.

human mind, or from the appearance of design in nature, or from the existence of the world as a whole. They regard these reasonings as fine words which scholars at their ease coin in their studies, but which when the heart is tried by the sense of sin, and by the darkness of life, have really no persuasive power, but leave men in doubt whether God be indeed good, or whether He even so much as be. It is only when the eye is directed to Christ that there arises for the man who sitteth in darkness a great light by which he sees at once what God is and that God is.[1] This view is a revolt against the traditional method of theologians, which lays a foundation in natural theology for revelation, nothing doubting that its reasonings are sound, and its results sure. While not prepared to take sides with the authors of this revolt, or to accept offhand the philosophical presuppositions on which it rests, I feel considerable sympathy with the religious attitude therein assumed. How much or how little the so-called proofs of natural theology will actually prove for us depends on the state of mind in which we enter on their examination. We find what we bring. We are convinced at the end because we were convinced before we began; and that we were so convinced may be due to a Christian nurture which has saturated our whole spiritual nature with the idea of God from our earliest years. In this view even Dr. Martineau so far concurs. He holds that the order in which natural and revealed religion are usually placed must be inverted; that the reasonings of the natural theologian "lead to explicit theism because they start from implicit theism, which therefore stands as an initial revelation out of which is evolved the whole organism of natural religion."[2] The point of divergence between Dr. Martineau and the school

---

[1] So Professor Herrmann of Marburg in *Der Begriff der Offenbarung*, an address delivered at the conference in Giessen in 1887. The addresses were published in 1888 in collective form under the title *Vorträge der theologischen Konferenz zu Giessen*. Herrmann's essay is a very fresh discussion of the idea of revelation.

[2] *Seat of Authority in Religion*, pp. 312, 313.

of Ritschl, as represented, for example, by Herrmann, is this: For the English theologian "revealed religion" means the thoughts of God, which come to men intuitively through the natural action of their own reason; for the German theologians it means the thoughts of God which give rest to reason, conscience, and heart, but which came to us through the knowledge of Christ, and which but for His appearance in the world we never should have had as a living belief acting as an effective force on our lives.[1]

On the authority of the *Church* it is not necessary to say much in general apologetic. One who has, after a spiritual struggle, at last got himself grounded in the essentials of the Christian faith may be left to adjust his relations to the community of believers the best way he can. To those, on the other hand, who need help in fundamental problems, it would not be expedient to speak of the Church, except indeed in the way of apology, not as one claiming for her authority, but rather pleading that a considerate and generous view should be taken of her shortcomings. Pre judice against Christianity arising from the sins of the ecclesiastical organisation that bears Christ's name, and professes to be guided by His spirit, is certainly one of the facts with which a defender of the faith has to reckon. He may try to dispose of it as a source of unbelief by pointing out that the sins of the Church have to a large extent been sins of infirmity rather than of wilful disloyalty; that it is no presumption against the supernatural origin or initial purity of the Christian religion that in its subsequent development it was left to run its natural course, exposed to the degeneracy and corruption that are apt to befall everything that man has to do with; and that Christ Him self was under no misapprehension as to the future for tunes of the kingdom of God in this world, but predicted coming evils and described them in the most sombre colours.

[1] *Vide* the address referred to in note 1, p. 502,

That a society of men professing in common a religion must in the nature of things exercise over its members an influence in a very real sense authoritative, is self-evident. The claim of the Church to authority, viewed in the light of this axiom, is not exceptional; it is simply a particular instance of a universal law. What has to be remarked concerning the Church, considered ideally, is the peculiar reasonableness of her claim. What is the ideal Church? It is a body of men believing Jesus Christ to be the Son of God, with a faith not received by tradition but communicated directly by the Father in heaven to each believer. Each man for himself has clear insight into the divine worth of Jesus, passionately loves the goodness exhibited in His character, and with sincere, deep fervour reverences Him as the Lord. What a close, mighty bond of union this common relation to the Head! What a power the mutual cohesion thence arising gives the society as a whole over the individual member! How much he will bear in the way of authoritative decision of doubtful matters of opinion and conduct, rather than break away from so blessed a fellowship! And with what good right the society will be felt to decide, whether in formally assembled council, as when the question of circumcision was debated at Jerusalem, or by well understood, though not distinctly formulated, pervading sentiment! The pure in heart see God and truth clearly. Therefore what they bind or loose on earth shall be bound or loosed in heaven. Their judgments have real, not merely technical value. What they approve is worthy of approbation; what they condemn, of condemnation. If one or more members of the society find themselves out of accord with their brethren they will distrust their own judgment, and loyally acquiesce in the judgment of the majority, which will be made easy for them to do by the consideration of the latter for all sincere difference of opinion, and by the supreme desire on their part also to maintain at all hazards the fellowship unbroken In such a society it is not so much one part that rules over another, as love that rules over all ; now constraining the few to submit to the many, now constraining the many to defer to the few, all alike acting in a spirit of loyal devotion to the common Lord.

A fair ideal indeed, but it hardly ever existed on this earth, at least it exists no longer. If the "true" Church mean the Church of the ideal, then there is no "true" Church in this world. There are many religious societies called Christian Churches. They cannot all be right in their doctrine ; none of them may be altogether right in their spirit. In view of this possibility the important question is not the abstract one as to the nature and limits of Church authority, but what Church has the moral right to exercise authority ? Church members may answer the question in favour of their own communion, and by a mental effort invest it with the attributes of the ideal. That will some times be hard work, and what is more important, it may be dangerous. It is possible to be too submissive a son of mother Church. Circumstances are easily conceivable in which it might be said with truth : the more of a Church man the less of a Christian. In such circumstances it is necessary to rebel against the Church in order to be loyal to Jesus, to be anti-ecclesiastical in order to avoid being anti-Christian.

Speaking generally, with reference to the actual situation, it may be said that a believing man does well to be jealous of Church power for Christ's sake. The Church is a mother, and like that of all mothers her influence is helpful up to a certain point, and beyond that is apt to be a hindrance to spiritual development. She is fond of managing, and does not readily recognise that in the case of many of her grown-up sons the best thing she can do is to leave them to the guidance of a higher wisdom. The ecclesiastical spirit does not foster, or value, vigorous, intractable indi viduality. It has too often driven men of this type into dissent or into banishment, thinking it better they should be without than that the comfort of passive obedience should be disturbed within. Yet what is a Church without such men—men of earnest thought and robust moral senti ments, but a salt without a savour? To repress or oppress spiritual independence is to quench the spirit of Christ. It was observed of the men that had been with Jesus that they were bold: they had the courage of their opinions. God often speaks through minorities, even through solitary individuals who are in a minority of one. It was so in the Hebrew Church, even when the nation not the individual was the social unit, and when to break with national custom was considered a crime. It is so still in the Church of the New Testament. And the Church needs constantly to be reminded of the fact. The value of energetic personalities endowed with initiative is now fully recognised in science and in commerce. Dis-coverers and inventors are welcome. But in religion, more than in any other human interest, the power of custom is strong. The passion for solidarity, the intolerance of dissent, characteristic of uncivilised men, still survives there. In one aspect it commands respect, for there is conscience in it. But there is more than conscience; there is moral disease. It is the form which egotism assumes in the religious world. Church authority is enforced against individuals by men who are themselves, perhaps uncon sciously, guilty of individualism of the most offensive type.

No one who, with intelligence, asserts the supreme authority of Christ can possibly mean to disparage the Scriptures of either Testament. They are writings which "testify of Him," and in virtue of this fact must possess for every Christian a unique authoritative value. They are His own word, and the channel through which He exercises authority. In cherishing a high and reverent esteem for the Scriptures, we only follow Christ's own example. He ever spoke of the Hebrew writings in a manner involving express or implied recognition of their divine truth and worth. Thus, to take a single typical

instance, in the Sermon on the Mount, speaking as the
Herald and Legislator of the kingdom of heaven, He said :
"Think not that I am come to destroy the law or the
prophets : I am not come to destroy, but to fulfil ; " law
and prophets standing for the whole Old Testament.
Christ's sincere, deep reverence for the Scriptures becomes
invested with peculiar significance when viewed in con
nection with His intense antagonism to Rabbinism.   That
antagonism means that nothing in the piety of Jesus was a
matter of custom or mechanical acceptance of tradition.
He believed in nothing as true or good simply because it
passed for such in the religious world of His time.   His faith
and reverence were invariably based on spiritual insight
and personal conviction.   Not because the scribes busied
themselves about the sacred book as the one supremely
important subject of study, did He deem it worthy of
devout attention.   On the contrary, as used by them the
book must have been repulsive to Him.   He had to clear
His mind of whatever He knew of Rabbinical use that He
might be able to cherish a hearty liking for it, just as He
had to rid Himself of current ideas of the Messianic hope
and of the kingdom of God, before either could have any
reality or value for His religious consciousness.   As things
stood, He could take nothing for granted in the whole
range of morals and religion, but had to go back on first
principles, and with regard to all the spiritual treasures of
His people ask, What is the real as distinct from the cur
rent worth of these things ?   And when He entered on His
public ministry He appeared as one who had formed His
own estimates, and was in possession of transformed con
ceptions alike of Bible, kingdom, and Messiahship.   And
with regard to the first, His verdict was in effect : The
book is divine, full of the spirit of truth, wisdom, and good
ness, supremely useful for guidance in life, setting forth
views of God and man and duty to which one can with a
pure conscience say Amen.

Yet while infinitely more reverent as compared with

that of the Rabbis, Christ's attitude towards the Scriptures was not, like theirs, one of indiscriminate, idolatrous admiration. His use was critical. Some books He quoted often; others He did not quote at all. He had a graduated sense of the relative importance of the matters treated of. He distinguished between "weightier matters" in the law [1] and things of minor consequence. The *ethical* was in His esteem of far more importance than the *ritual;* it was for Him the supreme category. To it as a test He brought every custom or statute, however venerable; and if He found any wanting, judged by the royal law of love, He unhesitatingly pronounced them imperfect and transient, though they might have a place in the Mosaic code. In all this He differed from the Rabbis. For them all Scripture was alike important; all laws great or small alike binding in theory, in practice the small more than the great. Who dared presume to call any law small, defective, or temporary that God had commanded?

In all this we must follow Christ rather than the Rabbis. Recognising Him as an authority in His general attitude of reverence for the Scriptures, we must further recognise Him as an authority in His discriminating use of the Scriptures. Nay, in the very fact of that discriminating use we must recognise Christ setting Himself as an authority above the Scriptures. He judges them, teaches the right, reasonable, profitable method of using them, as opposed to the wrong. Loyalty to Him as the supreme authority requires that we should accept His verdict, and use the sacred writings in His spirit; *and above all, that we should be careful not so to use them that He shall be eclipsed and His own teaching made void.* To this caveat, in general terms, all will assent; the practically important matter is to realise the possibility of making the grave mistake, and to know in what directions danger is to be feared. As to the possibility, it is illustrated by the case of the Jews. They searched the Scriptures, as men only could who believed

[1] Matt. xxiii. 23.

that their salvation depended on the quest; yet they missed Christ.[1] On their way of using the Scriptures no other result was possible. How could worshippers of the letter accept as their Messiah one who valued only the spirit? what could men to whom the Bible was a book of law do but reject one for whom it was a book of inspira tion?

A tragic error; can it happen now? Is it possible by a wrong use of the Bible to-day to miss Christ; to miss Him, not in the sense of forfeiting all share in His salvation, but in the sense of utterly failing to do justice to His claims as the Supreme Master in religion? If we may accept evidence from the biography of modern religious doubt, we must conclude that it is possible to lose Christ in the Bible and through the Bible.[2] And if it be asked how that happens, the answer suggested both by experience and by theory is: It comes about through not realising that the Gospels are the core of the Bible. Here at last is the elect Man towards whom for many centuries the history of elect Israel has been pointing. Here is He who as one having the standing of a Son speaks God's final word to men. Surely one ought to give supreme attention to what He says by word, deed, character, and experience! Yet there are men who are constrained to confess that they have not done so. After years of search for truth, and with a good general knowledge of the Bible, they turn at last to the Gospels as to a *terra incognita*. The theoretical explanation of this experience offered by those who have duly reflected on the phenomenon is that in such cases the Bible as a whole, instead of Christ in particular, has been regarded as the authority in religion. The point is of such moment that it may be well to quote words in which it is

---

[1] John v. 39.

[2] Take one instance. Harrison (*Problems of Christianity and Scepticism*, p. 282), giving an account of his own experience, says : "How I found my way out of the darkness is easily told, for it was in fact the only way. It was by finding Christ Himself. I had lost Him even in the Bible. At last I turned to the four Gospels and stayed there."

stated with all needful breadth and clearness. Wendt writes :

"The view that the historical teaching of Jesus Christ was the perfect revelation of God for men has been always *theoretically* recognised in the Christian Church, and has had its place assigned it in dogmatic teaching in regard to the prophetic office of Christ. The necessary *practical* application of this view, however, has been cramped on the part of Catholicism by the theory of the infallible authority of Church teaching, and of Protestantism by the theory of the normative authority of the Holy Scriptures for Christian doctrine. When the Holy Scriptures, as a whole, are re garded as expressing the immediate revelation of God, the sayings and discourses of Jesus are, indeed, viewed as part of the contents of Scripture ; but there is no definite reason for emphasising their specific pre-eminence over the other con tents of Scripture. Even Paul has in reality had a much greater influence in moulding the form of Christian doctrine in Protestantism than Jesus Himself." [1]

The principle that some parts of Scripture are of more importance than others is not one which any party will be inclined to dispute. On the contrary, it has been to a wide extent expressly recognised,[2] and still more extensively acted on. The religious spirit has asserted the right to have regard to its own edification in the selection and use of Scripture. Its preferences have been on the whole pretty uniform. In the Old Testament it has done honour to the Psalms, the Song of Songs (spiritually interpreted), and Isaiah, specially the second part, neglecting Proverbs, Ecclesiastes, and the other prophets ; in the New it has favoured the Fourth Gospel, the leading Epistles of Paul, especially that to the Romans, and in certain circles the Apocalypse, and left the three first Gospels comparatively

---

[1] *The Teaching of Jesus*, author's preface, p. 2.

[2] *The Directory for the Public Worship of God*, prepared by the West minster Assembly, commends "the more frequent reading of such Scriptures as he that readeth shall think best for edification of his hearers, as the book of Psalms and such like."

in the background.[1] It is permissible, while conceding to faith the right of preference, to suggest respectful doubt as to the wisdom with which it has been exercised. In particular, it may be confidently asserted that the neglect of the Synoptical Gospels is a serious error, and a suicidal act of self-impoverishment.

It is an obvious corollary from the position stated by Wendt, that the teaching of Christ must guide us in estimating the religious value of the *Old Testament*. This view having been already enunciated,[2] it is not necessary here to enlarge on it; repetition, however, may be pardoned as tending to give it due and needful emphasis. Let it be understood then that it is not only our right but our duty to carry the ideas of God, man, and their relations taught by Jesus, back to the Old Testament, and to regard all herein not in conformity therewith as belonging to the defective element whose existence must be recognised as a matter of course by all who have grasped the idea of a progressive revelation. If, from a mistaken feeling of reverence, we fail to act on this principle, we allow the moonlight to eclipse the sunlight, and go contrary to the rational axiom of the Apostle Paul, " When that which is perfect is come, then that which is in part shall be done away."[3] Some of the phenomena coming under the cate gory of defect have been indicated in a previous chapter,[4] and the list admits of being extended.[5]

In the *New Testament* Christ is conceived to be the one Speaker. " God, who spake to the fathers by the pro phets, hath at the end of these days spoken unto us by a Son."[1] All other speakers, whether by voice or written page, are simply witnesses or interpreters. The several books of the New Testament have been admitted into the

---

[1] So Eibach in his Giessen Address (1888) on *The Scientific Treatment and Practical Use of the Holy Scripture.*

[2] *Vide* p. 323.   [3] 1 Cor. xiii. 10   [4] Book II chap x.

[5] *Vide* Clifford, *The Inspiration and the Authority of the Bible* (chap. v.), a small but suggestive and helpful book.

[6] Heb. i. 1

collection because they were believed by the early Church to be in harmony with the mind of Christ, and to be helpful to the understanding of His gospel. Formally the prin ciple by which canonicity was determined was apostolic authorship direct or indirect, it being assumed that all apostles, and all intimately associated with them, were in possession of an inspiration and spiritual intelligence which would guard them against misconception of whatever per tained to the Christian faith. In reality, however, the judgment of the Church was based on the conviction gained by devout perusal that the various books included in the canon were consistent with each other, and all together in harmony with the doctrine and spirit of the Master. And, speaking comprehensively, it may be affirmed that the judgment of the Church was right, though the reasons given in particular instances might be wrong, or at least pre carious. Thus no one possessing due insight doubts the right of the Epistle to the Hebrews to a place in the authoritative literature of the Christian religion. But few now set value on the reason which induced the ancient Church, after long hesitation, to recognise the canonicity of the Epistle, viz. that it had the Apostle Paul for its author.

The settlement of the canon of the New Testament was a weighty problem, demanding for its wise solution due acquaintance with historical traditions, and, still more, spiritual discernment and sober, unbiassed judgment. Without cherishing superstitious ideas of Church authority, we may rationally pay great deference to the final verdict of Fathers and Councils. Still such deference does not foreclose inquiry. Every Christian has a right to examine into the matter for himself, and to hold himself in suspense in regard to the canonicity of particular books, as tested by the principle of essential agreement with the mind of Christ in moral and religious teaching. It were better for a time to doubt the canonicity of a book, even under a misunder standing, than to allow its supposed teaching to obscure the light of great leading Christian truths. Luther was not a

heretic because, in his jealousy for the doctrine of justifica
tion by faith, he pronounced the Epistle of James a strawy
Epistle. He was simply a man who had made a mistake
in exegesis biassed by a one-sided, narrow conception of the
doctrine which he championed.

The question of the New Testament canon, while inter
esting and important, is not vital to faith. Faith could
live and even thrive with a very reduced New Testament :
the Synoptical Gospels and Paul's four all but universally
recognised Epistles might suffice to start with. Hence it is
not necessary in general apologetic, which concerns itself
only about what is urgent, to deal at length with the sub
ject of the canon, going into the history of its formation
and the claims of particular books to a place therein. For
all that relates to such matters the student must be referred
to books specially treating of them.[1] The Gospels have
received exceptional attention for obvious reasons. They
are the main source of our knowledge concerning Christ
and the Christian religion, and it is of urgent importance
to assist the inquirer to arrive at a satisfactory conviction
as to their substantial historicity, their fidelity to the spirit
of Christ, and their essential harmony. If Jesus be the
ultimate authority for the Christian, it is most needful to
know with all the exactness and fulness possible what He
was and what He taught as shown in the professed records
of His life in this world.

The sphere of Christ's authority is religion and morals,
not science, whether sacred or secular. In defining His
mission He said that He came not to destroy the law and
the prophets. It may also be said that He came not to
tell us who wrote the law or the prophecies, or when or in
what order the various books of the Hebrew Bible were
written. In this view the Christian intelligence of our
time acquiesces with increasing unanimity. Let it suffice

---

[1] *Vide* Westcott on *The Canon of the New Testament ;* Charteris, *Canon-icity ;* Reuss, *History of the Canon of Holy Scripture.* For the Old Testa-ment consult especially the work of Professor Ryle.

to state it without going into questions concerning the
limits of Christ's knowledge.

In the foregoing pages the authority of Christ has been
exalted above that of all other claimants. But it has not
been set in antagonism to any legitimate authority. Christ's
attitude is not one of zealous antagonism but of grand
comprehension. His teaching sums up and crowns the
best thought of the wise in all ages and lands. It is
throughout in affinity with reason. The just, wholesome
authority of the Church depends on the measure in which
Christ's spirit dwells in her. " The testimony of Jesus is
the spirit of prophecy." Therefore Christianity is the
absolute religion. It is indeed God's final word to men.
On the simple principle of the survival of the fittest, it is
destined to perpetuity and to ultimate universality.

GENERAL INDEX.

MORRISON AND GIBB, PRINTERS, EDINBURGH.

The International Theological Library

EDITED BY

STEWART D. F. SALMOND, D.D.,

Professor of Systematic Theology and New Testament Exegesis, Free Church College, Aberdeen ;

AND

CHARLES A. BRIGGS, D.D.,

Edward Robinson Professor of Biblical Theology, Union Theological Seminary, New York.

Now Ready (No. II. of the Series). Post 8vo, 10s. 6d.,

CHRISTIAN ETHICS.

By NEWMAN SMYTH, D.D.,

PASTOR OF THE FIRST CONGREGATIONAL CHURCH, NEW HAVEN, CONN. ;
AUTHOR OF 'OLD FAITHS IN NEW LIGHT,' 'THE REALITY OF FAITH,' ETC. ETC.

'A treatise on "Christian Ethics" very properly finds a place in the International Library of Theological Text-books, in which Canon Driver's book on the Old Testament Literature holds the honourable position of pioneer, and the preparation of such a treatise could not have been entrusted to better hands than those of Dr. Newman Smyth. . . . We cordially commend a work which we have perused with much pleasure, and not less instruction.'—Professor A. B. BRUCE, D.D., in *The Critical Review.*

'This series, which opened so auspiciously with Dr. Driver's famous "Introduction," has just been added to by another volume worthy to rank with that work as a solid contribution to modern theological literature. In his "Christian Ethics," Dr. Newman Smyth has admirably filled what was confessedly a gap in Anglo-American Protestant theology. . . . The publication of this work at the present time is specially opportune.' —*The Christian World.*

'This is a book which, we doubt not, will make something like an epoch in the ethical teaching of the English pulpit.'—*Independent.*

Now Ready (No. I. of the Series). Fourth Edition. Post 8vo, price 12s.,

AN INTRODUCTION TO THE LITERATURE OF THE OLD TESTAMENT.

By S. R. DRIVER, D.D.,

REGIUS PROFESSOR OF HEBREW, AND CANON OF CHRIST CHURCH, OXFORD.

'The service which Canon Driver's book will render in the present confusion of mind on this great subject, can scarcely be over-estimated.'—*The Times.*

'By far the best account of the great critical problems connected with the Old Testament that has yet been written. . . . It is a perfect marvel of compression and lucidity combined. A monument of learning and well-balanced judgment.'—*The Guardian.*

EDINBURGH: T. & T. CLARK, 38 GEORGE STREET.

LONDON : SIMPKIN, MARSHALL, HAMILTON, KENT, & CO.

A book that no student can afford to neglect.'—*Review of the Churches.*

Just published, in demy 8vo, price 10s. 6d.,

COMMENTARY ON ST. PAUL'S EPISTLE TO THE EPHESIANS.

By Rev. JOHN MACPHERSON, M.A., Findhorn.

'It is an advance, and a great one, on anything we yet possess. . . . The author goes to the root, and neglects nothing that usually comes under the eye of a careful student. . . . Besides all this, the book is a living book. One is conscious of the heart of a man in it, as well as the brains.' *Methodist Times.*

'This is a very handsome volume which Mr. Macpherson has given us, and without any doubt it will take the first place among the commentaries devoted to this Epistle. The Introduction is fuller far than we have ever had. It is quite in touch with the latest literary and archæological results—results which, in this particular Epistle, have recently come in with unusual richness. That alone is sufficient to give this volume the pre-eminence.'—*The Expository Times.*

In demy 8vo, price 7s. 6d.,

CANON AND TEXT OF THE OLD TESTAMENT.

By Dr. FRANTS BUHL,
PROFESSOR OF THEOLOGY AT LEIPZIG.

TRANSLATED BY Rev. JOHN MACPHERSON, M.A.

** *Professor Buhl is successor to the late Prof. Franz Delitzsch, at Leipzig.*

'Students will find this an extremely useful book. There is not a subject connected with the text of the Old Testament, its history and condition, on which it does not afford all needful information. It is written with great clearness and commendable brevity, and is by far the best manual that exists on the subject of which it treats.'— Prof. A. B. DAVIDSON, D.D., in *The Expositor.*

'It would be difficult to find a more comprehensive, succinct, and lucid digest of the results of recent study of the Old Testament canon and text than is given in this volume. Instead of bewildering us with a crowd of discordant opinions, the author sifts the evidence and indicates the right conclusion. The discussion in the text is kept clear by the relegation of further references and quotations to supplementary paragraphs These paragraphs are a perfect mine of exact, detailed information.'—Prof. J. S. BANKS in *The Critical Review.*

EDINBURGH: T. & T. CLARK, 38 GEORGE STREET.

WORKS BY PROFESSOR A. B. BRUCE, D.D.

In post 8vo, New Edition, Revised, price 7s. 6d.,

THE KINGDOM OF GOD;

OR, CHRIST'S TEACHING ACCORDING TO THE SYNOPTICAL GOSPELS.

BY A. B. BRUCE, D.D.,

PROFESSOR OF NEW TESTAMENT EXEGESIS IN THE
FREE CHURCH COLLEGE, GLASGOW.

'To Dr. Bruce belongs the honour of giving to English-speaking Christians the first really scientific treatment of this transcendent theme . . . his book is the best monograph on the subject in existence. . . . He is evidently in love with his subject, and every page exhibits the intense enthusiasm of a strong nature for the Divine Teacher.'—Rev. JAMES STALKER, D.D. in *The British Weekly.*

BY THE SAME AUTHOR.

In demy 8vo, Fourth Edition, price 10s. 6d.,

THE TRAINING OF THE TWELVE;

OR,

EXPOSITION OF PASSAGES IN THE GOSPELS EXHIBITING THE TWELVE DISCIPLES OF JESUS UNDER DISCIPLINE FOR THE APOSTLESHIP.

'Here we have a really great book on an important, large, and attractive subject—a book full of loving, wholesome, profound thoughts about the fundamentals of Christian faith and practice.'—*British and Foreign Evangelical Review.*

BY THE SAME AUTHOR.

In demy 8vo, Third Edition, price 10s. 6d.,

THE HUMILIATION OF CHRIST,

IN ITS PHYSICAL, ETHICAL, AND OFFICIAL ASPECTS.

'We have not for a long time met with a work so fresh and suggestive as this of Professor Bruce. . . . We do not know where to look at our English Universities for a treatise so calm, logical, and scholarly.'—*English Independent.*

'The title of the book gives but a faint conception of the value and wealth of its contents. . . . Dr. Bruce's work is really one of exceptional value; and no one can read it without perceptible gain in theological knowledge.'—*English Churchman.*

In post 8vo, price 7s. 6d.,

THE PREACHERS OF SCOTLAND,

FROM THE

Sixth to the Nineteenth Century.

(Twelfth Series of the 'Cunningham Lectures.')

By WILLIAM GARDEN BLAIKIE, D.D., LL.D.,
PROFESSOR OF APOLOGETICAL AND OF PASTORAL THEOLOGY, NEW COLLEGE, EDINBURGH

CONTENTS.—CHAP. I. Introductory. II. The Early Celtic Church. III. Preachers of the Reformation. IV. The Successors of Knox. V., VI. The Covenanting Period. VII. The Field Preachers. VIII. The Secession Period. IX. The Moderate School. X. Evangelical Church Preachers in the Eighteenth Century. XI. The Evangelical Revival. XII. The Pulpit of to-day. Appendix.—On the Method of Preaching adapted to the Age.

'Incomparably the best and most popularly written book on the subject that has appeared for many years.'—*Spectator.*

'Exceedingly interesting and well worth reading, both for information and pleasure. . . . A better review of Scottish preaching from an evangelical standpoint could not be desired.'—*Scotsman.*

In crown 8vo, price 3s. 6d., SECOND EDITION, REVISED,

THE THEOLOGY AND THEOLOGIANS OF SCOTLAND,

CHIEFLY OF THE

Seventeenth and Eighteenth Centuries.

Being one of the 'Cunningham Lectures.'

By JAMES WALKER, D.D., CARNWATH.

CONTENTS:—CHAP. I. Survey of the Field. II. Predestination and Providence. III. The Atonement. IV. The Doctrine of the Visible Church. V. The Headship of Christ and Erastianism. VI. Present Misrepresentation of Scottish Religion. VII. Do Presbyterians hold Apostolical Succession ?

'These pages glow with fervent and eloquent rejoinder to the cheap scorn and scurrilous satire poured out upon evangelical theology as it has been developed north of the Tweed.'—*British Quarterly Review.*

'We do not wonder that in their delivery Dr. Walker's lectures excited great interest; we should have wondered far more if they had not done so.'— Mr. SPURGEON in *Sword and Trowel.*

'As an able and eloquent vindication of Scottish theology, the work is one of very great interest—an interest by no means necessarily confined to theologians. The history of Scotland, and the character of her people, cannot be understood without an intelligent and sympathetic study of her theology, and in this Dr. Walker's little book will be found to render unique assistance.'—*Scotsman.*

Just published, in demy 8vo, price 10s. 6d.,

BOOKS WHICH INFLUENCED OUR LORD AND HIS APOSTLES:

Being a Critical Review of Jewish Apocalyptic Literature.

BY

J. E. H. THOMSON, B.D.

CONTENTS:—Introduction.—Book I. Background of Apocalyptic.—II. Evolution of Apocalyptic.—III. Criticism of Apocalyptic.—IV. Theological Result.

' Mr. Thomson moves easily under his load of learning, and uses it skilfully. His language is clear and vigorous, and often eloquent and picturesque.'— *Scotsman.*

In demy 8vo, price 10s. 6d.,

THE JEWISH

AND

THE CHRISTIAN MESSIAH.

A STUDY IN THE EARLIEST HISTORY OF CHRISTIANITY.

By Professor VINCENT HENRY STANTON, M.A., TRINITY COLLEGE, CAMBRIDGE.

' Mr. Stanton's book answers a real want, and will be indispensable to students of the origin of Christianity. We hope that Mr. Stanton will be able to continue his labours in that most obscure and most important period, of his competency to deal with which he has given such good proof in this book.'— *Guardian.*

' We welcome this book as a valuable addition to the literature of a most important subject. . . . The book is remarkable for the clearness of its style. Mr. Stanton is never obscure from beginning to end, and we think that no reader of average attainments will be able to put the book down without having learnt much from his lucid and scholarly exposition.'— *Ecclesiastical Gazette.*

Just published, in post 8vo, price 7s. 6d.,

MESSIANIC PROPHECY:

Its Origin, Historical Growth, and Relation to New Testament Fulfilment.

By Dr. EDWARD RIEHM.

New Edition, Translated by Rev. LEWIS A. MUIRHEAD, B.D.

With an Introduction by Professor A. B. DAVIDSON, D.D.

'No work of the same compass could be named that contains so much that is instructive on the nature of prophecy in general, and particularly on the branch of it specially treated in the book.'—Professor A. B. DAVIDSON, D.D.

'I would venture to recommend "Riehm's Messianic Prophecy" (Clark's translation) as a summary account of prophecy both reverent and critical.'— Principal GORE in *Lux Mundi*.

Just published, in crown 8vo, price 5s.,

MESSIANIC PROPHECIES IN HISTORICAL SUCCESSION.

By FRANZ DELITZSCH.

Translated by SAMUEL IVES CURTISS,
PROFESSOR IN CHICAGO THEOLOGICAL SEMINARY.

—

'The proofs of this volume were corrected by the author on his deathbed, and the Preface was dictated by him five days before his death. There is something sacred about such a book. It embodies the results of the most recent scholarly investigation, and at the same time breathes the spirit of deep and fervent Christian faith. In times when it needs the greatest care to handle wisely the subject of Messianic Prophecy, the student could not well have a better guide than this short but comprehensive volume. It is as full of instruction as it is a help to discriminating faith. We heartily wish it a wide circulation.'— *Methodist Recorder*.

HERZOG'S BIBLICAL ENCYCLOPÆDIA.

Now complete, in Three Vols. imp. 8vo, price 24s. each,

ENCYCLOPÆDIA OR DICTIONARY

OF

Biblical, Historical, Doctrinal, and Practical Theology.

Based on the Real-Encyclopädie of Herzog, Plitt, and Hauck.

EDITED BY PHILIP SCHAFF, D.D., LL.D.

'A well-designed, meritorious work, on which neither industry nor expense has been spared.'—*Guardian.*

'This certainly is a remarkable work. . . . It will be one without which no general or theological or biographical library will be complete.'—*Freeman.*

'The need of such a work as this must be very often felt, and it ought to find its way into all college libraries, and into many private studies.'—*Christian World.*

'As a comprehensive work of reference, within a moderate compass, we know nothing at all equal to it in the large department which it deals with.'—*Church Bells.*

SUPPLEMENT TO HERZOG'S ENCYCLOPÆDIA.

In Imperial 8vo, price 8s.,

ENCYCLOPÆDIA OF LIVING DIVINES.

'A very useful Encyclopædia. I am very glad to have it for frequent reference.'—Right Rev. BISHOP LIGHTFOOT.

Now complete, in Four Vols. imp. 8vo, price 12s. 6d. each,

COMMENTARY ON THE NEW TESTAMENT.

With Illustrations and Maps.

EDITED BY PHILIP SCHAFF, D.D., LL.D.

Volume I.	*Volume II.*
THE SYNOPTICAL GOSPELS.	**ST. JOHN GOSPEL**
	AND THE
Volume III.	**ACTS OF THE APOSTLES.**
	Volume IV.
ROMANS to PHILEMON.	**HEBREWS to REVELATION.**

'A useful, valuable, and instructive commentary. The interpretation is set forth with clearness and cogency, and in a manner calculated to commend the volumes to the thoughtful reader. The book is beautifully got up, and reflects great credit on the publishers as well as the writers.'—THE BISHOP OF GLOUCESTER.

'There are few better commentaries having a similar scope and object; indeed, within the same limits, we do not know of one so good, upon the whole, of the New Testament.'—*Literary World.*

'External beauty and intrinsic worth combine in the work here completed. Good paper, good type, good illustrations, good binding please the eye, as accuracy and thoroughness in matter of treatment satisfy the judgment. Everywhere the workmanship is careful, solid, harmonious.—*Methodist Recorder.*

LOTZE'S MICROCOSMUS.

In Two Vols. 8vo, FOURTH EDITION, price 36s.,

MICROCOSMUS:

CONCERNING MAN AND HIS RELATION TO THE WORLD.

By HERMANN LOTZE.

CONTENTS: — Book I. The Body. II. The Soul. III. Life. IV. Man
V. Mind. VI. The Microcosmic Order; or, The Course of Human Life
VII. History. VIII. Progress. IX. The Unity of Things.

' These are indeed two masterly volumes, vigorous in intellectual power,
and translated with rare ability. . . . This work will doubtless find a place
on the shelves of all the foremost thinkers and students of modern times.'—
Evangelical Magazine.

' The English public have now before them the greatest philosophic work
produced in Germany by the generation just past. The translation comes at
an opportune time, for the circumstances of English thought, just at the
present moment, are peculiarly those with which Lotze attempted to deal
when he wrote his "Microcosmus," a quarter of a century ago. . . . Few
philosophic books of the century are so attractive both in style and matter.'—
Athenæum.

' Lotze is the ablest, the most brilliant, and most renowned of the German
philosophers of to-day. . . . He has rendered invaluable and splendid service
to Christian thinkers, and has given them a work which cannot fail to equip
them for the sturdiest intellectual conflicts and to ensure their victory.'—
Baptist Magazine.

In Two Vols. 8vo, price 21s.,

NATURE AND THE BIBLE:

LECTURES ON THE MOSAIC HISTORY OF CREATION IN ITS RELATION TO NATURAL SCIENCE.

By Dr. FR. H. REUSCH.

REVISED AND CORRECTED BY THE AUTHOR.

Translated from the Fourth Edition

By KATHLEEN LYTTELTON.

' Other champions much more competent and learned than myself might
have been placed in the field; I will only name one of the most recent
Dr. Reusch, author of "Nature and the Bible."'—The Right Hon. W. E
GLADSTONE.

' The work, we need hardly say, is of profound and perennial interest, and
it can scarcely be too highly commended as, in many respects, a very success
ful attempt to settle one of the most perplexing questions of the day. It i
impossible to read it without obtaining larger views of theology, and mor
accurate opinions respecting its relations to science, and no one will rise from
its perusal without feeling a deep sense of gratitude to its author.'—*Scottis
Review.*

PROFESSOR GODET'S WORKS.

(Copyright, by arrangement with the Author.)

In Two Volumes, demy 8vo, price 21s.,

COMMENTARY ON ST. PAUL'S FIRST EPISTLE TO THE CORINTHIANS.

By F. GODET, D.D.,
PROFESSOR OF THEOLOGY, NEUCHATEL.

'A perfect masterpiece of theological toil and thought. . . . Scholarly, evangelical, exhaustive, and able.'—*Evangelical Review.*

'To say a word in praise of any of Professor Godet's productions is almost like "gilding refined gold." All who are familiar with his commentaries know how full they are of rich suggestion. . . . This volume fully sustains the high reputation Godet has made for himself as a biblical scholar, and devout expositor of the will of God. Every page is radiant with light, and gives forth heat as well.'—*Methodist New Connexion Magazine.*

In Three Volumes, 8vo, price 31s. 6d.,

A COMMENTARY ON THE GOSPEL OF ST. JOHN.
A New Edition, Revised throughout by the Author.

'This work forms one of the battle-fields of modern inquiry, and is itself so rich in spiritual truth, that it is impossible to examine it too closely; and we welcome this treatise from the pen of Dr. Godet. We have no more com petent exegete; and this new volume shows all the learning and vivacity for which the author is distinguished.'—*Freeman.*

In Two Volumes, 8vo, price 21s.,

A COMMENTARY ON THE GOSPEL OF ST. LUKE.

'Marked by clearness and good sense, it will be found to possess value and interest as one of the most recent and copious works specially designed to illustrate this Gospel.'—*Guardian.*

In Two Volumes, 8vo, price 21s.,

A COMMENTARY ON ST. PAUL'S EPISTLE TO THE ROMANS.

'We prefer this commentary to any other we have seen on the subject. . . . We have great pleasure in recommending it as not only rendering invaluable aid in the critical study of the text, but affording practical and deeply suggestive assistance in the exposition of the doctrine.'—*British and Foreign Evangelical Review.*

In crown 8vo, Second Edition, price 6s.,

DEFENCE OF THE CHRISTIAN FAITH.
TRANSLATED BY THE HON. AND REV. CANON LYTTELTON, M.A.,
RECTOR OF HAGLEY.

'There is trenchant argument and resistless logic in these lectures; but withal, there is cultured imagination and felicitous eloquence, which carry home the appeals to the heart as well as the head.'—*Sword and Trowel.*

✳

HISTORY OF THE CHRISTIAN CHURCH.

By PHILIP SCHAFF, D.D., L⟨.D.

New Edition, Re-written and Enlarged.

1. **APOSTOLIC CHRISTIANITY, A.D. 1-100.** Two Vols. Ex. demy 8vo, price 21s.
2. **ANTE-NICENE CHRISTIANITY, A.D. 100-325.** Two Vols. Ex. demy 8vo, price 21s.
3. **NICENE AND POST-NICENE CHRISTIANITY, A.D. 325-600.** Two Vols. Ex. demy 8vo, price 21s.
4. **MEDIÆVAL CHRISTIANITY, A.D. 590-1073.** Two Vols. Ex. demy 8vo, price 21s. (Completion of this Period, 1073-1517, in preparation.)
5. **MODERN CHRISTIANITY The German Reformation, A.D. 1517-1530.** Two Vols. Ex. demy 8vo, price 21s.

'*Dr Schaff's "History of the Christian Church" is the most valuable contribution to Ecclesiastical History that has ever been published in this country. When com pleted it will have no rival in point of comprehensiveness, and in presenting the results of the most advanced scholarship and the latest discoveries. Each division covers a separate and distinct epoch, and is complete in itself.*'

'We have read those volumes with the most unmingled satisfaction. . . . For the student, who wants to get at facts, to understand the *rationale* of the facts, and to have the means of verifying them, there is no book so good as this.'—*Church Bells.*

Now complete, in Five Volumes, 8vo, price 10s. 6d. each,

HISTORY OF THE JEWISH PEOPLE IN THE TIME OF OUR LORD.

By Dr. EMIL SCHURER,

PROFESSOR OF THEOLOGY IN THE UNIVERSITY OF KIEL.

TRANSLATED FROM THE SECOND EDITION (REVISED THROUGH-OUT AND GREATLY ENLARGED) OF '*HISTORY OF THE NEW TESTAMENT TIMES.*'

* * Professor Schurer has prepared an exhaustive INDEX to this work, to which he attaches great value. The Translation is now ready, and is issued in a separate Volume (100 pp. 8vo). Price 2s. 6d. *nett.*

'Under Professor Schürer's guidance we are enabled to a large extent to construct a social and political framework for the Gospel History and to set it in such a light as to see new evidences of the truthfulness of that history and of its contemporaneousness. . . . The length of our notice shows our estimate of the value of his work.'—*English Churchman.*

'Messrs. Clark have afresh earned the thanks of all students of the New Testament in England, by undertaking to present Schurer s masterly work in a form easily accessible to the English reader · · · In every case the amount of research displayed is very great, truly German in its proportions while the style of Professor Schurer is by no means cumbrous after the manner of some of his countrymen. We have inadequately described a most valuable work, but we hope we have said enough to induce our readers who do not know this book to seek it out forthwith.'—*Methodist Recorder.*

Printed in Great Britain
by Amazon.co.uk, Ltd.,
Marston Gate.